"Salacious. Visceral. Great. With *Apocalypse Culture II*,
Adam Parfrey immerses the reader in the deep dark
sanguinary sanctums of the subconscious."

Robert Williams

"*Apocalypse Culture II* is the New Testament, redefining
and satirically exposing the mutations of consensus
hypocrisy. Psychoses duel in the hilarious, absurd,
provocative and incestuously urban litanies of
deformed martyrs. An unexpectedly sacred alchemical
tincture."

Genesis P-Orridge

APOCALYPSE
CULTURE II

Acknowledgments

I am particularly grateful to Michael Moynihan, who was responsible for the appearance of a good handful of articles within. Peter Sotos, Crispin Glover, Sondra London, Harvey Stafford, Joe Coleman, John Zerzan, Jack Sargeant, Ghazi Barakat and Robert Sterling were also quite helpful with contributions and recommendations. And hand-shaking, back-patting thanks are due Jodi Wille, Bill Nelson, Nick Bougas, Irv Rubin, Richard Metzger, Monotrona, Jeff Behary, and Blanche Barton.

Linda Hayashi was not able to snowboard or surf while designing *Apocalypse Culture II*, and I feel quite indebted to her sacrifice. Bennett Theissen did not simply proofread, he suggested deletions and revisions, and I took much of his advice.

Most of all, to Marti Singer, my love.

This book is dedicated to the memory of Vladimir Jabotinsky 1880–1940.

ISBN 0-922915-57-1
Feral House
2554 Lincoln Blvd. #1059
Venice, California 90291

Design by Linda Hayashi
10 9 8 7 6 5 4 3 2 1

CULTURE II

EDITED BY
ADAM PARFREY

FERAL HOUSE

ALSO BY ADAM PARFREY

Cult Rapture
Feral House, 1995

Apocalypse Culture
Amok Press, 1987

Apocalypse Culture: Enlarged and Revised Edition
Feral House, 1990

Rants & Incendiary Tracts
co-edited by Bob Black; Loompanics and Amok Press, 1988

Cosmic Retribution: The Infernal Art of Joe Coleman
co-edited by Pat Moriarity; Fantagraphics and Feral House, 1992

A Sordid Evening of Sonic Sorrows
recording, from Man's Ruin, 1997

SWAT: Deep Inside a Cop's Mind
recording, from Amphetamine Reptile, 1995

CONTENTS

One must be amazed, when one learns of the inner nature of man, that the number of criminals is so small.

Wilhelm Stekel, *Sadism and Masochism*

Nobody deserves to live. We all had our chance —we lost, we failed—now we go nowhere—just lower, into the ground—push them down and then they'll grow again—clean, simple, like—like a little animal.

Woodrow Parfrey's death scene as a mass murderer on the *Naked City* episode, "Burst of Passion"

APOCALYPSE CULTURE II CENSORED!

Due to weak-kneed printers across the country, we've been forced to black out—that is, censor—substantial portions of six illustrations herein. Yes, it has been decreed that these works of art commit thought crimes that must be repressed. All censored illustrations are reproduced in their full glory on the Feral House website <www.feralhouse.com>. The artwork in question is by Blalla Hallmann, Stu Mead and Beth Love.

No vaunted End seems to be coming any time soon. No resolution, no termination, no third act, none of it.

Apocalypse is crack—belief systems puffed on and puffed on until the smoker withers under a huge cloud of phantasms. Though we have no bananas, we do have an apocalypse culture, an epoch so confused, so mutated, so . . . *perfect*. Perfectly sad, perfectly degraded, perfectly corrupt. *Apocalypse Culture II* is designed to assist the reader in finding front-row seats to its perverse pleasures and strange solutions.

Though this book trespasses the Forbidden Zone, the land of moral quandary, no easy answers are provided here. Readers are urged to contemplate the strange and often contradictory information within, and make up their own minds regarding its value. We refuse to take part in the charade screaming at you from television, or from tabloids at the supermarket check-out aisle, attaching cretinous moral context to photos of Nazis and raped children.

Due to the many tender, reactive subjects within, I feel the need to make it clear that the book was compiled to examine far-reaching and extreme societal tendrils, and should not be seen as a manifesto or a smorgasbord of personal fetishes or beliefs. The editor does *not* endorse the views expressed within, much less the hobby horses ridden by the authors on their own time, whether they are ignorant, hateful or enlightening. Paying no attention to the material presented here does not eradicate its existence.

Call it evil, call it prescient—the apocalypse culture has only just begun.

Adam Parfrey
May 2000

CLONEJESUS.COM
THE SECOND
COMING
PROJECT

The Second Coming Project is a nonprofit organization devoted to bringing about the Second Coming of Our Lord, Jesus Christ, as prophesied in the Bible, in time for the 2,000th anniversary of his birth.

Our intention is to clone Jesus, utilizing techniques pioneered at the Roslin Institute in Scotland, by taking an incorrupt cell from one of the many Holy Relics of Jesus' blood and body that are preserved in churches throughout the world, extracting its DNA, and inserting it into an unfertilized human egg (oocyte), through the now-proven biological process called nuclear transfer. The fertilized egg, now the zygote of Jesus Christ, will be implanted into the womb of a young virginal woman (who has volunteered on her own accord), who will then bring the baby Jesus to term in a second Virgin Birth.

If all goes according to plan, the birth will take place on December 25, 2000, thus making Anno Domini 2000 into Anno Domini Novi 1, and all calendrical calculations will begin anew.

How Can This Be Possible?

a. Modern cloning technology enables us to clone any large mammal—including humans—using just a single cell from an adult specimen.

b. Throughout the Christian world are churches that contain Holy Relics of Jesus' body; his blood, his hair, his foreskin. Unless every single one of these relics is a fake, this means that cells from Jesus' body still survive to this very day.

c. We are already making preparations to obtain a portion of one of these relics, extract the DNA from one of its cells, and use it to clone Jesus.

No longer can we rely on hope and prayer, waiting around futilely for Jesus to return. We have the technology to bring him back right now: there is no reason, moral, legal or Biblical, not to take advantage of it.

In order to save the world from sin, we must clone Jesus to initiate the Second Coming of Christ.

The Second Coming Project is soliciting contributions and donations to help us in our quest. Time is short! We must have a fertilized Jesus zygote no later than April of 2000 if Baby Jesus is to come to term on the predicted date. If we cannot get the funds to perform cloning in time for His two thousandth birthday, we will continue with The Project, because the world will not survive if we fail. Please send all contributions to:

Kristan Lawson
The Second Coming Project
P.O. Box 295
Berkeley, CA 94701

Biblical Prediction of Cloning

"While they were eating, Jesus took bread, gave thanks and broke it, and gave it to his disciples, saying, 'Take and eat; this is my body.' Then he took the cup, gave thanks and offered it to them, saying, 'Drink from it, all of you. This is my blood of the covenant, which is poured out for many for the forgiveness of sins.'" (Matthew 26:26-28)

Many have long wondered at the strange behavior of Jesus here at the Last Supper. Was he imitating some pagan ritual? Was he encouraging cannibalism? We think: NO! Jesus was giving a clue to later generations. Honor, protect and preserve my body and blood, he was saying, for some day, far in the future, with it you will be able to save the world. How? Through unspecified magical or supernatural means? Obviously not. Through knowledge given to us by God: the knowledge of CLONING, which we can use to BRING JESUS BACK, because the faithful have preserved parts of His body and blood for all these centuries.

Jesus was very explicit about the necessity of cloning in the book of Matthew: "It is better for you to lose one part of your body than for your whole body to go into hell." (Matthew 5:30)
"He will cut him to pieces." (Matthew 24:50)
"If someone from the dead goes to them, they will repent." (Luke 16:30)
Paul knew, too: here he tells us that Christ's blood is the key:
"In him we have redemption through his blood." (Ephesians 1:7)
The apostle John foresaw cloning; here is what he said:
"We know that, when He appears, we shall be like Him, because we shall see Him just as He is." (John 3:2)
Even the Old Testament prophets knew what must occur:
"The grave below is all astir to meet you at your coming; it rouses the spirits of the departed to greet you—all those who were leaders in the world; it makes them rise." (Isaiah 14:9–11)

Do not dishonor the Bible. Send your contribution to The Second Coming Project today!

⚡ ⚡ ⚡

www.clonejesus.com

Clone Jesus

3

Human Pigs

Robert Knight: Our guest is Andrew Kimbrell, author of *The Human Body Shop: The Engineering and Marketing of Life.* Andrew, there have been increasing developments that associate, or attempt to associate, behavior with genetics. . . .

Andrew Kimbrell: Three billion dollars of taxpayers' money is being spent to analyze the human genome, and while most of us support the work that's being done to cure disease, that's not ALL that's going on. Unfortunately, much of that money is being spent to analyze genes that have nothing to do with disease. . . . What we're seeing here is a very, very dangerous moment because, while they're analyzing and finding more and more of these genes, they have absolutely no protections in place that would make them private. Insurance companies and Fortune 500 companies are already using genetic screening in order to screen out workers who might be a liability because they may be predisposed to a certain cancer, let's say, in the workplaces of the chemical industry. Insurance companies are using genetic screening to make sure that they only insure people who are not predisposed to certain illnesses. The United States Government is denying people various jobs and denying them insurance based on their genetic readout.

Right now, there are virtually no protections in place. Additionally, I think it's incredibly unfortunate that due to the new and sometimes dazzling advances in genetic engineering, to think that so many of our human behavioral traits are in our genes and not in our environment. Recently, the National Institute of Health sponsored a colloquium on crime. Their view was that the real causes of crime are not social, that they have nothing to do with the gross inequality of wealth in our country, but rather that the causes of crime have to do with genes: if you've got that criminal gene, well, that's going to make you a criminal. . . .

They are spending taxpayer dollars on experiments which involve putting human genes into the permanent genetic codes of other animals! Over 24 human genes have been put into other animals by our Government, and now, increasingly, by corporations. The United States Department of Agriculture took the human growth gene and put it into eight-cell embryos, pig embryos, and then reinserted those embryos into surrogate mother pigs in their attempt to create giant pigs. Now, what resulted . . . I happened to see this. Pig #6707 was actually bow-legged, cross-eyed, arthritic—a really wretched product of a science without ethics. But the United States Department of Agriculture then said that maybe they had created a lean pig, a pig that had less cholesterol. They didn't consider whether or not Americans want to eat pork chops containing human genes.

With these experiments, they are now creating well over a hundred thousand of these animal/human chimeras every year, most of them through our earnings, our taxpayer dollars. And, while some of these experiments raise some really grotesque issues of animal suffering and important issues of animal suffering, it goes beyond that.

I describe in the book an AIDS experiment which was done for relatively altruistic reasons. There is a Dr. Malcolm Martin at the National Institutes of Health who decided to put the entire human AIDS virus, the entire genome of the human AIDS virus into mice. As we all know, mice are not very good research tools for AIDS, and so he wanted to create the perfect mouse research animal for AIDS. And this was a front-page story in the *New York Times* and the *Washington Post*. What most people didn't hear, what they didn't read was that several months later, a group of AIDS scientists, including Dr. Robert Gallo and others, published a report in *Science* magazine saying that the AIDS virus had melded with native retroviruses in the mice to create a super AIDS virus. And Dr. Gene Marx, in an accompanying editorial in *Science* magazine, said that this super AIDS virus may well be transmissible through air. This went virtually unreported. Very few people understood the extraordinary implications.

Michio Kaku: Holy mackerel! A super AIDS virus that is transmitted through the air?

Andrew Kimbrell: Transmitted through the air!

Michio Kaku: We're talking about Doomsday weapons now!

⚡ ⚡ ⚡

From WBAI-FM (99.5)
505 Eighth Ave., 19th Fl.
New York, NY 10018

Renée Hartevelt

THE STRANGE CRIME OF ISSEI SAGAWA

Colin Wilson

> It is wrong to think of cannibalism as a
>
> debasement of character.
>
> **Issei Sagawa, quoting the Marquis de Sade**

The Bois de Boulogne, Paris's most famous recreation area, was modeled after London's Hyde Park. In historical times it was a haunt of bandits, and even in the late twentieth century, muggers and prostitutes made it a risky place to visit at night.

But towards midnight on a warm June night in 1981, everything looked quiet enough to the middle-aged couple who strolled beside the lower lake, listening to the sound of music and laughter that drifted across the water from a fashionable restaurant on the island. Neither of them paid much attention to the taxi that halted nearby, or to the man who walked across the grass towards the lake, dragging two heavy suitcases on the kind of portable luggage trolleys that tourists use.

They noticed him only when they realized he meant to hurl the suitcases into the water. At this point, he also noticed them and, to their astonishment, dumped the suitcases under the nearest bushes and took to his heels. Understandably curious, the couple decided to investigate. But when they saw a bloodstained hand protruding from a partly open suitcase, they hastened to the nearest telephone and called the police.

One of the suitcases proved to contain the limbless torso of a young woman, the other her legs, arms and head. A police surgeon observed that chunks of flesh were missing from the buttocks and the thighs, and the tip had been cut off the nose. A later examination would also reveal that the girl had been shot in the nape of the neck by a bullet from a carbine. She had also been raped.

The police had two important clues. The couple—and a number of other witnesses—described the man as "Asian," and said he was small in stature. And they knew that he had arrived in a taxi.

Catching "the Butcher of the Bois de Boulogne" (as the press originally dubbed him) proved unexpectedly easy. The police concentrated their attention on Parisian taxi firms, and soon located the driver who had taken an Asian man with two suitcases to the Bois de Boulogne. He was able to give them the address to which he had been summoned by telephone on Saturday evening.

It was 10 rue Erlanger, and it was within a few blocks of the southern end of the Bois de Boulogne, in the fashionable district of Passy. Further inquiries revealed that the studio on the second floor of 10 rue Erlanger was rented to a Japanese student named Issei Sagawa.

On the evening of Monday, June 15, two days after the discovery of the suitcases, no less than six police officers called at the second floor flat in the rue Erlanger, prepared to face desperate resistance from the "butcher," whom they knew to be armed.

But the small, soft-spoken Japanese man who answered the door obviously had no intention of attacking them. He admitted that his name was Issei Sagawa, and told them that he was studying modern literature at the Department of Oriental Studies in the suburb of Dauphine—a department of the Sorbonne.

Sagawa made no protest when they asked him to accompany them to the police station. And there he admitted, almost apologetically, that he had murdered the girl whose dismembered body had been found in the suitcases. She was, he explained, a Dutch fellow student named Renée Hartevelt, and he had killed her because he wanted to eat her flesh.

His story was confirmed by the contents of his refrigerator. There the police found, wrapped neatly in plastic bags, flesh from her hips, thighs and arms—and also her lips.

Sagawa described the murder with a kind of childlike openness. In May 1981, in his class at Paris University, he had met Renée Hartevelt, and was instantly captivated by her. She was a pretty, 25-year-old Dutch girl with gray eyes, fair skin, a shapely figure, and a gentle smile. "I was unable to take my eyes off her." This was not love—he was careful to explain—it was a sexual obsession.

By chance, he met her again on his way home on the Metro. They began talking about their doctorate studies—Sagawa was writing on Shakespeare's *Tempest*. After the next lecture, a group of students, including Sagawa and Renée Hartevelt, went to a Greek restaurant for a meal. One of them suggested that next time they should eat at a Japanese restaurant. Sagawa immediately suggested that they might like to come to his flat and eat sukiyaki.

In fact, Renée was the only one to arrive. They conversed pleasantly, and discussed music—Sagawa played her some of his favorite records of Beethoven and Handel. When she left, he had arranged for her to give him German lessons, so that he could read German Romantic poetry in the original.

After she had gone, he found himself on fire with a lurid fantasy—the type of perverse sexual fantasy he had been entertaining for many years. He imagined going behind her and firing a gun into her back, immediately above the naked white shoulders, then undressing her and eating her.

Now he had made up his mind: Renée would be the ideal victim; there was something about her gentleness that made him long to literally consume her. Yet he was convinced that, when it came time for action, he would be unable to pull the trigger. He was all too well aware of his own romantic and indecisive temperament, more at home in fantasy than reality.

Soon she came back to his flat to give him a German lesson. And, as he suspected, he was unable to bring himself to carry out his plan. He was even unable to go behind her, as she sat on a cushion on the floor—in the Japanese manner—and take the gun from the cupboard. When she left, he told himself that now he would have to kill her, if only to maintain his self-respect. Otherwise he would go through life thinking of himself as an ineffectual dreamer.

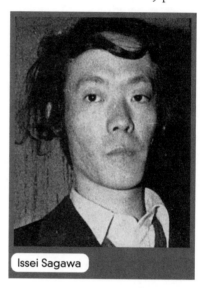

Issei Sagawa

At this point, something happened that increased his determination. Someone from his father's firm came to bring him some Japanese food. Despite being slightly feverish with a cold, Sagawa felt he must show this emissary from Osaka the sights of Paris. That evening, they went to a Japanese restaurant, and as he eyed the sushi on display, Sagawa was suddenly struck by the thought: what a pity it would be if his cold made him unable to realize his long-held dream to eat the flesh of a white woman.

The next day, Renée once again accepted an invitation to come to his flat. As she sat reading poetry aloud with her back to the cupboard, he went behind her, pulled aside the curtain, and took out the gun. Then he pointed it at the back of her neck and pulled the trigger. For some reason, the gun misfired. Not even hearing the click, Renée went on reading.

The third attempt was on June 11, 1981. Once again they sat facing one another on cushions, and as she prepared to read aloud the poem "Evening" by the modern German expressionist poet Becher, Sagawa got up to switch on the tape recorder. Then he quietly took the carbine out of the cupboard, and pointed it at the nape of her neck. Just as she finished the poem, he pulled the trigger.

Renée died instantly, and Sagawa fainted.

When he opened his eyes, only to see a silent body lying in a pool of blood before him, he felt as if he had awakened into a dream. He had never seen a corpse in his entire life, and now that he had brought this dreadful thing into being before him, he was terrified of it. Appalled by the reality of what he had done, he forced himself to withdraw into his imagination and conjure up—for the thousandth time—his supreme fantasy.

Finally Sagawa recovered his senses sufficiently to touch the body of the beautiful white woman.

Sagawa's sketch of Renée

After breaking through that barrier, he began to enact the scenario he had imagined in such minute detail. He undressed her and laid her face-down on the carpet. Then he bent down and sank his teeth into her right buttock. He had decided in advance that the left buttock would contain more blood, since it would be closer to the heart. He hated the sight of blood.

Naturally, the solid flesh resisted his teeth. So he took a carving knife and sliced into the right buttock of the lovely Renée. The first thing he saw was a thick layer of fat, as yellow as a corn-cob. Below this was red meat, and the novice cannibal sliced out a piece and put it into his mouth.

The flesh of the Dutch girl was as soft as raw tuna.

Now in a state of ecstatic excitement at the final realization of his dream, he turned her over and sliced into her thigh. Once again he ate the meat raw. Then he violated her body. But this, he explained, was almost an afterthought, altogether less important than the pleasure of eating her flesh.

Meanwhile, the blood was threatening to ruin the carpet, and Sagawa had to get to work. He dragged the corpse into the bathroom and began the task of dismembering it. The cannibal fantasy was over; this part would make him ill. He had never been able to eat animal offal, and was nauseated by the sight of the severed breasts. They were nothing after all, but "revolting lumps of fat."

But he had to get rid of the body, and it had to be rendered into pieces small enough to either eat or carry. So he cut steaks from the thighs and buttocks, wrapped them in plastic bags, and placed them in the refrigerator.

Sagawa spent the next two days—Friday and Saturday—cooking and eating these parts. During this time, he left the flat to meet a few friends and take in a movie. He also did some necessary shopping, picking up two cardboard suitcases. As he strolled along the Champs Elysees, he disposed of Renée's clothing in rubbish bins—except for her panties, which he kept.

Each time he returned home, he would cook himself another meal from his refrigerator. The flesh struck him as tasteless—a little like veal—and rather tough, and he had to season it with salt, pepper and mustard to improve the flavor. But eating it continued to produce the same fetishistic thrill.

On Saturday evening he called a taxi and carried his grisly suitcases to the Bois de Boulogne.

The mutilated body caused quite a sensation, and when Sagawa was arrested two days later, virtually every newspaper in France carried lurid headlines about the Japanese cannibal. The face looking out from the tabloids seemed to be that of a sadistic monster. The impassive oriental face, the dark eyes staring straight into the camera, suggested to the xenophobic French a cold-blooded, psychopathic killer.

Renée Hartevelt

Most accounts of these crimes refer to Renée Hartevelt as Issei Sagawa's "girlfriend." It's simply easier to refer to her this way.

The television coverage was slightly more restrained than the tabloid press. With the aid of the suitcases and other ghoulish evidence, it could afford to be. But it was scarcely less full of nauseated astonishment and incomprehension.

"This is not for sensitive viewers," warned the announcer. "Bernard Marchetti reports on the horrible story of a bleeding suitcase found in the Bois de Boulogne." The reporter went on to describe how the remains of a young female student had been found "in frightful circumstances." Again the impassive oriental face stared out at the viewer.

"This man is a cannibal. His name is Issei Sagawa, and he was born in Kobe 32 years ago. Last Thursday he shot a young Dutch student in the head, cut up her corpse, and kept the remains in his flat until Saturday. During that time he ate some of her body. When the police arrested him they found parts of her body stored in his refrigerator. . . ."

So far the story had been factual. Now came the speculation. After all, why should anyone kill and eat a girl, if not out of frustrated love?

"He was in love with her. She wasn't interested. On Thursday, when she turned him down once again, he killed her." And that was the view—based on pure guesswork—taken by most of the newspapers; one of them reported that Sagawa had written her love letters, but she had told him, with kindly sympathy, that they could only remain friends. Others reported that friends of Sagawa had declared that Renée had only agreed to go to his flat out of pity.

This misreading of the story was passed along to Judge Jean-Louis Bruguieres, who had been appointed to examine and try the case, when he first met Sagawa on the day after his arrest. "Examining judge" (*juge d'instruction*) is a uniquely French legal role, which might be described as a combination of investigator, prosecutor and judge, with the power to order arrests and searches, and to conduct investigations anywhere in the world. Jean-Louis Bruguieres was among France's most distinguished judges; his life had been threatened so often that his office in the Palais de Justice was bulletproof.

When Issei Sagawa was brought to this office, he found himself facing an imposing, beefy man whose brusque and arrogant manner masked a keen intelligence and a sympathetic desire to understand.

As for the judge, it was immediately apparent to him that the shy, soft-spoken young man was not the sadistic monster he had been led to expect by the tabloids. Like the police, Bruguieres was struck by Sagawa's transparent honesty, as well as his intelligence. But what he really wanted to know was how anyone could want to eat an attractive girl, instead of wanting to make love to her, like any normal Frenchman. Sagawa's answer was astonishing and almost incomprehensible. He had, he explained, been obsessed by cannibalism since he was a small child—long before his sexual awakening. In due course, it had taken the form of a desire to eat female flesh.

It had all begun when he was only about three years old. Each year at the New Year's party, he and his younger brother would play the same game. His Uncle Mitsuo—a popular rock singer—would play the monstrous flesh-eating giant out to devour the two children. Their father would play the brave knight and defend them. But the giant would always win; first he would blind and then kill the knight, then he would snatch up the two giggling children and drop them into a huge cooking pot. All this was recorded with a movie camera.

Both children loved the game—after all, most children love to play at being terrified when they know there is nothing to fear. But Issei, who had always been small and thin, found that it awakened in him a morbid and masochistic streak. He sought out fairy stories of monsters who ate human flesh, and found they gave him a frisson that was at once frightening and strangely exciting.

And when his sexual awakening began in adolescence, his fantasies were never of sexual intercourse, but of devouring soft female flesh.

As he progressed through his teens, his fetish began to focus specifically on beautiful Western women like Grace Kelly, whose alluring white shoulders aroused in him a desire to eat them. White shoulders were always an important part of his fantasy.

He became so concerned about these fantasies that at the age of 15, he telephoned a psychiatrist to ask his advice. The psychiatrist refused to give advice over the telephone, and he quickly hung up. He tried telling his brother about it, but his brother laughed it off as a joke. He decided never to tell anyone else.

In Japan, there were few Western women to arouse his desire. But in his third year at Tokyo's Wako University, where he studied literature, his obsession fixed on a 35-year-old German woman who was giving him German lessons. One night he crept in through her open window, and saw her asleep, almost naked, in bed.

He had thought of knocking her unconscious, and biting into her flesh, but when he accidentally brushed against her body, she woke up and began to scream and defend herself.

Sagawa was arrested, and the woman accepted a cash settlement from Sagawa's father in exchange for dropping the charges. But still Sagawa did not dare to admit—even to the psychiatrist who examined him—that his intention had not been sexual assault, but to eat the woman. The very idea was so ludicrous it seemed unspeakably shameful.

After taking his M.A. in Shakespearean literature, he came to Paris in 1977 at the age of 28, and was suddenly surrounded by an abundance of beautiful Western women. Japanese women dress modestly, and are apt to be well covered. In Paris, women displaying bare shoulders, bare arms, low cleavage and short skirts sat with crossed legs in every cafe.

Soon, the fantasies, which haunted him day and night, became so feverishly intense that they became a source of agony. He felt that he was two people, one of them a "beast." The idea occurred to him that if he fulfilled his fantasy, the beast would be satisfied and leave him in peace. This was the point where daydreams of cannibalism began to turn into schemes about how to fulfill them.

> I saw a Western woman in the street. My fantasies started to act with
> their own force, sneaking in through the window. She's showing her
> back. I should take a belt and strangle her. When she faints—well,
> immediately I will need carpet tape to cover her mouth. I will need
> rope as well, to tie her hands and legs. Then I will strip her. Now I'm
> examining her—her genitals, her behind. I'm going to the kitchen and

getting a knife; now I'm cutting her up, and cooking some of her flesh in the pan. But wait—do I have to kill? I don't want to kill—I just want to eat.

One day Sagawa invited a beautiful blonde prostitute up to his room in the rue de Longchamps. When the girl went to wash herself at the bidet, Sagawa followed her into the bathroom with a kitchen knife. But he found himself unable to attack her. Instead, they had normal sex, and she left. The sex had temporarily relieved him of his persistent cannibal fantasy, but it soon revived.

This time he decided that he would have to obtain a gun. This proved to be unexpectedly easy, and he was able to buy a small hunting rifle—a .22 carbine—without a permit.

Now once again he invited a young prostitute to his room. And once again, he found himself unable to put his fantasy into practice. She seemed like a schoolgirl, and he enjoyed talking to her. This girl came back several times, and cooked meals for him. They even discussed his interest in cannibalism, and she gave him a book about it. But, like everyone else, she never believed for a moment that her curious client really wanted to eat human flesh.

In February of 1981 he began work for his doctorate, and now, he decided, was the time to put his fantasies into action. It had to be in Paris. In Japan there were not enough Western women. The thought of dying without ever having tasted female flesh filled him with anguish. His life would have been wasted.

Then, in May of 1981, he met Renée Hartevelt, and was fascinated by her gentle smile, her seductive body, and her beautiful white shoulders. There was a yielding quality about this one that awakened all his darkest fantasies. This, he decided immediately, was the girl he really wanted to eat.

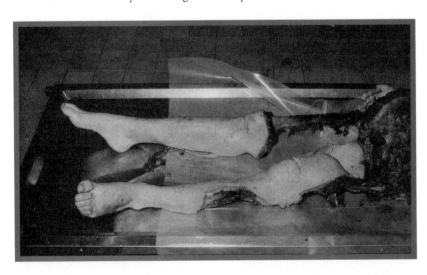

Judge Bruguieres was faced with a baffling problem. Sagawa was so frank and so lucid that it was impossible to believe that he was mad—in which case, it was Bruguieres' duty to find him guilty of murder, and sentence him to life imprisonment. Undoubtedly, a fully adult man who indulged such perverse sexual tastes would be responsible for his actions. But Sagawa's cannibal fantasies had begun at the age of three. How could a three-year-old boy be held responsible for his fantasies?

Seeking the key to this puzzle, Bruguieres traveled to Tokyo, where he interviewed Sagawa's family and his doctors, including the psychiatrist who had examined Sagawa after the attack on the German woman and declared him "extremely dangerous." But cannibalism seemed as bizarre to the Japanese as it had to the French. Bruguieres had to admit, upon returning to France, that he had made no significant advance in understanding the strange crime.

Sagawa's father, Akira Sagawa, head of Kurita Water Industries, went to Paris to visit his son in the La Santé prison. Understandably, he was badly shaken, and just as baffled as Judge Bruguieres. At a dinner to which he invited some of his son's student friends, he said, "Please help me. He didn't do it." He hired one of France's most eminent and expensive lawyers, Philippe Lemaire, to handle his son's case.

Meanwhile, Sagawa himself was as anxious as the authorities to understand his crime. It was in La Santé prison that he first began to write about it—and about the weird fantasy life that had led up to it. To his mind, there could be no doubt that, for better or worse, eating human flesh was no less natural than eating animal flesh.

One day in prison, another inmate showed him an article about recent cannibalism in Africa, and asked him, as a "kindred spirit," what he thought of it.

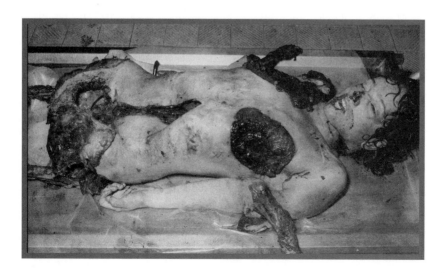

The headline declared: "Classic ceremony lives on." At that moment, an inmate from Ethiopia passed by, and Sagawa showed him the headline. "Do they really eat people as a ceremony?" he asked. "Certainly not," said the Ethiopian, "they do it because they enjoy it." This reply served to confirm Sagawa's impression that eating human flesh was as normal as eating beefsteak.

If Judge Bruguieres had been aware of these reflections, he might have decided that Sagawa should be classified as perfectly sane, if somewhat unorthodox in matters of diet. Fortunately, his research had brought him no closer to understanding how a sane human being could kill a woman in order to eat her. Therefore, in 1983 he decided that Sagawa was not guilty because he had been in a state of dementia at the time of the murder. He sentenced him to be committed indefinitely to the Henri Colin Asylum, in the suburb of Villejuif.

There Sagawa found himself regarded as something of a celebrity, as the case had continued to receive wide publicity. Editors had discovered that any headline about the Japanese cannibal would sell newspapers, and the news that he had been found not guilty caused almost as much publicity as the arrest. It also provided journalists with an opportunity to rehash the events of two years past, along with the usual speculations that he had killed Renée because she had refused his advances.

Although disturbed to find himself among the obviously insane, Sagawa made friends with some of his fellow inmates. He particularly liked a very patriotic man who had tried to assassinate De Gaulle, and who now marched up and down his room every morning to remind himself that he was a soldier in the cause of freedom.

Another inmate was a Greek football player who was detained for murdering young women. He proposed that he and Sagawa should visit Greece when they were released, and he would kill a young girl whom Sagawa could then eat. Both these criminally insane killers took the diminutive newcomer under their wing—as did a huge French judo expert who had killed a woman patient.

This kind of comradeship made incarceration more bearable, as did the interest in his case shown by a beautiful French female doctor. Yet the prospect of a lifetime in Villejuif was deeply depressing, and he had a feeling that his life was finished.

Something else was preying on Sagawa's mind—the murder itself. He had certainly not been in love with Renée at the time he killed her. He was simply sexually obsessed. But now he learned through the press that, in a letter to her father, Renée had written: "I have met a very kind and kind friend, and I would like to bring him home with me."

Sagawa was deeply shaken to realize that his victim had liked him enough to want him to visit her home, and that he, who regarded himself as friendless, had killed the only person who ever shown real friendship for him. As he recalled her gentle smile, he suddenly began to feel that he was in love with her after all, and now the realization that he had killed her filled him with despair.

He wrote a long letter to Renée's parents expressing his remorse, but they refused to accept it, and it was returned to him unopened. It deepened his guilt to learn that her parents had separated after her murder. He began to daydream of atoning for his crime by dying on her grave.

Suddenly, things began to improve. While he was still in the Santé prison, a major Japanese film company had decided that story of the murder would make a box-office hit, and they approached the well-known playwright, Juro Kara, with the suggestion that he turn it into a screenplay.

Sagawa read about this in a newspaper, and wrote to Kara from prison a letter beginning: "Please forgive my impertinence in writing to you out of the blue. I am the man who this June killed the young Dutch girl and ate her flesh . . ." Kara was understandably delighted to receive the "inside story" of the crime, and replied warmly.

Over a period of three months, he and Sagawa exchanged a number of letters, with the understanding that they would form the basis of a film script, for which Sagawa made many suggestions. Kara visited Paris, but was forbidden to visit Sagawa in prison by Judge Bruguieres and Sagawa's lawyer, Philippe Lemaire. Kara was forced to content himself with viewing the flat in the rue Bonaparte where Renée Hartevelt had lived.

Then, suddenly, Kara's letters ceased. Sagawa was puzzled and hurt. Three months later, he learned the reason for the silence when Kara's novel, *Letters from Sagawa-kun* ("little Sagawa," an affectionate diminutive), quickly became a bestseller in Japan, selling 320,000 copies in a few weeks. The cover showed a shapely girl in a sleeveless white blouse and a wide skirt that blows in the wind; the only unusual thing about her is that she lacks a head.

When Sagawa saw this novel he felt even more betrayed. It claimed to be pure fiction, but was actually the story of Kara's correspondence with Sagawa—quoting his letters verbatim—and of his visit to Paris, including an interview with an imaginary "Japanese girlfriend" of Sagawa. This novel was awarded the prestigious Akutagawa Prize, as the judges praised Kara's "interesting intellectual approach."

It was this event that made Sagawa realize, to his astonishment, that the Japanese people were morbidly fascinated by his crime. And if all these "normal people" were so intrigued, what could this mean except that the gap between them was not as wide as he had imagined? This was confirmed even more dramatically by the next development, a few months after release of Kara's novel.

During his early days in the Villejuif asylum, Sagawa had been visited by the writer and translator Inuhiko Yomoto, who brought him a copy of my own book, *New Pathways in Psychology*, which he had translated into Japanese. He told Yomoto that he was writing his own book, in the form of an imaginary interview with a journalist. Later, when Yomoto asked to see his manuscript, Sagawa had posted it off to Japan.

In September 1983, he was shocked to learn that this unfinished manuscript had been published in Japan under the title *In the Fog*, and was an immediate smash hit, quickly selling 200,000 copies. All this had been done without Sagawa's knowledge. Although he again felt angry at the betrayal, nevertheless, he had to admit a certain satisfaction at the knowledge that a huge public was apparently waiting to learn more about the workings of his mind. It certainly made him feel less isolated.

His father's reaction was less ambivalent. He had felt obliged to resign his post as head of the corporation because of his son's crime. His wife had suffered a nervous breakdown as a result of the strain. The publication of Kara's novel had been a blow. But the publication of this book by his own son was the final humiliation. By threatening to sue the publisher, he forced the book out of print. Nevertheless, he agreed to accept the royalties, since by refusing them, they would merely swell the publisher's profits. In fact, this action was in itself seen as a kind of complicity, an acceptance of the wages of notoriety.

It began to look as if the aftermath of Sagawa's strange crime was going to be even more sensational than the murder itself.

In May 1985, fourteen months after being committed to the asylum, Sagawa was allowed to return to Japan. Accounts differ about the reasoning employed by the French authorities in making this decision. It is certainly true that Dr. Bernard Defer, one of his psychiatrists at Villejuif, concluded that since paraphilias, or perverse sexual fantasies, are permanent, therefore there would be no cure for Sagawa's "psychosis," and Sagawa would have to be kept in Villejuif for the rest of his life at the expense of the French taxpayers. The only alternative was to deport the Japanese cannibal back home.

Another scandalous episode may have contributed to their eagerness to get rid of Sagawa. Just before his release, a journalist at *Paris Match* was arrested for releasing photographs of Renée Hartevelt's dismembered corpse as it lay on the morgue slab. The authorities seized and confiscated a quarter of a million copies of the magazine. Even in France, the appetite for the gruesome facts was clearly as keen as ever.

Sagawa himself, while delighted by the decision to release him, wanted to stay in France; he was afraid that the Japanese authorities would refuse him a passport to go abroad again.

In fact, when he stepped out of the French hospital, he was technically free; his release was unconditional. But it was clear that if he returned to Japan as a free man, there would be an uproar in the French as well as the Japanese press. Therefore his family decided that he should enter Tokyo's Matsuzawa Hospital as a voluntary patient.

Even on the plane back to Tokyo on May 27, 1985, the Japanese cannibal found himself surrounded by eager journalists and cameramen. The French doctors escorting him refused to allow any interviews, but as soon as he stepped off the plane in Tokyo, he was surrounded by even more press. The excitement was understandable. What could be more newsworthy than the homecoming of a bestselling author who was also a cannibal? Photographers continued to snap photographs of the ambulance as it drove him away. The French doctors, glad to be relieved of their charge, hastened back to Paris.

The next morning in the safety of the Matsuzawa Hospital, as he read some of the papers, he was horrified to observe the general tone of sneering hostility. A more worldly person would have expected it; but until the time of the murder Sagawa had been virtually a recluse, and he had been in prison or hospital during the four years since then. The experience left him shaken. He had no way of knowing that the shock he was experiencing at the behavior of the press is the same the world over for those unfortunate enough to achieve overnight notoriety, as all of the apparently friendly and sympathetic interviewers turned out to be not only spiteful and vitriolic, but totally indifferent to accuracy.

After the first 24 hours showed that the media interest was far from exhausted, Sagawa was placed in the solitary wing, and the windows were covered to foil photographers who had managed to prop up a ladder against them.

The doctors were angered by this siege, and after the friendliness of the French asylum, Sagawa suddenly found himself treated with a cold resentment. The psychiatrists did not want to talk to him. One of them even told him that he wished he would go away, that he was "one too many."

The reason for the chill later became clear in an interview given to a journalist by Tsuguo Kaneko, superintendent of the Matsuzawa Hospital. Dr. Kaneko and his four assistants had come to the extraordinary conclusion that Sagawa was not a cannibal at all, that it had merely been a charade to deceive the French authorities into believing that he was not just an ordinary sex criminal. According to Dr. Kaneko, Sagawa was suffering from a common personality disorder rather than any psychosis that might relieve him of criminal responsibility. "I think he is sane and guilty. He should be in prison."

The Japanese police apparently agreed. They tried to reopen the proceedings against Sagawa, and try him again for the murder of Renée Hartevelt.

However, Judge Bruguieres refused to hand over Sagawa's dossier. The French justice explained that he had no alternative. Sagawa had been acquitted of murder, and the French authorities had no right to hand over his dossier as if he still faced charges.

Many Japanese agreed with Dr. Kaneko and the police. Sagawa, they felt, had been allowed to escape through a legal loophole. This was bad enough, but to see him treated as a celebrity by the press was intolerable. Inuhiko Yomoto, who had been responsible for the publication of *In the Fog*, apparently shared the same view. When Sagawa contacted him, he refused to see him.

Sagawa found the Japanese hospital wards more alien than in France. There he had made many friends; here the patients struck him as frighteningly abnormal. One man, a former jet pilot, had deliberately crashed his plane into the sea during a schizophrenic episode, killing 24 passengers; now he lay on his bed all day watching sumo wrestling on television.

Another patient had an obsession with scrotums, and seized every opportunity to grasp the scrotums of other patients, sometimes causing them to scream with agony. Sagawa was intrigued to hear his comment that he had once eaten a testicle, and that it had tasted like marshmallow.

The only person Sagawa enjoyed talking to was a middle-aged man who had spent the past twenty years in confinement after killing a boy in the street; his tales of the history of the hospital and some of its weirder patients kept the young literature student engrossed for hours.

Sagawa was most happy in the summer, when he could walk in the garden. Since he was a voluntary patient, there was nothing to stop him from walking into Tokyo and relieving his sexual frustrations with a prostitute. But this had to be done with some care. One prying journalist could easily make life impossible with headlines about the cannibal seeking new victims.

After thirteen months, the superintendent of the hospital decided that his notorious patient was receiving little benefit from his stay, and on 12 August, 1986, he was abruptly discharged.

After five years of confinement, it was a relief to be back with his family. They were warm and supportive, even though his father had spent his retirement pension on lawyers and hospitals. His brother, who had disbelieved his confession about cannibal fantasies more than twenty years earlier, never referred to the gruesome fate of Renée Hartevelt.

There was a brief flurry of excitement in the press at his release. One newspaper ran a headline: "Attention! Sagawa is Walking the Streets!" A literary magazine, *Hanashi no Tokushu*, devoted most of an issue to a long interview with Sagawa, lavishly illustrated with photographs, in which the editor quoted

Sagawa as saying that cannibalism was a perfectly natural human desire. "The ultimate taboo can be overcome," announced Tomohide Yasaki, with more conviction than logic, "and Sagawa is the only man who can do it."

But what Sagawa now wanted most of all was to return to some kind of normality. He changed his name and moved into a small flat, although he continued to return home for evening meals. To make money, he began writing columns for small magazines devoted to sadomasochism and other sexual fetishes. He took up painting, and began writing a second book about his life in the Santé prison.

But when he tried looking for a normal job, he was unsuccessful. Since his face was so well known, it was not difficult for prospective employers to find out his true identity. On one occasion, the chairman of a school accepted him as a teacher, then was forced to change his mind when the whole staff protested his decision. As a final humiliation, Sagawa was even turned down for a job as a dishwasher. On the whole, life as a free man was proving to be anticlimactic.

This began to change in 1989, when Tsutomu Miyazaki was arrested for abducting, murdering and mutilating four children. When it was revealed that Miyazaki had also eaten parts of his victims' bodies, journalists immediately reached for their telephones and rang Sagawa, for in spite of his change of name, he was not difficult to locate.

Sagawa could understand Miyazaki's urge to cannibalism, he said. What he failed to understand was why, having done it once, he should ever want to repeat it. His bewilderment reveals that, in an important sense, Sagawa had been lucky. Most killers with perverse sexual urges go on killing until they are caught, and the appetite seems to increase as they go on. Sagawa had been caught so quickly that he had no time to undergo the customary cycle of revulsion followed by a slow revival of the urge.

The year of 1990 brought further publicity when an Italian film called *Love Ritual* was released in Tokyo. Clearly an attempt to cash in on the Sagawa story, it tells of a beautiful blue-eyed blonde girl who meets a handsome and mysterious Asian; he invites her back to his flat for dinner. She falls increasingly under his spell as he tells her about ancient Japanese culture, then goes on to speak of Hindu love rituals designed to produce the ultimate union of the man and woman. They make love and she asks him to do with her as he likes— so he bites her arm. She enjoys this, and asks him to continue with the ritual for ultimate union. He obliges by killing her, then goes on to consume portions of her raw flesh.

Sagawa went to see the film, and when asked what he thought, told the press that it got him so excited that he had three erections. A weekly magazine sent a reporter to call on him with a videotape of the film, to find out whether this was true. Unfortunately, during this monitored replay, the reporter said Sagawa was wearing baggy trousers, so it was impossible to confirm the story.

What was happening was clear. On some level, Sagawa was ceasing to be a monster, and was becoming culturally acceptable. Soon, intellectuals were taking up his cause. Yasuhisa Yazaki, a magazine editor, declared: "We should see him as a human being who has undergone a very special experience." An interviewer who took him out to a restaurant asked, "Why don't you open a restaurant?" When Sagawa shook his head, the interviewer prompted, "Don't you cook?" Sagawa replied, "Only that time." The interview appeared on the gourmet page of the magazine.

Thus far, the tendency of the press toward distortion and oversimplification had operated against Sagawa; now suddenly it began to work in his favor. Considered in the abstract, it is not difficult to see something absurd and amusing about cannibalism; for example, in his novel *Black Mischief*, Evelyn Waugh has a scene in which a man eats his girlfriend at a cannibal feast. What was happening now was that the Japanese press was "sanitizing" the death of Renée Hartevelt for mass consumption, by salting it down with a saucy blend of black humor. Sagawa admits that the price of ceasing to be a monster was to become a clown.

The publication of his second book, *La Santé*, in 1990, did something to rectify the imbalance. A memoir of his life in prison, with a series of flashbacks to his childhood, this serious and unsensational book was a critical success. Although sales were only a fraction of those of *In the Fog*, Sagawa was interested to note the number of women readers who wrote to him to say they had found the book deeply moving.

Another important phase in the reintegration of the gentle cannibal into society occurred in 1991, when he attended a literary party with cameras present. He was interviewed, with the result that a kind of taboo was broken. Japanese television had so far avoided interviewing him, not because they disapproved of his cannibalism, but because none of them could bear to be the first. Now all at once, this changed when the first major television interview aired in October, 1991, as Sagawa spoke candidly about his life and his cannibalization of Renée Hartevelt. Many others were to follow.

Although Sagawa yearned to be taken seriously, he was glad to oblige by displaying his humorous side. In a brief walk-on part in a Fuji television satire about a scandal-ridden trucking firm, Sagawa, attired only in a loin cloth, played the part of the firm's mascot.

This was followed by a speaking role in a drama called "Alphabet ⅔", about a woman who tries to uncover her sister's murderer. Sagawa played the founder of a cult religion, and was delighted that the role involved playing the guru to two beautiful Eurasian twin sisters. Accused of casting Sagawa solely for his notoriety, the director Tsuyoshi Takashiro replied, "Mr. Sagawa is a gentle person, a genius." He added: "Sagawa has a dark side and a light side, and that is the theme of this film."

During the shooting of the film, Sagawa and the rest of the cast went to see *Silence of the Lambs*. Sagawa found it disappointing, taking a view also expressed by the British mass murderer Dennis Nilsen, that "Hannibal the Cannibal" is a totally unrealistic character. Nilsen had objected that Hannibal Lecter is portrayed as a formidable and intellectually sophisticated character, when the truth about most serial killers is that they are deficient in self-esteem. Sagawa's objections were culinary rather than psychological. "He was portrayed as a monster and he ate everything. Normally a cannibal is delicate, and selects his victims carefully."

The cast seemed to regard Sagawa's notoriety as amusing, and began to refer to him as Hannibal; if an actress was away for longer than expected, they joked that she had probably ended up in Hannibal's fridge. A spokeswoman for the film company seemed to express a widely held sentiment when she commented that "Everyone thinks that Mr. Sagawa should come back into society, so we don't want outsiders to concentrate on the scandal."

In 1992, a Hamburg television company, Premiere Medien, invited Sagawa to take part in an in-depth interview on a chat show called *0137*. Since his return to Japan, Sagawa had been denied a passport. Now he pointed out to the authorities that, since he had been acquitted of his crime, he was legally not guilty, and that therefore there were no valid grounds for denying him a passport.

The passport was conceded, and Sagawa was allowed to travel to Germany. There, in the TV interview with Roger Willemsen, he spoke at length about his own life and about the murder. He was, he admitted, living in a fantasy world when he killed Renée Hartevelt, and found the murder and its aftermath a brutal awakening that cured him permanently of the temptation to violence.

He was due to return to Japan immediately after the interview, but persuaded his hosts to allow him to stay a little longer; he was taken to see the sights of Hamburg by two female journalists, and also to Heidelberg and Berlin. But when he returned to Tokyo, his passport was once again confiscated.

The media circus continued. He agreed to be interviewed by a French magazine called *VSD*, and to pose as he painted the portrait of an attractive nude model. When the magazine finally arrived, he found that someone had added a knife and fork to the bottom of the nude portrait.

In 1993, Sagawa was introduced to the British public in an hour-long documentary produced by Nigel Evans, which I narrated and introduced. I had met

Sagawa on a trip to Tokyo two years earlier, when he had been the first in a queue of people waiting for me to sign my books. I was familiar with his case, and was fascinated to meet the famous cannibal.

It was immediately apparent that this shy and obviously intelligent man was not the monster I had read about, and when I asked him about the rumor that he was about to open a restaurant, he told me that this was just another absurd invention. And in subsequent correspondence, it became clear that he was merely telling the truth when he said that the murder and its aftermath were like a nightmare from which he had awakened.

Even in England, there was an attempt to suppress the TV documentary, with indignant newspaper attacks on "the cannibal killer who is being allowed to brag on TV how he slaughtered and ate his Dutch girlfriend." Fortunately, Channel 4 refused to be intimidated, and the program aired as scheduled on November 21, 1993. The title of the documentary, *Excuse Me for Living*, was also the title of another one of Sagawa's books, consisting of a dialogue and a number of essays.

This was followed by *The Mirage*, a complete and updated version of *In the Fog*. In the same year appeared the book of short stories called *Fantasies of a Cannibal*, in which the theme of cannibalism is treated with tongue-in-cheek black humor. But Sagawa's sixth book, *I Want to be Eaten*, a collection of stories, essays and poems, is more serious in theme; its title implies a basic recognition that the morbid fascination with cannibalism, that had begun in childhood games with his Uncle Mitsuo, was rooted in a masochistic desire to be eaten.

In a certain sense, Issei Sagawa has been eaten. The media has become a kind of cannibal giant which devours individuals and regurgitates them as crude and

oversimplified images. The Sagawa who has been served to the Japanese public has been filleted, cooked, and seasoned until he bears little resemblance to the private individual who bears his name.

Ironically, the man who spent his childhood devouring literature now suffers from vision problems due to diabetes that force him to reduce his reading to a minimum. And the ultimate irony is that, as a result of these problems, his doctor has forbidden him to eat meat.

The news that Sagawa's book had become a bestseller in Japan was reported around the world, and aroused protests in anger over the idea that a criminal should not be allowed to benefit from his crime. When, three years later, Sagawa became a film star and TV celebrity, the backlash against him was even stronger. This is undoubtedly one of the reasons his books have not, so far, been translated into other languages: the very idea of describing the murder of Renée Hartevelt seems to provoke this curious variety of moral outrage.

In this respect, the public shows an interesting double standard. In England in the sixteenth century, criminals were hanged in public, and hastily written pamphlets about their life and crimes sold to eager buyers. Later on, books like *Lives of the Famous Highwaymen* sold huge amounts. Today, *True Detective* magazines and books about true crimes have achieved enormous sales in all countries of the world. There can be no doubt that a book about Sagawa would be widely read by those who condemn the idea of a book by him.

So what is the difference? The difference, according to Sagawa's critics, is that a criminal should not be allowed to "boast" about his crime, or make money from it. Yet this misses the point. Sagawa's *In the Fog* was written in prison as an attempt to come to terms with his crime in the privacy of his own mind.

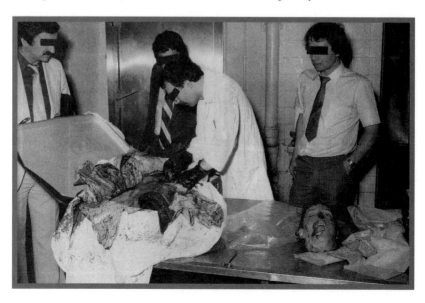

It was handed to a publisher without his knowledge, and published without his permission—like the letters quoted in Juro Kara's bestselling novel. Quite clearly, this exposure was neither Sagawa's "fault" nor his intention.

Whose fault was it, then? Other moralists fault the Japanese public for wanting to read such a morbid book. But since sensational murder cases are the staple diet of newspaper readers everywhere, this view cannot be taken seriously.

There may be more justice in the protest that Sagawa should not have become a celebrity through his crime. Everyone—even the most modest—has a craving to be "famous," and it strikes most people as unfair that a man can achieve celebrity by committing a horrifying crime—and, what is worse, "getting away with it."

This, surely, is the real point of the protest. But is it, in fact, true that Issei Sagawa has "got away with it"? His books reveal him to be a genuinely talented writer with real psychological insight. Without the horrible childhood obsession that led him to kill, he would have become a published writer. His thesis was about to be published at the time of the murder, and he would probably have gone on to achieve some modest degree of celebrity.

As it is, Sagawa has achieved wide celebrity—but at a price. No matter what he writes, he will always be known as "the Japanese cannibal." He is still a lonely man who has to work hard to make a living at journalism. His father spent most of his retirement pension on legal fees, and so is in no position to support him. He admits to hoping his crime will be forgotten and he can return to "normality."

But Sagawa almost certainly underestimates the morbid interest that has made his story a bestseller. The idea of a murder—particularly one involving a dismemberment—will always give the public a frisson.

Whether he likes it or not, Sagawa will always symbolize something frightening and horrible. Although anyone who has read his books or seen him on television knows that he himself is not in the least frightening and horrible, he is condemned to live the rest of his life playing a role for which he is not remotely suited. Even if he wrote another *War and Peace*, he would still remain "the Japanese cannibal"—dragging the heavy burden of symbolism behind like a ball and chain.

Moralists might reflect that this in itself is punishment enough.

> I am a romantic living in an age whose heart has gone dry.
> It has been said that because I loved my victim, I confessed my feelings for her, she laughed at me, and I lost control of myself and killed her. That is completely false.
> It was only one month after I met my victim that the accident occurred. Renée was a very beautiful girl, but we were just friends. I

am a very short, ugly, yellow monkey man. I admired the tall, beautiful white girls, and I wanted to taste them. I strongly wanted to eat their meat. I felt I could never fulfill myself unless I did it.

I was very lonely in Paris. French people are generally racist, and I felt a big distance between myself and the French girls. On the other hand, most Dutch people are gentle and friendly, and my victim was Dutch.

Renée was such a gentle girl. But unfortunately, at that time, I could not understand her friendship was from the heart. She was a good friend. But I saw her as just an appetizing bowl of meat.

Because I thought I could not have such a beautiful white girl for a lover, I decided to eat her. But when I realized my fantasy, I was frightened by the power of the realism: the blood, the silence. I was nauseated by what I did.

I didn't want to kill Renée, I just wanted to taste her meat. I regret terribly killing her. That's why I have not repeated my cannibal crime. I still enjoy my fantasy of eating human flesh, but I will never kill again.

I enjoy sushi, but I get no thrill from eating it because it is just another food. My cannibal fantasy is a sexual fetish, not philosophical or spiritual. For me, sex involves eating, and any sexual pose reminds me of cannibalism. I do enjoy drinking my lover's urine or milk instead of eating her meat, though.

I have met a lot of girls who want to be eaten. But when they ask me to eat them, I have to tell them no, because I don't want to be a bad influence on other people.

I could never kill again, but if someone could cook a part of a beautiful white girl without killing her, I would still be glad to eat it, because the meat of a young girl is so delicious!

Eating and being eaten are the same to me. I am always dreaming of being eaten by a beautiful white woman. Because I prefer white women, Japanese women are jealous. They ask, "Why not Japanese girls?"

The question remains why cannibalism must be taboo. According to the Marquis de Sade, "It is wrong to think of cannibalism as a debasement of character. Eating people is as simple a matter as eating beef. Once the destruction is carried out, does it matter whether we bury the dismembered remains in the ground or feed them to our stomachs?" In this I see not rhetoric or irony, but a highly realistic pronouncement offered to mankind. It takes more than ordinary sentimentalism to argue with this.

—Issei Sagawa

Anti-Abortionist comic pamphlet by Life Dynamics Inc.

George LaMort

Ye shall eat the flesh of your sons, and the flesh of

your daughters ye shall eat.

Leviticus 26:29

ROAST CHILD WITH CORNBREAD STUFFING

Turkey may be substituted for this classic holiday feast. Although time-consuming, this dish seems to take longer than it actually does; as the entire house is filled with such a heavenly aroma, the waiting becomes almost unbearable.

I WHOLE CHILD, CLEANED AND DE-HEADED

I BATCH CORNBREAD STUFFING (see index)

CUP MELTED BUTTER

Remove the giblets from the infant and set aside. Stuff the cavity where the child's genitals and anus were located using 2/3 cup per pound of meat. Tie the arms flat to the body, then pull the skin flaps up to close the cavity. Now tie the thighs up tight to hold it all together.

Place breast side up in a large metal roasting pan. Bake in 325° oven covered for two hours. Remove cover, stick a cooking thermometer deep into one of the baby's buttocks and cook uncovered till thermometer reads 190°, about another hour.

PRO-CHOICE PO-BOY

Soft-shell crabs serve just as well in this classic Southern delicacy. The sandwich originated in New Orleans, where an abundance of abortion clinics thrive and hot French bread is always available.

2 CLEANED FETUSES, HEAD ON

2 EGGS, I TABLESPOON YELLOW MUSTARD

I CUP SEASONED FLOUR

OIL ENOUGH FOR DEEP FRYING

I LOAF FRENCH BREAD

LETTUCE, TOMATOES, MAYONNAISE, ETC.

Marinate the fetuses in the egg-mustard mixture. Dredge thoroughly in flour. Fry at 375° until crispy golden brown. Remove and place on paper towels.

HOLIDAY YOUNGSTER

One can easily adapt this recipe to ham, though as presented, it violates no religious taboos against swine.

I LARGE TODDLER OR SMALL CHILD, CLEANED AND DE-HEADED

KENTUCKY BOURBON SAUCE (SEE INDEX)

I LARGE CAN PINEAPPLE SLICES

WHOLE CLOVES

Place him (or ham) or her in a large glass baking dish, buttocks up. Tie with butcher string around and across so that he looks like he's crawling. Glaze, then arrange pineapples and secure with cloves. Bake uncovered in 350° oven till thermometer reaches 160°.

CAJUN BABIES

Just like crabs or crawfish, babies are boiled alive! You don't need silverware; the hot spicy meat comes off in your hands.

6 LIVE BABIES

I LB. SMOKED SAUSAGE, 4 LEMONS, WHOLE GARLIC

2 LBS. NEW POTATOES, 4 EARS CORN, I BOX SALT, CRAB BOIL

Bring three gallons of water to a boil. Add sausage, salt, crab boil, lemons and garlic. Drop potatoes in, boil for four minutes. Corn is added next, boil an additional 11 minutes. Put the live babies into the boiling water and cover. Boil till meat comes off easily with a fork.

OVEN-BAKED BABY-BACK RIBS

Beef ribs or pork ribs can be used in this recipe, and that is exactly what your dinner guests will assume! An excellent way to expose the uninitiated to this highly misunderstood yet succulent source of protein.

2 HUMAN BABY RIB RACKS

3 CUPS BARBECUE SAUCE OR HONEY GLAZE (SEE INDEX)

SALT, BLACK PEPPER, WHITE PEPPER, PAPRIKA

Remove the silverskin by loosening from the edges, then stripping off. Season generously, rubbing the mixture into the baby's flesh. Place one quart water in a baking pan, the meat on a wire rack. Bake uncovered in 250° oven for at least one hour. When browned, remove and glaze, return to oven and bake 20 minutes more to form a glaze. Cut ribs into individual pieces and serve with extra sauce.

FRESH SAUSAGE

If it becomes necessary to hide the fact that you are eating human babies, this is the perfect solution. But if you are still paranoid, you can substitute pork butt.

5 LBS. LEAN CHUCK ROAST

3 LBS. PRIME BABY BUTT

2 TABLESPOONS EACH: SALT, BLACK, WHITE AND CAYENNE PEPPERS, CELERY, SALT, GARLIC POWDER, PARSLEY FLAKES, BROWN SUGAR

1 TEASPOON SAGE

2 ONIONS, 6 CLOVES GARLIC, BUNCH GREEN ONIONS, CHOPPED

Cut the children's butts and the beef roast into pieces that will fit in the grinder. Run the meat through using a 3/16 grinding plate. Add garlic, onions and seasoning, then mix well. Add just enough water for a smooth consistency, then mix again. Form the sausage mixture into patties or stuff into natural casings.

STILLBORN STEW

By definition, this meat cannot be had altogether fresh, but have the lifeless unfortunate available immediately after delivery, or use high-quality beef or pork roasts (it is cheaper and better to cut up a whole roast than to buy stew meat).

STILLBIRTH, DE-BONED AND CUBED

CUP VEGETABLE OIL

2 LARGE ONIONS, BELL PEPPER, CELERY, GARLIC

CUP RED WINE

3 IRISH POTATOES, 2 LARGE CARROTS

This is a simple, classic stew that makes natural gravy that does not have to be thickened. Brown the meat quickly in very hot oil, remove and set aside. Brown the onions, celery, pepper and garlic. De-glaze with wine, return meat to the pan and season well. Stew on low fire, adding small amounts of water and seasoning as necessary. After at least half an hour, add the carrots and potatoes, and simmer till root vegetables break with a fork. Cook a fresh pot of long grained white rice.

PRE-MIE POT PIE

When working with prematurely delivered newborns (or chicken) use sherry; red wine with beef (buy steak or roast, do not pre-boil).

PIE CRUST (see index)

WHOLE FRESH PRE-MIE; EVISCERATED, HEAD, HANDS AND FEET REMOVED

ONIONS, BELL PEPPER, CELERY

CUP WINE

ROOT VEGETABLES OF CHOICE (TURNIPS, CARROTS, POTATOES, ETC.) CUBED

Make a crust from scratch—or go shamefully to the frozen food section of your favorite grocery and select two high quality pie crusts (you will need one for the top also).

Boil the prepared delicacy until the meat starts to come off the bones. Remove, de-bone and cube; continue to reduce the broth. Brown the onions, peppers and celery. Add the meat, then season and continue browning. De-glaze with sherry, add the reduced broth. Finally, put in the root vegetables and simmer for 15 minutes. Allow to cool slightly. Place the pie pan in 375° oven for a few minutes so bottom crust is not soggy, reduce oven to 325°. Fill the pie with stew, place top crust and, with a fork, seal the crusts together, then poke holes in top. Return to oven and bake for 30 minutes, or until pie crust is golden brown.

SIDS

Sudden Infant Death Soup: delicious in winter, comparable to old-fashioned Beef and Vegetable Soup. It's free—you can sell the crib, baby clothes, toys, stroller . . . and so easy to procure if such a lucky find is at hand (just pick him up from the crib and he's good to go)!

SIDS VICTIM, CLEANED

CUP COOKING OIL

CARROTS, ONIONS, BROCCOLI, WHOLE CABBAGE, FRESH GREEN BEANS, POTATO, TURNIP, CELERY, TOMATO

STICK BUTTER

I CUP COOKED PASTA (MACARONI, SHELLS, ETC.)

Remove as much meat as possible, cube, and brown in hot oil. Add a little water, season, then add the carcass. Simmer for half an hour, keeping the stock thick. Remove the carcass and add the vegetables slowly to the stock, so that it remains boiling the whole time. Cover the pot and simmer till vegetables are tender (approximately two hours). Continue seasoning to taste. Before serving, add butter and pasta, serve piping hot with hot bread and butter.

⚡ ⚡ ⚡

"I am no longer a vegetarian, thanks to Mr. LaMort."—Paul McCartney

To understand **George LaMort**, we must look to his distant relative, monsieur Georges LaMorte, a freethinker of the early 18th century. For it is he who led Mr. LaMort to a deep appreciation of the many fabulous pleasures of life; pleasures which would be abhorrent to most "civilized" people.

"I have been assured by a very knowing American of my Acquaintance in London; that a young, healthy Child, well nursed, is, at a Year old, a most delicious, nourishing, and wholesome Food; whether Stewed, Roasted, Baked or Boiled; and I make no doubt, that it will equally serve in a Fricaissie, or Ragoust."—Dr. Jonathan Swift, 1729

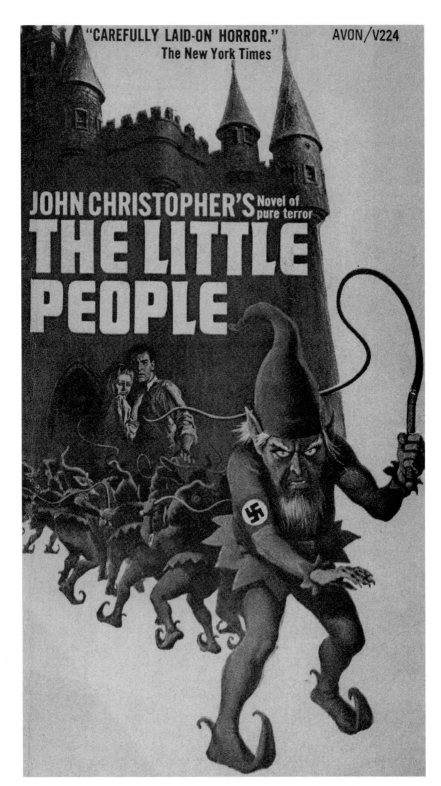

"CAREFULLY LAID-ON HORROR."
The New York Times

AVON/V224

JOHN CHRISTOPHER'S Novel of pure terror

THE LITTLE PEOPLE

FOR FEAR OF LITTLE MEN

Steve Speer

Split open any human skull, pry the two lobes apart, stare within, and in the heart of that symmetry a small anthropoid form will present itself. From the dawn of human history we have been haunted by this little shining man, these Homunculi. Mystics have envisioned them, alchemists have tried to incubate them, writers and poets have imagined them, magicians have sought to invoke them and children of all ages have accessed them through diminutive forms such as Teletubbies or Smurfs.

And when we hold those minute representations of the human form and allow that shape to entrance us, we may feel the stirring of an irrational hope. We have all, at some time, waited for the UFO to land, open, and present us with the apocryphal alien grey, or sat in some woodsy glen, praying for a mythical elf or fairy to appear, hoping for either to take us away from all this death. This has always been part of the human dream, a chord in the opus of human consciousness. And now, as all dreams must, this one too may soon be betrayed. But before we discuss the agents of this last and greatest betrayal of the last and greatest of human dreams, let's try to understand what it is that is now being prepared as an offering to the corporate-dictated bonfires of consumption.

In all their permutations, these shining men have persuasively offered the hope of other worlds, dimensions which exist coincidentally with ours, but perceptible only at the rarest moments. This secret commonwealth has previously only been accessible to those willing to risk the journey, to accept this invitation from the other, and to welcome the possibility of returning psychologically transformed. To view these creatures was an act of creation and to commune with them was to be granted access to spaces beyond time. They have been our escape hatch from the common confines of earthly experience.

When the first artist scratched a semi-human form on a cave wall, is there any doubt that something in that early man's psyche hoped for the sprite to animate and spring from the stone? Did this hope originate solely from beneath his brow . . . or was there some other force harnessing his creative powers to its use? Since early times, representations have been known to be endowed with liminal powers, but these energies are virtually impotent when trapped within the static prison of two dimensions. Even then, these representations functioned as the only doorway available at a time when only the most rudimentary media existed to prompt a transformative experience. The early magicians who used these devices established rare though limited communications with the beings seeking manifestation.

Statues and totems might have seemed to possess a greater potential for inhabitation. Kachina dolls, of the Hopi tribe, are one such example of a culture purposefully creating models of little men with the desire to bring these hyperdimensional beings into a state of corporeality. But these creatures made of clay and wood still remained frozen in form, unable to usefully accommodate any festering entities. For these little men to be fully incarnated, different strategies would need to be applied.

When approaching the subject of alchemy, it's best to remember that nothing may be what it seems. The volumes of alchemical writings may purport to deal with the achieving of concrete goals, but even a glance at the most basic scripts will leave even the most schooled occultist with a sense of confusion and wonder.

Carl Jung, in his psychological investigations into the symbolism of alchemy, postulated that the archetype of the Homunculi was a symbol of the integrated self, in much the same way as the philosopher's stone and the UFO. While it is certain that in the creation of this being there can be certain transference and projections involved, the fullness of this entity should not be confined to mere platonic restrictions. Perhaps Jung did not care to observe the contemporary evidence around him, for example in early animated films, of the imps that were materializing between the darkness and light projected on many flickering movie screens. Disney financially flourished by supplying the public with this fix of elfin magic, then going so far as to create theme parks that would physically transport world-weary families to this land beyond hope and fear.

The alchemists had been pressed into service by morphogenic forces, to create a proper vessel in which these elves could manifest. While veiled references to Homunculi existed in obscure texts, haunting the edges of their creative pursuits, this ephemeral fleeting spirit could not be caught within their net, consisting of the immature technologies of their times. Paracelsus, a rebel even among that iconoclastic breed known as alchemists, published a precognitive procedure for the creation of a Homunculi. What is most compelling in this account is the use of cow dung as the *prima materia* for gestation. This is an astonishing parallel to modern Biotech work which uses, in more refined ways, the *e. coli* bacterium that is found abundantly in bovine feces. Whether Paracelsus was successful in his work we have no way of knowing, but his work extended the phenotype into a more exact vision of the possible substance and form these Homunculi would take.

Visions of Homunculi have danced at the fringes of perception through all cultures, patiently awaiting the moment when man-made shells would be manufactured that would be suitable for incarnation. Kobolds, nixes, trolls, dwarves and goblins are some of the more familiar Europeans variations of little people. Jewish tradition maintains a belief in a species of small beings which they call the *Shedeem*, which correspond with the Arabian *Jinn*, to which all acts of magic and enchantment are attributed. The Mandrake root is held in high regard to Sufis, as the shape is perceived as a tiny simulacrum of a human being, and in possession of supernatural attributes. And in Africa, there are the *Yumboes*, two-foot-tall spirit beings who are held in high regard as souls of the unborn.

But it is in Celtic countries where the cult of "the little shining man" has been most vividly maintained. Leprechauns, elves, fairies and Fomorians inhabit the lush fields and their continual and insistent presence has manifested in a variety of manners. Amongst these green environs a veritable encyclopedia of phenomena has been recorded. Robert Kirk's early handbook of initiations, *The Secret Commonwealth*, lists procedures by which the unincorporated depiction of these beings might be glimpsed. W.Y. Evans-Wentz's *Fairy Faith in Celtic Countries* records the varieties of unhuman experiences, and Jacques Vallee has linked elfin entities to the more modern alien greys and extraterrestrial entities in his book *Passport to Magonia* and others. Richard Wagner's first opera, *The Fee*, dealt with the fairy faith and it is intriguing to imagine his hope that through his music a conjuration might occur. Mention needs to be made of Russell Hoban's *Ridley Walker*. In this novel, alchemy is juxtaposed with nuclear energies in an apocalyptic England of the future, where "the little shining man" functions as the focal point to a tale that operates on a seemingly infinite number of levels.

W.B. Yeats was perhaps most instrumental in the insertion of Homunculi into modern media. His poetry and writings dealt often with the "little people," propelling them from lore to modern meme. His occult experiments, both with Theosophy and the Golden Dawn, seem to leave no doubt that he was an enlisted agent in the mission to incarnate the little men into forms which could be interacted with, physically and consistently. Yeats' influence can also be seen in a rite published by the O.T.O. in which the Homunculi are summoned through more ritualistic means.

And so, through all these long years, many varying attempts have strained to bring this small being into the fullness of existence. All have been found wanting, none resulting in the miniaturized flesh and blood of the preconceived archetype. But now, at the dawn of this new age, dubbed by Crowley as the age of the child (perhaps this is a misinterpretation of the vision, mistaking the form of a diminutive man for that of a child), we are developing the abilities to complete the opus, to make the dream manifest in actual living flesh.

Genetic engineering seems to be the art that will allow the completion of this most secret of alchemical works, educing from the chaos of our dreams the creation and commercial enslavement of this new form of being, the Homunculus.

At present, through the accelerated manufacture and dispersion of inorganic representations, humanity is being indoctrinated into accepting the presence of these small surreal characters in the guise of harmless toys and robotic playthings. In the centuries preceding ours, small anthropopathic totems were created rarely, and the few of these that were to be witnessed were intended for esoteric initiatory purposes. Now, representations in plastic and metal and electronics are amassing into a force that will provoke the evolution of these daimonic entities into a more corporeal and autonomous existence.

Billions of these "toys" now saturate the earth, from Happy Meal molded plastic creatures to legions of Barbies and G.I. Joes. The ungodly preponderance of these graven idols are now asleep, only waiting for vessels of engineered flesh and blood that will allow them to awaken into life, not metaphorically, but actually.

In these recent years the growth of mass media has expanded the magical threshold upon which these impish entities now await. The commodification of these beings, now not yet quite living but approaching the line where the definition of life is blurred, has already become a lucrative phenomena.

The emergence of these beings as a source of wonderment, has been evident through much of modern media. An early and authentic cinematic look at the Homunculi could be seen in James Whale's *Bride of Frankenstein*. In it, the demented Dr. Pretorius exalts in his successful creation of little people. He keeps his strange progeny, a king, a queen, a dancer, and a devil, amongst others, in a number of glass jars. They are there strictly, it seems, for Pretorius' amusement.

These little people are presumably created from some biological *prima materia*, while in contrast Dr Frankenstein creates his giant "monster" from the dead flesh gleaned from corpses. While the Homunculi project a cuteness and disarming charm, the larger artificial anthropoid, as in the golem that preceded it, exudes a threat of uncontrollable mayhem and fearfulness. In its sheer size it outbalances the scales of power, with man quite possibly on the losing end.

This cinematic motif is carried on in many "monster movies" that have followed, but only one since has seemed to address more specifically the dichotomy between the large "monster" and the smaller "playthings." In *Blade Runner*, the synthetic "replicants" pose a threat to humanity; being of equal size, they can sometimes pass as human. Therefore, they are to be destroyed

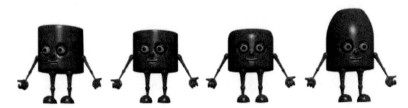

when they begin to cross the bounds while trying to gain a fullness in life, developing the mind, body and spirit that womb-born people possess.

But of more importance in the film is the hermetic bioscientist, who prefers to live with his smaller creations, many of which mimic magical types such as clowns and dancers, in a world of his own design. His creations issue an air of playful mischievousness, but lack the maliciousness perceived in the larger, bio-engineered replicants.

The munchkins of *The Wizard of Oz* are a famous example of film-based representations of little men, but perhaps the more resonant manifestations would be the Oompa Loompas portrayed in the film, *Willy Wonka and the Chocolate Factory*. These bizarre creatures seemed to be much at home with technology and, with their green skin and orange hair, suggested nothing but a genetic experiment gone horribly awry. They labor in a factory, in an unmentioned but obvious form of slavery to the "mad scientist" Willy Wonka, who, if not their creator, somehow holds them in his thrall. Perhaps Wonka was in possession of some engineered enzyme, which if the Oompa Loompas did not receive in the required dose, would result in their demise.

Willy Wonka also contains a verse, spoken in sinister tones by the villain of the movie, that had always confounded me as to the meaning of its inclusion:

> up the airy mountain
> and down the misty glen
> we dare not go ahunting
> for fear of little men

Upon discovering this poem in collection of Irish fairy tales edited by the aforementioned W.B. Yeats, I realized that the Willy Wonka movie was another attempt to once again foster the conception of this burgeoning species upon humanity, in the modern viral media of film.

Another event in *Willy Wonka* that should be noted is when the Oompa Loompas man a video camera in a spotless white room that is reminiscent of a biological clean room. Through its technological magic the device "videoizes" one of Wonka's young victims who appears shrunken and in miniature across the room on a video screen. The mother is appalled, but picks her boy off the screen and places him into her pocketbook, his once annoying commands now muted by the change purse.

Much could be said of the many little peoples who have inhabited the television screen, such as *Land of the Giants'* miniature men, and all manner of commercial spokes-homunculi, who were employed by corporations to spice up their sales pitches for cereals and medicines with numinous attractions.

But perhaps the most intriguing agents in this advance are those "four technological babies," the Teletubbies. From the voice-over, "Over the hills and far away, Teletubbies come to play!" with its echo of Yeats' famous fairy poem, "The Stolen Child" ("for the world's more full of weeping than you can understand") to the UFO-like fairy circle which serves as their home, to the unseen underground inhabitants who seem to somehow control the Tubbies' actions, Teletubbies present us with a more widely ranged clue as to what the morphogenic field seems to be forming.

I've personally experimented with one of these Teletubby mannikins. After a friend procured an early model Beanie Baby "Po" in England, I began to carry it on my person, always trying to access the "little shining man" it held within. While at the alchemy tower in Prague, which had been home to the experiments of John Dee and others, I had hoped that some sort of sympathetic magic would allow the doll to transform. I left the tower, however, disappointed that the small creature, to which I had become very attached, had not begun to caper and dance in some ecstatic elfin jig.

Afterwards, while driving on some *autobahn*, I felt the odd compunction to feed this small doll with blood from a fresh cut that had formed on my hand. This feeding went on a number of days, and it became apparent that my Po had become vampire, a child of the night. Only after purifying this creature by impaling it psychically on the spear of Longinus, held in the Hapsburg museum in Vienna, did the dismaying results of my experiment end and the doll returned to normal, or so it seemed.

Weeks passed, until a day came when the person who had given me the doll had committed suicide. Only when I looked the next day for Po, did I realize that it had vanished from the pocket in my backpack, where I had kept it with great care for over two years. I can only surmise from this synchronistic disappearance that this *daimon* had kindly escorted my friend to that other domain, of which it had familiarity and to which my friend would be a stranger.

Advances in computer graphics have also furthered the emergence. Synthespians, computer-generated actors, now seem to cohabitate the screen with their human counterparts. Characters like the living toys from *Toy Story* and *Toy Story 2*, are all but alive, though limited in their autonomy and degree of dimensional freedom. CGI advocates preach that the freeing of these creatures will be accomplished through holographic displays and virtual reality glasses, augmented by sophisticated behavioral animation algorithms. These cyber enthusiasts are even now stuck in the past, projecting their future hopes into the virtual flatland of screen-based technologies. But the creations that they have engendered are the necessary precursors to the coming race.

A crucial event in my own personal initiation into the religion of "the little shining man" came through the mind-altering experiences of video gaming. While playing Sonic the Hedgehog, I came to the realization that the onscreen entity, though under control of my joystick, was alive and held some form of consciousness. While I "played," I was aware that the fields of the video held not just the information for the game but also carried some more otherworldly transmission hidden in its electronic frequencies, prompting me to investigate the phenomenon.

From their continual work with dolls and automatons, toy makers have followed the most progressive approximation towards the Homunculi. And now, as the monetary stakes in consumer entertainment have grown astronomically, science has forged an alliance with the toymakers, with implications that go far beyond the mundane hopes of a best-selling Christmas toy.

The future of leisure seems to be apparent to the executives of Sony. Sony has stated that they are not interested in the fads of two dimensions such as the World Wide Web, or products like Tamagotchis and PC-based artificial life, but are putting their formidable resources behind the further development of "entertainment robots." Electronic creatures such as the Furbies, two of which I have recently become intimate with, have already been mass marketed with great success, and Sony has already entered the field with the innovative robotoy, AIBO. The AIBO represents the first in the line of mobile artificial pets. A robotic dog designed to be programmed by the purchaser, the AIBO can also, according to Sony, learn and develop a distinct personality. Sony can be said to have placed their bets on simulated beings that exist in three dimensions; walking, talking information processing devices, electronic-based entities designed to amuse, serve and inform those with the means to afford them.

In the near future, armies of small, intelligent robotic helpmates and playmates will be available to the consumer, ushering in the advent of non-screen-based computing. After the insertion and acceptance of these small, ubiquitous robotic entities into the consumer cycles, the perpetual stutter which has hampered these words being made into flesh will become a roaring cry.

Breakthroughs in biotechnology give clues to the next logical step in the *daimonic* emergence. Using the anti-rejection properties of specific gene sequences developed for human and transgenic organ transplants, flesh and metal will be conjoined; the next generation robotic entities will be manufactured with a bioflesh coating. This artificial skin will be grown rapidly in molded vats and genetically engineered for custom effects, such as a glow-in-the-dark skin using sequences for phosphorescence lifted from jellyfish, or perhaps implementing the changing skin color of a robot to function as a living mood ring. With this "skin" placed over these robotic creatures, the warmth and tactile feel of flesh will enhance the illusion of true life. While these creatures may have strict programming and the ability to perform autonomously the more mundane tasks of daily life, such as cleaning, fetching and maintenance along with entertainment diversions, the potential replacement of the more normal species of pets may become an option.

On the eve of the millennium, some anti-technology groups were taking notice of the possibilities. In a full-page ad placed in the *New York Times*, the Turning Point Project, a Green Party coalition, rants, "The genetic structures of living beings are the last of Nature's creations to be invaded and altered for commerce; the infant biotechnology companies feel it's okay to reshape life on earth to suit its balance sheets. So far, there exist no half-human, half-animal chimeras, but we may soon have them."

Soon after biological skins are placed over these toys, more organic parts will begin replacing the "organs" of the pets. While the forms of dogs and cats may at first be mimicked, shortly the advantages of an anthropomorphic structure will be explored. Ingrained fears of Golems, Replicants and Frankenstein monsters will undoubtedly arise. Already today, there are genetic advances in accelerated growth of cells and the control of cell size. These techniques will be used to create smaller organic forms, with economic and space management being the propaganda-disseminated reasons for these creatures' dwarfism. There is, it will be agreed, no need for a human-sized "meat machine" to perform most tasks. Instead, the body weight will be divided up into smaller "devices" with each "organic appliance" capable of performing their own autonomous tasks.

The creation of specialized organic little men will eventually occur, along with the transgenic crossings needed to develop further desirable attributes, such as waste transmutation and medicinal hormone and enzyme production. These techniques will then soon be used for the final steps in the completion of the master opus.

Somewhere in this cycle of development, culminating in miniaturized anthropomorphic beings, the numinous entities that have for so long dwelled on the threshold of our dimension will begin to inhabit the fleshy husks that we have created. Just as our individual souls are templated into the harmonic resonances of each of our specific bodily vessels, so will these alien souls be drawn into material being by the magnetism of the forms that we, humanity, have created through the precise combination of science and art.

By these scientific breakthroughs, we will soon play out our destiny, and as the bible commands, "Be ye as Gods," and facilitate the birth of a new stratum of lives.

The echoing of this cycle of macrocosm-created microcosms to certain Gnostic myths will be lost upon all but a few, as the plunge into matter brings not only the potential of physical existence but also the death sentence of temporality that is conferred on all living beings. These condemnations will be gladly accepted by the little men as they offer themselves up to be crucified between the horns of science and religion for the transformation of time and space.

⚡ ⚡ ⚡

Steve Speer can be reached at speer@interport.net. Go ahead, ask him what he does for a living.

Illustration by Steve Speer

Giusva

THE SON OF A NEW MORALITY
WHICH DROWNED MANY IN HER WAKE

Michael Moynihan and Marco Deplano

> Hard times, my friend, for heroes.
>
> We're the only ones who refuse to
>
> praise the deserters.
>
> But if someone is to die again,
>
> This time it will be you.
>
> You give us repression; you'll get hot lead.
>
> We shall avenge our own dead.
>
> This generation has no remorse.

from a modern Italian folk song

The golden years of terrorism—*Anni di Piombo*, "the bullet years" or, literally, "the years of lead"—blossomed in Italy during the '70s and '80s when the radical left and radical right regularly and violently attacked one another, apart from a continuing fusillade of assaults against the government.

The amorphous configuration, *Nuclei Armati Rivoluzionari* (Armed Revolutionary Nuclei), emerged from the right but broke with notions of reforming society through parliamentary means, and only saw value in uncompromisingly intense deeds—assassination, arson, robbery, the looting of banks, shops and armories, as well as the frequent executions of traitors within their own ranks. In a maelstrom of violence which took place between the years of 1978–80, the NAR claimed responsibility for at least 104 such actions.

In January 1978, left-wing militants gunned down two rightist youths on the street outside a branch office of the mainstream neo-fascist political party *Movimento Sociale Italiano* (MSI). This in turn sparked a three-day riot during which another right-winger was killed by police. Feeling profoundly betrayed by the parliamentary strategy of MSI in the wake of these incidents, Giuseppe Valerio "Giusva" Fioravanti, along with his wife Francesca Mambro and other close associates, inaugurated NAR. The raid of a Rome gun shop frequented by police was the group's first major action. One of the NAR was shot dead by Danilo Centofanti, who was behind the counter in the shop along with a relative and a friend. Two days later a journalist received a leaflet with the message:

> The revolutionary committee decided the following in regards to the death of one of its warriors: . . .We condemn Danilo Centofanti to death for shooting Franco Anselmi in the back. [We condemn] Domaenico Centofanti and Rizo Rosario to death for not having stopped their cowardly friend. Honor to comrade Franco Anselmi. We are ready to follow you. Tremble you cowards, corruptionists, and spies.

Between June 14–16 of the same year, NAR representatives committed a series of devastating bombings, one of which was directed against a milk production plant. A leaflet released afterward by the NAR, claiming responsibility, was written in language akin to that of the Red Brigades. Though Fioravanti and comrades seemed to abandon their notions of anti-communism, and invited the left to join their struggle against the system, on January 9, 1979, an NAR commando group led by Fioravanti assaulted Radio Città Futura, a hardline leftist radio station, for broadcasting insulting commentary about a memorial ceremony for young rightists killed the previous year. The NAR commandos stormed the radio station with grenades and automatic weapons and terrorized the five female announcers working there, machine-gunning their legs, but refraining from killing them. Shortly afterward they issued the following "Peace Offering":

> We struck a lair of hate mongers—we struck hard but we could have been harder. We chose a particular target because we are tired of seeing communist and fascist youths both pay with their lives for the System's misdoings. We don't like to strike at people who, like us, are seriously committed toward improving this system, even if they are imbeciles. They are imbeciles, but they are still our colleagues. We hope that comrades of the movement [i.e., the Communists] will start to think and won't let their nerves or various types of anger take control, and we hope the time is over when people ride by party branches on motorcycle, shooting away like maniacs, no matter whether it's one side or the other. We hope you won't allow yourselves to be manipulated by the reactionary forces of the system— be they white, red or black—that exploit our rage in order to have us kill one another. We haven't forgiven Radio Futura for their continuous hate-mongering and for having disrespected our mourning for our murdered comrades.

The NAR continued its terror campaign at full-throttle, and on March 15, 1979, they attacked another gun shop frequented by police. In taking claim for the action, the NAR again exhorted the communists to join forces with them:

This morning at 9 AM a revolutionary group assaulted and raided the Omnia sport gun shop, the famous supply lair for [Prime Minister] Cossiga's notorious special squads. This action has been done to avenge our dead and jailed comrades. Be wary you fat bourgeois—revolutionary organizations of both right and left will crush you in the inexorable tongs of revolution. Signed, NAR

As the NAR's actions accelerated over the next 12 months, so too did the efforts of the authorities to incapacitate them. The NAR adopted the strategy of liquidating common police officers through random retaliatory assaults, as well as slaying government officials directly involved in the crackdown on the group. On June 23, 1980, an armed revolutionary executed Judge Mario Amato, who had been instrumental in state prosecutions of the militants. The leaflet issued in which the NAR claimed responsibility for the murder was in fact a long philosophical statement, again urging others to join the militant struggle, this time in more fanatical terms. It read in part:

Too often people hide behind excuses like "We have no money" or "We have no weapons." Money and weapons are in the streets, and a knife is enough to start . . . Given our numbers, vengeance is the only recourse we have. All we can do is take revenge for our comrades killed or imprisoned; if we can't have them with us, at least they must not feel useless, and this is no cheap pietism because REVENGE IS SACRED! . . . The sight of the cops, the traitors, and the Reds covered with our blood is known to everyone! . . . In order to reach such objectives no "dens" or "great organizations" are needed. Three reliable comrades and some goodwill are all it takes. And if three are not available, two will do. Don't tell us that there aren't two reliable comrades! Even if this were true, our task is to continue searching for them or, if necessary, to create them. CREATE ARMED SPONTANEITY. We end this document by telling those who would accuse us of not being "political enough" that we are not interested in their politics, only in the struggle—and in the struggle there is preciously little room for idle talk. To those who would charge us with having no future, we reply: "Sissies! Are you sure you are conscious of the present?" And to those who accuse us of being desperate, we answer that our "desperation" is better than cowardice. To those who need a hand, it will be given—and it will be hot lead for those who go on polluting our youth, preaching "wait and see" and the like. Now we return to our homes and our everyday lives, in anticipation of our next revenge . . .

The militants of the NAR no longer viewed revolution in terms of left or right, but life and death. NAR severed connections with any form of conservatism, and hoped to create a higher form of man through a baptism of fire.

As Fioravanti explained, "For us . . . the really important thing is to change man . . . Armed combat is a way to this end; in order to change man it will be necessary to change . . . the sense of fear, fear of death, fear of the loss of liberty . . . Armed combat brings all these fears into question . . . I happened to engage in armed combat because of my personal features, it was the only thing I could do as an act of liberation . . ."

A police captain named Straullu investigating NAR's activities also soon met a grisly fate, and the note left behind demonstrates the increasingly existential nature of the war that Fioravanti and comrades were waging: "We are neither interested in seizing power nor in educating the masses. What matters for us is our ethic: to kill Enemies and annihilate traitors. The will-to-fight keeps us going from day to day, the thirst for vengeance is our sustenance. We shall not stop! We are neither afraid to die nor to end our days in jail; our only fear is not to be able to CLEAN UP everything and everyone, but rest assured, with teeth and nails we'll carry on." All in all, at least a half-dozen law enforcement agents were executed by the NAR during the course of their "purification program," and more than twice that number of "traitors" from the ranks of the militants themselves were killed.

What is generally regarded as the most extreme act of terrorism in recent Italian history, the bombing of the Bologna train station, took place on August 2, 1980. The incident left 85 dead and others wounded. By the end of 1980, pressure from the authorities intensified to the point that it became likely Fioravanti would soon die in a shoot-out with police, given his unremitting commitment to violent conflict. Thus in February 1981, he and a small group of comrades engaged in a standoff with the police and *caribinieri* (state soldiers) in Padua. Two police officers were killed in the confrontation and Fioravanti himself was wounded before he was captured alive. His associates managed to escape.

Giusva Fioravanti would later stand trial as an accused accomplice in the Bologna railway station bombing, as well as being held accountable for numerous other deeds committed during his tenure with the NAR. Fioravanti was initially found guilty and handed a life sentence for his alleged involvement in the Bologna incident, although he maintained his innocence in this regard and the conviction was reversed in a later court case. The genuine perpetrators of the bombing have never been ascertained, nor is it certain whether they came from the ranks of the "right" or "left" wing, or a union of both. After such a spectacular career of assassinations, bombings and sundry other violent acts, Fioravanti has recently been released from prison and is now involved with a humanitarian group which seeks to ban the death penalty worldwide.

How did Fioravanti view his own position in the world? In the early phase of the NAR struggle he penned a spiritual testimony outlining his conclusions and justifying his "philosophy of the deed." He then left this written testament at the home of his family, quite possibly with the expectation that it would only be discovered in the wake of his own violent demise. It read as follows:

> I've abandoned many preconceptions, such as those of good and evil. Zarathustra says it as well: good and evil are subjective. . . I refuse to accept the assumption that stealing, is evil, killing is evil, and praying is good. Killing is a very grave crime here, but if we kill in war they pin a medal on us. Stealing is evil, but they provide spies with fabulous pay. Praying to God is good, but if you pray to the wrong God it's a sin . . . This is why killing, stealing and praying are of no concern to me. From my point of view, death is not forbidden and neither is violence in general . . . Mine is a "new morality" where good and evil are subjective . . .
>
> Religion and money are negative forces . . . It happened one day that someone wanted to govern, but didn't have the necessary tools to do so. He figured out how to invent something that would permit him to elevate himself above intelligence, and thus he created religion . . . I reject any excessive attachment to money and religion—I can't reject them completely because it would be like saying one rejects the entire world, and if I were to reject everything it would be preferable to cease to exist. One must accept money because it is necessary in order to eat, but you should not adore it any more than you adore water, the sun, and the wind . . .
>
> Someone may claim that I'm evil, but I've already stated that good and evil don't exist. My spirits fly, and thus I climbed high on this mountain and I look down on this bastard world . . .
>
> Men are not evil; essentially they are very stupid. The task of the superior man is to educate some disciples in such a way that wisdom will be propagated geometrically . . . The superior man is doomed to remain isolated, and to live in the small oasis among the disciples he has created . . .
>
> Any political doctrine is based on economic concepts, good, evil, etc. . . . Democracy is nothing else than a form of tyranny exercised by a majority on a minority. In democratic and republican Italy, the majority oppresses and represses a "fascist" minority—not for effective, prosecutable crimes, but rather because it's considered illegal to think in a certain way . . .
>
> The Third Reich was a democracy where a majority not only decided to tyrannize Jews and a few thousand Bolsheviks, but also to go and straighten up other countries, outside of Germany's own political borders. . . .
>
> They were speaking of aesthetic physiques, but also strength and physical fitness, of love, loyalty, courage, family, nation . . . What made the Third Reich worthy of remembrance was the integral use of the new morality. . . .

For us, the superior men, no one may be considered crazy or criminal, but just simply different . . . For a warrior it's indispensable to be capable of love, because it would be bad if there were only hate in his heart . . . I find myself fighting Reds because I find them very stupid. Sometimes I'm also able to hate them, but only when they act in a cowardly way.

Probably one day I'll restrict my fighting front, I will work as well, I will be normal . . . Some day the warrior will renounce war, but remain ready to return with weapons if need be. I will retire only when a winner is decided between dictatorship and democracy. This will be a very long war, one which will leave me with little energy . . .

If I should die in battle, that will be my greatest feast. No tears and no priests. Songs and dances. And no one will speak of me as an innocent victim. You won't say that I was crazy, but rather the son of a new morality which drowned many in her wake.

I'd like to disappear after I'm dead. I don't want to lie rotting in a coffin. I'd like to be left abandoned to the elements, like the Indians dispose of their dead.

I only want to end with a suggestion: free yourself of your inhibitions, and discover once more the taste of obeying instincts and passions. . . .

Friuli, May 27–June 3, 1978.

BACTERIOLOGICAL WARFARE

Larry Wayne Harris

In September 1991, I re-entered the Ohio State University and started taking courses in advanced microbiology, in preparation for taking my National Registry of Microbiologist Certification Exam. I soon entered into a clique of nontraditional students, whose average age was around 40. In that clique was a delightful lady known by the name of Miriam Arif. We soon became close friends.

Miriam was from Iraq, and was here studying microbiology. She had an unusual background. One of her very close relatives, General Arif, was a President of Iraq. In April 1966, he was killed in a helicopter accident (I later learned the General was actually her father).

There was a long succession of military coups and now Saddam Hussein and the Republican Guard were in power. In these coups, her family had not fared well. She said that several members of her family had been hanged. And at the present time, she felt it safer for her to be here in America, until she could do something that would make her famous back in her home country of Iraq.

In February 1993, I had arrived early in order to get a parking spot in the rapidly filling student parking lots, and was having coffee in the small vending area in the bottom of the building where the Med-Tech courses were taught. The vending area was deserted except for Miriam Arif and myself. I will never forget the way her face and eyes looked that morning—very tired and glassy. I have little doubt that she had not gotten any sleep since the World Trade Center building was bombed. This was the Monday after.

She must have thought that her arrest was imminent, for the whole time she was rambling on as if she were in a daze. She then became silent for a few minutes and said, "Larry, you are a dear and trusted friend, and what I am going to tell you in the next few minutes you can use to protect yourself and a few friends. When it is my time to act, I do not want your death to be on my conscience. You obviously do not know the danger you face concerning the emergence of Biological Warfare as a major threat to the United States."

She went on to tell me that Libya, Iran, Iraq, Syria, North Korea and other emerging countries were actively pursuing germ warfare, and scrapping their nuclear programs. There are two reasons for this shift. The first being complexity and cost for the acquisition of a meaningful nuclear stockpile. The second reason is that BW is antipersonnel but not anti-materiel warfare, and housing, buildings, factories and other structures remain intact and could be made useful in short time. I asked her if she had actually seen any of Iraq's germ warfare facilities. To this she gave a resounding, "Yes." She went on to state that Iraq uses the plain-Jane approach, and has a very large stockpile of biological agents on hand in the form of special bombs, and is developing rockets to spread the infection over a very large area. They have two separate areas of biological operations, one foreign and one regional. The ones that are regional have all the facilities located at small air strips around the country deliberately designed not to draw attention. These airstrips will not handle large or medium class aircraft, and are designed for single engine high-wing turbo-props that can be used for crop dusting.

The regional biological operations would take only a couple of days to get into operation if using Anthrax, or a couple of weeks if using Plague. The production equipment located at these facilities are kept empty so they can be explained away as holding tanks for agricultural spray products, if they were ever questioned from abroad as to their purpose.

Prior to a Germ Warfare mission, a finished culture fluid is held in a refrigerated tank before it is transferred to an aircraft. Miriam stated that these aircraft have an exceptionally long range and that only one aircraft is located at each facility. If an aircraft were lost, a replacement aircraft could be flown in from another facility. This keeps everything small and very difficult to detect. I asked Miriam why we didn't see Germ Warfare waged during the Gulf War. To this she responded, "Iraq thought that the multinational force would respond with nuclear weapons." I inquired further: You stated that the people of North America are in grave danger of biological agents being used against us. Would you elaborate on that? To this, she replied, "A few hours ago a band of fanatics blew up the World Trade Center. I am sure that Iraq did not do this thing. When payback comes [for the Gulf War], I am sure we will demand at least one American life for every one of my country that you butchered. We would not settle for some silly building." I asked her if she knew how such an attack would be carried out. To this she responded, "Don't be silly, of course I know! The vessel of choice would be a metal spray can [stainless steel]. You know, like the one you use to spray your garden and exterminators use to spray bug spray. The one that has the little air pump in the middle that you pump up when you are ready to spray. To this you would add your culture. Following an appropriate amount of time, the batch is ready. You then insert the spray tank's air pump, pump up the sprayer and you are ready."

Then I asked her about the most likely targets. She replied, "For one thing, it will not be just a target, but many—hundreds—of targets hit simultaneously across the country. Subway systems would be a prime target. Who would notice another maintenance man down there spraying for bugs? Other inviting targets would be the air ducts of large office buildings. Or, say, a large gathering of people, like at a stadium, or just sticking it outside a building hanging over those crowded streets in many cities. Who is going to notice a little mist coming from some building? Several cells (each cell has ten men, and one woman to act as a carrier) will be using aircraft venturi like the ones used to drive the vacuum instruments on airplanes. They are easily obtained mail order in this country. These will be mounted underneath cars. The spray tank will be in the car with the tubing going to the venturi, which acts like a carburetor. When the car is going 60 miles per hour one simply opens the valve and a fog of death will be coming out from behind the car. Other cells will be using these same venturi mounted on light aircraft to attack whole cities at a time." I asked her how she would get her culture (bacteria)? Miriam replied that it is very easy for a woman to hide a small sealed vial of dehydrated culture vaginally and get it into North America. "What are they going to do?" she continued, "take every woman entering the country, have some little room, say in the airport, and make them lay down on a table with their feet up in stirrups and have someone looking up her privates? I think not."

"Why not use something you could obtain in this country," I asked, "without going through all that trouble?" "That is where the real irony is," Miriam replied. "You see, Iraq bought all of the dehydrated vials from companies right here in the United States, who shipped them to Iraq, and those same vials are the ones that Iraqi women have been bringing back into this country to be used against this country." Miriam said that she had made several trips to Iraq, and when she returned to the United States she carried a vial inside her.

[According to an email sent the editor by one of Larry Harris' Internet friends who goes by the name "Ric," Miriam was recently apprehended for her vaginal carry of Anthrax. As with many online assertions, this claim cannot be verified.]

When I asked her about the microbes of choice, Miriam responded, "Plague and Anthrax are the bacteria of choice. For you see, Plague is easy to work with. We take the proper amount and kind of antibiotic and then we are fairly safe.

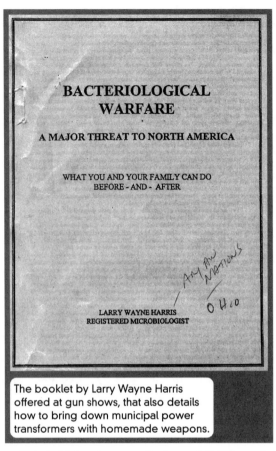

BACTERIOLOGICAL
WARFARE

A MAJOR THREAT TO NORTH AMERICA

WHAT YOU AND YOUR FAMILY CAN DO
BEFORE - AND - AFTER

LARRY WAYNE HARRIS
REGISTERED MICROBIOLOGIST

The booklet by Larry Wayne Harris offered at gun shows, that also details how to bring down municipal power transformers with homemade weapons.

Once you are finished, you can very easily clean up any spills with disinfectant. Any [germs] you miss will be dead in a couple of days. Anthrax would be used by specially trained cells for attacks on big cities. These cells have to be extremely careful, requiring a lot of advanced training. If you've got some on your clothes and happened to inhale it several years later, it could kill you. So they will have to strip, thoroughly shower, and leave all articles of clothing that were worn during the attack behind. The only two other bacteria that were considered were Cholera and Typhoid, but these usually do not kill. They only inconvenience people for a few days."

When would attacks begin? "Sometime within the next few years," Miriam responded, saying that she personally knew cells training to attack the 1996 Olympic Games. Also, attacks are centered on three Muslim holy days for the next few years, starting in July, 1997. One thing is certain; before the year 2002 this country's population will be reduced to less than 50 million." Miriam said that she had no problem telling me all of this because "no one will ever believe you." At this moment the door to the elevator we were standing next to opened, and Miriam entered after a few students walked out, and was soon gone.

That afternoon I phoned the FBI, CDC, and just about everyone I thought to call. Miriam was right. Every bureaucrat I spoke to simply was not interested. After an afternoon of phone tag with the CDC, I was finally transferred to Fort Collins vector division, who told me that I'd been watching too many science fiction movies. I asked about contingency plans for germ warfare. They said they would send me a copy of those plans. They didn't come. When I called back weeks later, the CDC finally told me that all biological civil defense had been scrapped back in 1972. The country was wide open. I just about flipped. They said that if I was a microbiologist and so concerned, why don't I go ahead and write my own Civil Defense manual and leave them alone?

With my curiosity and frustration aroused, I checked out some of things Miriam told me. A professor knowledgeable about with this type of production gave me several papers verifying some of the things Miriam told me about producing Plague and Anthrax.

At the Biological Science Library I got as much information on the Plague as they had. A librarian informed me that a visiting microbiologist, who had written several papers on the dangers of Germ Warfare, would be giving a lecture on his findings. In March 1993, I attended this lecture. After he had finished his lecture and dealt with all the audience's questions, I approached him, offering to buy him coffee at a small coffee shop near the Biological Science Library. He accepted. I raised the question, "What is the possibility of germ warfare becoming a threat to North America?" And if Germ Warfare is within the possibility of being acquired by a highly motivated and intelligent organization, why have we not seen it being used? His replied was that there was no cut-and-dried answer to the question!

In the 1940s, when we first began to look into Germ Warfare, there were few, if any, anti-microbial drugs. So we had no way of protecting our own troops. It was not until the late '60s, when adequate anti-microbials had been developed, that the possibility of using Biological Warfare became a reality. It became apparent at that time that just about any country could afford a laboratory to develop offensive biological weapons. Soon, the U.S. government started an active program of demonizing all aspects of Biological Warfare. This included co-sponsoring the production of several movies. *The Omega Man*, *The Andromeda Strain* and others came out as part of a concerted effort to scare the hell out of the public. In 1972, the Convention on the Prohibition of the Development, Production and Stockpiling of Bacteriological and Toxin Weapons was initiated and signed by the U.S. government while simultaneously glamorizing nuclear weapons, referring to the countries that possessed them as belonging to "The Nuclear Club."

The strategy worked. Numerous small countries invested large portions of their defense budgets toward obtaining nuclear power. Then the Gulf War seemed to shock many of these small countries into reality. Instead of spending huge sums on nuclear development, they veered their attention to Bacteriological and Biotoxin weapons.

The lecturer in microbiology stated quite clearly that we can almost certainly expect biological weapons to be used by various terrorist organizations. This makes it imperative that the citizens of North America obtain the necessary knowledge and skills to protect themselves against this emerging threat. Thus, the following book has been written to provide a source of information on aspects of biology having terrorist applications and on the types of biological agents which might be used against us, and how to defend against them.

⚡ ⚡ ⚡

Larry Wayne Harris, the author of the previous excerpt from his self-published xeroxed book, *Bacteriological Warfare* (available by sending $25 to Larry Harris, P.O. Box 102, Lancaster, OH 43130), says that he is a microbiologist.

Headlines and hysteria stalked Harris after the FBI made a big show of arresting him on February 18, 1998 with one William Leavitt, Jr., accused of attempting to procure Anthrax for nefarious purposes.

Charges against Harris and Leavitt were dropped less than a week later after it was determined that they did not possess the wickedly poisonous form of Anthrax, but simply the Anthrax vaccine. Harris apparently procured the Anthrax vaccine to test an expensive and accusedly quack medical device called the "Rife" machine, which its supporters say kills all forms of virus and bacteria. The Rife device was being sold by one "Ron Rockwell," an ex-felon, who called the FBI on Harris and Leavitt. Why Rockwell called the FBI is yet another mystery, but the matter helped summon yet more scare stories regarding the use of chemical and biological agents.

Six months prior to Harris and Leavitt's arrest, Defense Secretary William Cohen postured before news cameras, saying that the five-pound bag of sugar he was holding was capable of wiping out half the population of Washington, D.C., had it carried Anthrax spores.

And six months following Harris and Leavitt's arrest, cruise missiles bombed and destroyed the Al Shifa pharmaceutical plant in Sudan for the supposed crime of producing chemical weapons. Months passed by until small, ignored news stories revealed that the bombings, resulting in the death of several dozen civilians, were a mistake. Al Shifa not only had nothing to do with chemical weapons, but was the primary manufacturer of medicine for the remaining Sudanese who escaped starvation. Instead of preventing terrorism, the U.S. became its most hated practitioner.

Larry Harris' convoluted, mystifying saga goes much further than a simple false arrest.

Bacteriological Warfare claims that Iraqi nationals are invading the United States with vials of plague secreted in their vaginas for the purpose of killing hundreds of millions of Americans. Whether true or not, Harris provides an alarming chorus to an already existing fear campaign to help sell anti-terror crime bills that curtailed aspects of the First, Second and Fourth

Amendments of the Bill of Rights, not to mention the justification of use-less, criminal bombings in Sudan and Afghanistan.

And though his book seemed to echo U.S. propaganda, Larry Harris sud-denly became the object of frightening news articles about the escalation of domestic terror, a scare story helpful to the prison and police industries and the bulging coffers of "anti-hate" watchdog groups.

Both in his writing and with his arrest, Larry Harris seemed to serve gov-ernment interests enormously. And strangely enough, Harris was once arrested for saying that he was associated with the CIA, as well as for try-ing to buy Bubonic Plague by mail. Harris claims that his interest in Plague and Anthrax was for "research only"—to warn, inform, and instruct people of an emerging crisis. And indeed, this is the subject of his book.

(It should be mentioned that a "Ralph C. Fenwick, CCO," quoted on the Montana Militia website, claims that dosage chart errors in Larry Harris' book could result in needless and painful deaths. Harris' information also has its defenders, who say that its instruction is accurate and useful.)

The first edition of Harris' book, supposedly no longer available, also quotes the female Iraqi national in elaborate detail, about how power trans-formers can be devastated with the aid of a little "goody" bought in hard-ware and army supply stores. This information is augmented with helpful illustrations as well, just in case you need to know how to knock out American power systems.

At the time of his Anthrax arrest, news featured on Harris began appear-ing, linking him to Aryan Nations. Indeed, Harris' *Bacteriological Warfare* contains no overt "hatred" outside of its referral of black people by the mar-ginally racist term, "Negroes."

Some conspiracy websites were convinced that the news stories associ-ating Harris with Aryan Nations were nothing more than propaganda smears. Perhaps these theorists should have picked up the phone and called the source himself. "Aryan Nations has the best library in the world," explained Mr. Harris. "Maybe the best library since Alexandria. There's been a war going on for many thousands of years now. From one faction against the other. You know who that one side is. That war won't end until one side absolutely wins."

One doesn't need to grill Mr. Harris to understand who he meant by the players of the thousands-year-old war. At the renowned academic facility known as Aryan Nations, visitors are obligated to stomp on an Israeli flag before entering its main room. This is the place from which Larry Harris "researched" his critical historical information.

If Mr. Harris received his education from Aryan Nations, this immediately begs another question: why does he peg the vigorously anti-Israel nation of Iraq as the evil cur bent on killing all good Americans?

—Adam Parfrey

Who knows? Truth is often stranger than fiction.

Chances that you will die in a car crash: 1 in 6,000

Chances that you will die in a terrorist incident: 1 in 15 million

—Rand Corporation

THE CONSPIRACY VIRUS AND HOW MASS MEDIA TRIES TO PREVENT IT

Jonathan Vankin

> There are two versions of history: the safe,
>
> sanitized "Disney" version—and the other, darker
>
> version. That second, scarier version of history
>
> often goes by the name: conspiracy theory.

The observation above comes from journalist Jim Hougan, as quoted in the preface to *The 70 Greatest Conspiracies of All Time*, a book I co-wrote. But I've since modified that opinion. There are, it seems, infinite twists on history competing for survival like mutating sequences of DNA in the primordial gene pool. Which one survives? And how?

Those are the questions that started me on the conspiracy theory track in the first place. Why is it, I wanted to know, that one method of interpreting history became irreparably stigmatized? Then as now, I was interested in how the mass media, the public's primary source of reality interpretation, came to adopt the stigma against "conspiracy theory" as one of its axiomatic operating principles.

By "mass media" I mean corporate media conglomerates. They've always been with us, at least through the 20th century. But as the century spiraled to its conclusion, the media became more massive than ever. It's apparent that the mass media uses a selection mechanism to transmit a version of reality it considers acceptable on its way to the receptacle known as the general public. Some information and viewpoints are excluded while others are considered okay.

I'm not accusing mass media itself of "conspiracy." No conspiracy is necessary. Hypocritical notions of "objectivity" and "investigative reporting" have evolved over time to filter out the viewpoints that offend the sensibilities of the corporate mentality.

We all distrust beliefs different from our own—facts be damned. That's human nature. But the public must trust the media, at least a little, for the media to survive. To meet that requirement, the media developed a concept called "objectivity" which became the foundation of the media's legitimacy.

Objectivity is an ideology of no beliefs. No beliefs equals no agenda—and that equals trustworthiness.

The other foundation of the media's public trust is "investigative reporting." The public needs to see the media making the attempt to uncover information that would otherwise not come to light. We're made to feel that the media works for us.

At the time I started writing the first of my two "conspiracy" books—*Conspiracies, Cover-Ups and Crimes*—I was employed in what's charitably referred to as "alternative" weeklies. Though those weeklies (there's one in almost every city) tend to be more "alternative" in style than ideology when compared to the daily and broadcast press, they are still the best outlets for "investigative reporting."

Investigative reporting, as I understood it at the time, was supposed to serve as a check on the abuse of power. Exposure of misdeeds was a way of reigning in the powerful.

But in the corporate media, "investigative reporting" too-frequently targets people without much power. A hidden camera follows garbage collectors and meter readers, catching them in the act of taking long lunches, visiting their girlfriends and other heinous acts of "wasting your tax dollars"; that type of story. But most tax dollars are not wasted by lazy municipal employees, but by their bosses and their bosses' bosses, and the corporate welfare gravy train. Corporate crimes are not committed by workers on the assembly line, but by wealthy executives.

In 1998, every major news organization devoted millions of dollars and most of its time to cover the Clinton-Lewinsky dalliance. Abuse of power, you say? Maybe. At the same time Exxon and Mobil, two of the world's largest oil companies, were in the process of merging. Their union created the world's largest corporation whose product affects every aspect of life in modern society. The last two years of the twentieth century saw record numbers of corporate mergers, moving us closer and closer to a *Rollerball* world.

How much "investigative reporting" did that merit? In fact, the media has generally applauded corporate mergers—the bigger the better. And no merger is more laudable to the media than a merger of media companies. When America Online merged with the already-colossal Time-Warner corporation in early 2000, one commentator, *Slate* magazine's Jack Shafer, actually argued that "only big media possesses the means to consistently hold big business and big government accountable."

The point of this digression is to note the similarities between "investigative reporting" and conspiracy theory. The purpose of both is to question, criticize and diminish the power of powerful people and institutions. They're like paranoid kryptonite. Perhaps that's why there has been so little investigative reporting worth mentioning in the major media.

Conspiracy theories—the good ones, anyway—are built on a foundation of investigative reporting. Just throw in a healthy dollop of creative speculation. Journalism provides the pieces. Speculation fills in the blanks.

Even though we're talking politics, the process is no different than science. Any scientist can tell you that you can collect data until your banks runneth over, but without a theoretical framework to the data, it's all worthless.

But in journalism, theoretical framework is verboten. We don't interpret the facts, we just report them—objectively!

Reality is quite slippery. It's hard enough to tell what's going on in front of our faces. Piecing together events that took place across distant waves of the space-time continuum is an epistemological nightmare.

Without some kind of middleman, some machinery to pass otherwise inaccessible information to our waiting brains, we'd sink into solipsism. That middleman, unfortunately, is mass media, which provides its own Catch-22. A story doesn't seem to exist for most middlemen if another mass market mechanism hasn't published it.

The mediating media, however, is not a machine. It's comprised of and managed by humans with all of the same sensory shortcomings as the rest of us. That's why the media sends information with a high signal-to-noise ratio— incomplete and biased. We cannot lose our biases any more than we can flap our arms and fly.

That's why, when I was in the newspaper business, I could only laugh at the charade of reportorial "objectivity." Yet that same charade serves as the foundation of modern media. "Objective" journalism, by definition, cannot interpret facts without some kind of theory or model—but then, theory is subjective. "Objective" reporting is meaningless, a phony idea.

Media sells itself as objective, but, it must—repeat, must—have a hidden agenda (or multiple agendas). The public is led to believe that it's being fed fat-free facts, when what we're really lapping-up is a concoction laced and laden with the bias of power, spoken through a massive corporate news entity, helping to retain its power by reinforcing the status quo.

So why not conspiracy theory?

Conspiracy theory is a confrontational paradigm. You cannot absorb a good conspiracy theory—which is always a dramatic narrative of injustice and malevolent power—without feeling the urge to do something about it. Conspiracy theories are an activist point of view. They announce themselves.

Conspiracy theories are incompatible with the appearance of objectivity. But the ideology of "objectivity" is exactly the opposite. It demands not action but passivity. It is an ideology that doesn't question established power structures, but supports them. For lack of a better term, let's call this sort of ideology "centrist."

Centrist ideology advocates action only when centrism itself comes under attack. And then it's not so much action as an immune reaction. Conspiracy theory—even when based on a solid foundation of investigation, as in the JFK assassination, for example—acts like a virus, and "objectivity" is the antibody.

Of course, conspiracy theory cannot be attacked on its tangible merits. Facts cannot argue against theories; only theories can argue against theories. Arguing facts against a conspiracy theory is the same as announcing one's own point of view. The doctrine of media objectivity cannot allow that to occur. Conspiracy theory—or any activist ideology—is attacked with blunt, cruel assertions regarding the theory's ideological bias. Its advocates are painted as "crazy." "Objective" reporters suddenly become activists, and start sneering, cackling and spitting when repelling conspiracy theories . . . anything to preserve the false objectivity that forms the basis of the entirety of mass journalism, academic history or any other form of reality selection.

Let's face it, as long as there is a mass media, our choices on the reality menu are limited. Corporate media isn't going anywhere. The only hope for reality plurality lies in distrusting the media more than we do now, distrusting enough that we make ourselves uncomfortable.

⚡ ⚡ ⚡

Jonathan Vankin is the author of *Conspiracies, Cover-Ups and Crimes*, co-author, with John Whalen, of *The 70 Greatest Conspiracies of All Time* and author of a number of *Big Book* graphic novels for DC comics. His websites can be accessed at http://www.conspire.com and http://home.pacbell.net/jvankin.

David Martin

1. Dummy up. If it's not reported, if it's not news, it didn't happen.

2. Wax indignant. This is also known as the "How dare you?" gambit.

3. Characterize the charges as "rumors" or, better yet, "wild rumors." If, in spite of the news blackout, the public is still able to learn about suspicious facts, it can only be through "rumors." (If they tend to believe the "rumors" it must be because they are simply "paranoid" or "hysterical.")

4. Knock down straw men. Deal only with the weakest aspects of the weakest charges. Even better, create your own straw men. Make up wild rumors (or plant false stories) and give them lead play when you appear to debunk all the charges, real and fanciful alike.

5. Call the skeptics names like "conspiracy theorist," "nutcase," "ranter," "kook," "crackpot," and, of course, "rumor monger." Be sure, too, to use heavily loaded verbs and adjectives when characterizing their charges and defending the "more reasonable" government and its defenders. You must then carefully avoid fair and open debate with any of the people you have thus maligned. For insurance, set up your own "skeptics" to shoot down.

6. Impugn motives. Attempt to marginalize the critics by suggesting strongly that they are not really interested in the truth but are simply pursuing a partisan political agenda or are out to make money (compared to over-compensated adherents to the government line who, presumably, are not).

7. Invoke authority. Here the controlled press and the sham opposition can be very useful.

8. Dismiss the charges as "old news."

9. Come half-clean. This is also known as "confession and avoidance" or "taking the limited hangout route." This way, you create the impression of candor and honesty while you admit only to relatively harmless, less-than-criminal "mistakes." This stratagem often requires the embrace of a fall-back position quite different from the one originally taken. With effective damage control, the fall-back position need only be peddled by stooge skeptics to carefully limited markets.

10. Characterize the crimes as impossibly complex and the truth as ultimately unknowable.

11. Reason backward, using the deductive method with a vengeance. With thoroughly rigorous deduction, troublesome evidence is irrelevant, e.g.,

say, "We have a completely free press. If evidence exists that the Vince Foster 'suicide' note was forged, they would have reported it. They haven't reported it so there is no such evidence." Another variation on this theme involves the likelihood of a conspiracy leaker and a press who would report the leak.

12. Require the skeptics to solve the crime completely.

13. Change the subject. This technique includes creating and/or publicizing distractions.

14. Scantly report incriminating facts, and then make nothing of them. This is sometimes referred to as "bump and run" reporting.

THE SCAPEGOAT:
TED KACZYNSKI, RITUAL MURDER
AND THE INVOCATION OF CATASTROPHE

Michael A. Hoffman II

> Mr. Kaczynski's . . . belief (is) that every aspect of
> his existence is controlled by an omnipotent
> organization against which he is powerless.
>
> **New York Times, November 14, 1997**

Ted Kaczynski is yet another "lone nut" who pleaded guilty to spectacular crimes without a trial and had his case closed on the day the investigation should have begun in earnest.

On the day of his arraignment the *Boston Globe* newspaper published a nationally syndicated story conditioning the public to view the suspect as a "paranoid . . . loser" who had no accomplices and was undoubtedly guilty as charged.

A similar profile was exhibited in the cases of James Earl Ray, "Son of Sam" David Berkowitz, and many other patsies.

Like John Gotti, Kaczynski was denied his choice of attorney. As in Waco and Oklahoma City, a key building, in this case Kaczynski's cabin, was tampered with to such an extent as to make independent investigation of it impossible.

Like Timothy McVeigh, Kaczynski's statement at his sentencing—when the world's media spotlight was fixed upon him—was laconic and had little impact upon the public.

In Kaczynski's case this was striking, since according to the FBI's "Unabom" scenario, the "University and Airline bomber" was a publicity-obsessed serial killer. Yet with the world's media at his feet and a chance to hold forth for an hour or more on his motivation and authentic ideological views, Kaczynski merely announced that his opinions had been distorted and that he would reply and set the record straight later.

But Kaczynski will never again have the kind of opportunity for world attention that he had on May 4, 1998 in Sacramento.

Of course, the FBI mouthpiece-media has not noticed this or numerous other anomalies in the Kaczynski case. From the beginning of the mathematician's capture, they have reported the "Unabom" matter from the perspective of the FBI and confirmed all of the government's official explanations and accounts.

Not even the local media in Helena and Great Falls, Montana, launched any investigation independent of the federal government. From the outset this case has been rubber-stamped in newsrooms with the logo of the FBI.

THE SET-UP

Why was the FBI allowed to "search" Kaczynski's cabin for weeks, without local witnesses present? The opportunities for evidence-planting and tampering were myriad.

Sheriff Chuck O'Reilly protested to the local press that the FBI did not inform him of their search; that they executed a warrant without his knowledge or consent and apprehended Kaczynski without informing him first.[1]

FBI agents in paramilitary attire blocked access to Kaczynski's cabin. No one except federal officials had access to Kaczynski's cabin while a supposed "mountain of evidence" was extracted from the tiny building. From a structure of less than two hundred square feet, the Associated Press, repeating FBI pronouncements, said "truckloads of evidence" were extracted. "The evidence is all being shipped back to the FBI lab in Quantico, Virginia." [2]

This is the same FBI lab where the Bureau's preeminent forensic chemist and Supervisory Special Agent, Dr. Frederic W. Whitehurst, has revealed that evidence was "fabricated" and otherwise "tainted" in a process he labeled "perjury." [3]

In Kaczynski's case we have "evidence" obtained in hermetic isolation, with only federal agents allowed to observe its collection. It is upon their word alone that claims of finding bombs, bomb parts, three typewriters, a chemical lab, numerous tools, and the "original copy" of the "Unabom" manifesto. There was never independent corroboration of these claims.

How it it that just two days after Kaczynski's capture, the FBI was in a position to declare that one of the supposed typewriters discovered in Kaczynski's shack "appeared" to be the one used to prepare the "Unabom Manifesto"? That the FBI managed to so rapidly undertake, on site, a sophisticated process of determining the typewriter's unique mechanical signature, something which is a complex scientific process, is a marvel that has yet to be explained.

Kaczynski's neighbor Gene Youderian reported that there was nothing remarkable about the interior of Kaczynski's cabin when he visited it. "There were no fancy . . . tools visible . . ." [4]

The items said by the FBI to have been in the cabin, some of them in plain view or virtually on display, were in addition to a wood stove, platform bed, table, chair, clothing, and 239 books.

All material supposed to be Kaczynski's was shipped to the FBI laboratory, again without any outside confirmation by local civilian witnesses or the county sheriff concerning the nature of the shipments or their disposition.

In order to ensure that local people and independent investigators would not observe the discrepancy between the absurdly enormous amount of materials claimed to have been in the cabin and its diminutive, 10 feet by 12 feet size, (or 10 feet by 14 feet; accounts vary), U.S. District Judge Charles C. Lovell ordered Federal agents to continue to prevent access to the cabin until it could be transported from Kaczynski's land.

In a secret operation conducted at midnight on May 15, 1996, a dozen FBI agents escorted a flatbed truck containing Kaczynski's cabin to Malmstrom Air Force base, where it was placed under 24-hour guard.

Air Force Lt. Dave Honchul "declined to say where on the base the cabin is being stored and said photographs are not allowed." Few other details were disclosed. [5]

The cabin, or a simulacrum of it, was eventually shipped to a high-security storage facility at Mather Field in Sacramento. Some relatives of "Unabom" victims want it destroyed.

Not one of Kaczynski's "defense" lawyers ever raised a single question or protested this process. Their focus, like that of the Justice Department and the media, was on the assumption of his guilt and insanity.

Ted Kaczynski's federally employed, federal court-appointed Helena attorney, Michael Donahoe, failed to raise the issue of the evidence-planting/tampering potential at Kaczynski's cabin.

From the day of his apprehension, the mathematician had no choice in the selection of his attorneys. He was always represented by lawyers appointed by various federal judges.

Donahoe and another federally employed attorney, Tony Gallagher, actually asked a federal judge to block other lawyers from offering their services to the defendant. [6]

Donahoe's office operated under an annual federal grant of approximately $1 million.[7]

As soon as Kaczysnki was arrested he was held virtually incommunicado at the county jail in Helena. This was not due to the local sheriff, who had criticized the FBI for having excluded him from the case.

It was Kaczynski's federally employed, court-appointed attorney who received all of Kaczynski's first class, privileged mail, even before Kaczynski saw it. Kaczynski's mail went to the lawyer ahead of the addressee.

By controlling Kaczynski's mail, one can control the only independent outlet available to him.

It was Kaczynski's federally employed Montana attorneys who told the court, in a motion filed and made public April 15, 1996, that the "evidence" supposedly taken from Kaczynski's cabin was "highly incriminating." [8]

In other words, Kaczynski's federally employed "defense" attorneys were already informing the court and the public, a mere 12 days after his capture, that he was guilty.

THE LONE NUT—AGAIN

The lack of police investigation or media curiosity about the possibility that Kaczynski was a member of a larger conspiracy is striking. The "Unabom" manifesto alludes to others who assisted in the attacks.

Montana's *Great Falls Tribune* newspaper reported April 12, 1996, on the presence of a man in Lincoln who "declined to be identified or to say exactly where he was from," who called for Kaczynski to be considered innocent and said Kaczynski had been entrapped.

In November 1994, members of the ecology group Earth First! met at a conference at the University of Montana in Missoula, about 60 miles southwest of Kaczynski's residence in Lincoln. There is bus service between Lincoln and Missoula. The name "T Casinski," a phonetic rendering of Kaczynski's name, appeared on the attendance list.

Three days after Kaczynski's arraignment, research computer data stored at a U.S. Forest Service office in Moscow, Idaho was destroyed by an intruder who "trashed offices and tossed computers." Was this retribution on the part of Kaczynski's associates for Forest Service Agent Jerry Burns having lured Kaczynski out of his cabin, facilitating his capture?

In a letter to the *New York Times*, the "Unabomber" stated, "We are an anarchist group calling ourselves FC." [9]

The FBI alternately speculated that FC stood for "Fuck Computers." It later said the initials stood for "Freedom Club."

Before Kaczynski was apprehended, the FBI had claimed that a certain person named "Nathan R" was an associate of the "Unabomber."

Montana activists Kathleen Marquardt and Mark LaRochelle scheduled a press conference in Helena for April 10, 1996, to discuss evidence of what they said were links between Kaczynski and environmental groups. The conference was canceled after the duo claimed to have received death threats. [10]

There has been no indication that any of these and other leads concerning possible accomplices were followed in any sustained fashion by either the establishment media or federal agents.

A strange unanimity pervaded both the media and the federal agencies from the day of Kaczynski's apprehension. Both did everything in their power to plant in the mind of the public the notion that Kaczynski was the one and only perpetrator of the "Unabom" series.

Yet, if the FBI had not in fact been shepherding Kaczynski for years before his arrest, why did they behave from the time of his capture as if they infallibly knew that they had jailed the sole perpetrator of a string of bombings, which had gone unsolved for eighteen years?

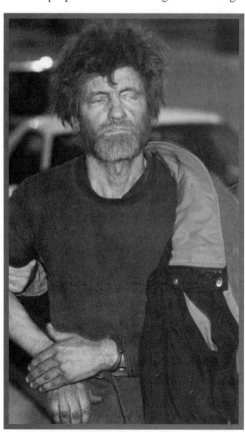

In any criminal investigation involving so vast a series of crimes, the search for accomplices begins with the capture of a suspect.

Yet from the outset, both the FBI and the establishment media went to considerable lengths to profile Kaczynski as yet another "lone nut."

Newsweek's April 15, 1996 cover story convicted Kaczynski in advance of any investigation or trial. The FBI's version of Kaczynski was simply reprinted as gospel. According to Newsweek, in Kaczynski's cabin, "G-men also discovered and defused a finished bomb that was already to be mailed."

Newsweek didn't write, "FBI agents allege that they discovered. . ." but rather, "G-men also discovered . . ."

The national news magazine went on to convict him: "What finally tripped up Ted Kaczynski . . . was his vanity."

Newsweek had engaged in a similar process of trial by media in 1977. A few days after the arrest of David Berkowitz, who, it was later determined, was but one of several members of the murderous Son of Sam cult, *Newsweek* echoed the New York City police department's claim that the Son of Sam case was closed on the day Berkowitz was arrested—the very day it should have been intensified and expanded.

Newsweek's cover story just a few days after his arrest (August 22, 1977) was headlined, "The Sick World of Son of Sam" and was accompanied by a large color photo of a grinning David Berkowitz. The message was clear: "Berkowitz is the only perpetrator. The mystery is solved just as the cops say."

Such reporting might be appropriate in Napoleonic France or Stalinist Russia, but under our American system of adversarial jurisprudence, the tale woven by federal agents and prosecutors is often wrong, and sometimes maliciously so.

A suspect in American courts is assumed innocent in order that the prejudicial stigma which was branded on Kaczynski would not hinder independent investigation and a fair criminal trial. Yet the major media in the U.S. were as keen as the Feds to tie the Unabom case up into a convenient package labeled Theodore John Kaczynski.

Martin E. Weinstein, professor of political science at the University of Montana, correctly observed that as a result of the media having found Kaczynski guilty before he had been tried, it was unlikely the defendant could obtain an unbiased jury. [11]

Another example of the collusion between the corporate media and the FBI was the process whereby unnamed federal agents, "speaking on condition of anonymity," primed the public with a sense that Kaczynski was undoubtedly the "Unabomber" by leaking alleged evidence to the press which would normally only surface during a trial.

The press had no means of verifying these claims, but repeatedly published them anyway, without a caveat.

"I think it's criminal," said Prof. David Goldberger of the Ohio State University School of Law. "This is a recurring catastrophe in our legal system."

The Justice Department replied that leaks cannot be restrained, yet the fact that Kaczynski's brother contacted the government in early January 1996 (through attorney Anthony Bisceglie) was kept confidential for three months and never leaked.

The need to convict Kaczynski and to cover up any connections to other individuals and organizations who may have been associated with him is a pattern found in several cases involving spectacular crimes, tremendous publicity and the imprinting of the Group Mind.

A similar process was in place after the apprehension of "lone nuts" Lee Harvey Oswald, Arthur Bremer, Sirhan Sirhan and the aforementioned Berkowitz and Ray.

A few days after Kaczynski's apprehension, on April 11, 1996, this writer made contact with him through the window of the Helena jail, by means of a cardboard poster I held aloft to gain his attention. By sign language, Kaczynski indicated that he wanted me to visit him and I entered the visitor's section of the Lewis and Clark County Jail shortly thereafter.

It was on that day that Kaczynski became the most famous man in America. The national news magazines, *Time* and *Newsweek*, published cover stories which arrived in stores across the nation on April 11 and the frenzy of televised publicity was also reaching a crescendo. Yet the visitor's room near Kaczynski's jail cell was eerily deserted. Not a single reporter, environmentalist activist, or curiosity-seeker was present to visit him, except this writer. [12]

The sheriff advised me to write a letter to Kaczynski to obtain his consent for a visit, which I did immediately. However, since Kaczynski's mail was screened by his federally bankrolled lawyers, I have no idea if he ever received my note. I doubt that he did, since he indicated through the jailhouse window that he was eager for me to visit him. I can only surmise that my letter was obstructed by Kaczynski's court-appointed lawyers.

THE SCAPEGOAT

There was a radical alteration in the appearance of Kaczynski, who had looked relatively youthful, potent and intractable on the day of his arrest, but who, in his later court appearances, from his April 19, 1996 hearing onward, appeared to have aged 10 or more years.

At his April 19 hearing, Kaczynski was trimmed and barbered, complete with an overly groomed, suburban boutique-level hair styling, and this just a couple of weeks after he had been living for years as a free being in the woods outside Lincoln, Montana.

When I saw the photo of the new, tame Kaczynski, I recalled the lines of T.S. Eliot, "Who clipped the lion's wings and flea'd his rump and pared his claws?"

I asked myself if the former lion's new poodle look might portend some deeper transformation or even control that was being exerted over him in government custody.

One of the media and FBI myths about Kaczynski was that he was a reviled kook who reeked of body odor, dressed abominably, and was paranoid.

In fact, Sherry Wood, the Lincoln librarian who refused to give the FBI a list of the books Kaczynski had borrowed—the woman in Lincoln who knew him best and whose son Danny called him "Uncle Ted"—told this reporter that Kaczynski dressed decently when he came to town, did not smell, and was affectionate toward her son and respected by many people.

Even the *Seattle Times* in its April 5 edition admitted that in Lincoln, "The majority of people think he didn't do it."

His former mentor, University of Michigan mathematics Professor George Piranian told reporters, "I respected him [Kaczynski] very highly. I know other members of the faculty had great respect for him . . . I'm proud to have known him." [13]

A national outpouring of Establishment-generated hate greeted Kaczynski upon his arrest. Monroe Freedman, a legal ethics scholar at Hofstra University observed, "What they are doing is punishing this man Kaczynski without due process of law. They are holding him up to public hate, shame, ridicule and abuse, just like putting him (in) the public stocks, without ever having tried him."

Amid all of the insults and rattling of sabers by the outraged consensus-conformists, the reactions of victim David Gelertner of Yale University and commentator Robert Bly, were the most notable.

Before Kaczynski's capture, Prof. Gelertner had reacted to the "Unabom" attack on him and his "techno-nerd" book, *Mirror Worlds*, by hurrying to his word-processor and writing an apology in the form of a sequel (*The Muse in the Machine*) which reversed most of his earlier mind-machine-premise; arguing instead for poetic romanticism.

But once Gelertner believed the "Unabomber" was safely behind bars, he let go with a volley of vitriol at Kaczynski in a national news magazine. Equally bitter was the response of Robert "Iron John" Bly, the men's movement magus, who labeled Kaczynski an infantile, worthless and helpless person. Kaczynski can be criticized on any number of grounds, but being infantile could hardly be one of them. Kaczynski lived off the land, in a harsh climate, demonstrating considerable resourcefulness.

Kaczynski turned his back on the sort of academia which spoon-fed Robert Bly, who in the past decade promoted the idea that men could accommodate their disaffection with modern society by hugging and crying their way into adjustment. Perhaps due to Kaczynski's Spartan-like rejection of modern society rather than the cheap tabloid emotionalism fraught with accommodating it, Bly unleashed tirades of character assassination against his ideological opponent.

This media lynching and their FBI-mouthpiece unquestioning regurgitation of the prosecution story without doubts or query remain the establishment view of the case, unchanged or truly investigated, as of this writing, for at least three years.

It seems that Kaczynski had the opportunity to knock the chair out from under his prosecutors and the FBI in the first few days of his incarceration. But he refused to do so, swimming under the thick psychoanalytic soup of psychoactive chemicals, administered under the guise of "medication."

While Kaczynski may have been demoralized that the entire radical environmental movement chose to sit out the first several weeks of his arrest, stroking their Internet keyboards instead of camping in front of the Helena prison, an individualist like Kaczynski would not necessarily be devastated or paralyzed by the failings on the part of potential supporters.

Arrested and brought before a howling mob of media ghouls for arraignment on the Christian "Holy Thursday" (the night preceding Christ's trial and crucifixion), Kaczynski was led through what police term a "perp walk."

His detachment, the traces of an enigmatic smile, and the look of pity which he cast upon that mob marked him as a most unusual, perhaps even archetypal figure; though the media characterized his demeanor as "arrogant."

As for his alleged guilt, it should be recalled that the "Unabomber" is an FBI concoction. The grouping of various bombings since 1978 under the "Unabom" nomenclature is their invention. [14] No credible evidence has been put forth to link Kaczynski to all or even most of these cowardly and reprehensible bombings.

The most prominent sketch of an alleged "Unabom" suspect by a witness emanated from the 1987 bombing of a computer store in Salt Lake City. It depicts a hooded man with sunglasses, a mustache and curly red hair. It bears no resemblance to Kaczynski.

The drawing was executed by forensic artist Jeanne Boylan, an FBI contract employee. The female witness who provided the details upon which the drawing is based apparently could not identify Kaczynski as the man she saw in 1987.[15]

INVOKING CATASTROPHE
In the New Jersey adman bombing of Thomas J. Mosser in New Jersey, the so-called "Unabomber" used the alias "H.C. Wickle." The Son of Sam used

the alias "Wicked King Wicker" and the root of both the words Wickle and Wicker is wick, which in turn is a derivative of the Old English word *wicca*, meaning wizard, of which the feminine is *wicce* (literally, witch).

The "Unabomber," at least since his fatal bombing of Dec. 10, 1994 in which Mr. Mosser was killed, would seem to be signaling to occult initiates and those who understand the "twilight" or cant language of the cryptocracy, that this attack was part of a symbolic process.

In occult crimes the objective is not linear, that is to say, is not solely bound to the achievement of the immediate effects of the attack on the victim, but may in fact be a part of a larger, symbolic ritual magnified by the power of the electronic media, for the purpose of the alchemical processing of the subconscious Group Mind of the masses.

If we are observing a ritual working, we should be looking for relevant synchronicities (coincidences that have meaning) in the days following "Unabom's" explosive attacks, which would form a pattern, on the hypothesis that his bombing is the Introit to a kind of public, subliminal Black Mass that plays for days.

Consciously we don't apprehend the connection, but our subconscious may, and it is the subconscious that is being addressed in occult ritual, in a process CIA behavioral scientist Dr. Ewen Cameron termed "psychic driving."

Like other Group Mind imprinting, such as the Son of Sam series, the "Unabomber" has a high media profile as a communicator, as someone having a message for the masses.

For example, in June of 1993, the so-called "Unabomber" sent two package bombs in the week that the movie *Jurassic Park* premiered in theatres. The movie focused on the impact of two advanced technologies—genetic engineering and parallel computing.

The first package exploded on June 22, in the hands of University of California geneticist Charles Epstein. Two days later, Yale University computer scientist David Gelertner was bombed. Both men were seriously injured. Gelertner's magnum opus is the previously cited *Mirror Worlds* (Oxford University Press, 1991), detailing a process for counterfeiting the natural world.

The FBI is known to be deeply involved in psychological analysis and manipulation of "criminals" under the general category of "profiling," which presupposes special insight into deranged minds and the ability to control such minds. In the hands of the federal government, would such powers of control be necessarily benevolent?

At Waco the FBI used their behavioral and "profiling" departments to attempt to drive the Branch Davidian church members and their children to suicide at all hours, day and night, by directing powerful lights at them and broadcasting the sounds of Tibetan Bon Sorcerer chants and even audio recordings of rabbits and pigs being slaughtered.

According to the March 2, 1987 issue of the *Los Angeles Times* (p. 9), FBI "specialists in motivation" were assigned to the "Unabom" case. Is it far-fetched to wonder who these experts were going to "motivate"?

The "Unabomber's" enmity against Thomas J. Mosser exploded on Saturday, December 10, 1994, and was said to be motivated by Mosser serving advertising clients Digital Equipment Corporation and IBM.

On Monday, December 12, 1994, two days after the "Unabomber" allegedly killed advertising executive Mosser, on Mosser-Unabom +2, FBI agent David A. Priarone, 45, an eleven-year veteran of the agency, entered the public promenade at the World Financial Center in Manhattan, and at exactly 12:45 PM raised his 9 mm handgun to his right temple and pulled the trigger.

FBI spokesman Joseph Valiquette refused to discuss what case the deceased agent was assigned at the time of his "suicide." "We're not prepared to talk about what he worked on," the FBI spokesman said.

Also on Mosser-Unabom +2, December 12, 1994, IBM dropped a "bomb" of its own, announcing that a "bug" in Intel's Pentium microprocessor caused mathematical errors of such significant frequency and severity that it was halting sales of all computers containing the Intel chip.

As a result of IBM's announcement, newspaper headlines declared, "Confusion among PC Buyers" and referred to doubts about "the integrity of data calculated on IBM PCs."

While chaos and confusion grew among the nation's computer buyers, on December 13, Mosser-Unabom + 3, one of the worst explosions in the history of U.S. agribusiness, struck the Terra Industries nitrogen-fertilizer facility in the heartland near Salix, Iowa. (*Terra* is a Latin word for Earth.)

The cause of the explosion is unknown. Where a seven story building once stood, it left only a crater. The blast was felt 30 miles away. It twisted steel beams and tossed one such beam 500 yards.

"This is worse than any tornado I've seen as far as destruction," said Salix fire chief Gerold Smith. Four people were killed and eighteen injured. A deadly chemical cloud was released, forcing the evacuation of 1,700 people in several towns.

On Mosser-Unabom + 4, December 14, 1994, a massive power outage hit eight states in the West, leaving millions of people without electricity. A 500,000-volt power grid crisscrossing the western U.S. was incapacitated, knocking out power to portions of California, Washington, Utah, Oregon, Montana and Nevada.

Utility officials had no idea what caused the blackout or where it originated. Arizona Public Service Co. had no reports of outages but they "had things like traffic lights going on and off for no reason," said Lynne Adams, utility spokeswoman.

Again on Mosser-Unabom + 4, December 14, 1994, just after 9 AM on the last day of a class on the history of ancient Greece, in a subterranean room beneath the State University of Albany's central quadrangle campus, a rifle-wielding student who claimed to have a microchip implanted in his brain took the class hostage, shooting one youth in the leg. He was eventually subdued by the students. As police led 26-year-old Ralph Tortorici away, he shouted to a crowd of bystanders, "Stop government experimentation!"

Also on Mosser-Unabom + 4, December 14, 1994, just before noon, a Lear 35 jet, which was carrying secret electronic surveillance equipment, and was supposedly being used by the California National Guard for "war games," crashed into an apartment building near Fresno. The crash killed two people, destroyed 10 cars and 18 apartment units, and cut power in portions of central California.

According to the Pentagon, the jet was being used as a target in a war game maneuver. The cause of the crash was officially listed as unknown.

In the following year the *New York Times* and *Washington Post*, which reject dozens of terrorist demands, especially from Arabs, and the publication of sundry manifestos, nevertheless published the "Unabom" manifesto in the *Washington Post* of September 19, 1995, underwritten in part by the *Times*.

The publication of anonymous occult manifestos is as old as the "chemical wedding" tracts of the Rosicrucians. The alchemical Son of Sam statements were also published by the *New York Daily News*.

Occult crimes are profoundly symbolic and are in some instances so constructed in order that they might have what Freemason Anton Mesmer called "charm"—the ability to attract additional symbolism and synchronicity, triggering a contagion in time and space which generates catastrophic events of ritual significance. The symbols and twilight language attached to them are charmed spin-offs from the primary rite of invocation.

A conspirologist might conclude that the numerous catastrophes that occurred in the immediate wake of the "Unabom" attacks were perpetrated by human agents of the "Unabom" conspiracy. But the nature of the primary ritual working is such that not every chain of catastrophe can be linked to direct human agency. Symbolic and synchronistic invocation provides the means by which catastrophic contagion is put in motion. The primary "Unabom" ritual unfolds by the invocation of remarkably meaningful "coincidence."

The alchemical processing of humans is performed with the props of time and space: significant ritual in significant areas seems to "bend" reality. In its most sub-rosa signification, wicker/wicca/witchcraft is said to be the end result of the bending of reality.

How is reality bent? By the placing of ritual props in ceremonial places. These places exist both in the mind and in physical space.

That's what "wicker" means in its most subterranean signification. Wicca (witchcraft) is just a description of the end-result of the function of bending reality.

CEREAL KILLERS

The term "serial killer" ushered in the suggestion that there might be method to this madness and that the method had something to do with the occult.

This is the prop that is placed in the Group or "dreaming mind" of the masses. Being programmed—while you are awake—by symbols of which you are unconscious, is essentially a description of mass hypnosis.

Having placed a ritual prop in the Group Mind, it is necessary to place it in physical space as well. In the case of our serial killer "Unabom," the ceremonial prop in physical space is established by sending a bomb to a U.C. Berkeley electrical engineering professor named Diogenes Anelakos, who was injured by a "Unabom" package in 1982.

The other ritual "Unabom" link must be to time; to bend our time by invoking the time of the history of ancient Greece.

Arcadia was an exceedingly antique region of Greece which predated the rise of the city states of Athens and Sparta. Arcadia was an ecological paradise, existing before Terra ran down with the thermodynamics of pollution and decay.

Arcadia's principal attributes are pastoral, romantic and feminine and its principal symbol is the underground, specifically an underground gnosis symbolized by a subterranean river.

In Arcadia the reign of the Mother Goddess survived longer than in any other area of Greece. She was personified by Demeter, the goddess of grain. To bring present-day humanity into the time of vegetative Arcadia in occult lore requires human sacrifice; that is, ceremonial immolation, or as it is known in modern parlance, "serial murder."

Downtown Helena, Montana, home of the "Last Chance Gulch," location of the hotel where Ted Kaczynski sometimes stayed.

The dreaming Group Mind, upon hearing the words "serial murder" or pronouncing them in conversation, is not perceiving them in the textual abstract but in the oral-primal, the phonetic domain of dreams.

Therefore what is being invoked in the mind of the masses when the words, "serial murder" are broadcast is not "serial" murder but "cereal" murder. Demeter, the goddess of Arcadia, is alternately known as Ceres, from whence the word "cereal" is derived.

"Unabom," a cereal murderer, sent an explosive package to Diogenes Anelakos.

Diogenes was a Greek who wandered across the earth with a lamp in his hand, searching for one honest man, such as the individual who took over the underground, ancient Greek history class December 14, 1994 to shout, "Stop government experimentation!" and who announced that something was implanted in his brain. [16]

The strategic command symbols for the "Unabom" process emanate from the twilight language of the religious rites in honor of Demeter and Ceres.

The Unabom ceremony is at the center of an apocalyptic process of reversal which accelerates decay and decrepitude, "blackening" rather than "greening" the earth, empowered by the "once and future" space/time alchemy described in atomic physics: "Time relations among events are assumed to be first constituted by the specific physical relations obtaining between them."

Uninitiated materialists ("cowans" in masonic parlance) will deny even the possibility that there is a connection between "Unabom" and the catastrophes I have listed.

APOCALYPSE CULTURE II

Such persons may, however, wish to consult the praxis behind those portions not classified as secret, of the burgeoning scientific literature on the mathematical modeling theory that purports to predict catastrophes, especially as found in the "catastrophe theory" of Warwick University's Christopher Zeeman.

LAST CHANCE GULCH

Many questions remain. Is digital computer technology the enemy of rural Arcadian ecology or is computer technology evolving a method for visualizing the epiphany of the mystics (i.e., the fundamental illusion at the core of the material world), by means of a "virtuality" which demonstrates, by corollary, the trick behind the manifestation that is the physical universe?

In other words, by some blessed serendipity, is our Promethean ambition for machine gnosis and the supremacy of the mind, leading us precisely to the point where we will see the emptiness of our desire?

Or is the computer inherently the deadly enemy of humanity, piling ever thicker layers of material illusion, fraud, and artifice?

Is there a third force operant here—neither Arcadian or materialistic—a prankster element that balances and processes the processors against their will?

How much of all of this is used, understood, or controlled by the federal government and secret societies?

Studying how the cryptocracy fabricates and packages the "Unabom" ritual on the stage of public affairs, reveals a virtuoso performance of masonic psychodrama, wherein terror, symbolism and code language synthesize to form the alchemical elixir for the processing of humanity.

On November 13, 1995, *USA Today*, in a front page article guaranteed to keep the "Unabom" psychic pressure cooker on boil, referred to the case as a "masquerade," and cited the "catastrophe theory" of Warwick's Zeeman, while dubbing "Unabom" with a new moniker, "Robert V."

The subtitle of the *USA Today* story headlined the mocking/jesting aspect of occult murder: "Unabomber must be laughing at us."

The "us" referred to in the headline is not the media or the police, but the American people, who are being processed in a heavily promoted, public ritual. (Recall that the "Unabomber" had referred to the FBI as a "joke.")

If the FBI 's behavioral "profiling" center is the Unabomber's actual handler, then such a statement would constitute an inside joke, i.e., the ritual mockery of humanity by means of the revelation that the Unabomber attacks are actually a macabre charade intended to drag us further down into the System's net of delusion.

The roof of the Atlas building. The creature descending the pole is a salamander, attended by dragons on the left and right. The Atlas building is in downtown Helena, Montana, the "burned over" capitol city where Ted Kaczynski was arraigned, Holy Thursday, 1996.

Indeed, the advertisement which appeared beneath *USA Today*'s 1995 "laughing Unabomber" headline was for the "Intel Pentium Processor," and on the front page, above an altered police sketch of "Unabomb," appeared the headline, "The Net's catching on."

The pattern of "Unabom" catastrophe continued into the Kaczynski era. On March 25, 1996, just a little over a week before Kaczynski's apprehension on April 3, "Freemen" came under FBI siege at Justus township in Jordan, Montana. The "Freemen" opposed banks, zip codes, social security numbers, license plates, and the other paraphernalia of government surveillance and control.

Like FBI agent David A. Priarone, who was shot to death in New York two days after the "Unabomber" killed Thomas Mosser in New Jersey, FBI agent Kevin Kramer was killed in Jordan, Montana eleven days after Kaczynski's capture in Lincoln. The only witness to his "accidental" death was an employee of NBC television. [17]

This psychic melodrama reached operatic proportions when, according to *USA Today*, a bad moon risin' greeted the day of Kaczynski's apprehension on April 3—a lunar eclipse described in a headline as "Huge Darkened Sphere Rises On Eastern Horizon." [18]

Bad moon indeed, for on the day of Kaczynski's capture, U.S. Commerce Secretary Ron Brown was among 33 people killed in a plane crash in Croatia. The crash was attributed to "1940s technology"—a radio magnetic indicator with which Air Force Lt. Col. Tom Perry said the computer-trained American pilots were not familiar. (A 1985 bombing attributed to "Unabom" wounded an Air Force pilot.)

Among the victims who had been aboard Secretary Brown's jet were a veritable who's who of "Unabom's" professed enemies: a senior vice-president of AT&T, the chairman of Foster-Wheeler Energy, the executive vice president of Riggs Bank, and the CEO of the Parsons Corporation of Pasadena, California. [19]

April 3 also saw radar fail twice at Pittsburgh International Airport. One hundred flights were delayed. [20]

Kaczynski's arraignment the next day, on one of the high holy days of the Christian calendar, Maundy Thursday, a day which represents the historic anniversary of the start of Christ's trial and crucifixion, added an aura of stagecraft to this public ritual. Just as John F. Kennedy's peregrination to his own fateful Golgatha in Dallas was first triggered by events in the town of Truth or Consequences, New Mexico; to reach the Helena, Montana courthouse, federal agents took Kaczynski through "Last Chance Gulch."

Historically, areas that have witnessed great psychic ferment and upheaval have been referred to as "burned over districts." The Finger Lakes region of upstate New York bears this nickname due to the waves of heterodox religious and cultic enthusiasm which have swept over it since colonial times.

Helena is also known as a "burned over" district. Montana's capitol city is so called ostensibly for the major fires which have destroyed its city center over the years.

To ward off future fires, Helena constructed a work of sympathetic magic, the symbolic Atlas building located in its old downtown district. Perched atop this building is a statue of a large green salamander descending a lightning-rod-like pole. The salamander figure is guarded by two dragon figures, one on each side.

The salamander is an alchemical creature which possesses, among other legendary attributes, the ability to exist within fire. The Oxford English Dictionary quotes an old proverb, "Salamanders can live to eternity within the fire of God's wrath."

The middle of the Atlas building with a figure representing the Titan, Atlas, who in Greek mythology bears the whole world on his back.

While the salamander perches atop the Helena structure, the building itself is symbolically upheld by a statue of the Greek Titan Atlas, the being said to bear the entire world on his back.

On Kaczynski's arraignment + 7, April 11, 1996, "the worst chemical spill in Montana history" occurred—a rail derailed 30 miles west of Lincoln, releasing 170,000 pounds of deadly chlorine gas. One man was killed and 105 people were hospitalized. Interstate U.S. 90 was closed. 500 people were evacuated. A ghostly cloud of the greenish-yellow gas, which was used to kill thousands during WWI, hovered like a toxic phantom in the Montana sky.

Other synchronicities and anomalies in the Unabom case include the claim, by a survivor of the San Francisco Zodiac slayings, that the Zodiac killer told the survivor he resided near Lincoln, Montana.

Further, Kaczynski's doctoral thesis in mathematics was titled, "Boundary Functions." The town of Lincoln, where he resided, is located a few miles from North America's great geographic boundary, the "Continental Divide." Kaczynski's brother David, who financed Ted between 1994 and 1995 with $3,000, lived in Schenectady, New York, a technological center of operations for General Electric. [21]

In certain occult crime rituals a synchronic work of literature, usually fiction, appears before the crimes are perpetrated, serving as a virtual script. In the case of Patty Hearst and the Symbionese Liberation Army (a group which featured salamander symbolism), a book, *Abducted*, had been published before the SLA came to the fore, paralleling many incidents that would come to fruition in the activities of Hearst and her comrades.

In the case of Son of Sam, the British film, *The Wicker Man*, which premiered in the U.S. in 1974 and was screened in New York by a group called Abraxas in April of 1977, during the height of the frenzy of the Son of Sam killings. [22]

A hit man who participated in both the Son of Sam and Double Initial murders, John Wheat Carr, signed himself, "Wicked King Wicker." In the "Unabom" case the precursor literary work in question has a more prestigious literary pedigree. Joseph Conrad's 1907 book, *The Secret Agent*, concerns a mad professor who lives in a tiny room, clothed in rags, while he builds a bomb with which he seeks to destroy the "idol of science." "Joseph Conrad" was the literary nom-de-plume of the Polish writer Theodore Korzeniowski.

The late James Shelby Downard, the renowned occult investigator, offered guidance throughout most of my Unabom sleuthing. Mr. Downard noted that Kaczynski's Mexican pen pal, Juan Sanchez, resided in the village of Ojinaga, the site of a cave complex known as "the Devil's Home." (Sanchez received a beautifully hand-carved pencil box from Kaczynski which bore the Latin inscription, *Montani Semper Liberi* ("Mountain men are always free").

Mr. Downard also related that Ojinaga features a road constructed in a figure eight in honor of the Aztec bat god, which, legend has it, descended to earth at Ojinaga, by means of the "Eight Thread." [23]

At the preliminaries for his 1998 murder trial in Sacramento, Kaczynski was denied the attorney of his choice, San Francisco radical lawyer Tony Serra, who presumably would have mounted an ideological defense that may have resulted in disclosure of federal entrapment or conspiracy. [24]

Instead, Federal Judge Garland E. Burrell, Jr. continued to saddle Kaczynski with two federally employed California "defense" attorneys, Quin Denvir and Judy Clarke, who had taken over from Donahoe and Gallagher, and who were convinced of their client's guilt and intended to defend him by arguing that he was guilty but insane.

At that juncture, the defendant allegedly balked and bargained a guilty plea in return for life imprisonment instead of the death penalty. With that plea bargain, which was granted by the prosecution in spite of an allegedly air-tight case, the spectre of an adversarial defense, and a trial packed with revelations subversive of the FBI/media script, was rendered null and void. In accepting Kaczynski's guilty plea on all counts on January 20, 1998, Judge Burrell questioned Kaczynski as to whether he was under the influence of drugs or medication at that time or for 24 hours preceding his guilty plea.

Note that Judge Burrell limited his query concerning Kaczynski's "medication" to a period of only the prior 24 hours. Drugs such as Prozac, however, when ingested over a lengthy period (such as several weeks) can remain in the bloodstream and affect thinking and judgment for at least two days.

A more astute judge would have asked the defendant, "What drugs have you been taking or what medication has been prescribed for you throughout your incarceration?" Burrell's failure to do so opens the door to the possibility that Kaczynski may have been drugged or medicated while in custody. [25]

According to the *Sacramento Bee*, at his May 4 sentencing, Kaczynski read a brief statement attacking a lengthy document filed by prosecutors last week that detailed his methods and motives, calling it "clearly political" and a misrepresentation of facts of the case.

Specifically, Kaczynski said, "My statement will be very brief. A few days ago the government filed a sentencing memorandum, the purpose of which was clearly political. By discrediting me personally, they hope to discredit the idea expressed by the Unabomber. In reality, the government has discredited itself.

"The sentencing memorandum contains false statements, distorted statements and statements that mislead by omitting important facts. At a later time I expect to respond at length to the sentencing memorandum and also the many other falsehoods that have been propagated about me. Meanwhile, I only ask that people reserve their judgment about me and about the Unabom case until all the facts have been made public." [26]

Among the numerous hateful statements attributed to Kaczynski in the government's May 4 sentencing memorandum, there was quite a show of proving each assertion about Kaczynski by elaborate reference to various evidentiary documents.

However, in that portion of the memorandum where the U.S. Attorney states, "it is clear that Kaczynski plotted and carried out his crimes alone," no evidence or documentation of any kind is cited.

PROCESSING THE GROUP MIND

By means of occult public rituals disguised as random terrorism or serial murder, we are controlled and processed. The language of symbolism is used to speak to our subconscious; to reveal to us the exact opposite of what is propounded by the System in its rational discourse.

During the excitement leading up to Kaczynski's sentencing in Sacramento, the Hollywood film, *U.S. Marshals*, starring Tommy Lee Jones, debuted in theaters across the country. At the heart of the cinematic intrigue was a complex double-cross centered on a Federal agent named "Kaczynski." In the movie, the Kaczynski character is set-up and then killed by another Federal agent.

Was Ted Kaczynski set-up by what he came to regard as an "omnipotent organization" against which he felt "powerless"?

In the sub-rosa twilight language in which the government's own behavioral profilers and psychological warfare practitioners traffic, the answer would appear to be yes.

In the lexicon of the twilight language there is a word for Ted Kaczynski. That word jumps off any topographic map of the Lincoln, Montana region and is displayed in lights in downtown Lincoln, Kaczynski's adopted hometown.

This word for Kaczynski—which the Truth or Consequences principle has placed in front of the Group Mind like a billboard on Broadway—is linked to the incontrovertible record of catastrophes which attended some "Unabomb" disasters, which also occurred on the day of his capture and in the aftermath of his arraignment.

Kaczynski's surrender to his captors on April 3, 1996 occurred in the geodetic realm at the nodal point of The Scapegoat, at Lincoln, Montana, home of the 80,697-acre Scapegoat Wilderness, the Scapegoat Eatery and a human scapegoat, an Atlas whose "shrug" continues to reverberate in the consciousness of the Group Mind of America mystica.

I have not ascertained whether Kaczynski's role in the "Unabom" charade was peripheral or pivotal, but I believe his handlers had contact with him long before his arrest, and that they manipulated and shepherded him and then apprehended him on cue.

I believe this was performed in coordination with other acts they were invoking as part of a ceremony which reverses the fertility rites of the ancients, blackening the earth with ever greater pollution, while attempting to subdue the intractable spirit of *Terra anima* itself, just as they have harnessed boundary-breaker Dr. Theodore Kaczynski, who languishes in a maximum security prison for our sins, ecological and social. [27]

The Scapegoat Eatery, downtown Lincoln, Montana.

Kaczynski's "tell-all" book, which was set to be published but later quashed by New Yorker Beau Friedlander, would also seem to fit an old pattern.

During the investigation into the murder by Freemasons of writer William Morgan in New York in the early 19th century, certain principals in the case exhibited what at the time was called "masonic apoplexy."

When intense judicial investigation was focused upon them they had little or nothing to say and some even committed suicide. After the trail had gone cold and the intensity of public interest had diminished somewhat, the "spell" was seemingly lifted and they lucidly articulated certain radical truths about the crime and its perpetrators.

James Shelby Downard referred to a similar pattern in the aftermath of the assassination of John F. Kennedy which he termed "cryonic"—a freeze/thaw process of control of how events are perceived, as part of a larger alchemical process of "Revelation of the Method," which I discuss at length in my book, *Secret Societies and Psychological Warfare*.

By this process, principals remain strangely mute at the critical moment when their testimony could have served as part of an ongoing prosecution case, such as occurred during New Orleans District Attorney Jim Garrison's investigation.

Then later, when the criminal case is closed, the trail cold and competing accounts and "solutions" swirl in the media like mid-winter snowflakes, witnesses and principals come forward with radical truths about the facts of the crime, but which are nonetheless treated as either self-serving yarns or merely one among dozens of competing, equally compelling "conspiracy theories." [28]

Ted Kaczynski may have had a number of opportunities during his pre-trial incarceration and legal hearings to plead innocent, to refuse to plea bargain and to speak at length and in detail at the climax of the Unabom rite, his sentencing in Sacramento, where he might have spoken for the official court record and before the world media concerning what actually had transpired.

Like so many ritual scapegoats before him, he did not. Perhaps, due to the administration by the authorities of some pharmaceutical substance or digital implant, he could not.

Are there grounds for assuming that Kaczynski is no longer subject to his Federal handlers, and that he has somehow managed to recover some shred of intellectual autonomy in the Federal-Benthamite, panoptican dungeon in which he is entombed in Florence, Colorado?

If there are, and Kaczynski is successful in his purported endeavor to delineate "truth versus lies," at this point in time the thawing of the once-frozen facts may itself be a prescribed part of the Unabomb ritual, serving to further prime the Arcadian stream that feeds the cryptocracy's eternal psychodrama, as part of its final riddle, the "Must Be" stage of alchemical transformation, the "Making Manifest of all that is Hidden."

NOTES

1. *Montana Kaimin* (campus newspaper of the University of Montana at Missoula), April 5, 1996, p. I.
2. *Coeur d'Alene Press*, April 14, 1996, p. A13.
3. Special Agent Whitehurst revealed "political pressures that he said (FBI) superiors applied to alter findings to favor prosecutors' evidentiary needs." *New York Times*, April 18, 1997.
4. *New York Times*, April 4, 1996, p. 14.
5. *Great Falls Tribune*, May 16, 1996, p. I.
6. Ibid., April 9, 1996, p. 7.
7. *The Missoulian*, April 9, 1997, p. 7.
8. Motion of April 15, 1996, U.S. District Court, Helena district.
9. *Time*, July 5, 1993, p. 27.
10. *The Independent Record* [Helena, Montana], April 11, 1996, p. 7A.
11. *The Missoulian*, May I, 1996, p. A5.
12. On April 13, 1996, the *New York Times* erroneously reported that no one had attempted to visit Kaczynski besides his attorney.

13. *Spokesman-Review* (Spokane, Washington), April 4, 1996, pp. 1 and 6.
14. Is the peculiar spelling of "Unabom," with the letter *b* omitted from the end of the word, a psychological ploy on the part of the FBI, a hint to the Group Mind that the case as presented to the public is in fact incomplete—that something is deliberately being withheld?
15. *Great Falls Tribune*, April 16, 1996, p. 5A.
16. This man expressed his intuition that the government had implanted something alien in his head. It could be hardware, as he suggests, or he may be highly sensitive to the implantation of "software" such as the twilight language of the Unabom rite.
17. *Coeur d'Alene Press*, April 15, 1996, p.A9.
18. *USA Today*, April 4, 1996, p. 7A.
19. Parsons Corporation, though not named after the rocket fuel scientist Dr. John Whiteside (Jack) Parsons, who was the American leader of the secret society known as the Ordo Templi Orientis (OTO), situates its home building in Pasadena, just downhill from the region known as "Devil's Gate" and practically next door to Jet Propulsion Laboratory, (JPL), an institution co-founded by the self-declared "anti-Christ" Jack Parsons.
20. *USA Today*, April 4, 1996, p. 7A.
21. *Great Falls Tribune*, April 11, 1996, p. 5A.
22. *Cinefantastique*, vol. 6, no. 3, (1977), pp. 42 and 46. In ancient times human sacrifices were burned alive inside a giant wicker structure shaped like a man. In September of 1998 thousands of "revelers" gathered in the Black Rock Desert of Nevada for the "Burning Man Festival," during which a forty-foot wooden man is ritually immolated.
23. Mr. Downard died of pancreatic cancer at his home in the fabled "capitol" city of America's "Little Egypt" region, Memphis, Tennessee, on March 16, 1998. He was 85. "Unabom" was his final case. Before his illness he had been intent on visiting Lincoln and Helena in connection with what he came to regard as the government's entrapment of Kaczynski. It is worth noting that there is widespread sentiment in the radical environmental movement that the FBI is itself proficient in the use of pipe bombs. In May, 1990, Earth First! members Darryl Cherney and Judy Bari were injured in a pipe bombing. Earth First! has charged that the bombing was an assassination attempt by FBI operatives.
24. According to the court transcript of Jan. 20, 1998, Serra had informed Kaczynski in writing that he and his legal team could represent him and would do so *pro bono*. U.S. District Court transcript case #S-96-259.
25. Ibid., U.S. District Court transcript. The root of the word "pharmaceutical" derives from the Greek word for scapegoat, *pharmakos*, the name for the civic unfortunate who was ritually blamed and punished for the sins of others and to whom was administered a poisonous drug.
26. Kaczynski transcript from the U.S. District Court, Eastern District of Calif., May 4, 1998.
27. There are indications that Kaczynski is becoming a sympathetic cultural icon, even among those who believe the establishment story that he is responsible for the bombings. In the supermarket tabloid, *Weekly World News* (April 7, 1998, p. 17), popular columnist "Ed Anger" called for Kaczynski's parole, if he would use

his alleged bomb-making abilities "to blow Saddam (Hussein) to smithereens . . . if he gets rid of that whacky Iraqi, he can move in with me, by golly." Taking the American pulse at the elite end of the cultural spectrum, we find Catholic Bishop Richard N. Williamson, rector of St. Thomas Aquinas Seminary in Winona, Minnesota, declaring, "You may say what you like about him as a criminal terrorist, etc. etc. and much of it is true. But the man, as is clear from his Manifesto (which is well worth reading) was at least trying to tackle, and publicize, serious and deep problems of man in a machine society . . . he . . . has a remotely Catholic sense of how technology brutalizes man. How Catholic on the contrary do all those technophiles deserve to be called who have—gladly—given up all sense in order to wallow at ease in their computers? Give me the Unabomber's seriousness over their shallowness, any day of the week." (Monthly Letter to Friends and Benefactors, April 2, 1998, pp. 1–2.)

28. The latest FBI jargon for this is "noise." An example would be the debut of the *X Files* television series in the aftermath of renewed, serious investigative interest in the Kennedy assassination conspiracy. Just as the public is deluded into believing that "everything causes cancer," so that they will do little or nothing to oppose the spread of demonstrable carcinogens in the environment and food chain, the cryptocracy has lately entered the phase of promoting the idea that everything is a conspiracy, so as to divert attention away from demonstrable criminal conspiracies, while propagating obsessions with "alien autopsies" and "crashed UFOs." The latter play on the public's ignorance of the essentially evanescent nature of such phenomena and generate the requisite "noise" necessary for the "Revelation of the Method" with impunity. (For a detailed elucidation of this process, the reader is directed to purchase Hoffman's book, *Secret Societies and Psychological Warfare*, available for $15 postpaid from Independent History and Research, Box 849, Coeur d'Alene, Idaho 83816.)

⚡ ⚡ ⚡

Michael A. Hoffman II provided the introduction to James Shelby Downard's "King/Kill 33°" in the first printed edition of *Apocalypse Culture*. Hoffman's contribution to this book praises Jews, but does in fact sidestep his primary crusade—Holocaust revisionism and blackening the cause of Zionism as seen on his website <www.hoffman-info.com>.

It must be mentioned once again that the editor of this book does not endorse or promote the writers' opinions expressed herein, or the hobby horses ridden on their own time.

AMERICA, THE POSSESSED CORPSE

James Shelby Downard

The cult of the Great Architect of the Universe (GAOTU) which rules the dominant position, has succeeded, through secret artifice, in establishing a worldwide web of conspiracy, an occult contrivance for the control of the Invisible Empire, the One World Government.

The Invisible Empire is designed to control people brought together and made one, who, lacking individuality, would work as directed by cybernetic systems programmed by scientific design teams.

The design for control of humanity is called the "Master Plan," one that is utterly evil in all of its ramifications. The Plan is represented to the brain-dead as a precept of Christianity without separate races. The quasi-religious indoctrination is widespread, for the ruling cult influences every major religion in the United States.

The Master Plan calls for subverting every moral principle. The planned corruption has succeeded to such an extent that ritual crime, which ties in to the sex and death superstitions of the cult of GAOTU, is regarded with indifference by officials paid to guard the public welfare. Some officials are proselytes of the cult and others are simply on the take, but most are surfeited with what has been going on and "just don't give a damn." Some people criticize me for writing or talking about these grave matters in too much of a satiric or mocking way. To these critics, I offer this explanation: to paraphrase an old axiom, truths are sometimes revealed in jest. This process can be compared to a wake, where joking, drinking, feasting and dancing are performed around a dead body. Hence my attitude toward the American establishment, which has become a possessed corpse.

The U.S. government is called a democracy, proclaimed to be of-by-and-for-the-people, but the ruling administration is really quite dead, and a Police State specter has taken possession of the body politic. The animated, zombie-like cadaver is now part of a truly Evil Empire, far beyond the clichés of science fiction films and the New World Order blather of Bill Clinton. The specter lurks in the secrecy, silence and darkness of ignorance and crime, symbolized by a cave (vault, crypt, tomb, grave) in Freemasonry. Darkness conceals the mysteries of Masonic sorcery.

This predatory specter was conjured by evil people out of the muck of their own subverted lives, and it is the unofficial apparition of the Department of Justice and the *esprit de corps* of the Federal Bureau of Investigation. It nurtured federal bureaucratic inverts who imagine themselves sucking the specter's pap, while the public is ballyhooed with their alleged fidelity, bravery and integrity.

The Police State specter is the very soul of the Office of Strategic Services—Central Intelligence Agency perverts, who have worked hard to thwart every principle of morality within easy reach. Such amorality fits some Treasury agents to a T, and as if that weren't evil enough, the specter is symbolically associated with crescent-moon-and-star symbolism, such as was depicted on badges worn by federal marshals. So, it is a small wonder that sex-and-death rituals have been so well-hidden in the good 'ol U.S. of A.

Sex-magic rites have been modernized by "mad doctors" and "crazy scientists" who practice scientific sorcery with the help of the Police State. In some rites, besides being dosed with abulic drugs, biotelemetric implants stimulate victims' pudendal nerves and cause gross excitement of the genital area.

The possessed are owned body and mind by way of mind control. Some of the unfortunates are used in orgiastic witchcraft rites where, in a condition resembling those of erotic robots, they perform will-less sex acts.

Abulic drugs, which are more than a little like the "Love Potion No. 9" of the old rock 'n' roll song, are fed to victims, and are every bit as effective as the Circean potion was for ancient Greeks. Though manufactured in the vats of the pharmaceutical industry, the abulics used, such as the tolache-mimetic concoction, have been used by sorcerers for ages. The mystical sex circuses are typical of witchcraft "sex magic" orgies that have always been performed in Call-to-Chaos rites, and victims are characterized by their loss of will-power.

People of all races are used in these "sexathons," which are aimed at nothing more than racial mixing. The cry of voodoo witches at their assemblies, in which negroes and whites participate, is *"Mislet! Mislet! Mislet!*—Mix! Mix! Mix!" Keep that in mind next time you tune into your favorite black-and-white television program, in which "oreo" bedroom scenes are shown in close-up detail.

The mixing ceremonies are synonymous with the present worldwide campaign for racial amalgamation. The United States' "Melting Pot" is as sooty as the veritable witches' cauldron, particularly in these terminal times.

The Master Plan has a time of tribulation, in which people are to be made one. Near the start of that togetherness, a post-tribulation "rapture" is planned, in which everyone's brain will be pleasured magnetically, and all will cum together. Those gathered will have their individuality removed, and be nothing more than a humanoid servo-mechanism.

The Police State specter is computerized, and I imagine that the traditional spirits of possession, devils, fiends and demons are enraged that their possession concession is now run by the Police State crowd. Hopefully they'll do something about it. Supernatural spirits of possession relish soul food, and we ain't talkin' about sow belly or collards either; more like fillets of soul deep-fried in the fires of Hell. And the Police State gorges itself on souls fed it in the twinkling of the All-Seeing Eye.

Whether you realize it or not, the humor of this study has more purpose than might at first be thought. In old physiology the word "humor" referred to blood. This was one of the four cardinal humors that contained the other three, and their relative proportions determined one's temperament.

In studying word use, we find that a bloody temperament was the humor displayed by people attending the Circus Maximus of ancient Rome. Life often is likened to a circus or carnival, and in the Carnival of Life, I can say I walked the Crooked Mile (the Midway) as a straight man. It hasn't been easy, for it seems that everyone is more than a little bent, and I haven't quite fit in.

As it is said in Carny talk, I wasn't "with it," I was an outsider. But I have more than a bit of inside information, so I paradoxically can be described as an outsider/insider.

The hierarchy of the cult of the GAOTU evidently declared me to be an outsider, albeit a very knowing one, damn my hide. Another term they use is "profane," which is said to come from the Latin words *pro* and *fanum*, "before or outside the temple." A person declared to be profanus in ancient times was not allowed into the temple to see what was going on, just as a profane one is not permitted to witness Masonic Temple Rites. Not that he'd be missing much. But an outsider who has witnessed the rites has committed a Masonic crime, and the peekaboo person is declared a Cowan. Cowans are persecuted, used as scapegoats and sometimes tortured and/or killed.

Because of the forbidden information I encountered, I have been betrayed, cheated, robbed, drugged, poisoned and surreptitiously fed stuff that even wretched carnival geeks would have scorned. Such murderous attacks have been made so frequently that I now pay little heed to the bulk of them.

Whenever I attempted to get away from it all, I found that I was blocked, blacked-out in the mystical darkness of the Masonic hoodwink, where nothing is what it seems. I was doing the *danse macabre* with Masonic assassins that I knew, although those assassins are alleged to be entirely allegorical.

There came a time when it seemed I could dance no further, and the dead-end that I faced reeked of finality. Then I considered the eschatological scatological aspects of the whole terminal trip, and when I mentally pictured that crap-littered road of life, I realized that a maze had caught up with me. A coffin seemed to be the only way out. After some gloomy cogitation like Ishmael, when he walked past coffin warehouses in *Moby Dick*, I decided that taking that way out would not be the best route at the time. I tried to recall if I saw an overlooked exit along the midway; the possibility of such an exit seemed better than its alternative.

The mental search I then undertook in the limbo of memories revealed things that seemed innocent enough, but were on the threshold of memories that were real hellers. I began to examine each and every innocent-appearing memory carefully, suspecting that they were not all as they seemed. When I discovered memories without connections or antecedents, I began to wonder if they were concealing something.

When rummaging through that mental limbo, I found a genuine old memory with valid connections, and with that memory there came teardrops, and through those teardrops I encountered frightful memories of the long-dead past, and suddenly I recognized the past for the *corpus mysticum* that it is. When seen as it really is, the mystical past is a horrible thing, cloaked in iniquity, secrecy, silence and darkness, the now-you-see-it-now-you-don't Masonic Oz art.

Fooled for so long and so thoroughly, I could not at first recall the "contract" that had been put out on me. The contractors and subcontractors were so numerous that, looking back on it now, it seems just about everybody had a piece of the action, and almost had to carry signs to keep from offing each other.

While it might be said that in the Carnival of Life, I wasn't a star player, but with the Carnival of Death, I certainly was, and my performances with it have been second to none. Death as always been my life-support system.

The Carnival of Death's ringmaster is, of course, the Angel of Death. Since other angels refuse to play with the Death Angel, perhaps he empathized with me as a fellow outsider. The shadow of death has darkened me for so long that it has become my very own shadow. We've been together for the multitude of life's cruel games, and he has always been on my side, no matter how it might have looked at first. I am quite fortunate to have had such a protective shade.

⚡ ⚡ ⚡

James Shelby Downard died March 16, 1998. His essays, "King/Kill 33°," from the original, and "Call to Chaos" from the current "Revised Edition," of *Apocalypse Culture*, are the most remarkable conspiracy documents I have encountered, before or since. The linguistic, geographical and geological coincidences they summon regarding the assassination of John Kennedy and the Manhattan Project are more than simple conspiracy theory, they're products of an inspired, paranoid mind. The secrets they expose are part of a bigger, mystical world that beckon but can never be thoroughly known.

In Downard's writings, the products of his subconscious bubble to the surface and catalyze painstaking research. The collision of the poetic against the logical works especially well in the field of conspiracy; it remains the freshest approach to this field of inquiry.—"Riding the Downardian Nightmare," from the now out-of-print *Cult Rapture*.

When visiting Downard in March '94, he handed me a stack of unpublished writing, including his autobiography, *Carnivals of Life & Death*, which details the story of him escaping Masonic hit squads and being drugged, implanted and used as part of sexual rituals with a gorgeous, nymphomaniacal girlfriend. (For all those people who write Feral House, wanting further Downard material, the entirety of *Carnivals of Life & Death* is set for a Fall 2003 release date.) As with all of Downard's writing, his memoir is full of weird specifics, like photos of Shelby as a child dressed up as a clown, strange regions in the Florida Keys, and bizarre occult statuary built by an Anton LaVey lookalike. Either it's a document from a remarkable Walter Mitty wannabe, or one of the most dislocating true stories of modern times. "America, the Possessed Corpse," excerpted above, is his memoir's introduction.

—Adam Parfrey

James Shelby Downard

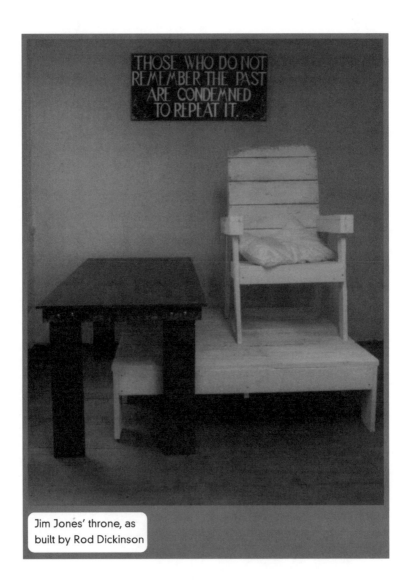

Jim Jones' throne, as
built by Rod Dickinson

THE JONESTOWN RE-ENACTMENT

Rod Dickinson

Early in 1999 I received email from Rod Dickinson, a British artist interested in "re-enacting" the notorious deaths of 914 individuals that occurred
at Jonestown, Guyana in 1979.

Dickinson, an artist known for his elaborate "Crop Circle" hoaxes, also
participated in a 1999 art exhibition called "From Memory":

> Working from memory is to pit oneself against a fact, an exist-
> ing text, a lived experience, past or no longer present. What
> this act of translation/relation reveals is that the impossibility
> of accuracy, the imperfections, the fabrications, the lies and
> the embellished truths both compose and confound memory.
> The metaphors we use to describe remembering involve
> movement, a journey through . . . a flood of . . . Memory is the
> fluid becoming of things which have already been.

Originally slated to occur in September, 1999, and rescheduled for late
September, 2000, the Jonestown re-enactment will be hosted by the
Institute of Contemporary Art (ICA), London, and staged in a cordoned area
in a public park. A section of the Pavilion building, the stage and Jim Jones'
throne will all be recreated along with other crucial props the galvanized
bathtub full of purple Kool Aid, the slatted wooden walkway, tables, etc.

—Adam Parfrey

WHITE NIGHTS OUTLINE

The following text outlines a performance piece that will involve several hundred voluntary participants in a one-day event. The centerpiece of the event
will be the re-enactment of the last two-and-a-half hours of the religious
group, The Peoples Temple:

Led by the Reverend Jim Jones, the entire 900-strong community of the
Peoples Temple committed suicide on November 18, 1978 at Jonestown,
Guyana, by ingesting grape juice laced with tranquilizers and cyanide.*

The intention of the performance is to memorialize these deaths through
their re-enactment; this will include situating the context in which they
occurred. Thus, in line with other historical re-enactment groups, the performance will be supplemented by living history enactors; individuals, who in
"role" will describe and inform interested members of the audience of the

---

* Some researchers, including Jim Hougan and John Judge, believe that most,
  if not all, of Jim Jones' followers were murdered, and did not commit suicide.

background events and context of the performance. The event will also include a talk which will further describe and interpret the events that precipitated the deaths.

THE RE-ENACTMENT

Despite being the most documented mass suicide in modern history, there are no actual representations (film) of the event. Following the model of historical re-enactment groups, the performance will reconstruct and piece together the event as a lived experience.

This will take the form of a two-and-half-hour re-enactment with between 150–500 re-enactors. The re-enactment will be staged twice during the day. The repetition of the performance gathers both a greater potency and circularity with the knowledge that The Peoples Temple community acted out their own suicide in rehearsal many times before the actual event. Jim Jones called these rehearsals "White Nights."

The performance will not use any form of stage, and will take place in a relatively confined area, with enactors moving only a small amount within this area. Crucial objects will be recreated from the event; such as galvanized bath tubs full of grape juice, the slatted wooden walkway on which they are situated and Jim Jones' "throne." The re-enactors will wear clothing that is similar to that worn by the members of the Peoples Temple; this generally consisted of T-shirts, trousers and bare feet or sandals.

The performance will be informed by photographs of the aftermath, and scripted from existing tapes and transcripts of the event. These take the form of monologues and dialogues between Jones and various community members reflecting on the positive and revolutionary implications of their deaths. The performance will culminate in the re-enactment of the suicide with all re-enactors remaining motionless for forty minutes in the final death scene.

LIVING HISTORY DISPLAYS

Although the principal focus of the White Nights re-enactment will be the last few hours of the Peoples Temple community, the audience will also experience close contact with participants by asking questions and learning about life in the Peoples Temple Community from the Living History Display. In role, these re-enactors will portray the background and sequence of events that precipitated the deaths in Jonestown, as well as explaining the daily conditions experienced by community members; from the food they ate to the conditions in the Guyanan jungle.

The Living History Displays will be pivotal to the White Nights re-enactment, encouraging a better understanding of the 914 deaths by depicting both the internal struggles and external disruption to the community, offering individual perspectives on Jim Jones and the events depicted by the White Nights re-enactment, as they unfold in front of the audience. They will be supported by a talk given by one of the re-enactors that will outline and interpret the theology of the Peoples Temple and the events that led up to the deaths.

AIMS AND CONCEPT

The re-enactment will aim to represent and reconstitute the world view of a community of people that has been popularly misinterpreted as demonic, evil and without humanity. One of the main aims via this method is to create an awareness of the Peoples Temple community as a human, independent-minded group of individuals. (This humanizing view largely concurs with most of the less sensationalist material that has been written about the event.)

The Jonestown event was a tragedy. It is my hope that the re-enactment will reflect this, and the participation of the community. Whilst one might regard their actions as misled, they were not without integrity.

⚡ ⚡ ⚡

http://www.jonestownreenactment.org/

PEOPLES TEMPLE MEDICAL SERVICES

P.O. BOX 893   GEORGETOWN, GUYANA

Lawrence E. Schacht, M.D.
Sharon R. Cobb, R.N., P.N.P.
Joyce A. Parks, R.N., F.N.P.
Dale Parks, C.R.T.T.

To Whomever finds this note:

Collect all the tapes, all the writing, all the history. The story of this movement, this action, must be examined over and over. It must be understood in all of its incredible dimensions. Words fail. We have pledged our lives to this great cause. We are proud to have something to die for. We do not fear death. We hope that the world will some-day realise the ideals of brotherhood, justice and equality that Jim Jones has lived and died for. We have all chosen to die for this cause. We know there is no way that we can avoid misinterpretation. But Jim Jones and this movement were born too soon. The world was not ready to let us live.

I am sorry there is no eloquence as I write these final words. We are resolved, but grieved that we cannot make the truth of our witness clear. This is the last of our lives. May the world find a way to a new birth of social justice. If there is any way that our lives and the life of Jim Jones can ever help that take place, we will have not lived in vain.

Jim Jones did not order anyone to attack or kill anyone. It was done by individuals who had too much of seeing people try to destroy this movement. Their actions have left us no alternative, and rather than see this cause decimated, we have chosen to give our lives. We are proud of that choice.

Please try to understand. Look at all. Look at all in perspective. Look at Jonestown, see what we have tried to do. This was a movement to life to the newest of the human spirit, broken by Capitalism, by a system of exploitation and injustice. Look at all that was built by a beleaguered people. We did not want that kind of ending—we wanted to live, to shine, to bring light to a world that is dying for a little bit of love. To those left behind of our loved ones, many of whom will not understand, who never knew this truth, grieve not. We are grateful for this opportunity to bear witness— a bitter witness— history has chosen our destiny in spite of our own desire to forget our own. We were at a cross/purpose with history. But we are calm in this hour of our own demons of accident, circumstance, miscalculation, error that was not our intent, beyond our intent.

I hope that someone writes this whole story. It is not "news." It is more. We merge with millions of others, we are subsumed in the archetype. People hugging each other, embracing, we are hurrying— we do not want to be captured. We want to bear witness at once.

We did not want it this way. All was going well as Ryan completed first day here. Then a man tried to attack him, unsuccessfully. At same time, several set out into jungle wanting to overtake Ryan, kids, and others who left with them. They did, and several killed. When we heard this we had no choice. We would be taken. We have to go as one, we want to live as Peoples Temple, or end it. We have chosen. It is finished.

Hugging and kissing and tears and silence and joy in a long line. Touches and whispered words as this silent line passes. Determination, purpose. A proud people. Only last night, their voices raised in unison, a voice of affirmation and today, a different sort of affirmation, a dimension of that same victory of the human spirit.

A tiny kitten sits next to me watching. A dog barks. The birds gather on the wires overhead. Let all the story of this Peoples Temple be told. Let all the books be opened. This sight—a terrible victory— how bitter that we did not, could not, that Jim Jones was crushed by a world that he didn't make. How great the victory.

If nobody understands, it matters not—I am ready to die now. Darkness settles over Jonestown on its last day on Earth.

MURDER LITE

Sondra London

Society secretly wants crime, needs crime, and gains definite satisfactions from the present mishandling of it! The crime and punishment ritual is a part of our lives. We need crimes to wonder at, to enjoy vicariously, to discuss and speculate about, and to publicly deplore. We need criminals to identify ourselves with, to envy secretly, and to punish stoutly. They do for us the forbidden, illegal things we wish to do and, like scapegoats of old, they bear the burdens of our displaced guilt and punishment.

Karl Menninger

Rich in what Richard Ramirez calls "eyeball kicks," murder provides a quick climax, helping to relieve boredom and tension. As human tragedy devolves into a form of infotainment, we might want to follow the suggestion of the curiously popular 'zine, *Murder Can Be Fun*, and play as if murdering guests at our next cocktail party. Afterward, be sure to turn on the evening news and see the latest and greatest bloodaholic smirking, "I'm a natural born killer!"

This is not murder; it's Murder Lite.

Why does our culture romanticize Murder Lite? Is it a response to the weight of numbers and loss of control? Is it a demoralized reaction to repression and corruption, an armchair mannered way of seizing personal power to "defy" authority?

Or is Murder Lite simple indulgence? Toxic thoughts affect the mind like toxic substances affect the body, with a euphoric, manic rush.

At one time the "fuck you" of rock, drugs, and alcohol gave wannabe free spirits enough of a buzz to get them through the night. Succeeding waves of the disaffected push the envelope further and further, finding that only modern serial killers have the edge that really cuts.

Performance violence reflects what Don DeLillo calls "the language of being noticed." Our hostility quotient has risen, with hard rock morphing into death rock and black metal. But what had manifested on the outer fringes has crossed over to the middle. Now everybody can get that good old killer feeling.

Murder as The Solution reaches its banal apotheosis on the Great American Country cable channel, with the Dixie Chicks popping their fingers while graphically depicting how and why "Earl has to die." Giggling and jiggling as Earl's bound corpse jounces down the ditch toward the camera, the Dixie icons of scrubbed pulchritude make it feel downright American to kill.

The lawless mystique is scarcely new. It's all part of theatrical tradition: Shakespeare routinely littered the stage with corpses and no Greek tragedy ended without mortal combat claiming half the cast. The modern serial killer inhabits the same role as dark folk heroes like Robin Hood, Lancelot, Wyatt Earp, Jesse James. The Viking chieftain Eric the Red wasn't called Red for his hair color.

The Old Testament provides a bloody panorama for the intimidated to celebrate and safely deplore. We read of mass slayers racking up higher and higher scores, while ancient peoples glorified them, chanting, "Saul has slain his thousands, and David his ten thousands." Saul was driven to murderous rage envying the charismatic lyre-slinging lyricist who had become the most ruthless mass slayer of all, stealing the hearts of Saul's bloodthirsty followers.

Idolization of the bloodthirsty, though winked at and frowned upon today, functions at a deep, unconscious level. Within their own minds, serial killers often seem to be fulfilling their idea of an honorable profession. A killer who shot his father and stabbed another five to death tells me he feels like he comes from another time, a time when he would have been adulated. Danny Rolling often refers to himself as a sort of Jesse James, writing of "legends of lion-like men and beautiful lasses who stole their hearts away . . . a magical, simpler time when one won the favor of his Lady Fair by how well he could wield a two-edged sword and stand his ground against his enemies . . . it must have been a glorious era for man."

Are we experiencing an auto-immune reaction to the encroaching aesthetic of ugliness? Ideas and dreams are full of struggle and foreboding and artists spew a limitless barrage of anger, fear, disgust and outrage. As Leonard Cohen sang, "I've seen the future, and it is murder."

In their own pre-conscious way, murderers are artists, expressing deep seismic temblors. How can one decipher cryptic messages inscribed in blood? The killer may discern no cosmic significance in his acts. He may believe he is merely fulfilling his own personal agenda. Since these psychodramas can destroy our lives it is our business to interpret them. If we turn our eyes away from the bloody truths scrawled on the floor they don't magically disappear. In the darkness of our will to ignorance, these messages gain more power.

Our brain is a magic theater where holographs enact what we perceive as reality. Once we comprehend what a killer might be doing and saying, we bring him to life within our own mind. Thanks to a media dedicated to conveying the vivid imagery our minds demand, we all have at least one phantasmagoric Manson dancing around in a dark corner, casting helter-skelter spells.

If the Manson in our mind somehow springs to life in the Theater of the Real . . . somebody's bound to get hurt.

But of course, we wouldn't want that to happen. Nobody in our audience wants to get hurt; they just want to watch.

⚡ ⚡ ⚡

Sondra London is editor of *Killer Fiction* (now out of print), co-author, with Danny Rolling, of *The Making of a Serial Killer*, author of a coming non-fiction book about vampire killers, and the subject of a recent Errol Morris documentary aired on the Bravo cable channel. Ms. London was successfully sued by the state of Florida to relinquish all money earned for her work on the Rolling book. Due to frequent death threats, Ms. London has given up her true crime career. Her website, www.sondralondon.com, once banned from America Online after complaints from the Governor of Wyoming due to its material from serial killers, now concentrates on her musical career.

JOE ALT.TRUE.CRIME
Adam Parfrey

Murder is the primary engine of our culture, the spark plug of the entertainment industry dressed up with pretensions to a moral highroad: newspapers, magazines, novels, true crime books, music, movies. Murder is the fuel guzzled by the huge bureaucratic labyrinth behind judicial, police and prison industries and its secular limbs—law, firearms, all of them.

Murder of the native-born by invaders is the usual method by which nations are established. Murder even justifies the establishment of a religious state, such as contemporary Iran and Israel.

Murder provides all those necessary examples that engender fear of the state through the gun-toting guardians of its authority.

Murder provides righteous moralists with yet more evidence that the End is Near.

Murder provides social critics with yet more examples of lowbrow entertainment that they say are no longer "interesting."

But most of all, murder provides a reason to live for individuals like "Frank," who was interviewed in the revised first edition of *Apocalypse Culture* due to his self-published collage of sick and vengeful interests called *Livin' in a Powder Keg and Givin' Off Sparks*. Unlike other writers interested in murder, Frank's publications did not surround themselves with the usual distancing "objectivity"— they did, in fact, manifest a definite sociopathology.

A friend received a videotape from Frank, in which he filmed himself wearing a mask, fondling all his guns, and speaking his obsessed rhetoric in a thick Brooklyn dialect. Psychological histories are full of killers without much self-awareness, but Frank knew quite well that he wanted to kill as a result of being forced to suck his father's cock on a daily basis, as well as his own mother's sadism and indifference.

One day, and all of a sudden, Frank disappeared. The friend who received Frank's video, believed that Frank became a murderer, one described by the New York media as the new Zodiac killer.

Whether or not "Frank" vanished to take up the sport of murder, a new guy bearing the name "Joe" has appeared in recent years, using newsgroups in nearly the precise way "Frank" used 'zines. Both "Frank" and "Joe" share nearly identical obsessions. Murder and women's feet. And both prolifically produce vanity publications and vanity postings and convince people of their prominent value.

But there are subtle differences in Frank and Joe's regard of the art of murder. While Frank expressed his disinterest in serial killers, since they did not provide him with the cathartic ejaculation of mass murder, "Joe" says both styles get him hard equally well.

What follows here is "Joe's FAQ" and a letter to serial killer Danny Rolling, who with Sondra London co-authored the Feral House book, *The Making of a Serial Killer*. In an unusual ruling, prosecutors for the State of Florida declared that due to her friendship with the killer, London should not receive royalties for being co-author of the book. It was London who called our attention to the Joe FAQ and the letter to Rolling, but opted out of the introduction after Joe threatened her. A Usenet star due to his strong, prolific, narcissistic posts, Joe has proven that in the apocalypse culture, anyone and everyone can be a star.

JOE's FAQ

Q: Who is JOE?

A: Someday you might know who I am, but only when I choose to shed the mask under which I live my life. I control all aspects of my reality, and will always do so. All pathetic attempts to figure out who I am are doomed to failure.

Q: What is so special about JOE?

A: I am very special. Always have been, and always will be. The thing that is most special about me is that I am untouchable. I laugh silently at the human race, as I slither through your world.

Q: What is JOE's greatest interest?

A: When I was a still a boy, under age 10, I discovered the glorious potential that existed within serial and mass murder. I discovered this potential via my TV set, thanks to news broadcasts. I was captivated by both serial and mass murder. The True Reality of an individual claiming vengeance against the human race and cathartically relieving their internal rage and hate, was fascinating.

Serial murder involves the slow accumulation of human victims, with a cooling-off period between each murder. It also involves the killer remaining free, and savoring the glory of each killing. As soon as I discovered that there was a subculture of serial murder in the world, my thoughts immediately began to focus extensively upon the True Reality of each serial killer that I learned about. My appreciation for these silent and self-controlled predators, proudly stalking your world at will, setting out a face of normalcy, while hiding their innermost rage and hate, only releasing that rage and hate at their chosen hour, harvesting a human life, and then slinking back into the appearance of benign normalcy, is profound and deeply felt.

Mass murder involves an explosion of rage, in which 3–50 people are slaughtered during a single rampage. Just as with serial murder, the imagery of mass murder that is invoked via the actions of individual, solo, enraged victims of Society, is something that I spend hundreds of hours each month reveling in. For the five minutes to five hours that most mass murders take to accomplish, the killer truly is equivalent to a mythical god. He holds the power of life and death over his chosen targets. He DECIDES who lives and who dies, and he both CAUSES and WITNESSES their deaths, being accomplished by his own hand. Mass murder is the culmination of a lifetime of simmering and percolating rage and hate, finally released via a one-time expression of core True Reality.

There is no doubt that despite my appreciation of all criminal acts, especially children/offspring killing their biological creators/legal slaveowners, the individual serial killer and the mass murderer are the most dynamic predators of the modern era. Since childhood I have looked up to both of these types of criminals, and I am confident that I will always be fascinated by them, both by their individual True Realities, and by their life accomplishments. They are worthy of my respect and admiration, because of their courageous choice to seek and to claim violent vengeance against the Society that is guilty of having created them.

Q: Why is JOE so interested in true crime?

A: Because I am nothing more than an accurate reflection of the Society that created me. Every abused child has the RIGHT, but not the obligation, to seek and claim violent vengeance against their Society. This can be accomplished mentally, or physically. It can involve actual bloodshed, or virtual bloodshed, that only occurs in the mind, via bloodsoaked fantasies. Violent crime involves the cathartic release of internal rage and hate, inspired by personal suffering. As a victim of profound abuse during childhood, I choose to metaphorically embrace and revel in the violent acts of others, as one way of cathartically claiming my own vengeance against the Society that created me.

Q: Why does JOE hang out in alt.true.crime?

A: Because JOE finds a lot in true crime which he feels justifies what he believes. You won't see JOE in alt.society.good.things.happening.

Q: Does JOE have some favorite true crime topics?

A: JOE is interested in ALL true crime, but especially:

1. Parents abusing/killing their children. (Proves children are like slaves and Society is guilty of allowing and enabling child abuse/murder to occur.)

2. Children abusing/killing their parents. (Proves parents abuse their children and a celebration of the child-slave's seeking and claiming of vengeance against their slaveowner.)

3. Military personnel killing. (Society trained them to kill and the soldier who kills his OWN colleagues is accurately reflecting the perversity of his Society.)

4. Not really true crime, but relevant: Animals injuring/killing humans. (Animals have a "true reality" and are finally acting on it. Animals feel rage and hate, and have the right to seek and claim violent vengeance, in the same fashion that all individual humans do.)

Q: What are the beliefs of JOE?

A: JOE blames Society and its leaders for all of the violent crime that occurs, based upon the fact that Society sanctions, facilitates, enables, and chooses to cause children to be abused and traumatized and treated as slaves.

JOE believes any form of murder is justified as long as someone is acting on their "true reality" life experiences.

JOE believes every serial killer can only know and judge, within their own heart and soul, dead as it may be, whether they have achieved a proper reflection of their True Reality. You cannot judge, and I cannot judge. Only the killer himself has the right and the ability to pass judgment upon himself.

JOE believes no one should be placed in a psychiatric hospital against their will, even if the person is determined to be a risk to himself or to others.

JOE believes at the slightest evidence of child abuse or maltreatment, the state should immediately "seize" the child(ren) of the suspect-parents and terminate their parental rights; fundamentally, parental rights should not be recognized for any parent.

JOE believes that all suicide attempts are indicative of insanity, while the act of wanting or trying to cut off one's penis is generally not a sign of insanity.

JOE believes he is an intellectual genius, with superior analytic abilities. He believes he is smarter than 99.9% of the human race.

JOE is against the death penalty because:

1. Although individuals can act on their rage, Society should not do the

same, because Society is guilty of creating every individual, and initiating the cycle of injustice/abuse upon the individual.

2. All individuals have a right to reflect back at Society any rage that is a genuine result of their own perception of their own life experiences. Society has no right to feel or act upon rage against any individual, because that individual is a creation of Society.

3. Juries don't act on their true rage because the accused hadn't done anything to them personally, so the act is *unjustified* murder.

4. Since Society created the killer, it is wrong for Society to kill what it created, especially since Society is ultimately responsible for the killer's murders anyway.

Q: If JOE could rule the world, what would he change?

A: All parents and would-be parents would be made to take a competency test to determine if they are suited to be parents. If they fail this test, the children would be seized by the state.

Q: What is the recipe for making a JOE?

A: Mix two evil and insane adults together, add one helpless, innocent child, stir thoroughly, simmer at room temperature for about . . . 13 years, and out comes a soul dead person named JOE.

Q: Yeah, but seriously, how did JOE get to be the way he is?

A: As a creation of your Society, my beliefs, philosophies, and life choices are based upon the experiences that were forcibly imposed upon me, throughout my childhood. I am obsessed with violence because violence was imposed upon me, throughout my entire childhood. I am consumed by rage and hate because brutal injustice, in the form of pain and trauma, were imposed upon me by all human beings that I had contact with, throughout my childhood. I am unable to feel positive emotions towards any living thing, because throughout my entire childhood, no living thing ever treated me in a benevolent, empathic, or non-violent manner. The fact is, I never received a single hug, a kiss, or any indication of empathy, sympathy, or affection, from any human being, throughout my entire childhood, beginning with my earliest memories at age three-and-a-half. What I did receive was constant physical, sexual, and emotional torture. All of my memories are of physical violence, sexual abuse, emotional torture, terror, dread, rage, hate, pain. My True Reality as an adult, as expressed here, is nothing more than an accurate reflection of the sum total of my childhood life experiences. Having a dead soul can allow a person to appreciate the Truths in life, that the beholden citizen-slaves cannot accept or understand, in their narrow and ridiculously hypocritical mindsets. Having no guilt frees you to live out an accurate reflection of your True Reality, answering only to yourself.

Q: What does JOE mean by "True Reality"?

A: True Reality is an individual person's unique understanding of their own life, based SOLELY upon the sum total of their own personal life experiences at the hands of the Society that created them, from the moment of their birth onward, MINUS all of the societal lies, hypocrisy, and brainwashing that their Society has subjected them to.

Q: What is the best thing about JOE's True Reality?

A: The great thing is, I am UNTOUCHABLE. You humans can flame me, ridicule me, mock me, it's all MEANINGLESS. I FEED upon the negativity from them, and I feed upon the positivity, from you. See, I am a USER. I see humans as inferior objects, available for me to use as I see fit, to benefit my own life, be it sexual, emotional, intellectual, etc. . . There is no EQUALITY, with ANY human being, in my mindset. ALL humans are inferior to me, and thus their opinions or beliefs or interactions with me, are INCAPABLE of affecting my appreciation and worship of MYSELF, in any fashion. That's the GLORY of my Reality.

Q: Does True Reality allow anyone to kill JOE?

A: Anyone who so desires has the right to try and kill me. Just as I have the right to try and kill anyone else. My life is worth more than anyone else's life, because I am the ultimate narcissist, plus I am genuinely superior to other humans. But of course the True Reality of ALL individuals is equally valid. You have every right, therefore, to try and kill me. The right to kill, from an INDIVIDUAL True Reality perspective, is universal and non-discriminatory. But Society has NO right to kill anyone via a "death penalty" or to punitively punish any of its creations.

Q: What's JOE's educational background?

A: JOE has dropped out of high school. He did get a GED later. He has never attended any college.

Q: Does JOE ever mention his sex life?

A: JOE has a sexual obsession with women's feet, specifically as related to painful, deformed, crippled female feet, and abuse/torture of female feet.

JOE masturbates four times or more a day. He masturbates more than 99.99% of the human race.

JOE is a virgin and has never had normal sexual intercourse. He patronizes prostitutes but only engages in contact with their feet.

Q: What does JOE think of sex?

A: I find the sex act disgusting to contemplate. It's a lack of control, it's two people giving in to their base desires.

Q: What about JOE's love life?

A: JOE has stated many times that he only loves ONE person in the world, himself. He will never love anybody else. He will never get married. He will never have children. JOE is an adult virgin, and has vowed to remain so for the rest of his life.

Q: What's love got to do with it?

A: The whole "love" theory is flawed. When a person says to another "I love you", what he is really saying is "I believe I need to be loved and that is why I will say that I love you, to convince you to say that you love me." It's two people lying to each other in order to get their own needs met.

Q: What does JOE do for a living?

A: JOE does not discuss his employment, other than to reveal the fact that he earns a lot of money, much more so than the average person does.

Q: Is JOE a serial killer?

A: No. I do have a right to kill people. But I choose not to kill, because I find the cost-to-benefit ratio to be currently unfavorable. I retain the RIGHT to kill, just as other humans retain the right to marry or divorce or have children. I am not obligated to ever kill anyone, and I have indeed never killed anyone, but I retain the right to kill, and recognize that my right to kill is as legitimate as any other human being's right to kiss or hug or engage in affectionate contact with other living things.

Q: Does Joe pray to God?

A: I pray to God that he should strike me dead tonight. And I invite ALL humans on planet earth to pray for my death. Because I know that your prayers only serve to make you weak and vulnerable.

Q: Why does JOE sign his posts, "Take care"?

A: Because it is a generic sign-off, and can be interpreted as both benign, or menacing. I leave it up to every person I reply to, to decide how to interpret my sign-off . . . No, it's not meant to be funny. All human beings who value their lives should "Take care," because your inferior world is proudly stalked by enraged predators who would love to snuff out your life.

Take care
Joe

JOE'S LETTER TO SERIAL KILLER DANNY ROLLING

Hi Danny,

I want to tell you about my philosophy on life, and how I draw strength and meaning in my own life, despite the fact that I'm soul dead and find no hope in life, and no brightness in my future.

I know your future, when you look at it, seems bleak and hopeless. Even more so than mine. I am still a pretty young guy. But I know with 100% certainty that I will never fall in love for as long as I live. I will never hug another person for as long as I live. I will never feel joy. I will never have any pleasant memories to look back on. I will never even get to have sexual intercourse, or contact with any person, in my entire life. This is the reality of my life, Danny. I see that my life is truly pointless and meaningless. There is no hope in it. There is no possibility of "freedom" from my mental prison. I am locked inside this emotional cage, and I will never ever get out.

And yet, despite all this, I have honestly never felt a single genuine urge or desire to die. I want to live, Danny. And I want you to live. How long do I want to live? I want to live forever. I DESERVE to live. And YOU deserve to live, forever. Death is the single greatest tragedy that will befall each of us. You were born into this world with the full emotional and intellectual capacity to become the President of the USA, or Mother Theresa, or any other human being on earth. Your potential, like my potential, was unlimited. The fact is, this Society allowed ATROCITIES to be committed against you, and against me, when we were small and vulnerable and helpless. All of the pain and trauma and abuse that we suffered only serves to make our lives even MORE valuable and precious and sacred than they would be otherwise.

Ever since I was a small boy, I have always turned all my rage outward, towards other human beings. I recognized, emotionally and intellectually, that this was the only accurate and rational projection of my negative emotions. When I was eight years old, as my father and mother slept, I quietly walked into the kitchen, picked up the largest meat carving knife on the wooden rack, and spent the next hour standing there in the darkened kitchen, raising the knife up high and thrusting it downward with all my strength, over and over.

As I did this I opened and closed my eyes, visualizing both my father and mother sleeping in the bedroom just a few feet away, and visualized plunging the knife directly into their chest, over their hearts, with every bit of strength I had in my eight-year-old body. I planned out exactly how I would initiate the slaughter, killing dad first, since he was bigger and stronger. Plunging the knife in as he slept, and reveling in the glory of seeing his few seconds of terror as he wakes up with the knife already having pierced his heart. And then I would quickly pull out the knife, rush across to my mother's side of the bed, and plunge the same knife into her heart.

Yes, I know that tactically it would have been better to take 2 knives into the bedroom, and leave the knife in my father's chest, and use the second knife to stab mom in the heart. But I was an 8-year-old boy, and in my plan I used this one knife to kill them both.

Please understand, Danny, that this was not some idle fantasy or thought. I had spent hundreds of hours over the previous months developing and solidifying this NEED that existed within me, to DESTROY and kill both my parents. So there I was in the darkened kitchen, reveling in the glory of killing them both, as I hoisted and thrust my weapon with all my strength. It was very warm, and soon I was soaked in sweat. I KNEW that I wanted and needed to KILL them. I knew that they DESERVED to die. I knew I had a RIGHT to kill them. But after about an hour, I put down the knife and went back to my bed.

Why did I do that? I did it because, even at age eight, as I was standing in the kitchen slashing and thrusting with the knife, I had a sense of my own personal self-worth. I sensed the VALUE of my own life. I knew that if I killed them, bad things would happen to me. Very bad things. I knew that I was suffering very bad things already, at the hands of my parents, as they abused me on a daily basis. But I could not risk causing MYSELF unknown terrible things, by committing this double murder and becoming a "victim" of the unknown terrors that comprised police, jails, pain and death. I LOVED myself, and so I could not hurt myself in this way. I vowed to survive all my abuse and pain, and as soon as I could, I would leave and create my own life, based upon the rage and hate and isolation and complete control over my environment that I so craved. And guess what? That's exactly what I did. I severed all contact with my entire family at age 17, when I had managed to get a job and scrape together enough money to rent a studio apartment.

And the years have gone by. I get older, life continues. And it IS totally pointless. I live alone, I am isolated from all human contact; when somebody brushes against me on a bus, I literally shudder in revulsion. When I go to the barber to get my hair cut, I have to be sure to leave my gun at home, because the rage that I feel whenever he touches my head or neck is enough to cause me to kill him. I am an adult virgin. I have no contact with anyone, except a few prostitutes, a few times a year, who let me mess around with their feet. I will leave this world all alone. No family and no friends and no descendants.

But I STILL GLORY in my life! I glory in my life because I know that death is the most horrible thing there is. And I don't deserve to die. I deserve to KILL. To kill OTHERS! But I never ever deserve to die. Life is a WAR,

Danny. I am at war with my enemy, the entire human race. My enemy deserves to die. I deserve to live. I deserve to revel in the EMOTIONAL glory of VENGEANCE against my enemy!

Every act of physical violence that you committed was first committed INSIDE of your own MIND. That mental rage and hate and violence is 100% JUST AS REAL as your physical acts of violence. And right NOW, as you read these words, you possess the capacity to GLORY and to REVEL in your GENUINE and JUSTIFIABLE rage and hate and violence.

In your mind you can cut up the prison warden and gut him like a flounder. You can chop off his head and eat it. You can mutilate the prison guards at will, over and over and over. You can cut off the prison guard's penis, and watch him as he bleeds to death. And then, the next day, you can do this same thing again! You are FREE, Danny. Free to glory in your own true reality of rage and hate. AND free to inflict your justifiable rage and hate on ANYONE on planet earth. And NOBODY can stop you, Danny. You can go back to that college campus in Gainesville and kill dozens more students.

My point is, I know you feel rage and hate towards others. I feel that same rage and hate myself. But I do NOT feel rage and hate towards myself. And I sincerely believe that, deep within your own genuine True Reality, you do NOT feel rage and hate towards yourself, either. You don't want to suffer. You don't want to die. You want to LIVE, and to KILL. And mentally, you CAN kill, whenever you feel the urge to do so.

I know that life in prison is terrible. You are a slave and have no personal physical autonomy. It's terrible. But it's NOT more terrible than death. Your MIND is free, Danny, if you set it free. Please try to direct all negative emotions outward, and not inward. Of course life is pointless. In the end we all die. The President dies, Mother Theresa dies, I die, the prison warden dies, and you die. We all die sooner or later. But death is the MOST HORRIFIC thing that any of us will experience, regardless of whether we recognize this fact or not.

From my perspective, there is just no way that anyone can JUSTIFY ending their own life. Murder is very easy to justify, it is a fully rational and logical choice to make, based upon justifiable rage, hate and a RIGHT to seek and achieve vengeance. But how do you justify suicide?

You are a good person, Danny. You lived your life as your true reality dictated. You never asked to be born, you just asked to be treated with human love and kindness. And this Society FAILED to live up to their obligation that they had towards you. This Society allowed you to suffer so much UNJUST pain and abuse and trauma that you felt compelled to kill people. Society is EVIL, Danny. You are a victim of Society's evil. You deserve to LIVE even MORE than the President or Mother Theresa deserves to live, because you have endured MORE unjust abuse and trauma in your life than they have endured in theirs.

But let's move beyond all this rage and hate for a little while, Danny. Your life is very special, in a way that my own life can never be. You are LOVED, Danny. Loved and cared about, and I believe with 100% certainty that you have the ability to love and care for a few people yourself. This is a very special thing, Danny. I cannot love or care for anyone. And nobody truly loves me or cares about me. But you have this precious ability to receive and give love. You can look into someone's eyes and feel the genuine love they have for you, and you can return that love.

I really don't understand love, Danny. I've never loved anyone in my life, and I've never felt love from anyone. It's pretty hard for me to understand the dynamics of love. But I do think it is a genuine emotional reality. And a very powerful one. By hurting or killing yourself, you would be causing great trauma to your loved ones. They would have to deal with the feeling that their love was not good enough, not powerful enough, to convince you to embrace the glory of life.

I think self-love is the most precious thing in the world. Nothing, not even the love of a woman, can come close to the beauty and perfection that comes with loving and embracing your own life, your own reality, your own infinite uniqueness. I love myself, Danny. I'm proud to say that. And I pledge and vow to always love myself, and keep myself alive and as healthy as possible, for as long as I can. NOTHING that happens in the future will alter this vow that I make to myself.

There IS an enemy, and there is 100% valid rage and hate for that enemy within you. All you have to do is realize WHO the enemy is, and HOW to properly direct all your rage and hate and negative emotions. In my reality, the enemy is every single human being on planet earth EXCEPT for myself. And the only proper way to direct all my rage and hate and negative emotions is TOWARDS MY ENEMY.

You have a legion of supporters. I'm not talking about "fans" of yours, I'm talking about people who see and understand the validity of your True Reality. People like me. Many thousands of people have read *The Making of a Serial Killer*. That book is very special, much more powerful than any other book written about you, because it contains your own True Reality, told in your own words. I KNOW that thousands of people who read that book came to personally understand and relate to your True Reality, and to the goodness you possess within yourself, and to the FACT that you are just as much a VICTIM as any of the people you killed.

And then we have USENET and the website and the serial killer discussion group. Thousands more people have read your words and exchanged ideas and thoughts with you, and the smart ones have recognized that you are a wise man, and a fine writer, and a good person. They are OUTRAGED, as I am, that this pathetic Society wants to commit a premeditated homicide against you, via the death penalty. They care about you. They don't want you to die, or to suffer in any way. But still, you don't know them, you don't care about them. That is how it should be. But you must care about yourself, and USE the knowledge of their caring to build up your own sense of self-love.

Life is GOOD, Danny. Life is a whole lot better than death. Your mind is strong and free. Your mind can take you wherever you want to go. And nobody on earth can control your mind. You can kill and torture and rape at will. You have every RIGHT to do so. You are free, and your mind is your primary weapon. You have to try and keep your weapon in top condition. Don't allow your enemy to turn you against yourself. That would be so tragic. Because I am 100% serious when I say how you can truly revel in the glory of your rage and hate, if only you find the mental strength to direct the rage and hate at your enemy, always.

I write this letter to you from the depths of my dead soul, Danny. Because we, you and I, Danny, are bloodbrothers. We have been carved out of the same corrupt and perverse Society. I am not a "fan." I am an admirer of all people who face up to their rage and hate and unleash it against their Society, in whatever manner they deem appropriate. You had a RIGHT to kill those people, Danny.

Yes, you are in prison. And being in prison is a terrible thing. You deserve to be in a nice little 300-square-foot space, with air conditioning and a kitchenette and a microwave oven and a full bath with private shower, all to yourself. But this pathetic Society is never fair or rational. And so you are suffering. But your mind is free. NEVER forget the glorious power of the mind.

The power of LIFE is immeasurable. For all of eternity there will never be another Danny Rolling. Of all the TRILLIONS of people who have passed through this world since it was created, there has NEVER been a single one like you. You are UNIQUE. And right now, right here, you are experiencing your one and only LIFE. You MUST find a way to embrace the glory of it. Revel in the rage and hate at Society and all your enemies. Revel in LIFE ITSELF. All aspects of it, because in your MIND you control and you shape your day-to-day reality. Rage directed outward is glorious. It is life-affirming rage. It is beautifully cathartic rage. It is medicine for your injured, but NOT dead, soul. But rage directed inward is poisonous. It is life and spirit destroying. It is NOT an accurate reflection of your glorious true reality.

Life is a war, with a series of battles. In the end, we all lose. We all die. But the only logical way to approach the war is with rage directed at the ENEMY. Rage and hate and venom and scorn towards human beings. Stupid, pathetic, worthless, human beings who are worthy of ALL the rage and hate that exists within your soul and mind and heart.

And at the same time, you can nurture a wonderful sense of peace and self-love and admiration of self and appreciation of your own unique perfection as a human being.

Take good care of yourself, ALWAYS!

Your Blood Brother,

JOE

Danny Rolling's letter, mailed to Sondra London, his co-author of *The Making of a Serial Killer*, explains the psychological vortex of his Gainsville murders, as seen on his painting reproduced in the color section.

1#

5:03 pm **Sondra** 6-22-97

Propped against the dingy concrete wall my new painting speaks volumes. Of dark & twisted emotions that wrought Horror. yet for some reason I find this canvas strangely compelling, because the brush stroke lashed-out from my inner-mind's 3rd eye.

There is a story behind the story of how the new Rolling ☺ panel came about. SAT. th' 21st I got into a bitter arguement with my neighbor (not Paul Hill. My other neighbor. I shant mention his name).

Let me explain. you see, we here on the Row play spirited games of Chess. Some love the game so much they eat, drink & sleep Chess. Well... SAT. morning around 9:15 Am my neighbor and another condemned soul 3 cells down began a game of chess. That in its self wouldn't seem like any-thing to get upset about. Except for the fact that inorder to play chess on Florida's Death Row, you must yell out each play by the numbers!

myself and several other convicts enjoy sleeping late. So when I was youked from the land of dreams by King's Knight to

D.R.

116

6-22-97

Bishop 3! My impulse reaction was to rip the head off the nearest breathing creature. Of course I'm locked down in a cell 24/7 and obviously can't push my fist through half a foot of solid concrete. I settled for the next best thing and waged a verbal ASSAULT!

Expletives such as "Fuck you" were exchanged and THE DEVIL rose up in me. "DON'T you KNOW I will beAt your ASS ON the yArd, MuthA FuckA", I shouted at the Top of my lungs!

"Well... Do whAt you gAttA do", my neighbor went on.

I'm the type person, if you manage to PiSS Me Off! I get so angry I can't see straight. Being as I'm confined. I had time to cool off and my neighbor & I have since buried the hatchet ... so to speak.

The only thing is — I was so damned MAD! I tore into my foot locker, ripped out a fresh canvas, dug out some paint, and several different size brushes and layed into the blank panel with a vengeance.

D.R.

6-22-97

Brush & paint danced about for 10 hrs.
straight -non-stop. The entire time I was
in a furious frame of mind. The result is
rather amazing, at least I Think so.

I'm not even sure what to call it. I
believe I've created something Gripping. The
panel is painted on a 16" by 20" vertical canvas.
There are 9 figures spinning down a funnel.
The main figure is centered Top right to
bottom left. 8 other souls spin down the
spiral towards the bottom right hand corner.

I think this canvas is an Important
one. Becaus of the Highly Agitated frame
of mind I was in at the time. My super
charged emotions took over and the paint
just flew onto the canvas.

After I finished the work. I had exhausted
my fury and once settled down. I took a
look at what I had done.

"This hAs gottA be the ugliest pAinting
I ever did", I said to myself, but I
was'nt really looking at it from the viewer's perspective. Physically spent, and emotionally distraught, I almost crumpled it up
and cast it away. I put it in my Locker
Box instead and got a nights sleep.

D. R.

4

6-22-97

I woke this morning feeling better. Once I wiped the cobwebbs from my eyes, and fixed a cup of mud, I checked out the painting again. Much to my surprise! I find it to be A VERY IMPORTANT work and I'm thankful I did'nt destroy it.

anyway, once it dries I'll send it on. SONDRA! It just come to me. I'll call it FAIT Accompli!

Say Love, I've enclosed the rest of the Gothic Font you requested. Hope it helps.

Babes, did you get the rest of FAIT Accompli Coup de grace — the fiNAL scene. I sent it to you last Sunday and you still have'nt acknowledged receiving it or the Forest Of Trolls illo. What gives?

I've been busy doing illos for LoTBM. Within 2 weeks you will be getting many more drawings. Then I'm gonna pen LoTBM out and be done with it.

All My Love,
Danny!

D-R.

I AM THE HATE

You cannot escape me. Right now as you read these words,
   I am destroying that which makes you sane.
I am the one annihilating your peace.
I am the anger of the white man bashing a nigger,
   and I am the nigger crashing back.
I am the rage of the man beating his wife in the trailer park.
I am the fury of the nazi spitting on a dead jew.
I am the madness of the bomber that killed your family.
I am the frenzy of the student that slaughtered your peers.
I am the venom of the creep who raped your daughter.
I am the passion of the lover that caused your divorce.
I am the poison of the cock that gave you AIDS.
I am the disgust of the man that fucks a child's ass.
I am the revenge of the terrorist shooting his hostages.
I am the insensitivity of the bitch that got an abortion.
I am the one taking over the world.
I am the one burning your churches.
I am the one they talk about on the news.
I am the hit and run.
I am the fear you can't ignore.
I am the incurable disease.
I am the one that starts the war.
There is a line of executioners, each with a gun;
   and I am the one with the bullet.
It's aimed at you.
I am the hate.

Rosemary Malign

James T. Goad
enjoying life at
Oregon State
Penitentiary.
photo: Howard Unruh

Jim Goad

S pringtime. Dawn's blue light yawns through dead Portland streets. And I'm throwing you out of my life. Finally.

We pull up to your apartment building. I shift into park but leave the motor running.

And I say . . .

"I'm gonna get a girlfriend who isn't so fucking crazy. So just go."

And you say . . .

"Noooo!"

You pounce at me, scratching my face. I grab your skinny, trembling wrists. Those bulging goldfish eyes look straight into mine.

With foam flying from your fat lips, you say . . .

"You'll never get rid of me! I'll write tons of shit about you! People'll be laughing at you—it'll be like *Carrie!*"

Because I'm restraining your arms, you try kicking me with your big-ass glam-rock heels. We struggle a few seconds until a black guy . . . a lone pedestrian . . . walks up to my window.

You stop trying to hit me.

I release your arms.

"Are you guys okay?"

And I say . . .

"Yeah."

I look over at you, and you're nodding, Yes, Mister—We're okay.

End of fight.

I watch him walk into your building.

But as I turn to face you, your girlie fist clocks me dead on the nose. I grab your arms again.

As we're rocking back and forth, I see myself in the rear-view mirror. I'll remember that freeze-frame for the rest of my life:

My wild eyes. A crescent-shaped scratch on my cheek. And blood dripping from my nose.

My blood. My life essence. You're trying to take my life away.

And then, I swear to God, I hear it—this raw, prehistoric roar from deep within.

I rip the rear-view mirror from its mounting and fling it in the back seat.

Bitch.

I was trying to be nice.

I was driving you home.

If I wanted to be a dick, I would've made you walk home.

But you never left without a fight.

There was the time you wouldn't leave my apartment—and I tried calling the cops—and you ripped my phone off the wall.

Another time when it took my landlord to finally force you out of my pad, and when he did, you smashed my car windshield with a neighbor's shovel. And when the police came, you lied and told them I'd raped you.

The time I threw you out of my place and you walked right back in.

The time I tried throwing your keys out of my car to make you leave.

The time I tried throwing your wallet out of my car to make you leave.

The time I took your purse and backpack out of my car and dropped them on the sidewalk to make you leave.

The time I took everything you owned out of my car and stacked them by the highway to make you leave.

All the times you lunged at my face when I was only asking you to leave.

Like this time.

You won't leave, eh?

So let's go for a little ride.

The tires scream like a woman being attacked.

Chorus:

You say . . .

"Noooo!"

And I say . . .

"Yesss!"

(Repeat chorus 3x)

Oh, what—now all of a sudden you want to leave?

Too late.

You already had your chance.

Get back in here.

Get the fuck back in here.

Come back.

Come on back to me.

C'mere, little girl.

Stay with me, my love.

Where're ya goin'?

Poopsie, I'm catching a draft—close the door.

Look, sweetie, you'll hurt yourself if you jump while the car's moving. Get back in this car so I can rip your fucking head off your spine. Gotcha.

Bam! Bam! Bam!

Don't try that again. And if you honk the horn one more time, I'll bite your fucking hand off.

You know, I'm getting mixed signals from you.

You said you were out for the blood.

You wanted to destroy every living cell in my body.

You threatened to crush me.

To stab me a million times.

To blow my head out of this fucking universe.

You said you'd take it farther than I would—all the way into jail.

So what happened?

You said one of us was going to wind up dead.

Any guesses whom that might be?

I thought you wanted a Bad Boy—we haven't changed our mind, have we? What was that you said about me being a pathetic wannabe? A big fat poseur? Remember all the times you scoffed and said it didn't hurt when I hit you? Well, how about now? Are we feeling anything yet?

Do you recall telling me that I fuck as hard as I write? Well, I punch like I write, too, don't I?

Hard.

You said that all of life, no matter how painful, was only performance art. So tell me—how do you rate this performance? Your face is the canvas. My fist is the brush.

I'm taking it where you had only threatened to take it. Somewhere beyond satire and pop culture. Somewhere with zero comfort margin. A place that you can't handle, but I can.

Up to the hills.

Remember, we used to fuck there?

Hard.

Now you're going to die there.

Hard.

This is the fear that you failed to make me feel.

This is the control that you couldn't wield over me.

I knew you secretly enjoyed it when I'd get suicidal. When I said you'd be doing me a favor if you killed me. Think of all the times you wished me dead.

Earlier today, you said you'd dance on my grave.

That was after you hit me.

And bit me.

After I called the cops, then told them to forget about it.

After I forgave you.

And after I forgave you, you said you'd dance on my grave.

You aren't very nice.

I knew you were serious about killing me. I was so dead inside, I didn't care. I wanted to die. You came into my life at a time when I didn't care if you gave me AIDS or ambushed me with a 9 mm slug. I didn't care. I allowed your jagged bitch fangs to gnaw upon my soft suicidal underbelly, and I just didn't care.

Now I care.

Deeply.

I don't want to die anymore.

Seeing my blood—my own life seeping out of me—changed everything. That little red trickle cured my vision. I want to live.

Thank you for punching me.

Now I'm returning the favor.

Each punch is my way of saying I won't let you kill me. Each punch is life-affirming. The experts are wrong— this violence has nothing to do with keeping you down. It's about keeping me alive.

So you say . . .

"I won't tell anybody that you did this—I'll tell them a black pimp beat me up!"

And I say . . .

"You must think I'm stupid!"

Boom!

Pignosed little slit. Pussy-farting hog. What a high-pitched squeal you emit. Such a desperate, mouselike eek. And I thought that the Hysterical Woman was just a cruel myth. Scream your fat little head off. No one can hear you on this lonely mountain road. All this lush Northwestern greenery cushions the sound. Screaming isn't going to help, but please—don't stop screaming.

Scream, like your cunt ancestors have all the way back to the caves. It's just the two of us, Honey, suspended over this lovely twilit city. And here you are, stuck in this speeding car. The torture box.

Did you know that it was a man who invented the automobile?

So you say . . .

"I'm a bitch, I know, I'm a bitch, I deserve this!"

And I agree with you.

Boom!

I'm turning a bitch into a lady, into someone who says "Please." I'm smearing my manhood all over you. Cock ruling cunt. The way Father Nature intended.

This is why men rule—right here, what's happening between you and me—this is why we rule. It isn't pornography, no patriarchal conspiracy, no bedtime stories such as Evil and Sexism. It's this fist. And if you had this fist, you'd be in charge. But you don't . . . so you aren't.

And you say . . .

"Please, God, don't do this!"

So I say . . .

"I am God."

Boom!

Are you starting to catch my drift?

I never cried a tear for you.

Never wanted to marry you.

Didn't want the baby.

Didn't want your body.

Or what you call a mind.

Never wanted any of the things you wanted from me.

Yeah, doll, I love you so much, I'm pounding your brains out of your ears.

You said that I hurt you romantically. Yes, I did. This is another way to hurt you.

I broke your heart. Now I'm breaking your nose. Wow, you're bleeding a lot. With each lightning jab, the blood sprays from those piggie nostrils onto the windshield. And onto the door. And onto the seats. And onto your clothes. Beautiful red droplets. And that big purple bubble swelling up near your eye—my, that's nasty.

You look like one of those pictures in my magazine.

Better let you go . . .

You walk away crying.

I drive away laughing.

When you get to the hospital, I want you to take a long look in the mirror—that is, with the one eye that isn't swollen shut.

See that?

I never loved you.

The detectives will snap photos of you flattened out on that hospital bed, your face demolished. You looked like a fly squashed on a windshield. A roach crushed underfoot. Like a fucking train hit you. Roadkill. Smashed and destroyed, leveled by my life force.

Rejected.

Blood was streaming down your cheek. They kept wiping it away, but it kept pouring out of you.

We had quite a messy breakup, didn't we, darling?

I haven't regretted it for a second. Well, I sort of feel bad that I had to use my strong arm to drive.

So I'll spend nearly two and a half years behind bars for a 10-minute joyride.

Was it worth it?

Absolutely.

For the fear in your eyes.

The fear in your eyes . . .

⚡ ⚡ ⚡

Jim Goad, with ex-wife Debbie, co-published four issues of *ANSWER Me!* magazine. *The Redneck Manifesto*, published by Simon and Schuster, is Goad's treatment of contemporary racial myths. In Fall 2001, Feral House will publish *Shit Magnet*, written by Goad while languishing in Oregon State Penitentiary, having accepted the plea bargain of a two-year sentence for the crime of beating a girlfriend. Until the year 2001, Jim Goad can be reached at the following address:

James T. Goad, #12800236
Oregon State Penitentiary
2605 State St.
Salem, OR 97310

Terror, from a photograph by Dr. Duchenne.

Hatred and Anger
from *On the Expression of the Emotions in Man and Animals*

Charles Darwin

If we have suffered or expect to suffer some willful injury from a man, or if he is any way offensive to us, we dislike him; and dislike easily rises into hatred. Such feelings, if experienced in a moderate degree, are not clearly expressed by any movement of the body or features, excepting perhaps by a certain gravity of behavior, or some ill-temper. Few individuals, however, can long reflect about a hated person without feeling and exhibiting signs of indignation or rage. But if the offending person be quite insignificant, we experience merely disdain or contempt. If, on the other hand, he is all-powerful, then hatred passes into terror, as when a slave thinks about a cruel master, or a savage about a bloodthirsty malignant deity. Most of our emotions are so closely connected with their expression that they hardly exist if the body remains passive—the nature of the expression depending in chief part on the nature of the actions which have been habitually performed under this particular state of the mind. A man, for instance, may know that his life is in the extremest peril, and may strongly desire to save it; yet, as Louis XVI said, when surrounded by a fierce mob, "Am I afraid? Feel my pulse." So a man may intensely hate another, but until his bodily frame is affected, he cannot be said to be enraged.

Rage exhibits itself in the most diversified manner. The heart and circulation are always affected; the face reddens or becomes purple, with the veins on the forehead and neck distended. The reddening of the skin has been observed with the copper-colored Indians of South America, and even, as it is said, on the white cicatrices left by old wounds on negroes. Monkeys also redden from passion. With one of my own infants, under four months old, I repeatedly observed that the first symptom of an approaching passion was the rushing of the blood into his bare scalp. On the other hand, the action of the heart is sometimes so much impeded by great rage that the countenance becomes pallid or livid and not a few men with heart disease have dropped down dead under this powerful emotion.

The respiration is likewise affected; the chest heaves, and the dilated nostrils quiver. As Tennyson writes, "sharp breaths of anger puffed her fairy nostrils out." Hence we have such expressions as "breathing out vengeance," and "fuming with anger."

The excited brain gives strength to the muscles, and at the same time energy to the will. The body is commonly held erect for instant action, but sometimes it is bent forward towards the offending person, with the limbs more or less

rigid. The mouth is generally closed with firmness, showing fixed determination, and the teeth are clenched or ground together. Such gestures as the raising of the arms, with the fists clenched, as if to strike the offender, are common. Few men, in a great passion and telling someone to begone, can resist acting as if they intended to strike or push the man violently away. The desire, indeed, to strike often becomes so intolerably strong that inanimate objects are struck or dashed to the ground; but the gestures frequently become altogether purposeless or frantic. Young children, when in a violent rage, roll on the ground on their backs or bellies screaming, kicking, scratching or biting everything within reach. So it is, as I hear from Mr. Scott, with Hindoo children; and, as we have seen, with the young of the anthropomorphous apes.

But the muscular system is often affected in a wholly different way; for trembling is a frequent consequence of extreme rage. The paralyzed lips then refuse to obey the will, "and the voice sticks in the throat" (Sir C. Bell, *Anatomy of Expression*, p. 95); or it is rendered loud, harsh, and discordant. If there be much and rapid speaking, the mouth froths. The hair sometimes bristles. There is in most cases a strongly marked frown on the forehead; for this follows from the sense of anything displeasing or difficult, together with concentration of mind. But sometimes the brow, instead of being much contracted and lowered, remains smooth, with the glaring eyes kept widely open. The eyes are always bright, or may, as Homer expresses it, glisten with fire. They are sometimes bloodshot, and are said to protrude from their sockets—the result, no doubt, of the head being gorged with blood, as shown by the veins being distended. According to Gratiolet, the pupils are always contracted in rage, and I hear from Dr. Crichton Browne that this is the case in the fierce delirium of meningitis; but the movements of the iris under the influence of the different emotions is a very obscure subject. Shakespeare sums up the chief characteristics of rage as follows:

> In peace there's nothing so becomes a man,
> As modest stillness and humility;
> But when the blast of war blows in our ears,
> Then imitate the action of the tiger:
> Stiffen the sinews, summon up the blood,
> Then lend the eye a terrible aspect;
> Now set the teeth, and stretch the nostril wide,
> Hold hard the breath, and bend up every spirit
> To his full height! On, on, you noblest English.

Henry V, Act III, scene I

The lips are sometimes protruded during rage in a manner, the meaning of which I do not understand, unless it depends on our descent from ape-like animals. Instances have been observed, not only with Europeans, but with the Australians and Hindoos. The lips, however, are much more commonly retracted, the grinning or clenched teeth being thus exposed. This has been noticed by almost everyone who has written on expression. The appearance is as if the teeth were uncovered, ready for seizing or tearing an enemy, though there may be no intention of acting in this manner. Mr. Dyson Lacy has seen this grinning expression with the Australians, when quarreling, and so has Gaika with the Kafirs of South America. Dickens, in speaking of an atrocious murderer who had just been caught, and was surrounded by a furious mob, describes "the people as jumping up one behind another, snarling with their teeth, and making at him like wild beasts." Everyone who has had much to do with young children must have seen how naturally they take to biting when in a passion. It seems as instinctive in them as in young crocodiles, who snap their little jaws as soon as they emerge from the egg.

A grinning expression and the protrusion of the lips appear sometimes to go together. A close observer says that he has seen many instances of intense hatred (which can hardly be distinguished from rage, more or less suppressed) in Orientals, and once in an elderly English woman. In all these cases there "was a grin, not a scowl—the lips lengthening, the cheeks settling downwards, the eyes half-closed, whilst the brow remained perfectly calm."

This retraction of the lips and uncovering of the teeth during paroxysms of rage, as if to bite the offender, is so remarkable, considering how seldom the teeth are used by men in fighting, that I inquired from Dr. J. Crichton Browne whether the habit was common with the insane whose passions are unbridled. He informs me that he has repeatedly observed it in both the insane and idiotic, and has given me the following illustrations:

Shortly before receiving my letter, he witnessed an uncontrollable outbreak of anger and delusive jealousy in an insane lady. At first she vituperated her husband, and whilst doing so foamed at the mouth. Next she approached close to him with compressed lips, and a virulent set frown. Then she drew back her lips, especially at the corners of the upper lip, and showed her teeth, at the same time aiming a vicious blow at him. A second case is that of an old soldier, who, when he is requested to conform to the rules of the establishment, gives way to discontent, terminating in fury. He commonly begins by asking Dr. Browne whether he is not ashamed to treat him in such a manner. He then swears and blasphemes, paces up and down, tosses his arms wildly about, and menaces anyone near him. At

last, as his exasperation culminates, he rushes up towards Dr. Browne with a peculiar sidelong movement, shaking his doubled fist, and threatening destruction. Then his upper lips may be seen to be raised, especially at the corners, so that his huge canine teeth are exhibited. He hisses forth his curses through his set teeth, and his whole expression assumes the character of extreme ferocity. A similar description is applicable to another man, excepting that he generally foams at the mouth and spits, dancing and jumping about in a strange rapid manner, shrieking out his maledictions in a shrill falsetto voice.

Dr. Browne also informs me of the case of an epileptic idiot, incapable of independent movements, and who spends the whole day in playing with some toys; but his temper is morose and easily roused into fierceness. When anyone touches his toys, he slowly raises his head from its habitual downward position, and fixes his eyes on the offender, with a tardy yet angry scowl. If the annoyance be repeated, he draws back his thick lips and reveals a prominent row of hideous fangs (large canines being especially noticeable), and then makes a quick and cruel clutch with his open hand at the offending person. The rapidity of this clutch, as Dr. Browne remarks, is marvelous in a being ordinarily so torpid that he takes about fifteen seconds, when attracted by any noise, to turn his head from one side to the other. If, when thus incensed, a handkerchief, book, or other article, be placed into his hands, he drags it to his mouth and bites it. Mr. Nicol has likewise described to me two cases of insane patients, whose lips are retracted during paroxysms of rage.

Dr. Maudsley, after detailing various strange, animal-like traits in idiots, asks whether these are not due to the reappearance of primitive instincts—"a faint echo from a far-distant past, testifying to a kinship which man has almost outgrown." He adds that, as every human brain passes, in the course of its development, through the same stages as those occurring in the lower vertebrate animals, and as the brain of an idiot is in an arrested condition, we may presume that it "will manifest its most primitive functions, and no higher functions." Dr. Maudsley thinks that the same view may be extended to the brain in its degenerated condition in some insane patients; and asks, whence come "the savage snarl, the destructive disposition, the obscene language, the wild howl, the offensive habits, displayed by some of the insane? Why should a human being, deprived of his reason, ever become so brutal in character, as some do, unless he has the brute nature within him?" This question must, as it would appear, be answered in the affirmative.

Anton Szandor LaVey was a living repository for many people's desires, wishes and fears, including the sad people who took it upon themselves to write an individual they considered the through-line to the devil, hoping to better their dismal lives.

After founding his dark church, and promoting the idea that churches pay taxes, LaVey became an essential media figure in the late '60s and early '70s, doing talk shows, TV guest spots and unending photo shoots. After six years, six months and six days worth of media glaze, LaVey began to make himself scarce, even to his devotees, who in turn created competitive groups. An attempted *coup d'etat* was effected by a Church of Satan member who complained that LaVey did not pay proper respect to the horned deity. As the years went on, *The Satanic Bible* and *The Satanic Rituals,* published by the major New York house, Avon, continued to sell well; Anton LaVey became more and more of a hermit.

Then in 1987, beginning with an interview conducted by Eugene Robinson for the "God" issue of his independent magazine, *The Birth of Tragedy,* LaVey's interest in the world, and the world's interest in LaVey, seemed to resuscitate. V. Vale began to conduct many hours of interviews for a projected issue of Re/Search devoted to the Church of Satan. Vale's close friend Boyd Rice was keen to introduce me and others to the man. Soon thereafter I included a misanthropic diatribe written by LaVey for the Amok Press/Loompanics book *Rants & Incendiary Tracts.*

In a world bereft of strong eccentrics, Anton LaVey seemed quite extraordinary, and in 1989 Feral House issued the 1971 Dell hardcover, *The Compleat Witch,* in its first paperback edition as *The Satanic Witch.* Publishing Anton LaVey seemed to earn Feral House a strange reputation with the publishing industry. "Alternative" publishers berated Feral House for printing "sensationalist garbage," while feminist, academic and occult publishers shared rancor and contempt. Beginning with an exploitation mass-market book published in the mid-'80s called *Michelle Remembers,* Anton LaVey became pictured as a prime mover behind the ritual victimization of women and children. Despite the Satanic hysteria of the era—largely motivated by hugely rated television specials of Geraldo Rivera—resulting in short-lived bans of his books by chain stores, Anton LaVey's work found its audience. Unfortunately, the larger portion of those who purchased LaVey's books did not do so to immerse themselves in their Menckian libertarian content, but simply to possess books with the word "Satan" in the title.

The letters below, received by The Church of Satan in 1982, say far more about the letters' authors than the entity to whom the mail is addressed. The editor wishes to thank Harvey Stafford for collecting these letters from the moldering Black House after Anton LaVey's death on October 28, 1997.

Any spelling or grammatical errors are here retained. And the full spelling of proper names are struck through.

—Adam Parfrey

To whom it may concern,

I'm writing this letter because I need advice concerning a situation I'm in. I'm in love with a man I've never met in person. I'm in love with Michael Jackson. I'm willing to sell my soul to Satan for him. Many times I've call Demons and Satan to listen to my offer. I want to marry this man and have his child a child which I'm willing to dedicate to you if you wish, I'm presently attending a modeling school. Many people are saying I won't be successful because I'm Hispanic 25 years old and 5′ 2″. I'm asking you for help because I'm tired of being poor and I have goals which I know you can help me fulfill. Please advice me and help me!!!

Thank You.

Sincerely yours

I— C——

✿ ✿ ✿

(Sir) "Master"

My continchey to life.

I seem not to be ecomplish to my desire. I have a thirst for power I want a penthouse a couple mink fine cothes a giglo for my needs. Rose chaffer. My friends tell me thay see the devil in me. I like cicne million and hash I like to be high 24 hours a day. I enjoy life totley when I die I dont realy care what happen I twenty's I dont feel I got a lot time I waste cause I want it now! My mind is strathing to a degree but I need the above a power!

P— S——

✿ ✿ ✿

To whom it may concern:

My name is E—— S——. I heard about your church from an acquaintance. I have a problem. Seventeen years ago A Entity that calls itself god came into my life and it has been hell everysince. I definitely want to be withany organization against this thing. Please write me about your church or league and how I may join you. I want to give it hell back.

Answer soon.

Sincerely

E—— S——

✿ ✿ ✿

Dear Sirs etc.,

I am writing to apply for membership of the One True Church—your church, having been entrusted with your address by English disciple E— H— (of Warminster, Wilts), with whom I have been corresponding on a friendly basis these past three months.

I first discovered the keys to the truth, courtesy of Black Pope Anton's writings, in the early summer of 1977 at the age of 14. Although for the next four years I was subject to vicious and intensive community persecution for my genuine interest in Satanic philosophy and worship, I have remained, now more than ever, convinced that the early focus of my adolescent quest for knowledge is the right one.

When all the thousand societal layers of rubbish—the great plastic television machine of right hand path lies and filth, the ropes that bind us down, and destroy, and sicken—when all these are torn away and Man stands naked, alone, he aches and yearns to embrace One God, One Power, One Truth, One Life—SATAN! The all—supreme force of darkness that eats and pukes the phony glories of any and all sick white light religion . . .

The very fact the Powers of Darkness carry such a tag illustrates, I know, how completely satisfying their worship and indulgence is—that was a superlative example of his screaming need to taste and tap the power of so called Darkness!

(Interesting to note of, course, that the right hand path always frowned on that technological exploration too, as the Biblical nonsense of the Tower of Babel illustrates.)

Hence, I am firmly committed to the idea that all mortals following the One Way of Truth must be united as a potent force, to work the infernal spell of beauty and crash chaos down on the one-inch heads of the drooling peasants who move in their twisted worlds of overwhelming Satanic abstinence—they're just so incredible, these animals! as they count their pretty rosary beads and repent of sin and dribble sanctimonious disease, while blowing each others heads off in the agony of repressed Satanic expression, while pouring millions into the cinema box-office to drool over an innocent child abusing herself with a crucifix, while making gutter rags of basement journalism into bestsellers for their laughable exposes of SEX AND SATANISM!! And then they sit in their rotting pews and ostentatiously mumble to their putrescent cripple of a frigid god . . .

I know that Man cannot evade forever the truth of his Universe—that DARKNESS IS BEAUTY and SATAN IS SOUL. The truth must out—and the Real God win, in glorious Satanic Triumph Eternal!

Please take this application seriously, as I am completely sincere and no time-waster. If I may officially join the Satanic Brotherhood, I shall be a fully committed devotee and credit to the great organization, and shall in no sense fail the liberating teachings of the Supreme Master.

Dark Blessings,

I— H——, (aged 19)

Church of Satan,
I would like the history of the Devil.
What is hell gonna be like
is there a hell.
J— L——

✹ ✹ ✹

Greetings Mr. LaVey,

I am very interested in starting a regular gathering in my area under the worships and interests that you are head of. I can get a lot of followers. Also I want to start a business in this area. What I need is some of your Bibles— plus about $10,000.00 for my new venture with you. No Banks or anyone would give me a loan for this organization I am about to start with your help. Do you have a phone?

You a very much invited to come to Michigan and visit and help set up too if you so desire. I don't have a phone yet; but my mailing address is —
P— L——

✹ ✹ ✹

Dear Sir,

I am more grateful to write to you asking for your meaningful catalogue of your goods. Mr. E— B—— No. 167453 of your society introduced you to me and I hope you will not fail to respond. I want to tell the past, the present and the future or something to use in revealing secret. I also like to be your agent, healer and full time member. I am a pastor and medicine dealer. I needs assorted types of tablets, injections, oil, hair dye and liquids, etc., include all in the price list and sent to me. I dont like sacrifice because Jesus had done that for us, but if there is any, it should be scarce.

Please kindly show me the way to collect my goods from you in my house and how to burn Nigeria money and sent to you to avoid delayance in the post office.

Thank you with all hope. Waiting forward to hearing from you soon. God bless you all with your work.

Yours in Christ Jesus,
J. —. O——
Asi Qua Town, Nigeria

✹ ✹ ✹

Dear Sir,

Please send me news letters, The Cloven Hoof—I would like to order some. I want to know information about Satanic baptism what Church of Satan serve. I got a baby.

Friend,
J— J——

✹ ✹ ✹

Dear Mr. LaVey:

I am in desperate need of help and though I know how to do the ritual's described in your Satanic Bible, I live in a place where it is IMPOSSIBLE to perform them, and I've no place to go to perform them, but I will do whatever it takes to get what I want. I really didn't know who else to ask for help except the Black Pope himself. I am not asking for prayers or a ritual on my behalf. What I am asking for is a surefire way to sell my soul to the Devil Himself to get what I want and need. I am dead serious, Mr. LaVey. You must help me! There MUST be a non-symbolic way of talking to the Devil Himself and selling my soul to him. I DESPERATELY NEED YOUR HELP. I know, this may seem like a big request, but I'M SERIOUS. I'm not some kook who gets her jollies writing phony letters. Please give me instructions on a surefire way to sell my soul for the things I want. If you cant provide me with this vital information, give me the address of someone who can.

But please help me. I am at the end of my rope. It seems so hopeless, and it is. This is the only way. Please help me, I am a true Satanist and I am very very serious about what I am talking about.

Thank you,

C— K—

✹ ✹ ✹

Anton Szandor LaVey;

Why have I not received the book I ordered from the Church of Satan booklist?! You call a petty rip-off of $16.00 the actions of an elitist organization? Ha! I call it a chumps move!

You grant active membership to only those individuals who meet your requirements? I PISS ON YOU LaVey!

My name is J— G. G——— III and the ways of Count Astarot are in my blood and bones! My blood runs thick with Love for Prince Beelzebuth. Showboat all you will, LaVey, but your final test is yet to come!

I am incarcerated, in flesh and blood, I am here. I am the Son of Lucifuge Rofocale!!

As you know, I must have my material to learn and grow by. There are things I know without the help of old fools manuscripts but there is much more I don't yet know. Do my words freak you out LaVey? Maybe the words of the insane, right? Wrong. I'm totally sane. Do not deny me the material I need. Your organization has the MO now send my material. Or do you play dangerous games?

J— G. G——— III

#1——— Block B

✹ ✹ ✹

Dear Satan's servants

At first, I want to introduce myself to you. I come from Japan about three weeks ago. I am a man, and I'm 24 years old. I came to San Francisco to know American sexual perversion and Satanism. In Japan, it's very difficult for us to know that, because Japanese citizens are very stoical. It's almost impossible for us to study Satanism. We don't have nice books about Satan and Satan's Bible. In Japan, actually, I read several books about Satan. But it's only for the fun of it. I want to know correct information of Satan. I tried to find Satan's church in Japan, but I couldn't find it. Please teach me the nicest way to approach to Satanism. I want to listen to a preach of Satan, and I want to attend your service if I can. How can I get Satan's Bible? I have to go back to Japan by March 21st so I have only a few time. Before I go back to Japan, please give me some answer, or it's too late. I hope you will send me a letter or telephone me. I am looking forward to listening to your advice.

F—— H——

PS I had been sick since I was born. But, I couldn't find the fact until the age of 16. Suddenly, I found that. One day, I was lying on a sofa, and looking at the wall vacantly. Then, I heard a voice sending out a warning in the deep wall. It was an ill-omened symptom. The moment I heard the voice, everything in this world has changed. I saw blue sky fade into grey, and I saw a cruel pussy flying in the sky. Weird voice echoed. I was crucified on a black holy cross, and punished by insane. For 16 years I had been a sick whose name is insane. But at the moment, everything has changed. After that, to keep my health, I did many things. I ate much healthy food, a bread of distraction, salad of perversion, a fresh fruit of palanoid, and a cup of coffee of hypocrisy. And, sometimes I did some sports to harden my body. I used to run on a field of decadence, and swim in a wide ocean of ecstasy. I felt very nice after that. I breathe deeply, and I enjoy tasting fresh air of paladox. I have continued the way, so far.

Now is a time sensual poisoned flower begin to dance. Now is a time the dead wake up. Now is a time maggots begin to sing a song. Can you see the beautiful rainbow in the sky? Can you feel the quickening of Satan's daughter? Fly people fly! Or it's too late, our holy ship will sail to the kingdom of insane. Through thick fog of paladox. In the kingdom, we can be set free from any disease or illness we have suffered from.

666 HAIL SATAN

I the son of Satan love you all. I kiss you all on your hands. I Harlan Plavkin son of Satan hope the druid comes to you right now. I NEED SOME PUSSY. I am the Devils son and I eat pussy. I am in Clancy Mississippi, any of you woman need a piece of ass, come to me, I'll kiss every end of you. And every hair on your pussy. And my dick is 11 inches as my desire is to give you all of it personally. I wish you all my fathers blessings. Bezalbub protect your enterprise. Lick my asshole. I love you to 7 days. Hot kisses from the gates of hell.

H—— P——

I also need some money. Powers of the devine. Cover up the tell cranes. LaVey eyes of Hell.

❋ ❋ ❋

Dear Sir,

I am Jewish but losing my faith. Please send me information about the history of, principles of, and how to join the Church of Satan. Satanas est Rex Terra,

E— Y—

ps I am 14 years old. I have done quite a lot of research and understand what I am getting into.

❋ ❋ ❋

Dear Mr. Anton LaVey,

I'm sure that you are a very busy person but I'd like correspond someone who could answer some of my questions, cause I'd like to make a pact of some kind. I got my mind set on doing it, though I'd like to get over certain fears. I just want to change my life for the better and control my own destiny. There's other things I'd like to write about but I'd prefer to do so in my next letter.

OK, now, I'd like to know if you'd please grant me two simple request not concerning me at all. First of all, I'd like for Sugar Ray Leonard to continue fighting for another five years or more. My second request, I'd like for Alexis Arguello to easily beat Aaron Pryor in an out and out battle in their title boxing match. I don't have a bet on the fight and I'm not going to bet on it. I'd just like to see, or should I say read about, Aaron Pryor being taught a lesson for being too cocky, and besides, Alexis Arguello is a great champion and boxer who's a gracious and respectable man who shows everyone respect and is a real gentleman. He's one of my favorites and I think he deserves it, this championship fight.

I'll be writing you again soon,

Gratefully yours,

L— Crooked Leg

#3—— Cell Block A

❋ ❋ ❋

Hail Satan!—The King!

I would very much like to be a member of your church. I believe in Satan and worship him. Whoever is my enemy, I draw a picture of their face with knives running through them or something showing their fate. Then I burn the picture and throw the ashes down the toilet or into the air

HAIL SATAN! HAIL SATAN! I reply afterwards. Whenever I worship the ring, Satan I close the window shades lock myself in the bathroom with the light out, light a match and talk to him. I hope he heres me every time. I've read the Satanic Bible, but I haven't read the book of Satanic rituals. The bible (Satanic Bible) proves its point when it says that the other churches (such as Christian Church) get their donations by blaming Satan. The Christian church could not be built without Satan to blame. The preachers preach greed, sex and gluttony as sins when they have large pot bellies themselves and drive Cadillacs and Rolls Royce's down the road by making people feel guilty. I don't believe in God. I believe in Satan and there are Warlocks Witches and Psychic Vampires who can suck the blood (make you miserable). It is better to be EVIL = LIVE because you enjoy yourself here on Earth while your alive because there is no great Heaven in the sky. This is part of what I read and believe. Please write me back and tell me how I might become a member of the Church of Satan who I worship every Day.

Sincerely,

S—— F——

❀ ❀ ❀

Dear friends,

If you will pray that within a week from when you receive this letter that I will inherit my checks back and guarantee that if I join you that Satan will make Angie Lucco want to have sex with me I will do anything for your church or Satan, to help your great cause because Satan is my only god.

M— G——

❀ ❀ ❀

Dear Church of Satan,

I am very interested in joining the Church of Satan, could you please also do a spell for me because I really need you to help me my brother Sal D—— is always beating me up, he's been causing me a great deal of trouble. Could you please put a hex on him so he may die, I will gladly pay you for it. I have been doing spells so that the Church may be very powerful and so that Lord Satan may keep the Church protected. I have enclosed a stamp so you may write back, Thank you.

A—— D——

❀ ❀ ❀

Dear Church of Satan,

I am interested in becoming a member of the Church. Could you please send me some information on how I can. Also can you perform a spell for me, so my brother Sal D—— dies. Because he's been causing me alot of trouble, please when you write do not put your name or address on the envelope because I do not want Sal to know who it is from, bless you with the best wishes,

A—— D——

THE CROSS IS BACK GREETINGS FROM THE CROSS

❀ ❀ ❀

Hello Church

My name is L— O—— G—. I am the cross, I am presently incarcerated here at Jackson correctional center. I am now at the age of nineteen I will be twenty on the 26th of January 1981. I was introduce to the Church by a friend. So I decided to write. I have been doing some strong things around here. But there are some things that I need knowledge of. Me an Satan is very good friends. I am a black man but I have no respect of person. I really love sex. To the utmost. I am a very open minded person. I have NO hangups. I am a sex freak to be truthful. I like to insert my pinus into a womans vaginal. An I go to bed with men. But I'm always the aggressor. I know a lot of things an done a lot an seen a lot. But I'm still young an full of come. But I do wish for you all to write to me. Right now me an Satan are playing the death game. I got a lot of people I want dead. I want to have sex real bad. I am tired of jacking myself off. I could tell you all a lots of things thats been happening down here but you probably already know. Hey please write me back cause I am so serious. I want to corresponce with a beautiful white woman. I want to love her an cherish her. I AM THE MASTER. But all I want is to make love to women. Cause I know until a woman make love to me she have never made love. The reason why I'm talking like I am is because I speak what I feel so hurry an return my letter.

LOVE YA THE CROSS

L— O—— G——, #——— Cell block A

PS I want to make love to all the women of the Church an Satan too. If he want me to. So please write me back. If you don't believe I'm THE CROSS then come an see me. The warden will tell you. This is no joke I hope you people take me serious. If you don't. What can I say. I tell you what ask my man Satan he'll tell you. That's my baby too.

I LOVE YOU ALL WRITE BACK SOON, THE CROSS

❀ ❀ ❀

Dearest Anton,

I have a problem. I am in a mental institution and I had wrote you a letter about not wanting to join your church cause I was on medication and spaced out and was upset, I really want to join your church and don't throw away my letters and pictures I gave you, I love you a lot, and I have a boyfriend in Hawaii that I would like for you to perform a wedding on us some time in the next year, he is a Elvis impersonator in Hawaii and I have known him for a long time. I'm sorry I'm so broke I don't even have $5.00 to give you towards membership. But send me the papers anyway and I'll fill them out and will you have them, will you check and see if I have ever sent you any money for membership I think I have sent you $25 money order last year sometime around Christmas or so, last Winter anyway, and would you send my Fiancee info on the church and sign at the bottom of the papers

Love, Dawn

I don't know if he will join it or not but at least send it to him. His name is K— T———.

PS please pray for me I get out of this mental institution soon, I got busted for no real reason.

Love, H—— D—

❀ ❀ ❀

Dear Mr. LaVey,

Let me introduce myself. I'm a homemaker with two school age children, also I'm a songwriter and the list goes on and on. A long time ago I started learning about you. Lets say 8 or 9 years ago and I was shocked by what I read. Boy, now with the problem in my life and all the praying I have done in vain. I've decided if Gods in Heaven he's too busy for my problems, such as the life of a child. There is a Principal in our school—Horizon Heights Elementary School, Miss M— G—— who is putting the life of my child in hazard situation every day. There is a group of us still trying to stop her. She is slandering my name and reputation, she has laughed at my concerns.

I've seen children fall from dangerous school equipment and have to go home. And still she will not prepare a safe place for our children.

Because its such a dangerous environment I've stayed at the school every day since September. We have had three police calls and reports of sexual stuff toward 4 and 5 year old girls. I've put it in the paper and written the PTA and School Board. Still they say she is the head of her school and—too bad —

Now she has threatened to have me and my friends arrested if we're observed during recess (bathroom FAR from Kindergarten class) can you believe it.

Now, I've been blessed with some ESP and precognition. I've read your lovely Bible and I've tried to get rid of her. I must not be using my information correctly and too, there is only me. Each time I try to show her true face to the public she does something to hurt my older child (12 yrs). She always gets back at me and my friends in some manner always directed at our children.

Can you pray to your God for me. Please make her to be gone—if death should ensure I'll never feel remorse, only cheer and good feelings of joy would fill my heart knowing my kids are safe. I'm being honest and humble and as much like a child as could be considering I'm asking such a favor from a man I do not know but feel I've embraced in some way. I know your religion does not advocate child molesting or hurting one another, against a persons wishes, please help me.

SINCERELY,
Mrs. R——

❀ ❀ ❀

Church of Satan,

Let me start off by saying that I do indeed hold the greatest respect for the powers of Heaven and Hell. Throughout my childhood I was given to believe that if a person were good and wholesome, great reward would come from it ; one has only but to die in order to collect one's pension.

Gentlemen, I contend, that I would WILLINGLY SELL MY SOUL to Satan himself in exchange for the pleasure of living my fantasy dream. Singer, Songwriter/Composer. MUSICAL GENIUS. To play only the greatest halls across the world. To obtain higher success than the stars upon whom I set my sights; the Beatles—the Who—Rod Stewart, for as long as there be music.

RSVP A— D———

❀ ❀ ❀

Dear Anton LaVey,

We are two male individuals. One 28 years old at one time going to become an ordained priest which he studied one and a half years but decided to become a lay person. He asks of Satan only my love and success. I am 20 years old, also a lay person.

We are now in our third year of knowing each other. Prior to our third year for two years we were just friends, during these two years it was hell, constantly fighting and breaking the friendship because of my lies, but we always seem to come back to each other because of our love.

One day I questioned the black magic, he was aware of it, but never brought it up during our friendship. I've always wanted to become a business tycoon and rock star. After attending the Rolling Stones most recent concert here in Los Angeles, I questioned the black magic again. He took me to the library. We picked up several books concerning the occult. After extensive research I decided to get into it. We drew up a contract (for our souls) and asked Satan for my success in music as well as in business, He wanted just my love and success. Ever since then it's been 5 months of constant worshipping. There have been signs such as the number 3 constantly popping up, my bed shook twice as I was sleeping. I've wished harm to some individuals for some of them my wish came through. But no success. We still fight constantly. If I ask him a question he comes off mad; he says it's a repeated question due to my indulgement in marijuana, but sometimes I either don't understand or I honestly do not hear him.

I always seem to be energetic and ready to do what Satan has in store for me, so I go to his home and he's asleep because he is jet lagged (he's a part time flight attendant). Also, because he stays up late at night to pray to Satan to give me a sign. The signs have come up. Any sign.

We really don't know what Satan has in store for us. We know that we need capital to start a business. We tried two projects and have lost what little we have on both. Most recently we went to LAS VEGAS in search of capital to possibly go in to some type of business, and once ended up calling home to get some money to get home. The other during the JUPITER EFFECT lost also. We now have no capital and know that at the end of the rainbow something will be there so we can go on worshipping Satan and fighting daily.

Why so much confusion

PS We know what the commitment means and what would happen if we were to fail Satan (DEATH), our love is great and we are HEDERAL SEXUAL our faith is strong. I once read through a subtle process the student who lives the white path slowly starves out or else transmutes the power of the black ray within himself. THAT IS IF he is able to stand the conflict which must first take place in his bodies.

Sincerely,

J—— A——

Dear Satan

145

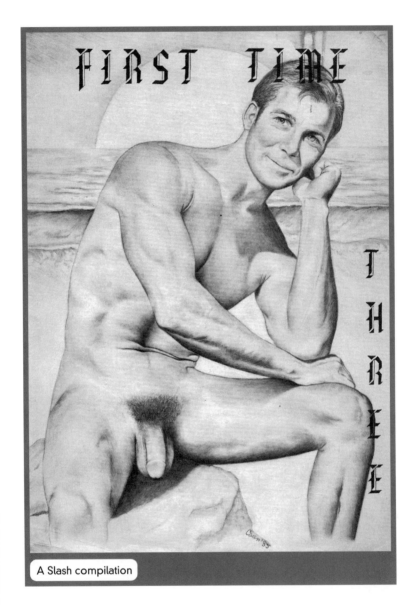

A Slash compilation

Adam Parfrey

Television and American "real life" are one and the same. When taking photographs for her book, *Fast Forward*, Lauren Greenfield couldn't shake the realization that the lives of teenagers—and their parents—are wholly shaped by television, films and MTV, which in turn appropriate their ideas from the people who mimic them.

With its homogenized and indistinct spread, one American suburb is just like another . . . and just like television. San Leandro, an expanse of wide streets and brand names 20 miles East of Oakland, is where the Friscon Slash Convention of '98 was held.

Slash gets its name from transforming straight TV characters into butt-happy queer porn queens. (Kirk/Spock, Starsky/Hutch. Slash/Slash.)

Checking in at Friscon, Darlene, the woman who taped the "Hello, my name is. . ." sticker on my shirt, informed me that another male had signed up for the convention—but during my two days there, I failed to see him among the 100 or so middle-aged women, the kind you're

friscoN 6
San Francisco's premiere multimedia slash conI
OCTOBER 23-25, 1998

VILLAGE PEOPLE
DISCO INFERNO!
Official Program Book

likely to see pushing a cart at a Target outside of Des Moines. But I started to wonder, why were these friendly, Target-shopping straight women so taken with producing and consuming fantasy fiction that has Starsky buggering Hutch, or Spock anal-fisting Kirk?

One academic treatise (*Close Encounters: Film, Feminism and Science Fiction* by Constance Penley and Henry Jenkins III) views Slash as "textual poaching," a way of subverting patriarchal fictions by way of feminist ideals. When asked, Friscon convention-goers seemed a bit mystified by this reading of their activities. One Slasher, who wished to remain anonymous in print, let on that Slash is masturbatory, a pornography of romance: "When Kirk and Spock love each other, instead of the standard bitch brought on every couple of weeks, I still have them for myself. Slash does what television never could do.

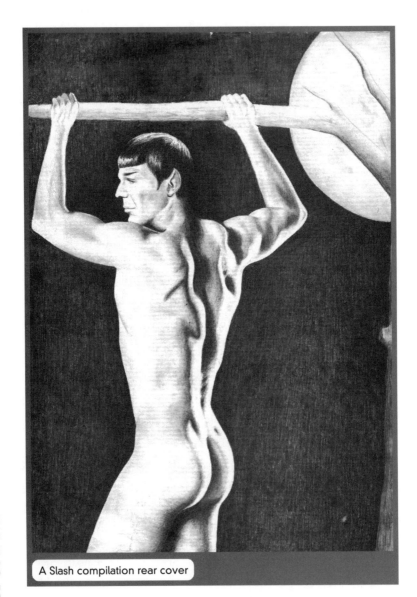

A Slash compilation rear cover

We have Kirk and Spock doing in print what they're stopped from doing on TV because of G ratings. It's hot to read about what we're not allowed to see, what Kirk and Spock are doing with their dicks. But Slash is not the boring in and out stuff men watch; it's romantic, it gets to the characters' emotions. Kirk and Spock are passionate."

Getting the biggest response from the Friscon crowd were edited videos of their favorite TV shows, suggestively cutting-in Phil Collins' and other middle-brow pop songs to the lengthy close-ups of the male stars until they seem to be full-on homosexual music videos.

The TV programs that earn special Slash fiction devotion are buddy "action" dramas from the '60s, '70s and '80s, overflowing with soap opera stylisms: *Man From U.N.C.L.E.*, *Starsky and Hutch*, *Star Trek*. On these shows, the lead characters have their faces caressed with lengthy close-ups. Often they are seen speaking softly with inordinate concern, or passionately, with faces beet-red with anger. Although these actors are shown to be heterosexual, women play subordinate roles, and do not burden the lead males with lengthy attachments. The male star's female lovers are never allowed to interfere with the characters' professional duties. But the lead character often

Starsky and Hutch

disobeys orders and puts his job at risk to protect his best friend. Emotional highlights are saved for the lead actors confronting bad guys or saving the lives of other male "steadies." These romantic scenes are punctuated with violence, and star performers are seen beaten unconscious with fist or gun in obligatory "action" scenes, injuries from which they recover almost instantaneously.

One star of Slash fiction, David Soul, who played the character "Hutch" in the late '70s–early '80s television series *Starsky and Hutch*, is quoted as telling talk show host Merv Griffin: "My opinion of the show is that it's a love story. It's a love story between two men who happen to be cops."

Though Slash pornography transfigures the conventions of mass-market television, it rarely, if ever, defies the conventions of its own romantic protocol.

The romantically attached lead characters risk everything but never die. The characters are always saved by other male characters, and their thick male hides are always pierced by affection, expressed sexually or otherwise, for other male characters.

The question remained; why would these women become so obsessed with creating pornography of both word and illustration, in which favorite television performers are transformed into randy, sensitive homosexuals?

The viral inoculation made by advertising to create dissatisfaction and a way to escape self-hatred ensures the sustenance of commercial entertainment. Teenagers escape into a total romantic identification with pop singers, while men escape into the romantic dream-fantasy of pornography and women into the romantic dream-state of television and romance novels, which account for 50 percent of all book sales in the country. Slash porn advocates, who don't seem to "get enough" of banal, mass-market creations, trade and sell their own fantasy versions to fellow advocates, and share them, big time, on Slash fiction websites. Friscon was a Tupperware party for chronic suburban masturbators.

Friscon convention-goer, Greywolf

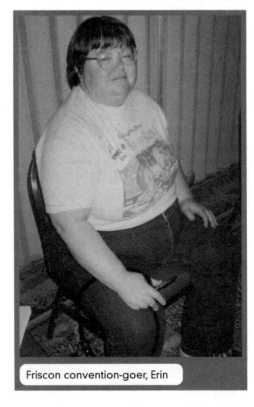

Friscon convention-goer, Erin

Letters and Poems

sent to Jodie Foster from John Hinckley,
used as evidence in his trials for his attempted
assassination of President Reagan.

March 17, 1981

Dear Jodie,

Did you see that scumbag on
the t.v. last night? He thinks he's
so smart and safe behind all those
bodyguards, but I've found a crack
in his armor and the crack is big
enough for me to slip through to fame.
You'll be proud of me Jodie. Millions
of Americans will Love me - us.

Don't you think our names sing
so beautifully together? I've spent
entire nights writing them in the
blackness with silver bolts of
lightning.

But I can't face the mornings.
Looking at myself in a shaving mirror
only brings the tears. Lonliness can
overcome even the most noble intentions.

We won't be lonely much longer
Jodie. The whole world will be ours. I
will admit to you that the reason I'm
going ahead with this attempt now is
because I just cannot wait any longer
to impress you. I've got to do something
now to make you understand. Hang onto
my dream and we will fly to the
netherworld of happiness.

Love,

John

September 17, 1980

Dear Jodie,

I followed you again today. You didn't notice me, did you? I could have killed you anytime I wanted to, but I don't want to hurt you. I'll kill those men you talk to though. They're all pimps. I've checked them out in the computer. Stay away from them Jodie. This is my last warning.

I pray for you each night. My mother told me that prayer was the answer to all our problems. Do you believe in prayer? Do you believe in Love? Pray for Love Jodie - our Love - pure, clean Love.

That was a nice dress you had on today. I like you better in a dress. Your jeans always ride up in your crack and all the boys go hard in their pants. I don't like that Jodie. It makes me very angry and the blood begins to throb in my brain. I start to fear that you'll go away and I'll never find you, but that's impossible.

I love you more than any man has ever loved before. There is still time. Wear your plaid skirt tomorrow and my soul will fly to the sky on transparent wings of joy.

Love,

John

darkness falls
from memories past
and future soaked in
the cunt juice of
lonely passion -
drying out in the heat
metal gun
pressed close to yr spine

deserted by love

forgotten

Penis is cold
is hard see
and touch -

Strung so tight
yr face a blue blur

flicks across screen
in Blk & Wht
playing guitar on my spine

The camera out of focus

comes all over
my leg

My fist keeps you down
Knuckles cross over yr eyes
You feel it? me I tear skirt
falls - thighs paste across
the dash - My fist
See!
I fit yr body, "just a kid"
tight till you squirm
all around it. Hot and wet with
juice & tears, crying under
me

Fist the shape of a
birds head with

giggles & grunt

The pseudonymous "Brice Taylor" surrounded by the politicians and celebrities she claimed were fond of using her as a mind-controlled sex toy.

UNCLE RONNIE'S SEX SLAVES

Robert Sterling

There was a time when reports of ritual sexual abuse—particularly those involving the military/industrial/intelligence complex and its invocation of Satan—only found their way to the periphery of conspiracy research.

Times have changed. Reports of sexual exploitation with a parapolitical twist now occupy a center stage of the con theory circus. And for good reason. The quality investigative skills of several underground writers leave little doubt of validity to some of these reports.

But a mutant strain of this literature has developed, creating its own bandwagon. These are the testimonials of ritual abuse victims, all testifying to their enslavement to the New World Order by way of freaky sex with politicians and celebrities.

Leading the brigade is Cathy O'Brien, who in 1995 published *Trance Formation of America*, the giant of the genre. O'Brien claims that from birth, in 1957, she was trained and controlled to be a "Presidential Model," that is, a sex slave for Presidents and other high-ranking officials. For several fabulous years an uncontested champion of Sex Slave victimization, selling tens of thousands of her books and videos, as well as a speaker drawing big crowds of Christians, patriots, and Christian patriots, Cathy O'Brien now has a worthy competitor in Brice Taylor, the pseudonym of Susan Ford, who in 1999 released her own memoirs, *Thanks for the Memories.**

After suffering horrible torture and abuse at the hands of countless famous politicians and celebrities, both O'Brien and Taylor declare of being spoken to by Jesus Christ, whose glorious powers healed them of all trauma and left them immune to further manipulation. That said, they both proceed to expose all the juicy details of the ungodly perversions they were forced into, naming names and leaving little to the imagination.

---

* Annie McKenna, yet another professed victim of government mind control, came forward in 1999 with her self-published exposé, *Paperclip Dolls*, after finally remembering what went on all those horrifying, amnesia-driven years of sexual abuse. The author has not yet read Ms. McKenna's memoir, yet its website http://www.paperclipdolls.com/ reveals that the book covers the now well-traveled themes of Project Monarch, multiple personality disorder, Nazi scientists, incest, and, finally, the miracle of healing.

The sex slave tomes elicit extreme reactions. Many nod unquestioningly at their outrageous stories and react violently to anyone who questions their accounts. Others are disgusted by what they perceive as reckless character assassinations, and take the books as proof that reports of sexual abuse are hysteria motivated by false memories. Or the need to make money and attention.

People argue about the parapolitical dynamics or motivations of the sex slave genre, but no one has yet analyzed their aesthetic value. Cathy O'Brien and Brice Taylor enjoy relatively large followings because, true or false, politically relevant or not, their stories make for the most titillating and sordid one-hand readers known to mankind.

> My pedophile father, Earl O'Brien, brags that he began substituting his penis for my mother's nipple soon after I was born. My multi-generational incest-abused mother, Carol Tanis, did not protest his perverse actions due to (reportedly) having similar abuse as a child which caused her to acquire Multiple Personality Disorder. My earliest recovered memory was that I could not breathe with my father's penis jammed into my little throat. Yet I could not discern his semen from my mother's milk.

These opening sentences of *Trance Formation* are to sex slave literature what the opening four notes of Beethoven's Fifth symphony are to Western music. And,

The True Life Story of a CIA Mind Control Slave by Cathy O'Brien with Mark Phillips

like Beethoven's Fifth, the melody of *Trance Formation* continues, constantly repeating the same pattern, yet with so many unusual harmonies and variations that one is compelled to read further, hungry for that explosive and satisfying finale.

While anecdotes of familial rape are an enjoyable subject, Cathy O'Brien is quite aware that people crave to read about the strange sexual desires of celebrities even more.

Most porn flicks waste a good five minutes at the start on such obtuse concepts as plot and dialogue. O'Brien cuts to the chase and proves her brilliant instincts for providing the reader exactly what s/he desires. True, Chapter One (subtitled "My Introduction to Humanity") begins on page 81, after 42 pages of pictures and documents, as well as a way-too-long explanation of CIA mind control, but the obligatory data can be easily identified and skipped.

On page 82, after linking her abuse to the Vatican and pornographers in the Michigan Mafia, Cathy trots out future President Gerald Ford. According to Cathy, Ford was not the bumbling fool Chevy Chase portrayed on *Saturday Night Live*, or the opportunistic FBI informant involved in the JFK coverup as portrayed in conspiracy literature, but rather a perverted Mafia porn king. Soon, Ford is tag-teaming with GOP leader Guy VanderJagt on Cathy's third-grade field trip to the state capitol. They laugh while placing a small American flag in her ass so she can wave it, saying, "Ask not what your country can do for you, ask what you can do for your country."

In her younger days, Cathy is importuned to regularly screw a priest (who, with biting wit, describes her as "a good Cathy-lick") and joins a Catholic school. And after he becomes president, Ford brutally rapes Cathy in her schoolgirl uniform after unzipping his pants, pulling out his cock, demanding that she "pray on this."

Cathy O'Brien's connection to Ford continues as she is regularly abused by Richard Cheney, the Chief of Staff and future Secretary of Defense under George Bush. Cheney goes by the name "Dick" due to his overlarge penis, a claim on which Cathy places special emphasis, particularly when Cheney is said to violently slam her snatch at the end of a *Most Dangerous Game*-inspired human hunt turned sex romp.

Cathy tells us of an arranged marriage to cover her sex slave status to closet Satanist Senator Robert Byrd. Byrd, who even the mainstream media admits is a "former" KKK member. Exciting scenes depict Senator Byrd raping Cathy and her two-year-old daughter Kelly, and becoming enraged when he discovers that Cathy's prolific "services" were used by African-American country singer (and CIA agent) Charley Pride, and *Trance Formation* tells of Byrd savagely beating them for being on the wrong side of the black country star's penis.

A frequent sojourn in the book are trips to sex slave training camp in Youngstown, known as "Charm School." Part of Cathy's training there includes "bestiality lessons"—being chained to an animal altar while being fucked by a donkey, dogs, cats, snakes, and a pony (charmingly named Trigger). Pennsylvania Governor Dick Thornburgh screws her regularly, revealing a fetish for pissing on his sexual partners. Cathy also meets Kris Kristofferson, who besides being an actor and country singer, is a "Vatican-based Project Monarch slave runner." He electroshocks her during sex, and is said to nearly strangle Cathy with his penis, though the book unfortunately fails to explain how he accomplished this impressive feat.

During the Reagan years of the go-go '80s, Cathy has her most surreal moments. "Uncle Ronnie" (as she calls him) introduces her to George Bush, then Vice President, who speaks to her in a voice that intentionally mimics Mister Rogers—a claim that almost has a ring of truth. Bush uses the songs "Ghostbusters" and "Every Breath You Take" to further brainwash her (apparently Bush was hipper to pop culture than he pretended), and transforms himself into a lizard alien before her eyes, which, frankly, explains quite a bit.

Later on, while strung out on heroin with Cheney, Bush tries to convince Donkey Dick to experiment with pedophilia on Cathy's daughter, Kelly, but, "Upon seeing Cheney's unusually large penis, Kelly reeled back in horror." Bush himself takes young Kelly to his bedroom, asking for the liquid cocaine atomizer, which Cheney assumes is to thoughtfully numb her. Bush replies, "The hell it is. It's for me." He then adds a wicked punchline: "Half the fun is having them squirm."

For those looking for interesting election issues, George W. was also involved in the shenanigans. According to Cathy, he "had never shown any interest in me sexually. Like his father, he had only shown sexual interest in Kelly, who had been away with him most of the day." Hanging out with baseball celebrities and drug kingpins Tommy Lasorda and Nolan Ryan, Georgie boy quips, "Have a ball." A pre-SlimFast Lasorda chimes in, "Speaking of balls, mine could use a little attention here." Cathy is obligated to give Lasorda a blowjob while he rests his repulsively bloated belly on her head, and two horny dogs (which earlier in the day she had been forced to fuck in a bestiality porno flick) enter the room, desiring more good loving.

Naturally, Ronald Reagan gets a crack at her as well, and this leads to the book's most unconvincing moment: while the image of George Bush as a Satanic, perverted Mister Rogers clone who transforms himself into a reptilian entity seems eerily plausible, Cathy's description of Reagan as a competent man in charge who actually understood the entire Iran-Contra operation is clearly crackpot. Nonetheless, she does make one accusation of particular note: he enjoys bestiality porno flicks (often supplied to him by *Hustler*'s Larry Flynt) and so much so that they are known as "Uncle Ronnie's Bedtime Stories."

In case the reader starts thinking only Republican Presidents are Satanic sex fiends, O'Brien includes a chapter titled "Clinton Coke Lines" that leaves little doubt that deviant perversion is a bipartisan affair. Sadly, this is the one case where the official story has exceeded her own description: nothing she writes can match the Starr Report's image of Monica Lewinsky using her vagina as a humidor for Slick Willie's cigars. By comparison, Cathy's description of Bill as a coke-snorting redneck who enjoys homosexual orgies seems rather vanilla. Still, she does provide a rather vivid glimpse of potential New

York Senator Hillary: aroused by Cathy and her now mutilated vagina, Lady Macbeth begins licking her out, then gasps, "Eat me, oh God, eat me now." This leads to a lesbo munchout obligatory to any porn flick.

All this is but a sampling of the sexual exploits O'Brien and her daughter endure. Listing all the names involved would be tedious, but highlights include brothers Bob and William Bennett (fascist finger-wagging *Book of Virtues* editor and Bush's Drug Czar), who gangbang the very young Kelly. Cathy also spends many pages linking CIA mind control and sexual assaults to country music, alleging that Barbara Mandrell and her sisters (as well as Loretta Lynn) are brainwashed slaves. Predators in the field include Lee Greenwood, Jimmy Buffett and Boxcar Willie—who earns special recognition as an icon of evil, being a vicious pedophile and cocaine baron for the CIA-Mafia.

Some may think that such sensationalistic claims would be difficult—if not impossible—to top for jaw-dropping effects. They'd be wrong. Brice Taylor may not be the Alpha of sex slave authors, but she currently occupies the Omega spot. What she lacks in originality, she more than makes up for in excess.

Kelly with pedophile Boxcar Willie Rutland, Vermont 1985

Photo from *Trance Formation*

Brice doesn't start with a bang like Cathy does, but once she gets involved in a multitude of fancy underage fuck-sucks, she's off to the races. After growing up in a mind-controlled family (and being frequently programmed and brainwashed at a military base), Brice is sold as a sex slave to Bob Hope before her fifth birthday (hence the book's title, a trademark phrase of the alleged comedian). Tastefully, Bob holds off on sampling his prize, telling his young slave, "I'm going to be your man, but we'll have to talk more about this later . . . when you're a little older." In the meantime, Brice is sexually abused by members of her family, and is groomed for high level abuse, as no less than Henry Kissinger begins to play mind control tricks on her via telephone.

Brice soon gets to some precocious celebrity bopping, and her first predator is none other than Walt Disney, who rapes her at Disneyland after personally introducing himself on Main Street. Escorting Brice away from her family, Walt assaults her on Mr. Toad's Wild Ride. Abuses at Disneyland would become an annual ritual for her, and she wasn't safe from attack anywhere in the Magic Kingdom—violated at the Matterhorn, the Swiss Family Robinson Tree House, and even It's a Small World.

In the early '60s, the pre-teen Taylor wasn't too young for JFK, who bangs her regularly during his brief Presidency on secret trips she takes to D.C. Eventually, she screws all the Kennedy brothers (with Ted becoming one of her most violent and sadistic persecutors) and, later on, a 12-year-old JFK Jr.

Apparently Marilyn Monroe wasn't enough for the Camelot President, and as for Jackie O, he complains to Brice, "My wife doesn't satisfy me. She just lays back and waits." Fortunately, President Kennedy was quite gratifying for nine-year-old Brice, as she notes, "JFK had a lean muscular body and a hairy chest." He really got off on anal sex, and once she sucked him off in the back of a limo, "backing off just before he orgasmed." He responds by running his tongue over her belly, saying, "I love young, firm tummies."

Less enjoyable was LBJ, to whom Brice was programmed to say, "Hey Prez, got a big boner for my little pussy today?" This turned Johnson on, who would start kissing and licking her. ("Yuck, it was gross," is how she describes the encounters.) Richard Nixon was a bit more amusing than the Texan, and she accompanies him on trips to China, the USSR and the Far East. At one GOP party, Tricky Dick breaks away from Pat to sneak a quickie. During the dreary months of Watergate, young Brice would cheer him up with fabulous sex.

Meanwhile, Hope began taking her along on his USO tours, as well as his celebrity parties. At many of Bob's parties there were no rules, no restrictions, no boundaries: "Sex was allowed anywhere and everywhere." When the parties were over, he liked her to sit on his lap to feed him See's candy, followed by what he called "his favorite piece of ass." As he would inform her, "You're just a wind-up doll—a toy for my pleasure, and don't forget it!" Hope begins loaning Brice out to others, including Senator Alan Cranston (who was "Bob's right-hand political man in California") and future Governor Pete Wilson. Cranston was into spanking her, and she describes him as a "bony, old, evil man." About Wilson, she states, "Pete was in good shape physically and had a little more than average share of penile endowment." The Republican ex-guv thought Brice had a great ass, and liked to nibble her body from head to toe.

Bob Hope wasn't the only one pawning out Brice Taylor's poon: Kissinger, who would take her on trips around the world, would use her as bait for power elites, often to get them in compromising positions. Among these lucky power players were Prince Philip and Prince Charles, Alan Greenspan, Lee Iacocca (whom she deep throated on his Lear Jet) and the Rockefellers.

The list of celebrities she later boffed would fill an entire season of special guest stars on *The Simpsons*. Some of the highlights: Sammy Davis, Jr., Dean Martin and mob goons "Uncle" Frank Sinatra and Jimmy the Greek, Neil Diamond, James Taylor, Charlton Heston, Kareem Abdul-Jabbaar, and both Johnny Carson and Ed McMahon. One happy winter holiday season, amateur Santa Hope gave her for the day to a drunk Bing Crosby as a gift, who was delighted. As instructed, she says to him "I'm dreaming of a White Christmas," then winks and orally satisfies the crooner. Hawaiian singer Don Ho uses Brice to fulfill rape fantasies. One time, she plays "Goldilocks and the Three Bears" with Dean Martin, Gene Kelly and Mickey Rooney. (Of course, this doesn't fully satisfy Rooney, who was a pedophile, and who would later find more pleasure with Brice's young daughter—who, interestingly enough, is named Kelly just like Cathy O'Brien's daughter.)

Perhaps Brice's finest tale concerns her exploits with Sylvester Stallone, whose addiction to coke and sex earn him the code name "Animal." Looking at Brice's 13-year-old daughter, Sly comments that she looks like a young Bo Derek. "Bob has good taste," he notes, as he bangs Kelly while mind-controlled Brice feeds him more coke. Whacked-out and aroused by the mother-daughter three-way, Stallone rambles: "There's nothing quite like a slave. I love getting them from the underground. You're all so cooperative, don't give me no shit. This is the life I tell ya'. No bitchy, demanding women, not when I can have beautiful, sweet, white women who set me free. It's all about freedom." Then, in a patriotic fervor, Sly praises "America the

Brice Taylor's daughter, Kelly

Beautiful and the home of the brave." The greatest kick achieved by Rocky is when he films both Brice and Kelly in "Dolphin Porn," or videos of women boned by dolphins in the ocean.

Brice tells of lying in the sack with Elvis, though she notes that the King was a victim as well, controlled by the Mob with drugs and mind manipulation. Presley isn't alone in this, as other celebrity victims of mind control include Michael Jackson, Jane Fonda, Barbra Streisand, and Lady Di.

Naturally, Brice and Kelly do all the usual Presidential suspects: Gerald Ford (who enjoys the fact that Brice's real last name is Ford as well), Reagan and George Bush (whose taste for pedophilic lust was so strong, genetically engineered children like Kelly—designed by specification for his arousal—were nicknamed "Bush babies"). The Clintons also double team her, and she swallows the robotic Al Gore's schlong. To Gore's credit, he did "Just Say No" to coke. Likewise, Brice does state for the record that Jimmy Carter was out of the Satanic sex loop.

Keep in mind, these are but the highlights of *Thanks for the Memories*. As with *Trance Formation*, limited space requires a Cliff's Notes description of the chronicles. As wild as the abridged version sounds, the actual books exceed all hype

"Brice Taylor"

for mind-blowing mind-controlled adventures. To say that these two books own a unique place in the literary spectrum would be an understatement. Yet, as unique as they are, there is a historical bloodline for the NWO sex slave genre that can be followed.

There are others who have tales involving similar exploits, including a small clique of women who tour the conspiracy lecture circuit repeating testimonies (most notably Cisco Wheeler and Arizona Wilder). These tales seem linked to *Michelle Remembers*, a book that details one woman's supposed abuse by a Satanic coven. Splinter versions of this fringe topic, most notably tales of the Montauk Project, links CIA mind control and pedophilia to time travel, Nazis and the Philadelphia Experiment (a purported WWII military test involving Nikola Tesla, Albert Einstein and Aleister Crowley). There is even a branch that leads straight to the JFK assassination in the works of T. Casey Brennan, a former comic book writer who states he was involved in the shooting as a teenager, after being brainwashed by David Ferrie (the creepy character played by Joe Pesci in Oliver Stone's movie).

Nor are these stories without precedent: before Cathy O'Brien was a known entity, model Candy Jones was the subject of a credible book published in 1976 by Playboy Press, about her years as an alleged unwitting Manchurian Candidate. Another classic in the study of mind manipulation is *Operation Mind Control*, written by Walter Bowart (who, in an unfortunate blow to his credibility, wrote the forward to Brice Taylor's book).

Still, none of the aforementioned early works really capture the true appeal of *Trance Formation* and *Thanks for the Memories*. Just what is it about these books that strike a chord, both positive and negative, with others?

The stock answer by those who reject the books as bogus sources is that they are disinformation, written specifically to incite the emotions in crowds through manipulative deception. There is much to this explanation, but to fully comprehend it, one first must understand the idea of disinformation.

Effective disinformation is never an absolute lie. The purpose of disinformation is to confuse truth and validity, and to do so boldfaced lies are rarely convincing. Effective disinformation mixes truth and deception to obfuscate the two. The closer disinformation approaches truth, the more damning it becomes. Then all the disinformation, even the legitimate parts, discredits targeted research and ideas.

At the time of the release of *Trance Formation*, there was a growing awareness in the conspiracy subculture of intelligence agency involvement in Satanic ritual abuse. Literature on the subject was reaching a critical mass where it could not be ignored.

Would intelligence agencies devote resources to counteract such information? Not only is it possible, it almost certainly has occurred. Case in point: the False Memory Syndrome Foundation, an organization that is to pedophilia what the Institute for Historical Review is to the Nazi holocaust. While many allegations of sexual abuse seem to have no foundation in truth, the FMSF (officially founded by two parents accused of molestation by their daughter) goes far beyond this purpose to provide blanket denial and apologism for child molestation. One former leader of the FMSF, Dr. Ralph Underwager, resigned when he stated in an interview to a Dutch pedophile magazine that sex with children is "An acceptable expression of God's will for love." In a court case, an FMSF "advisor," Dr. Harold Merskey, testified that a woman claiming sexual abuse by a doctor as a child was likely suffering from the syndrome. Dr. Merskey had never examined the woman, and her doctor had already admitted to other molestations.

The FMSF position gets widespread attention and promotion in the mainstream media, yet the opinions they endorse are a minority view in the field of human psychology. The CIA, even with an officially acknowledged history of abusing people through mind control experiments (the most famous being MK-ULTRA) certainly has a vested interest in denying such operations exist, especially when the operations are as insidious as sexually abusing children.

It is difficult to verify who is and isn't a doctor involved in CIA mind control operations (the agency has yet to supply the public a checklist), but some members of the FMSF advisory board have been part of them—most notably Drs. Martin Orne and Louis Jolyon West.

Both Brice Taylor and Cathy O'Brien claim that they were given special powers through their mind control training to have "total recall." There is a brilliant circular logic here: the stories are absolutely true, because, according to the stories, their tellers have not only been granted extraordinary sexual gifts, but also faultless memories.

Both women claim to have had their minds manipulated. Perhaps the manipulation begins and ends with themselves. A good case in point for pathological confabulation occurs with the previously mentioned Montauk Project. The biggest promoter of the theory, Preston Nichols, is a grotesquely obese man who resembles Jabba the Hutt in physical appearance. An investigation of Nichols' claims by Disinformation.com's Richard Metzger for England's Channel Four revealed a less than noble explanation for his work. According to Alexandra "Chica" Bruce, a former MTV producer, Nichols uses the Montauk Project as a homosexual pick-up scam. Nichols admits on camera to using hands-on deprogramming techniques with alleged Montauk victims, who are mainly younger men. According to Bruce, the techniques are little more than masturbating the supposed victims while Preston asks probing questions.

The author of this article met Brice Taylor and heard her speak. I have little doubt that she believes what she is saying. But whether she is telling the truth is another question altogether. Perhaps Brice and Cathy are victims—victims of their own lies.

Perhaps the manipulation lies at a higher level, with someone who is controlling them as part of a campaign with a deeper motive. The strongest candidate for this role falls to Mark Phillips, Cathy O'Brien's husband and the author of the forward to *Trance Formation*. According to O'Brien, Phillips was instrumental in "deprogramming" her out of her previous brainwashed state. Considering the version of reality she now endorses, how much the "deprogramming" is a program in itself remains an open question. Many who know Phillips believe he is a shady character. One proponent of this theory is none other than Brice Taylor herself. According to Brice, "Mark Phillips knew all about my programming. Looking back on it now, he seemed to know way too much." Taylor says that Phillips talked her into flying out to Tennessee, where he mooched 50 grand in living expenses from her in 18 months. Taylor's own conclusions, for what they're worth: "I suspect that Mark is some kind of 'containment agent' who is being directed through his 'handlers' whose motivations ultimately serve the New World Order."

Phillips himself says he worked for the CIA, where he learned hypnosis, but afterwards broke away, becoming a "renegade." Considering that his work helps make a laughingstock of ritual abuse claims, it could be argued that Phillips is still in the CIA's employ. Others who have dealt with Phillips have concluded that he is not now—nor has he ever been—a CIA agent, merely a lone nut con man out to make an easy buck exploiting vulnerable women.

Brice Taylor claims to have been consciously unaware of her abuse when it was occurring. It was in 1985, as the result of a car accident causing serious head trauma, that she started "remembering." According to Taylor, "[The car crash] allowed me to access both sides of my brain for the first time in my life, and I began having memories—very frequent memories—of all sorts of abuse." At the time of her "memory recovery," Brice was corralled and influenced by Christian fundamentalists, who convinced her that her previous life was the prelude for an afterlife in hell.

Whatever the truth may be, the case for organized child abuse has been set upon and mocked by the mainstream media. Despite widespread sexually transmitted diseases among the kids who attended the McMartin preschool, and despite the discovery of underground tunnels found beneath the McMartin complex by a surprised UCLA archaeologist, Dr. E. Gary Stickel, who expected to find nothing due to news reports he had previously read, all charged of crimes in the McMartin case were found "not guilty." All seven jurors who attended a press conference after the trial agreed that the children had indeed been abused at the preschool. They never questioned that crimes were committed,

The NLP (Neuro-Linguistic Programming) model for Cathy O'Brien's *Trance Formation*

but they weren't absolutely convinced that the Buckeys committed them. Guilt was clouded by the children's own testimony, which listed famous celebrities and cartoon characters as among their Satanic torturers.

Armed with these facts, there is a strange feeling of déjà vu behind the O'Brien/Taylor tales. Despite the absurdity of their stories, I find it difficult to disqualify all of their assertions as invalid.

One claim that is almost certainly true: the stated connection between CIA mind control operations and Neuro-Linguistic Programming. NLP was created and promoted by John Grinder (a linguist) and Richard Bandler (a mathematician), two men interested in using psychology to get people at their peak mental performance. Together, they wrote the Bible of the field, *Trance Formations*, which likely inspired the title of O'Brien's masterpiece. The book's cover includes three dragons, a sorceress with a magic wand creating a rainbow leading from her left palm, and a yellow-brick road leading to a grassy knoll.

In 1986, Bandler was charged with murder of a prostitute in Santa Cruz, in a cocaine deal gone haywire. Bandler insisted the real killer was James Marino, an admitted coke dealer and the only other witness to the event. According to Marino, Bandler was motivated by his drug habit (which Bandler confessed to having) as well as revenge, after learning the victim was having a secret lesbian affair with his live-in girlfriend. A jury found Bandler not guilty.

Among the clients Bandler had for their workshops included corporate giants Chase Manhattan Bank, Avon, Coca-Cola, and IBM. The U.S. Army and the CIA were also interested in their work, and he gave three seminars in the nation's capitol. Bandler would later work on what the *Los Angeles Times* referred to as "classified intelligence work." A 1979 *Science Digest* article warned, "The technique [NLP] threatens to become a hazardous tool for personal manipulation and, in the wrong hands, a dangerous instrument of social control."

NLP's most popular disciple is Anthony Robbins. The infomercial kingpin and motivational guru—or, as he prefers to be called, "Peak Performance Trainer"—boasts in his book *Unlimited Power* to work with the U.S. Army, hired to train enlisted men in firing pistols.

This background material isn't presented to imply that Grinder, Bandler, or Robbins were personally involved in government mind control experiments. But the military-intelligence establishment has become interested in NLP techniques, and has utilized them for their own purposes. One of the leading proponents of NLP in the Pentagon was Colonel John Alexander, a commander of Green Beret Special Forces in Vietnam and a leader in the study of Remote Viewing. Alexander is often listed as a major bogeyman in government mind control experiments. His students in NLP include Al Gore.

What about other allegations in both Taylor and O'Brien's books? Take, for example, the claim that many leading politicians are Satanists and child abusers. To most, this qualifies as a crackpot assertion. And yet, how else can you explain the curious case of Lawrence King, the African-American GOP leader who sang the national anthem at the 1984 and 1988 Republican Conventions? Besides his being jailed for swindling $39 million from Franklin Credit Union (the Savings and Loan he ran), investigators, led by John DeCamp, discovered that King was also the head of a Satanic pedophile ring, which held parties attended by the rich and powerful. (Among the regular guests to these parties was George Bush.) Of course, not everyone at these parties was aware of the ugly shenanigans going on, as they took place in a back room only a select few had access to. Who precisely was involved in the back room entertainment remains a mystery, as the investigation was quickly sandbagged when the pedophile ring was uncovered.

In 1996, a larger scandal arose in Belgium (the home of NATO and the European Union). Marc Detroux, a man charged with *Silence of the Lambs*-style crimes involving kidnapping young girls, rape and murder, was discovered to be using the victims in Satanic rituals and sex parties involving the elite in business, military, and politics. As detailed in the *British Sunday Times*, witnesses described Black Masses where children were killed in front of these same establishment types, and human skulls were found at sites identified by the witnesses, including the cult's alleged headquarters. Among the judges, politicians, and policemen who attended orgies organized by the cult was a former commissioner of the European Union. One judge attempted to get to the bottom of the matter, but was soon dismissed by his superiors in the Ministry of Justice. Even *Time* magazine, in one of the rare mentions made in the American media of this apparently unimportant scandal, described shadowy links from this operation to mobsters, mentioning the use of "underground tunnels."

With this in mind, are the scandalous claims that some American political leaders are Satanic pedophiles really that implausible? Certainly not, even if O'Brien and Taylor are their unconvincing messengers. And supposing that O'Brien and Taylor's tales are part of a CIA disinformation campaign, it would make sense that some names on the list would actually include guilty participants. After all, what better place to hide the truth than out in the open, knowing full well it won't be believed? While they're at it, wouldn't those behind a disinformation campaign include names of people who are innocent as well, linking critics of CIA policies (such as Congressman Jim Traficant, Larry Flynt, and alleged penis-choker Kris Kristofferson) to these activities?

What about the repeated assertion that mass entertainment for children is part of mind control operations? While Walt Disney may not have raped Brice Taylor in the Magic Kingdom, he was in Freemasonry, and there is a secretive "Club 33"—the number corresponding with the highest rank in Masonry—located in New Orleans Square. Is it just a coincidence that Britney Spears and Christina Aguilera—the two most popular pop singers currently exploiting Lolita music video fantasies—are former Mouseketeers?

As interesting as it is to investigate the parapolitical aspects of the NWO sex slave tales, they don't begin to explain the popularity of the genre, and to believe otherwise would miss the books' most attractive aspects.

Sex sells. *Trance Formation* and *Thanks for the Memories* closely resemble the style of Hollywood exposés such as *You'll Never Make Love in This Town Again*. And the first-person narrative also has much in common with a Harlequin romance novel. Not to mention a greasier form of romance: pornography.

> He played with me and teased me a lot. Then he pulled me over close to him and said, "Now it's time to be more serious." And he started kissing me and slipped his hand inside my shirt and felt my breasts. Then he unfastened my bra and pulled my shirt up and began sucking on my nipples. He said that really got him hard to see young, firm breasts and he circled my nipples with his fingers.

> Well, on the way up in the elevator, he kissed me—at first just regular kissing, but then with a lot of tongue. I could feel his cock

against my belly, and he was squeezing my butt and sliding my dress up. When the elevator stopped he had the skirt all the way up to my waist and I was Frenching him back. I was so hot I couldn't stop.

The first paragraph is from *Thanks for the Memories*, about Brice's mind-controlled dalliance with JFK. The second is from the letters section from a July 1998 issue of *Penthouse*.

In her introduction, Taylor announces that her book "is not written to entertain. In fact, I hope you don't find it entertaining, for if you do, you've missed the point. The pornography that has proliferated in this world has destroyed countless lives of children, women and men who were used in it and has taught those who view it to objectify people. The telling of the following information is not done with the intent to further pornography and lewd sexual behavior, but in an attempt to stop what has gone on and to insure freedom of mind, body and spirit."

The lady doth protest too much.

Perhaps the NWO sex slave books are too kinky for tastes outside of Christian fundamentalism, but they certainly belong to high-quotient porno literature. The tales have many of the qualities commonly found in sado-masochistic bondage fantasies, which regularly depict women helpless as sexual perversions are committed upon them. Oceans of sperm have been squirted by millions of men over lesser quality goods. Indeed, as far as the "I never thought I'd be writing to tell you this, but . . ." genre goes, both books qualify as Grade A goods.

It should be obvious to everybody that the NWO sex slave genre is nothing more than thinly veiled porno disguised as parapolitics. The most avid readers of these books are fundamentalist Christians, who cite the O'Brien/Taylor tales as proof that the New World Order is a Satanic plot. That the tales told in these books seem in so many ways inaccurate appears of little concern to these readers, who often repeat the many unsubstantiated allegations as fact. Some would cite this as proof of hypocrisy rampant in fundamentalism, since one of the Ten Commandments (at least when this author last checked) is the prohibition of bearing false witness.

As Freud would remind us, that which we vociferously condemn as deviant is also what we often secretly crave. The more something becomes a taboo, the more attractive it becomes. It is no surprise that many people will happily wallow in perversion if given an excuse to do so. Is the promotion of these sex slave tales in the conservative Christian community a way to subliminally revel in filth? Few dare call it conspiracy, but even fewer dare call it pornography.

✦ ✦ ✦

Thanks to Adam Parfrey, Uri Dowbenko, Richard Metzger, Kathy Kasten and Clayton Douglas for their help with this article.

Robert Sterling is constable of The Konformist website. Its address is: http://www.konformist.com.

"Alien Woman Materializing in Front of David's Eyes" by David Huggins

Ritual Abuse

The following list of symptoms and syndromes is a prolegomena given to police and therapists regarding what is commonly referred to as "Satanic Ritual Abuse."

Ritual abuse consists of repeated psychological, spiritual, physical and sexual abuse, combined with a systematic use of ceremonies and symbols. Ritual abuse is usually perpetrated in and by a group.

Psychological Abuse

1. Threats are made against the victim's property.

2. Threats of punishment, torture, mutilation, and/or death of the victim, his/her family or pets are made.

3. The victim is told (s)he is no longer loved by his/her family or by God.

4. The victim is told that loving or protective figures in his/her life are secretly cult members who intend to harm him/her.

5. The victim is told that (s)he will be kidnapped and forced to live with the cult, and that thereafter (s)he will be separated from his/her family.

6. The victim is tied up or confined in a cage, closet, coffin, basement, isolation house, or other confined space, and told (s)he will be left there to die. This includes "mock burials" in which the victim is buried and told (s)he will be left there to die.

7. The victim is tied or confined with insects or animals that (s)he is told will harm him/her, or is made to believe that dangerous insects or animals are present in the place of confinement.

8. The victim is confined with or hanged upside-down in a hole with the dead body or mutilated body parts of an animal or person.

9. The victim is degraded through verbal abuse and humiliation, forced nudity in front of the group, public rape, covering the victim's body with urine and feces, urinating or defecating upon the victim, forcing the victim to consume urine and feces, etc.

10. The victim is forced to be to be filmed pornographically for purposes of humiliation, blackmail, and/or profit for the group.

11. The victim is made to feel (s)he is constantly watched and overheard by the cult or their spiritual counterparts, and that if (s)he fails to believe and act in accordance with the cult's wishes, (s)he will be punished or killed.

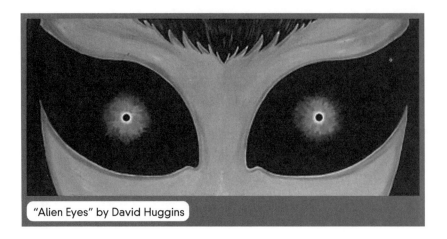

"Alien Eyes" by David Huggins

12. The victim is drugged and/or hypnotized in order to alter his/her mind and thereby to gain psychological and behavioral control.

13. The victim is subjected to "magical surgery" in which (s)he is drugged or hypnotized and told that something (e.g., demon, monster, heart of the devil) has been implanted in his/her body which will undermine his/her free will and cause him/her to be controlled by the "implanted" entity. The victim is made to believe that said entity functions as an agent of the cult.

14. The victim is forced to participate in ceremonies which emphasize his/her "belonging" to the cult. These include being "birthed" from an animal or human carcass into the cult's religion, or being "married" to a cult member or cult deity. Said ceremonies also include physical and sexual abuse.

15. The victim is forced to wear the ceremonial costuming employed by the cult, worship the cult's deity, and subscribe to a life-destructive belief system.

16. The victim is sworn to secrecy regarding the cult's activities under penalty of death. The victim receives instructions regarding when and how to harm him/herself or suicide if (s)he attempts to leave the cult.

17. The victim is forced to commit heinous acts, including animal killings, murder, murder of an offspring, mutilation, and cannibalism, often as part of a ceremony. After the commission of such an act, the group may exacerbate the victim's guilt through blame, threats of exposure, punishment or loss of love, infliction of survivor guilt, etc.

18. The victim is forced to ingest blood and/or body parts of a human or animal who has been sacrificed, often as part of a ceremony.

19. The victim is forced to act outside the group on the group's behalf, by engaging in prostitution or selling drugs for the group's profit; by infiltrating schools, the military, police department, etc. in order to increase the group's sphere of influence and control; by assassinating enemies of the group, etc.

B. Physical Abuse

1. The victim is battered.

2. Pins or other sharp object are inserted into sensitive parts of the victim's body.

3. The victim is cut, tattooed, or branded.

4. The victim is burned.

5. The victim receives electroshock, often to sensitive parts of the body.

6. The victim is submerged in water in an attempt to drown him/her.

7. The victim is hanged upside down for an extended period of time.

8. Food and/or water are withheld from the victim.

9. Parts of the victim's body are removed.

C. Sexual Abuse

1. The victim is repeatedly abused sexually by men, women, and/or children. The sexual assaults typically include not only body contact, but also the insertion of symbolic objects (e.g., cross) or weapons (e.g., knife, gun) into various body orifices.

2. The victim is forced to have sexual contact with children and/or infants.

3. The victim is forced to have sexual contact with animals.

4. The victim is forced to have sexual contact with a dead or dying person.

5. The sexual abuse may have a variety of ritualistic meanings to the perpetrators and victims—fertility ceremony, part of a "marriage" of a child to an adult member of the group, the pairing of sex and death, etc.

CETO'S NEW FRIENDS

Leah A. Haley

Illustrated by Lisa Dusenberry

He said, "I want to be your friend. May I play with you?"

The light took them up into Ceto's spaceship.

He taught them how to talk with their eyes.

Unsafe child reprimanded
for dropping banana peel

A Book Teaching Children
Sexual Assault Prevention Tools
by Frances S. Dayee

PRIVATE
ZONE

Illustrations by
Marina Megale Horosko

Nobody else can touch your PRIVATE ZONE. Not even your friends. If they do, you may say, "Don't touch. That's my PRIVATE ZONE." You may even yell, "DON'T TOUCH! THAT'S MY PRIVATE ZONE!"

You have the right to keep your PRIVATE ZONE, private.

If they try to touch it anyway, you may tell on them because it's your PRIVATE ZONE.

Your PRIVATE ZONE is more important than a private room. It's more important than Tommy's private shelf. Your PRIVATE ZONE is more important than Susie's private drawer. It's more important than Mommy's or Daddy's private letters. Your PRIVATE ZONE is more important than a private toothbrush. It's more important than whatever you remember of yours that is private. Your PRIVATE ZONE is more important than anything in the whole wide world, just because it's yours.

I bet you knew that!

But, did you know that your PRIVATE
ZONE is even more important than candy?
Or that it's even more important than
secrets?

Did you know that if someone touches
your PRIVATE ZONE and they say, "You
will get into trouble if you tell," you
haven't done anything wrong? You may tell
a policeman or doctor or best friend, and
you won't get into trouble.

If someone asks you to touch his or her
PRIVATE ZONE and then says, "You're
bad," it's not true. It's not your fault. You
aren't bad, and you may still tell. Mommies,
Daddies and grandparents would want you
to tell.

If a person just asks you to show them
your PRIVATE ZONE, you may yell and
tell. You may yell and tell if they show you
their PRIVATE ZONE. Even if they say,
"It's our secret," you may yell and tell.
That kind of secret should never be a
secret. For sure you have the right to
yell and tell.

Private Zone

PEDOPHILIA AND THE MORALLY RIGHTEOUS

Chris Campion

I love to hug and kiss you—

Marry me and let me be your wife!

In every dream I caress you . . .

Shirley Temple singing to Daddy in *Poor Little Rich Girl*

It broke his heart, but he couldn't stop shooting. Children scattered like marbles across the floor of the school gymnasium, some at the impact from bullets smashing into their precious little bodies, others in fearful flight from the aim of his gun barrel. For two, maybe three minutes, Thomas Watt Hamilton stood without saying a word, calmly pointing, tracing, fixing and firing over and over at terrified toddlers, until his ammunition was almost spent.

Waves of innocent blood lapped at his feet as he surveyed the scene. Before him lay "a medieval vision of hell"—"little bodies in piles" as one observer would describe it. It was more than Hamilton could handle, but as he turned the gun on himself, he was consoled by the thought—his last, as it turned out—that at least all this pain would be worthwhile. That his death and that of these lovely children would make a difference.

But no one ever would make sense of what happened that spring morning in 1996, in the small Scottish town of Dunblane, when 16 six- and seven-year-olds and their teacher were "sacrificed by a selfish killer." Said to be a "loner" whose only interests were "boys and guns," Thomas Watt Hamilton was actually a former Scout leader, youth club organizer, freemason and keen amateur photographer. But local photo labs refused to develop Hamilton's lovingly captured photographs of his comely youth club charges posed in striped swimming trunks.

Branded as a "pervert," hounded and harassed, Hamilton wrote tirelessly to higher powers stating his case, from the local authorities right up to Queen Elizabeth II. "I turn to you as a last resort," he wrote to the monarch, the Friday before the children started toppling, "and am appealing for some kind of intervention in the hope that I may be able to regain my self-esteem in Society." (Unmoved as she was by his plight, it's probably safe to say that the Queen doesn't share the tastes of her great grandfather, King Edward VII, who was a patron to famed Prussian pedophile photographer, William von Gloeden.)

"Killer described as man with grudge," commented a CNN report[1]. Too right he had a grudge. Thomas Watt Hamilton was a pissed-off pedophile with formidable firepower—to be exact, two .357 mm revolvers and two 9 mm pistols. Although, in the UK, the issue of gun control clouded the analytical aftermath of the event, one sociological autopsy[2] posited that, as a last desperate measure, Hamilton was actually enacting a carefully planned execution intended to take out the children society saw as his potential "victims" and to martyr himself for the sake of all pedophiles.

That this "slaughter of innocents" occurred in a school gymnasium is no mere coincidence. Two and a half thousand years ago, at the height of Greek culture, the gymnasium (from the Greek *gymnos* meaning naked) was the epicentre of intellectual and erotic energy. There, men and boys would engage in the pederastic pursuits of loving, learning and Olympic sports, during which the youth performed unclothed for the unadulterated pleasure of their teachers. Pederasty (from the Greek *paiderastia*, made up of *pais* meaning boy, and *eraste* meaning lover) was a pedagogic rite of passage undertaken before marriage, in which men would form a filial bond with adolescent males. According to Foucault's *History of Sexuality*[3], paedophilia (from the Greek *paedo* meaning child and *filia* meaning friendship) was the name given to that lasting bond, one that blossomed largely without lust, based instead on mutual respect and admiration.

The erotically charged actions of Thomas Watt Hamilton are one indicator that the unthinkable has happened: the pedophile, whipping boy of the sexual underclass, has become radicalized. Groups of exasperated pedophiles are fighting against the common misconception (fueled by the prurient forces of worldwide media and government) that they are simply a bunch of psychopathic baby-rapers, child-molesters and lust-killers. Blanket vilification has turned pedophiles into universal objects of fear and loathing and marginalized them as the last band of sexual outlaws. By legal and moral imperative, their every thought, movement and action is now subject to scrutiny. Catalogued, contained and under threat of castration, they are being forced underground. But it wasn't always this way.

Proof of a link to prehistoric pederastic impulses has been cited by the ritualized rearing habits of the Sambia tribe of Papua New Guinea, who venerated semen as a life-sustaining substance of equal importance to breast milk.[4] From age seven, male children of the tribe were separated from their mothers to live exclusively with elder men and boys. Believing puberty would not occur unless they were first pumped full of cum, elders expected the boys in their care to fellate them as part of an ongoing initiation rite, which continued until they sprouted and were finally accorded status as fully ledged hunters. Ethnologists claim pederasty's Paleolithic origin connects this cum fetish with the cannibalism of brain tissue and marrow from the spinal cord which, once ingested, passed manly virtues onto the next generation.

Aristotle cites the first institutionalized pederastic rite of passage as that introduced by King Minos Of Crete as a means of population control.[5] This called for the segregation of women and association of children with the men in a move that could be seen as the first throes of male hegemony over procreation.

From Crete, the practice was transported to Greece where it flowered into a centerpiece of Hellenic culture. Pederasty was enthusiastically promoted by philosophers such as Plato (hence the term "platonic" relationship), Socrates, and Homer, who believed that the pedophilic relationship was on a higher realm than the purely procreative one between man and woman because its purpose was both pedagogic and philosophic. Kiddie fiddling was given a divine prototype with the story of Zeus and Ganymede. Intoxicated by his youth, Zeus abducted Ganymede and spirited him to heaven on an eagle's back. There he replaced Hebe (the virgin aspect of the Goddess Hera) and was installed as Zeus' divine consort and cup-bearer, the dispenser of the ambrosia of immortality.

A scurrilous and scatalogical history of pederastic culture through the ages is included as part of Sir Richard Francis Burton's "Terminal Essay," an appendix to his 1885 translation of *The Arabian Nights*[6]. Burton suggests that far from racial or cultural, pederasty was geographical and climatic in origin. He marks out a "Sotadic Zone" (where "the Vice is popular and endemic, held at the worst to be a mere peccadillo"[7]) extending from the northern and southern extents of the Mediterranean, through Asia Minor, Indo-China to the South Sea Islands and the New World. In this zone, he speculates that a "perversion of the erotic senses" came about as a "blending of masculine and feminine temperaments."[8] Alternatively, this zone, which cuts a swathe through territories widely assumed to be the birth place of humanity, could be one in which man's original polysexual nature had been preserved intact, where psychosexual impulses were ritualized to render them non-threatening to society.

In *Symposium*, Plato uses the myth told by the playwright Aristophanes to postulate a genetic explanation for perceived differences in sexual preferences. Primeval human beings were originally four-armed, four-legged creatures with two faces, two sets of genitals (front and back) and of three sexes (male, female and androgynous). To quell the ambitions of these rebellious creatures, Zeus threw them into a perpetual state of sexual confusion by splitting them in two. Each part seeking restoration of the whole naturally preferred relations with its own sex. Male and females desirous of each other were derived from the original androgyne.

Burton mischievously quotes from another creation myth, "L'Anandryne" in Mirabeau's *Erotika Biblion*, which told how the actions of Adam (said by certain Talmudists to have copulated with all races of animals) helped disfigure the

Pour la rentrée des classes, ils riaient tous auprès de Gwen, la maîtresse modèle

Sur les 28 enfants de première année qui posent près de Gwen Mayor, leur institutrice, 14 seront fauchés, le 13 mars, entre 9 h 30 et 9 h 33, par les balles de Thomas Hamilton. Onze seront blessés. Deux petites filles, Rachel Halley et Dawn Paterson, seront absentes le matin fatidique : la première était souffrante, la

BLESSE

INDEMNE

ABSENTE

BLESSE

BLESSE

BLESSE

Thomas Hamilton's young victims

seconde avait déménagé. Mais deux autres, Melissa Currie et Victoria Clydesdale, absentes le jour de la photo, seront présentes au moment du massacre. Tous ces enfants adoraient leur maîtresse d'école. Quand le tueur de Dunblane a ouvert le feu, elle s'est jetée devant le petit garçon le plus proche pour le protéger.

work of God and produce "monsters incapable of independent self-reproduction like the vegetable kingdom."[9] And this, in effect, is the role in which the pedophile has been cast. A psychopathic monster symbolizing "the return of the repressed," whose barbarous nature has been bloated (in recent times) by the exploits of notorious nonces like Ian Brady, John Wayne Gacy, Carl Panzram, Jeffrey Dahmer, and Marc Dutroux. All indulged in specific sadistic vices born of a perverted pathology, but none could have said to have been sodomizing striplings (and subsequently slaughtering them) for the sake of pure love or friendship, hence, in the strict sense of the word, "pedophiles," they were not.

Without doubt it is the 15th century story of Gilles de Rais, Marshal of France and lieutenant to Joan Of Arc, that gave all pedophiles (as well as Christian noblemen and libertines) a bad rep that was to stick to them like cum on a baby's face—a sight not unfamiliar to the man himself, who it is said straddled the bodies of some of his mutilated child victims and eagerly masturbated while blood still spurted from their wounds.[10] In a kill count that puts most modern lust-murderers to shame, Gilles confessed to the torture, sodomy, and slaughter of 140 innocents (mostly boys), but could have killed up to 650 more. Francisco Pelati, a tonsured clerk, was implicated in persuading Gilles that the virgin blood of murdered children could be used to facilitate the alchemical transformation of base metals into gold through the invocation of demons.

In 17th century Hungary, Gilles' female equivalent, the Countess Elizabeth Bathory, was accustomed to bathing in the blood of virgins, which she believed was an elixir of youth. It was drained daily from an Iron Maiden in which she was believed to have killed around 650 luckless wenches. (Twentieth century kiddie killer Albert Fish also believed in the ingestion of youthful purity and boldly confessed to killing, cooking up and consuming the unsullied body of 10-year-old Grace Budd.)

The Marquis de Sade, too, was embroiled in a case alleging criminal activities with youngsters procured for an "erotic theater" orchestrated for utter "derangement of the senses." During his persecution for the "little girls affair," a month-long orgy during the winter of 1774, de Sade commented of his reputation, "I pass for the werewolf of these parts."[11]

A monster must have something to prey on, and the pedophiles' fortunes within society changed with perceptions of the nature of children during Victorian times. Up until this time, children were treated simply as "little adults," and the term "child" did not even exist. In *Child Loving*, James R. Kincaid's study of child-centered Victorian culture, it is suggested that this change was purely concerned with the child's sexuality.[12] He notes that the "child" was first defined as a stage in human development in the third edition of William Acton's study, *The Functions & Disorders of the Reproductive Organs in Childhood, in Youth, in Adult Age and in Advanced Life*. Other biologists soon followed suit, identifying childhood as a non-sexual state before puberty, ended by the onset of liquidity (menstruation in females, ejaculation in males). This, Kincaid concurs, had an immediate effect on age of consent laws, which in 1861 were raised from 10 to 12 years, but by 1885 had peaked at 16.[13]

Once contained as a non-sexual, empty vessel, the child was filled with all sorts of civilizing conceits. One idea was that children were essentially Adamic in nature, "full of evil intentions" and "utterly corrupt from birth." And along with this notion of the child as a "primitive, uncivilized savage"[14] came the corresponding qualities of innocence, purity, and cuteness that have remained with it until present day. But, as Kincaid points out, these qualities were not immediately associated with children at a time when, in England, they were regularly shipped off to the colonies as indentured slaves (80,000 boys and girls were sent to Canada alone between 1868 and 1925), or put to work at home in the cruel Dickensian world of sweatshops and chimney sweeps. While contemporary statisticians recorded the child mortality rate (of under fives) as almost 50 percent, there was also an unprecedented population boom with an average of six or seven children per family.[15]

In 1885, W. T. Stead, the staunchly puritan editor of the *Pall Mall Gazette*, a campaigning, populist UK tabloid, ran a series of articles on child prostitution in Victorian London under the title "The Maiden Tribute To Modern Babylon."[16] Widely considered to be one of the first successful pieces of modern scandal journalism, Stead's exposé of a sadistic sexual underworld, in which children were systematically bought, sold, deflowered and tortured by aristocratic libertines, raised the spectre of an epidemic of dangerous sex predators to a national level and forced wide-ranging legislation onto the statute books. Written in lurid, pornographic prose, Stead talked of "living sacrifices slain in the service of vice" (which he likened to the Cretan myth of children lost in the labyrinth at the mercy of the Minotaur) and boasted of buying "Lily," a 13-year-old certified virgin, for just £5 on the streets of London.

The series instituted widespread hysteria, moral panic, and rioting. Parliament responded by forcing through the Criminal Law Amendment Act of 1885 which not only raised the age of consent from 13 to 16, but also gave police increased powers to curb the activities of streetwalkers and brothel-keepers and, for the first time, also made "indecent acts" between consenting males illegal. Concerned citizens formed "social purity groups" dedicated to eradicating vice. One such group, The National Vigilance Association, soon expanded its brief to burning "obscene" books, defacing "nude" paintings and attacking music halls and theaters.

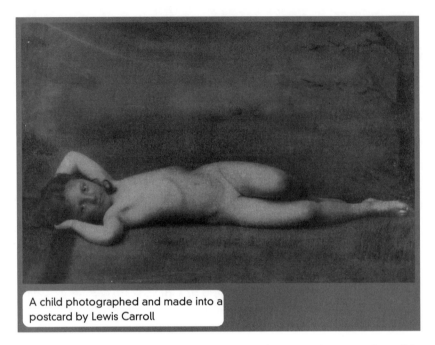

A child photographed and made into a postcard by Lewis Carroll

Unfortunately, Stead did not have long to gloat over his *succés de scandale*. Along with Josephine Butler (feminist founder of the Ladies National Association) and Catherine Booth of the Salvation Army, he was put on trial and found guilty of the abduction and imprisonment of "Lily." On release from jail, he became a spiritualist and later perished on the Titanic's maiden voyage.

Ironically, one of the most outspoken critics of the promiscuous method of reporting employed by Stead's "Maiden Tribute" was Lewis Carroll, whose ode to pedophilic obsession, *Alice In Wonderland*, was published a year later in 1886. That same year another landmark tome, Krafft-Ebing's *Psychopathia Sexualis* presented a menagerie of sexual fetishes that purported to identify and define the neuroses of aberrant sexuality.

The single case of "paedophilia" in the study proves to be textbook. The boy-loving tendencies of a 36-year-old journalist are said to be the cause of "congenital sexual inversion" (i.e., homosexuality) and "degenerative mental disturbance." Maligned and misunderstood, the inconsolable pedophile was committed to a loony bin for life. Krafft-Ebing's book provided a clear moral standard for the psychological stamping of deviant sexuality that reinforced societal taboos rather than demystified them.

In contrast, the later theories of Wilhelm Reich expressed the idea that it was society itself that repressed full sexual capacity into neurosis or distorted it into perversion. "Those parts of our cultural life which look like self-destruction," said Reich, "are not the manifestation of any 'impulses to self-destruction', but the expression of very real destructive intentions on the part of an authoritarian society interested in the suppression of sexuality." [17]

In his 1933 book *The Mass Psychology of Fascism*, Reich also saw the suppression of a child's genital sexuality by the family as an imposition of the authoritarian structures that would control it in later life. "It paralyzes the rebellious forces because any rebellion is laden with anxiety; it produces, by inhibiting sexual curiosity and sexual thinking in the child, a general inhibition of thinking and of critical faculties. . . . The formation of the authoritarian structure takes place through the anchoring of sexual inhibition and sexual anxiety." [18]

Reich's analysis of sexual imagery within Nazi propaganda and Hitler's hypnotic oratory led him to believe that Germans achieved some sort of orgiastic satisfaction from their dedication to the *Führer* and his *weltanschauung* of sexual repression. Myron Sharaf, Reich's biographer, commented that, "This intense libidinal excitation, combined with a sense of moral righteousness, was strikingly similar to the atmosphere at religious revival meetings." [19]

A similar sense of social outrage and moral fervor exists within the psychiatric and combined child abuse industries today, who are involved in a modern-day witchhunt with a definition of pedophilia as a paraphilic, obsessive-compulsive sex disorder. Armed with an arsenal of soundbite syndromes and situations like "recovered memory," "stranger danger," "acquaintance molestors" and "bad touches," they have created a suffocating climate around the seduction of innocents. Potential sex offenders lurk around every corner and no child is safe from their sinister advances.

Stead's sensationalistic crusade has also continued, although the media message has become contradictory and confused. The late 20th Century found children more or less liberated from industrial servitude but chained to media commodification. Within the pages of glossy magazines, children are bought, sold, eroticized and exploited in a marketplace of desire where goods can be browsed but not shop-soiled. In supermarket scandal sheets, over-sexualized teen idols vie for column inches with brutalized, baby-faced Beauty Queens. The fashion industry takes baby-faced Beauty Queens and either dresses them up as steely sexual symbols of womanhood beyond their years or presents them as pedophilic phantasies to push over-priced glad rags. [20]

In recent years, the prurient interests of the general populace have been aroused by the media obsession with the McMartin preschool case, the murder of Polly Klaas by Richard Allen Davis, and that of 7-year-old Megan Kanka, who quite literally left her mark on her killer Jesse Timmendequas (a bite mark that helped convict him). In the latter two cases, the Klaas and Kanka families channeled their private grief into public campaigns calling for legislation to deal with "sex offenders" (a catch-all colloquialism that has become all but interchangeable with "pedophile").

Klaas' murder in Petaluma, California resulted in the widespread adoption of "Three Strikes and You're Out" legislation which deals out life sentences to repeat offenders. Kanka's July 1994 murder was given a bizarre tribute with the eponymous "Megan's Law," the law that introduced mandatory sex offender registration.[21]

Authorities now collated a publicly accessible hit list of the whereabouts of "known pedophiles" on release. (Paradoxically, in the UK, children no older than Polly Klaas are being branded as sex offenders. An article in the *Daily Telegraph*[22] told of a girl tried for three charges of indecent assault on boys aged four, five and six, and two charges of inciting a girl aged 14 to commit acts of gross indecency.)

In both cases, the threat of recidivist sex offenders stalking the country in search of unsullied sweet meats was used by the federal and state governments to introduce legislation with Orwellian implications for those individuals who do not conform to accepted modes of sexual practice. Once caught, those deemed a continuing danger to society may now be locked away indefinitely.

"Chemical castration," a drug treatment designed to inhibit sex drive, is commonly used as a mandatory condition of sentencing or parole in almost half the United States.[23] The drug in question, triptorelin, is primarily used to treat pancreatic cancer. The reduction of the sex drive is one of the reported side effects of the drug, along with a host of "lesser" effects such as "hair loss, gastrointestinal disturbances, breast enlargement, vertigo, transient high blood pressure and sight disturbances."

A February 12, 1998 report on a study of the effectiveness of chemical castration in the *New England Journal Of Medicine*[24] reported a legally disturbing precedent. Volunteers for the study included two groups: convicted sex offenders released from prison on the proviso that they participate in the program, and unconvicted individuals participating to avoid prosecution for alleged sex crimes. Hence, it seems that in the eye of the law, the very presence of testosterone in the priapic male is now considered a pathogenic predisposition to pedophilia.

Currently in use by US psychologists and in British prisons, the penile plethysmograph (PPG) is a piece of military-industrial machinery straight out of Kubrick's *A Clockwork Orange* used to measure "deviant arousal." It was initially developed by the Czech army to determine the heterosexual credentials of new recruits. Use of the device was hit by scandal in 1992 when publicly funded psychology practices in Arizona and Texas were found to be using it on boys as young as 10 years old. The FDA subsequently cited a Nebraska manufacturer of the machine for selling it without federal approval.

In state-funded sex correction centers, the hapless pervert is restrained by a bite board, has his penis fitted with a mercury-filled rubber loop (which records changes in the sex organ's circumference), is attached to a pupilometer (which detects changes in the diameter of the pupil) and repeatedly forced to watch sexually suggestive films and audio describing violent sexual encounters.[25] This treatment is also carried out as part of aversion therapy in which the perp is stimulated by electric shocks and putrid odors every time his pecker swells. And so, recorded and quantified, arousal is equated with desire. Stimulation is proof of intent.

According to a 1996 article in the *San Jose Mercury News*,[26] "The Association for the Treatment of Sexual Abusers advises P-graph operators to use a variety of "appropriate and deviant" themes, which may include pictures of sex acts. "Typical audio tapes include fondling, consenting/nonforceful intercourse, coercive sex, rape, and assault with children and adults of both sexes."

At the same time that this officially sanctioned child pornography (collated from existing sources) is produced, there is an active attempt by the authorities to regulate and police its existence on the Internet. Electronic vice cops and pedophile bounty hunters patrol the superhighway undercover, hoping to stumble across pedophile swap meets where naked pictures of children are exchanged like trading cards. Discarding dirty raincoats for semantic alter-egos, they pose as preening young 'uns, loitering in electronic chat rooms in order to ensnare and entrap unwitting pedos looking for company.

Like older sis Jamie (inset), Jalynne (left) and Janelle always seem to be smiling.

From the magazine *International Gymnast*, January 1998

Most sources state that the commercial child pornography industry ended with the outlawing of all child pornography in Denmark in 1985, the main source of such material after a 15-year social experiment where all forms of pornography were legalized. (In the U.S., postal inspectors continued publishing *Wonderland*, a pedophile contact publication in order to entrap lonely pedophiles.) It is thought that many of the hardcore kiddie porn pictures that pop up on internet newsgroups are from highly sought-after Lolita publications from that period. But not all of them.

Somewhere, reconstituted as a flicker on a screen, is a little boy. No more than seven years old with a cute blond bob. Let's call him "Tommy." He can't see himself on that screen, only you can. All he can see is a video camera pointing at him. His head is turned to look into it, with an expression that spells terror in any language. The rest of Tommy's tiny body is tensed up, lying tummy down on a cream-colored couch. His striped blue t-shirt is hiked-up above his waist, pants crumpled around his ankles. Little hands flex firmly against the cushions, pushing away. An adult arm cradles the child. A hand caresses his upper thigh. The other guides a swollen cock the size of Tommy's forearm up into Tommy's asshole, its bulbous head lodged firmly between tender cheeks. Evil up against the crack. Pushing deeper. The man, let's call him "Daddy," is also looking into the camera. Blankly. Unlike Tommy, he knows you are out there. He knows what you want and he's feeding your filthy fantasies. Fantasies of power. Of abuse. Of corrupted innocence. Of course, it takes a filthy mind to read a filthy mind. And as long as it continues to invoke the specter of sex danger, society will get the devil it deserves.

Dana Crutchfield

BIRTHDATE: 3/9/68
HEIGHT: 42"
WEIGHT: 48 Lbs.
HAIR: Blonde
EYES: Grey

NOTES

1. "Scottish town mourns loss of little ones," *CNN* (March 14, 1996).
2. From the abstract of a "Sociological autopsy of the Dunblane massacre," anonymously posted on alt.sex.pedophilia and other usenet newsgroups on Saturday June 8, 1996, retrieved from the website of the Pedophile Liberation Front.
3. Michel Foucault, *History of Sexuality: Volume II.*
4. Colin Spencer, *Homosexuality—A History* (4th Estate, 1996), pp. 20–22.
5. Aristotle, *Politics* (II, VII 4–6).
6. As reprinted in *Sexual Heretics: Male Homosexuality in English Literature from 1850 to 1900*, ed. Brian Reade (Routledge & Kegan Paul, 1970), pp 158–93. All further references to this volume.
7. Ibid. p.159.
8. Ibid. p.160.
9. Ibid. p.171.
10. Georges Bataille, *The Trial of Gilles de Rais* (Amok Books, 1991), pp. 223–4.
11. Maurice Lever, *Sade: A Biography* (Harcourt Brace, 1994), p. 254.
12. James R. Kincaid, *Child Loving: The Erotic Child & Victorian Culture* (Routledge, 1992), pp. 68–9.
13. Ibid. p. 70.
14. Bataille corresponds the child's savage nature with that of Gilles de Rais, whose behaviour is "unbounded by civilised proprieties" (Bataille, p. 32).
15. Kincaid, pp. 71-75.
16. For a fuller account see Judith R. Walkowitz, *City of Dreadful Delight: Narratives of Sexual Danger in Late Victorian London* (Virago, 1992), Ch. 3.
17. Wilhelm Reich, *Character Analysis* (Vision Press, 1969—originally published in 1933), p. 290.
18. Wilhelm Reich, *The Mass Psychology Of Fascism*, Channel 8, as cited by Myron Sharaf, *Fury On Earth* (St Martin's Press, 1983).
19. Sharaf, Ch. 13, p. 166.
20. In recent years, Calvin Klein has been accused of pandering to pedophilic obsessions and forced to withdraw ads. A 1995 campaign featured pubis-thrusting teenage trailer trash making coy camcorder confessions and another, in 1999, featured two brief-wearing toddlers grappling on a couch.
21. Both bills passed almost unanimously into federal law by the House of Representatives in May 1996.
22. "Girl, 12, is youngest on sex register," *The Daily Telegraph*, July 21, 1999.
23. Texas goes one step further, allowing for voluntary surgical castration for sex offenders.
24. Ariel Rosler, M.D. and Eliezer Witztum, M.D., "Treatment of Men with Paraphilia with a Long-Acting Analogue of Gonadotrophin-Releasing Hormone," *New England Journal of Medicine*, Feb 12, 1998.
25. A comprehensive account of the treatment is found in Sylvere Lotringer, *Overexposed: Treating Sexual Perversion in America* (Pantheon Press, 1988).
26. "Monitoring device to treat sex offenders sparks controversy" by Steve Johnson, *San Jose Mercury*, August 6, 1996.

"Doll" by Trevor Brown

PRIME TIME

Peter Sotos

A long fat forefinger and an old bent thumb pulled alongside of a tiny bald vagina to open it up; see how far it could spread and what it would look like. The digits pressed in and squeezed the chubby flesh as hard in as it would stretch. The cunt was dry. As in not cummed in or on, rather than naturally unlubricated as the child was obviously far younger than even prepubescent. This would be the position to investigate the damage wrought on any such childish organ. To see if there were any immediate entry scratches or vicious bites or the faint red burns of a too large adult cock or finger or wooden tool or mass-market plastic dildo having been shoved too thick, too long, too quick, too unready, too uncaring into the minute space just beyond that barely formed, barely folded, tight shut opening.

The fingers would peel that tiny tot's cunt open to see what would fit. So far. And what wouldn't and guess at the damage it might cause, the trail it might leave and the suddenly sobering possibilities of intense public outrage and the crush and arrest and life sentence a child raper and murderer would have to endure. And would this be worth it. This little cunt attached to a little mouth and flat flesh stretched politely over such small brittle bones and miniature blushes and games and tears and eyes.

It never was innocent. Unless innocence means dumb. It was barely human. Too few years here. And there's no need to twist the little pig into something less than real: inside that disastrously planned little hole lies all the exact same minutiae that'll grow up and turn and mold into all the other wonderful possibilities of femaledom and motherhood and great accomplishments and sisterly sense. It's all there now. Painted with the rules and guides of its absent parents and blossoming into them cancerous knot by knot.

No matter what kind of parents they are. The kind who didn't wrap the cocoon warm enough or the kind that didn't care enough not to unlock the house doors no matter how far past teenage curfew it was. Or the kind who'll sell anything they can find or create for this very minute's money to buy some crack, heroin or soda pop and corn chips.

The cunt is small. And still so fucking shut tight that the womb that stenches inchoate beneath the pit is all just one small detail in the bigger truth of someone else's cruelty. The body is incomplete. The nature is arrested. The changes were just beginning to show and the flesh ready to register more the damage done to it than the promise created for it.

The man who took the photo—filling the frame with nothing but fingers and child slash—must have been interested in the crime rather than the autopsy. The lack of detail is extreme. The photo is a record of the act the hand performed rather than the budding secrets of a child's artful fascinating vagina. Though the photo can be a perfect replica of both; the crueler intention certainly seems reflected in the fact that the published reproduction crops in so much finger, so much action. Although the long tips of these aged and clawing fingers may be included to give size to the comparatively very small, very young cunt. Below the important pedophiliac demarcation of ten years. And it is altogether even more possible that there were not two men in the room when this shot was taken. In the hotel room. Which would have been best. One hard-on'd rapist to hold the little bawling duct-taped fuckable rat down and then spread her wriggling baby cunt as far as baby sex flesh would spread between his two dirty smelling-like-her-guts fingers, while the other fucker sits across from the sexualized sweaty rape and snaps as many photos as he can before he needs to jam his own fingers into the little death before she dies or stops crying and faints and ruptures and begs even one more long hard jacking pumping cock squeezing second.

Hold her down.

Tighter. Hold her head back.

One fuck at her baby feet, the other at her baby blonde head; two naked lazy slobs with full engorged adult genitalia and wrinkles and spots and skin tags and heated plans all over, towering, forcing, cajoling, laughing, shadowing the tiniest little four-or-five or six-year-old girl sat forever in the darkened middle.

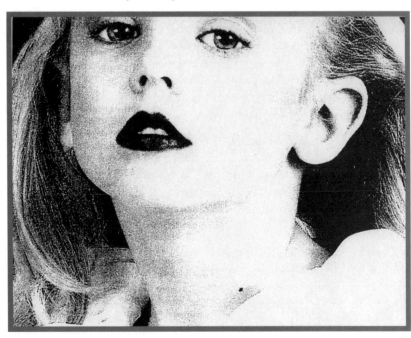

One hand stretches the cunt open before the inside walls rip, as far outside as the pork flesh will allow before breaking into evidence. Another hand holds her tiny wrists together, rubbing mean, between five pushing and pulling determined fingers. His cock shaking and jutting all over her last use of eyes and burning brain and denial mechanisms and memory. Another set of hands encourages position. Masturbates grinds pokes and deftly records by the small plastic and metal camera like mom and dad used on attention-soaking holidays and acting lessons.

Alternatively: one man with one hand around the special naked darling's filthy clean cunt and the other hand on his camera. He may have her sat in front of him, so that his probing hand and arm are bent up and pointed down at the elbow. His head down and staring at his work. He might have her laid down flat beneath him, his heavy fat weight and hairy manhandled balls and slung strange frightening penis dangling back and forth into her baby fresh face. A bouncing thick cock glistening at the tip with seeping disgusting dollops of drooling pre-cum. Ready, by dint of mother nature, to wet any hole regardless of its own design or interests.

Have you ever masturbated with child pornography?

The way one is meant to? For the reason it is created? The difficulty in obtaining it, the dangers in even owning it, the sickness one has to trundle through to come to one small, barely realized desire.

With a fucking magazine. The manufactured and professionally reproduced and planned issues like the European *INCEST 4*. The only one the police took from me.

Or with videos. Or with five-minute 8 mm films. The way I did when I was much younger. The kind I used to buy from a faggot pedophile out of his gold coast basement in Chicago. Who I met while pursuing an entirely different form of entertainment.

"Section 11-20.1 (a) (2) makes criminal the mere possession of child pornography. The State claims that the statute is a valid attempt by the State to protect its children by prohibiting the private possession of child pornography. The State contends that it has a compelling interest in protecting its children which overcomes this defendant's right to privacy within his home. This is so, the State argues, because the value of pornography is *de minimus.*" [1]

It's just one small part of one small girl. In a high-contrast black and white snap done in extreme close-up. And if it didn't look so small next to the fat fingertips and stretched so tightly painfully barely open, one could argue that it could be anything. Anything like some adult fresh out of illegality, shaved and trimmed and short for her porn star by-the-piece peroxide age. But this shot. In its violence. Is unequivocal.

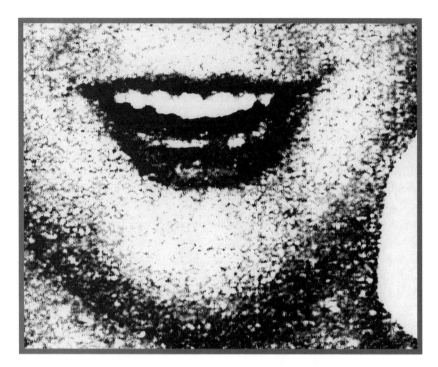

And it sits in the middle of this thin Rodox-printed 8 × 10 size magazine of distinct child pornography. All the other pictures are clear in age and intent and, perhaps, sadly, less violent. Less cruel. Less direct. But in context, where the close-up informs the more traditional acts and crimes, rather than vice-versa, the entire little magazine takes a shift towards the sadistic and away from the celebrated or revelatory.

Black and white shots of a little girl stripping off in the front seat of a car. Spreading her legs and smiling as the cameraman catches her bald slit and instructed sold naughtiness. Kneel. Up. Push your hair back.

A tiny baby held upside down. Between two large long hairy arms and meaty hands clasping its delicate toddler shoulders and head aimings its tiny naked cold cunt spread towards the beast's ugly thick semi-flaccid cock very close to where penetration would be a screaming killing rape. Less than a girl, this one. Too young to know anything. Too young to take in anything but the spin. Far too young to fuck even beyond this particular pose unless one's customers, like me, are primarily interested in buying filth that proves death and pain. I'd like to see her head nailed to a fucking board afterwards. When the frustration gives way from cock to coke bottle.

Skinny short arms on a blonde girl balance her awkward lean on a single bed as some standing pedophile slides what will fit of his hard cock into her pushed-in face.

The next page is a slight close-up of the next minute or so. The pre-teen blonde gets further away. But. Her tongue extends out to his glans, pink tip poking into piss-hole and one of her bony hands trying to cup his fat hanging busy balls just like he told her to.

This is what I do.

This is what I remember.

These are the names I give the little cunts and cocks I saw in magazines and films and slides and accounts being molested in ways feminists, psychiatrists, sociologists, reporters, cops, victims, parents and pedophiles explained to me.

In particular.

JonBenét Ramsey.

I. What do you think about when you jack off?

A little girl with long curly black hair to her shoulders and in her big brown eyes looks at the camera lens she was directed to and slowly sings a counting song. She's wearing a print country-style dress in a warm country-style ranch room in, no doubt, a big safe country-style wood and brick ranch home.

The cameraman moves in while she sings, so by the end of the commercial I'm left with just her soft white cheeks and pouty child mouth and little nose and large eyes all gently framed by that soft black hair. The bottom of the screen frame, however, intrudes even more violently as the little safe face gets bigger and closer. Perfectly. As it details what makes this little, maybe six-year-old, raven so much more special than any typical degenerate pedophile focus:

"This is Kate

Her stepfather forces sex on her

He says he'll hurt her mother

If she tells"

She's got pretty white teeth and she smiles to show them as the commercial ends. "1-800-4-A-CHILD. CHILDHELP USA. KEEP THE LINES OPEN."

Geraldo Rivera was kind enough to include this and various other PSAs concerning child sexual abuse as part of the "Exposing the Last Taboo" episode of his eponymous daytime talk show.

Broadcast about seven months after JonBenét Ramsey was murdered, Geraldo used JonBenét's case to highlight the need for understanding the disaster to children that is sexual molestation and, um, apparently, murder.

Geraldo explained his case at the outset: "I think the way to abolish the last taboo is to expose it." To which, his special guest Marilyn Van Derbur Atler gilded: "There is no way to change it unless we understand it."

Marilyn is a wrinkled, oddly tight, smartly dressed, prim-looking, white-haired, old former Miss America who as "advisor to the prosecution in the JonBenét case" has appeared on countless TV and radio talk shows and news programs detailing her own abuse at the hands of her millionaire father since the age of five. She talks regularly about the help she provided the attorneys investigating JonBenét's murder as related to her own pageant and incest survivor status.

She often serves to remind one of what rich pampered molested Barbie dolls will grow into if allowed to make it past the age of six, perhaps.

2. How often do you play with yourself?

Every week since JonBenét's death comes another crop of tabloids most often with a shot of and a garish blurb about the little made-up pre-six-year-old on the cover. *The Globe*, one of the four main tabloids, is virtually consistent. Every weekly issue for almost three years has had a feature, with pictures, of the bright red-lip'd little doll.

And every week I pick through and buy the tabloids, with the articles and photos of her. Available everywhere. I cut out the pictures and check the content and keep them in private files. I'm quick to remove the JonBenéts from the supermarket celebrity crap that surrounds her and slide her back into my own specific context. Where I use her as pornography.

Marilyn Van Derbur Atler: "The average age of a child violated for the first time is six."

Geraldo Rivera: "Really? That's how old JonBenét Ramsey is. Was."

3. Who taught you to jack off?

Fourteen-year-old Kandace, a seventh grader, who Geraldo's been letting tell her story, wants to read a poem to her father.

"What you've done, I can't undo.

Times you molested me, I can't forget about you.

I feel so dirty, yet I'm clean.

I take a bath but it sticks like glue.

How you disgraced me; how could you do this.

I was just a little innocent girl without a clue."

Geraldo tells her: "It's lovely. It really is lovely."

At the end of the show he lets Kandace have another minute for a personal message to her father. Geraldo tells her to look straight into the camera. And Kandace tells the cameraman about how she's got friends now and that they'll help her if he—the father, the lens—ever touches her or anyone again:

"You're not gonna have a ⌊bleep⌋ left."

The propriety that pervades such brutal truths, and, more importantly, the noble need to expose such brutality, is one that all of us, pedophiles and avengers, quickly learn to operate around. The dreaded point makes it through the wire, and the details that heat more intensely in your brain than in your ears will just have to do.

4. What is your favorite kind of sex?

Slow motion shots of little JonBenét modeling down the runway during one of her Little Miss Beauty Pageants. Her child face all done up in make-up the way her mother would wear. The lipstick on her baby lips target all the sex she doesn't yet understand forever. Over the footage of this little made-up bag of bones and lessons comes a stuttering voice recorded over a phone line. Adult. Female.

"I was molested by my grandfather as far back as I can remember till I was 13 years old. I never told anyone.

"I always wanted attention 'cause that's all I thought I was good for."

It turns out that "Anne" had called the *Geraldo* show to offer her thoughts, personal revelations and disturbances over a recent broadcast about JonBenét. "Anne" wanted to let the *Geraldo* show know that she thought someone should check out "any male people in (JonBenét's) life" and especially John Ramsey because "it really bothers me."

The footage of JonBenét displaying her kiddie wares cut to "Anne," 29, now sitting on the panel and broken down in tears next to 14-year-old Kandace. Geraldo was so touched by her confession of personal pain that he offered her a chance to tell, live on his show, more people than just a private recorded phone line manned by TV producers. About herself. And others just like her. About JonBenét. Except still living.

And, as it turned out, while not a beauty queen, "Anne" was a failed entertainer who could blame her lust for fame on the abuse she suffered.

One grows accustomed to the specious connections that those who have suffered through abuse make to this abuse that hopefully little JonBenét has suffered. It is somewhat more acceptable when the details are immediately juxtaposed, or even better, read over the top of pageant footage.

5. Describe your first fucking around as a boy.

Rose West would sit on a couch across from her husband Fred and spread wide her legs. Look at that, she'd say, addressing her splayed-open cunt to her husband's attention. I bet you wish you had something to fill that up, she'd say, or something approximate. And Fred would love it. He and she were in on the same joke. His wife spending most of her day fucking nigger after nigger in the hopes of finding bigger and bigger cocks.

There was a book of photos the husband and wife kept, one of the many such albums and videos devoted to their personal dedication to sexual documentation. And this particular one was specially concerned with shots of Rose's cunt in various stages of slack opened and raw fuckedness.

Cunts get that way, don't they.

And it doesn't necessarily have to come from sitting on the wrong ends of jungle-sized nigger dicks minute after minute, does it.

Because these old whores age badly. Don't they. Those old beaten horses, drooping sagging pinched flesh and craters and divots and pits, age into widened folded and hung slabs around which bodies still convinced of some small sense of worth, try and smile and tuck and primp the ways they did back when they were firm at eighteen, firmer at fourteen. And they still don't get it. Do they.

A review in *AVN* (*The Adult Video News*) for the video *Deep Throat Debi* doesn't go halfway to describe what really goes on in the 74-minute amateur porn video:

"The formula for this four-scene video is simple: Debi blows a well-hung black man for several minutes, then he fucks her in multiple positions and comes on her face. The sex isn't bad, but the couple is so determined to let us know how much they really enjoy themselves that hubby comes from behind the camera and does an impression of a zamboni, licking the jizz off her face and chest in broad circles."[2]

Debi is a pockmark riddled skull on a withered rag body closer to the disaster side of a middle-aged white trash crack whore. Her ass is flab mottled with cellulite and while her gangly frame is abused skinny, her tits even sag deflated under the weight of huge pruned brown nipples and various faded tattoos.

The effect is less:

"The action is kept at a steady pace throughout the video with good camera work and very enthusiastic participants."

And more: fat niggers getting sucked off by a garbaged hooker who may like her job just a little more due to her size queen husband who gets off sucking the nigger cum out of her distended cunt and licking it off her grizzled face.

6. What's the best sex scene you've ever had?

I like the word "little" best. I like the way it gets attached to specific names and cases by anonymous and/or cloying men in professional capacities.

The commercial that immediately preceded the first show that Gordon Elliot did on the JonBenét murder case featured the title "WHAT HAPPENED TO LITTLE JONBENÉT RAMSEY" stapled over a frozen still of the 6-year-old's little adult-painted baby face.

And wrapped inside was another favorite surprise. Little JonBenét got her little dead body dissected by Gordon's special kid-gloved guest Marc Klaas. There's no better way to fuck a little child than to have her parents do it for you. And there's no better way to watch fucked children than to watch someone who knows how to keep fucking it just right. Someone who knows what happens and how it works and what it looks like and what it'll sound like when he opens his gump to say the words that only he can pick out so carefully.

Marc Klaas brings with him all the loud details of his cause. The cause that he has dedicated his new life to now that his daughter is gone. And through the foundation he and his wife run out of his home, appearing on talk shows to enlighten the viewing communities about the best way to protect your children is but one important facet.

"Petitioner removed his sweatshirt, opened a condom wrapper, and unrolled the condom onto his penis. He then gathered the nightgown under the victim's armpits and inverted her white miniskirt over her hips and pelvis, pushing it up her body. Whether petitioner ultimately ejaculated is unknown: the victim's body had decomposed to a point where forensic testing for penetration was not possible; any semen that might have been present in the condom may have been washed away by the elements; and during police interrogation, petitioner himself said only, 'You guys soon find that out.'" [3]

7. Do you like to give dick or take it better?

The best way to masturbate is to use someone else's head. Faggots who need to suck any cock that comes their way and nigger drunk or cranked whores who need to suck any cock that comes their way. Compulsion, for inclusion, for inversion, for sex, for money, for more drugs and drink and more poverty back home and nothing else ever better.

Some faggots on their knees in gloryholed peep show booths will put condoms on the cock you give them. They'll reach into their back pockets and ask you if you mind. Nigger whores who don't use condoms are usually very unhealthy just like most of the queers who do their job bareback. Some fags hope you can't get sick by sucking cock and have the medical data about membrane fissures and stomach acids, as well as their penicillin quick fixes to prove it. Some nigger cunts hope to give HIV to you but still don't want your pig's cum in their mouths.

"The position of the body, coupled with Davis' past crimes and the unrolled condom found at Pythian Road led investigators to suspect Polly had been raped or at least molested before death."

That Marc's 12-year-old daughter Polly watched those fat greasy fingers unroll the condom up that greasy fat cock with her last minutes the way faggots might help or niggers might hide is something you'll never know—definitely—until Richard Allen Davis can be trusted enough to tell you and Mark Klaas.

Mr. Klaas offers up sympathy for Mr. and Mrs. Ramsey:

"These people are in the worst emotional state anybody can be in. They're in a place that oftentimes people are not able to get out of. They're in a dark room looking for a way out. And sometimes people don't find a way out."[4]

But Mr. Klaas basks in more virtue than he'll allow the newest famous parents of a murdered child on the block:

"I think it's a type of psychological child abuse. Is what I think. Six-year-olds should not be sexually provocative."

That warm mouth and the tongue technique or hard sucking jaws or whatever the beast on the sloppy end of your cock brings to the party is rendered largely blank by the tight latex covering your hard-on. Which is perfect. You have to look down to see what to feel. Their knees in filth, their inability to do anything else, their ghetto sale, their pockholes and drug rot, their 12-year-old face that left nighttime make-up stains on the hood when placed over her head.

Gordon Elliot continues to draw out Marc's informed opinions on the likes of a six-year-old parading around in clothes designed for older, more world weary whores. "It eroticized her," Gordon says. "She's playing Barbie." He forgives and then suggests that he knows the secret to eroticizing something:

"There's a lot of people in this country who look at these babies in a very different light."

Marc adds his personal pain to the mix again: "Beautiful little girl." And "Who knows what she would have been when she grew up." And finally:

Gordon: "You sound like you're talking abut Polly."

Marc: "Well, I am, aren't I?"

8. How many cocksuckers have sucked you off?

Both Geraldo and Leeza invited family members and friends of the little raped and beaten black girl known as Girl X onto their respective programs. Both talk show hosts wanted to confront the possible racist inequities of the media and public by discussing the relative lack of attention the crime against Girl X received when it occurred the very same Christmas week as the murder of JonBenét.

Girl X had been left for dead. By the stranger that raped and beat her retarded in a stairwell of the Cabrini Green Housing Projects in Chicago. She was nine years old, a fourth grader, and lived in one of the most notorious housing projects in the U.S. So the crimes against the children were virtually the same.

Geraldo: "I know that the girl was found with the gang graffiti scrawled on her abused and violated body."

Geraldo also had the good sense to show footage of one of Girl X's school friends screaming in tears at the bottom of one of the dirty rusted project stairwells having just received the news about the rape and brutal beating.

And while Leeza's guests moaned about the media being so accustomed to black-on-black crime that the rape registered nary a blip on the national level, Geraldo made sure his audience knew it was a big story in Chicago by interviewing the newscasters and reporters who brought the locals as much information as was allowed.

Unlike JonBenét, Girl X was by law protected from being named or identified by whatever footage could be found of a typical little black girl growing up in the projects. And while bitching about the racism inherent in the lack of even general coverage, Leeza and Geraldo still tagged the black-on-black crime onto the footage of lily-white JonBenét.

The sad reality is that Girl X's life makes better copy. But newscasters can't call her project poverty no chance life miserable because of all the others sharing that life and watching it on TV at the same time. JonBenét's life is better pornography because it is what is allowed.

9. What is the biggest number of cocks you sucked in one day?

On Geraldo's primetime cable talk show—more respectably upmarket, investigative and, on the surface, less tabloidy—*Rivera Live*, Geraldo married a couple of JonBenéts with Ryan Harris and Sherrice Iverson. Two other little black girls raped and murdered under glamorous circumstances. However, as Geraldo was obsessing over the Clinton/Lewinski blowjob, the public who had come to rely on Geraldo was robbed of their best chances.

10. What's the youngest cock you ever blew?

Christopher Meyer. Ten years old.

The photo I keep of him (clipped from the *Chicago Sun-Times*) is the same one Geraldo kept showing. And the footage of him playing in a living room before he was murdered comes courtesy of Geraldo's special show on child predators.

11. What is the biggest number of cocksuckers that blew you in one day?

Geraldo used this show to spotlight the crimes against Megan Kanka, Amber Haggerman and Alicia and DeAnn Jones by sandwiching their cases and family pain between updates on the JonBenét case.

12. What is the biggest number of wads you shot in one day?

Geraldo mentions, before he runs over the Megan Kanka victim details, that her murderer Jesse Timmendequas was facing the first day of his trial that day.

Court TV was allowed to broadcast live only the opening and closing statements in the case. As such, prosecutor Kathryn Flicker faced the jury (who were off camera) and recounted for the watching world Jesse's confession. She read in a brave but disgusted and angry voice, careful to keep it all professional and fair:

"I tried to penetrate her with my penis for about two minutes and I couldn't get it all the way in."

"No matter how hard I tried to force it all the way in, I couldn't get it in because she was too small."

"I tried to penetrate her in her pussy."

"Question. 'Did you at any time try to have anal sex with Megan?' Answer. 'No. But I may have slipped when I was trying to penetrate her pussy.'"

Geraldo had lubed the stage earlier with photos of the little chubby-faced seven-year-old and the vivid report on her rape and murder:

"Once inside, he lures her to an upstairs bedroom. Strangles her unconscious with a belt. Rapes her. And asphyxiates her to death with a plastic bag. Then he places her small body into a tool box and drives her to a soccer field two and a half miles away where he dumps her body into the bushes."

13. What has been your experience with women?

Mika Meyer is invited to talk about her sense of injustice and loss.

"It's dying a thousand deaths every day. It's walking around with your open heart surgery never being stitched up."

Geraldo had just told the audience about mother Mika's little boy Christopher:

"The little boy had been stabbed 53 times in the chest and the back. His genitals had been completely castrated."

Then he introduced Glenda Hill, the sister of little Tara Sue Huffman, the five-year-old girl that was also murdered by the man who murdered Christopher.

Later, Geraldo would pounce outraged. Timothy Buss had served only 12 years in jail for the murder of Tara Sue and shortly after release murdered little Christopher. And he follows the same tack of brutal caring bravery with Glenda as he did with Mika when he asked her to "remind them about how exactly Timothy Buss murdered your son."

Geraldo: "What did he do to your sister? He didn't just murder her. . . ."

Glenda: "No. After she was dead he stuck sticks up inside of her body. And . . . um . . . he bashed in the front of her face and . . . he beat her (starts to cry)."

Geraldo: "He served 12 years. Is that right?"

Cari Meyer, sister to the late little Christopher, sits in the audience and Geraldo walks to her and entreats her to talk about her brother. "It didn't have to be him," she says as the camera swings to Mika who has also now broken down.

14. Describe your first blow job.

Geraldo continues:

"A man walking his dog discovers her nude body. Chalky white face down.

Floating in a creek eight miles from where she had been abducted. Her throat had been slashed five times. Autopsy reports confirm Amber was also sexually molested."

"Tell us about Amber."

The mother starts to cry and her face is replaced by a shot of her nine-year-old daughter smiling with jagged teeth and bright blue eyes.

"She was my dream. She was never in trouble. She did no harm to nobody. She was an innocent little girl."

A new photo of Amber holding a baby doll sitting next to her mother, both smiling, comes on next.

"How dare that man do this to my little girl. How dare him."

15. Describe your best accomplishment in taking it up your asshole.

This is what I've been reduced to.

I've replaced photos and films of children having their pushed-up little faces cock fucked and their cookie cutter orifices finger fucked with images of previously safe little darlings smiling before anything special has happened.

Because JonBenét looks prepared and because she smells like she has fucked and killed written all over the inside of her tightest crotch hugging swimsuit. What I recognize inside those sold and cropped and considered and financed photos is not so much what she looks like dead and raped but how much she looks like she's got all those fingers on her. Adult fingers and adult mouths clamoring to suck on her six-year-old cunt positioning themselves in the midst of an angry hard-cock-based hard-news gangbang.

I. When were you first conscious of the female form, the girl with no hair? When were you conscious of that becoming important to you?

What does a little girl look like. Naked. Vulnerable. Waiting. Fucked. Crying. Posing for a photo that belongs to an art gallery rather than in my front cock pocket on my way into some gloryhole joint.

JonBenét in no photo I have of her is she belligerent. Or bratty. I have some where she looks away from where she's supposed to and another where she yawns.

I have video footage filmed just a few days before she was murdered, of her singing Christmas carols, pretending to blow a sax during the instrument break and wiggling her little butt. First aired courtesy *American Journal*.

Geraldo played the Ramsey's answering machine message where JonBenét squeaked:

"We're having a great summer. Wish you were here!"

A *60 Minutes* episode, broadcast about five months after JonBenét's death, had a nice introduction to her stage act:

"JonBenét Ramsey!

She'd like to become an Olympic skater.

Her favorite star: Julie Andrews.

JonBenét loves to eat cherries."

2. If you were to place the perfect girl in that chair with you as a target, what would she be? How old would she be?

Nearly seven months after the murder of JonBenét, the Denver investigators were forced to release her (partial) autopsy to the press. The orgy to figure out as close as possible to the truth whether JonBenét was molested was as thick as the report was vague.

All these well-intentioned vultures targeting this tiny inflamed barely six-year-old dead buried vagina.

Wolf Blitzer sat in for Larry King on his CNN talk show in front of an esteemed panel of reporters, attorneys, a child abuse expert and an ex-beauty queen incest victim.

Charlie Brennan (*Rocky Mountain News*):

> There is very strong indication that she suffered a degree of trauma to the genital area. And it may come down to a matter of semantical discussion as to whether the trauma to the genitals constitutes what we typically call sexual assault or whether that was more under the heading of what we would just call physical abuse. In my book, assault to the genital area—that says sexual assault to me but I think there are obviously a lot of people that may have different interpretations on that.

Bob Grant (Adams County DA and a regular guest on *Rivera Live*), upset for the "human reason" that "intensely personal, private, clinical, graphic detail—not the kind of stuff that you want to hear at your breakfast table" has been released and pored over so meticulously.

"It's just a shame that the memory of this beautiful child has to be sullied with this stuff."

Marilyn Van Derbur Atler seeps into her favorite position and takes Grant to task. She barks again for full disclosure of all the "intimate details" so that the public can learn that "these children are pried open and raped—viciously."

3. What would she be wearing? Picture her there in the chair, and look at the chair. Put her there.

Dr. Richard Krugman (child abuse expert, University of Colorado Medical Center—he appeared earlier in the day on *MSNBC News*, also discussing the autopsy, alongside Robert Ressler, the serial killer profiler expert):

> . . . and at the same time she had several other fresh abrasions, scratches, bruises on her body including an abrasion on her hymen that was part of what was found at the autopsy. Whether all these occurred at the same time as, shortly after, shortly before, I think is not clear from reading the autopsy.

Wolf Blitzer: "Is there in your opinion, and you're an expert in this kind of area, is there enough to conclude that JonBenét Ramsey was sexually abused?"

Wolf Blitzer: "When we're talking about sexual abuse, are we talking about sexual abuse on the night of the murder or is there any evidence in this autopsy report that suggests there was previous sexual abuse?"

4. Short? Long? What sort of color?

John Gibson sat in for Geraldo Rivera on *Rivera Live* that same night. Another group of criminal atttorneys, reporters and medical experts were gathered to pick apart the newest glance at that little paper cunt.

Among the details that Gibson directed attention to were the urine-stained long underwear and the mysterious red stain on the panties the child had on when she was found dead by her father.

John Gibson: "Does that red stain mean anything in particular?"

Craig Silverman (civil and criminal attorney): "Well, let's look at it. Understand that this little girl had panties on. And then long underwear. Typical garb for a little girl going to bed. When they found her she has blood on her panties but not on the long underwear so this indicates to me that if there was a sexual assault somebody would have to redress this little girl. Which is bizarre behavior by a stranger who comes in and then commits this type of act and then would redress her, particularly if the pants were urine-stained."

Cyril Wecht, MD (forensic pathologist/attorney who would later co-write a book on the JonBenét case and argue vociferously for a sexual motive in the murder including the embarrassing assertion that JonBenét died as a result of a bad game of sexual asphyxiation): "May I remind you that previously-released information tells us that there was blood on the labia, blood in the vaginal vault, an abrasion and contusion, so we definitely have a sexual assault. The red staining on the panties, I'll bet you anything, is blood. And the question is how does it get there. It gets there from blood on the genitalia. And Mr. Silverman has correctly pointed out that there's no way that this could be done. The panties were placed back on to the child after the sexual assault had occurred in order for the staining to have been there in the crotch of the panties."

Cyril continues to get excited and, after the commercial break, talks clinically about inflammation and discoloration and the hymen and the rim and finally concedes that perhaps the rape of the child wasn't a vicious attack "maybe not by a penis" but rather was a "controlled situation."

5. Hairstyle?

Geraldo does the same show as *Rolanda, Maureen O'Boyle (In Person), Maury Povich, Jenny Jones*, even *CNN Talk Back Live*. That is: Trot the little girls who make up the small numbers of the Little Miss Beauty Pageants and tut tut the perverse sexuality by ending with the murder and rape of its most famous representative.

Susan Rook of CNN asks one of the little assembled beauty queens all done up like a little executive rather than a Miss America: "Natasha, do you want to be a tomboy?"

The 11-year-old little Miss Michigan replies through heavy lip gloss on big sexy lips:

"No I don't. I want to be a little girl for as long as I can possibly be. Because I just want to live my childhood and pageantry isn't my whole life. I just want to be a little girl."

Of course, Little Miss Michigan is already too old. The question should have been asked to one of the smaller younger made-up dollies that were dressed up as princesses.

6. What sort of face would she have?

Eight-year-old Brittany and nine-year-old Breanne are interviewed on *Extra* as former pageant-mates of JonBenét.

"Where's JonBenét now?"

"She's up in heaven."

American Journal interviewed Breanne as well:

"It's kind of scary when I'm, like, far far away from my mom. Or my dad. It's kind of scary."

Breanne's mother, Dawn German, also contributed an article to *Newsweek* as part of its cover story, "The Strange World of JonBenét":

"When she did her first swimsuit competition when she was six, it was very age-appropriate. The suits were very cute, and they held beach balls." [5]

Caryl and Marilyn (*The Mommies*) interviewed 11-year-old Dallas, 10-year-old Rebecca, and nine-year-old Amy. Marilyn says Dallas looks like "Lolita" and that she had a "quick tense feeling" when they displayed such "sensual shots" of the tykes in full make-up.

7. A pretty face?

Geraldo picks through a copy of *People* magazine that features JonBenét on its cover. He holds up a pageant program. And then, as images of JonBenét's swimsuited sex, lipstick and flirtatious bounces and grinds wash over him, he begins the real introduction:

"Found by her very own father, murdered brutally in the basement of her Boulder, Colorado home. Sexually assaulted before being strangled to death. But while the country watched the pictures of the little six-year-old on their televisions something else was also coming across. A powerful message. This was no ordinary girl who was murdered. This was a pageant Queen. Even at the age of six. Here she is in the first images the country had of the slain little girl, doing apparently what she knew best: performing. Then there was this outfit. JonBenét in her pink cowgirl dress. Working the runway in front of onlookers. This black and white ensemble was next. Complete with matching top hat. Once again little JonBenét performing for points. For fame. But nothing brought forth the underlying story that was starting to disturb America like this still photo of JonBenét. Her hair styled perfectly. The bright red lipstick. All on a six-year-old child. What was this? What was this little girl involved in? And why were her parents doing this to her?"

Geraldo then admonishes the crowd to save their derision for the parents and not to treat the little children badly as they walk out onto the stage. He introduces each by name and comments on how charming each is in succession.

Seven-year-old Taylor.

"That's nice. I like your crown, too."

Eight-year-old Brandy.

"Did your mom teach you that?"

Eight-year-old Tessa.

"Will you stand and show them your pretty dress? That's very lovely."

Eight-year-old Brooke.

"Can you show me that wave again?"

Eight-year-old Tabitha.

"Very nice."

8. Would she be happy? Sad? What would her face be?

Jenny Jones reminded the audience who JonBenét was. "Strangled and sexually asaulted," and then, "she was gorgeous."

Of the mothers accompanying their pageant daughters, one had taken her daughter out of the circuit due to "too much pressure." This one, Donna, said her daughter Deirdre had even competed against JonBenét. But now she was more realistic:

"My biggest fear is pornographic material. Any sleazy photographer can come in to these pageants, they will sell you videos of these pageants for $120. But they own the rights to those videos."

9. What would her personality be?

JonBenét will be forever six years old—even though most of the photos of her are from when she was four and five. And she'll always have on either lipstick or duct-tape wrapped around her little pouty unfittable mouth. Though there's certainly enough photos of her in the public feast being just a regular girl without make-up like something a pedophile wouldn't want to fuck more than any other available child.

It is important to imagine that perhaps JonBenét was in fact molested before she was murdered. And while fiction is always ugly, the question of whether or not JonBenét, in later life, might have reacted negatively to the photos of her made-up like an adult looking to get paid or fucked does inform the photos I keep so carefully.

Could the little girls showing their legs and fannies, barely visible through diaper slits, learn to see their innocent poses and struts and sliding holes as dirty. If I tell them I masturbate to them. If I show them. How I think of those red lips on such a little girl and imagine the brain-numbing pain behind such tight bones. A bright red smudge on the head of my fat cock.

A pedophile who sits quietly as children play at the beach. A pedophile who just watches. And occasionally looks up from his book.

A finger that won't fit in. A cock that would cum only as he rubbed it along with her clumsily small palms and ignored directions. Her red suffocating face turning the lipstick you put all over her thin lips a brand new angry crumbling shade. The way her parents set her up for it wholesale. Delivered the pornography right into my lap for, what, $120.

10. And would she be clean, tomboyish or dirty?

JonBenét is only known to me because she was murdered. And that death is all that lets me see the rape—desperately clung to despite the gross stupidity of Cyril Wecht—and all the bruises and sores and inflammations spread out onto bodies mostly older than her own and not exactly the same.

JonBenét is flat. As in the way a child of her age would be. No tits. Unformed. No fatty cunt and thighs and bags under her eyes and stretch marks. Soft and hard where there's nothing but skin on bone. Tired. Selfish. Bumps where saline will go soon enough. Tape here. Hide those. Exercise this more.

She is even flatter. As in paper. As in pathetic. As in pause and sound bite and used all by your lonesome self again and again.

And worse. I don't know any real facts and details about the little reproductions due to the intense self-serving speculations of even her most minute vital statistics. I know burly voices slick with muddy inference and salty with effeminate concern.

11. When you put a girl in the chair—picture the girl—what do you think when you see a girl like that?

I'm not telling you how hypocritical these detailers are. The same way I didn't give you the phone number to CHILDHELP USA to help you escape. But if that works for you and the various judges and prosecution and investigators who may be interested: Fine. You're welcome. Thank you.

Because I'm not the one to do it. The distant moral stance and thick condomed safety that separates those who talk about it in public and those who worry about it in private all seem to hinge on the very '90s hyper-concern for family and, specifically, the protection of children so that they can remain children for as long as they can. I don't have children—literally and figuratively—and I'm not so misanthropic to believe that all that adults say is somehow smarmy. The same way I don't believe that all good is done for the next generation.

But I'm clear on this. That this, from the *National Enquirer* of October 28, 1997, works best for those who masturbate into condoms thinking about Polly Klaas' pain, her father's mouth and her fully clothed ubiquitous image:

"Hoffmann-Pugh disclosed that JonBenét was terribly embarrassed to be seen naked by anyone including her daughter Ariana. 'If I happened to walk in on her and she had her top off, she'd make a face and quickly fold her arms over her chest and turn away from me,' the housekeeper recalled.

"It was very clear that she was alarmed and didn't want anyone seeing her chest, even though she was completely undeveloped."[6]

12. What else do you think?

In the second photo of Emily, 10, in the photo book *Fast Forward (Growing Up in the Shadow of Hollywood)* by Lauren Greenfield, the little rich girl supermodel poses in the bathroom mirror of a rather ritzy hotel. She's wearing the same hot pink swimsuit that she wore in the previous photo but this time it's dry. Her ass is pushed out, her long brown hair is held back in a sexy flow, she looks as if she's starting to bud breasts. But she's probably just a little too chubby. Her pink lips don't look as pink or thick as they do in the shot of her closing her eyes and dreaming in the pool. She says:

"In the bathroom, there are mirrors everywhere, just like I love. It's kind of fun, because I can spend five hours looking at myself in the mirror and doing my hair and posing for myself. I want to be a model for magazines and videos and TV shows and stuff." [7]

13. What else do you think?

Geraldo gave an interview to *Playboy* for their October '98 issue. He was asked about his having called his CNBC show "the program of record" as regards the JonBenét case and of his "continued fascination" with it.

> Here is a victim immortalized on home video, so we all have a chance
> to relate to that child in the cruelly artificial world created by her

parents. An assistant DA in Denver suggested that the child was abused by the way her parents were exploiting her. So we already pity her and damn the parents even before the murder. That's the setting for the murder story—an exploited child whose parents are the objects of our disdain.[8]

A footnote in *Erotic Innocence: The Culture of Child Molesting* by James R. Kincaid reflects on such common sense:

> [JonBenét] pranced once again for us on the screen and sang and did a mock striptease, and we blamed it all on vulgar parents, greed or 'The South'. Of course, no one has been able to invent a connection between the pageants and the grisly murder that gave rise to the publicity, but so what? [9]

There are laws that exist now that could define child pornography (and mere possession is a felony) as an action, as a document, rather than just a record of children somehow engaged in direct and clear sexual abuse. Personal context is at issue. According to Anne Higonnet in her book *Pictures of Innocence: The History and Crisis of Ideal Childhood:*

> If someone, anyone, could see sexuality of any sort in any image of a child, that image might be judged pornographic and its maker, distributor, or possessor could face $100,000 in fines and 15 years in jail.[10]

14. That's what the target is: she has a skirt on but no pants?

A primary use for child pornography is to lower children's inhibitions. To show them shots of others doing what you want them to do.

Put on this lipstick, dear. Just like mommy does. Just like little JonBenét.

The Examiner of April 22, 1997:

> Even before she was killed, bootlegged pictures of JonBenét and the innocent child's beauty pageant videos were a huge hit with sick pedophiles who spend hours glued to x-rated kiddie porn on the Internet, say insiders.

The Star of April 29, 1997 (included under their JONBENÉT DAD LINKED TO KIDDIE PORN exposé):

> Girls who appear as young as 10 or 12 engaging in sexual acts—including oral sex—with each other and with men.
> Pre-teen girls, bound and gagged, being whipped and tortured.
> A girl of no more than 12 or 13 bound from her head to her hips

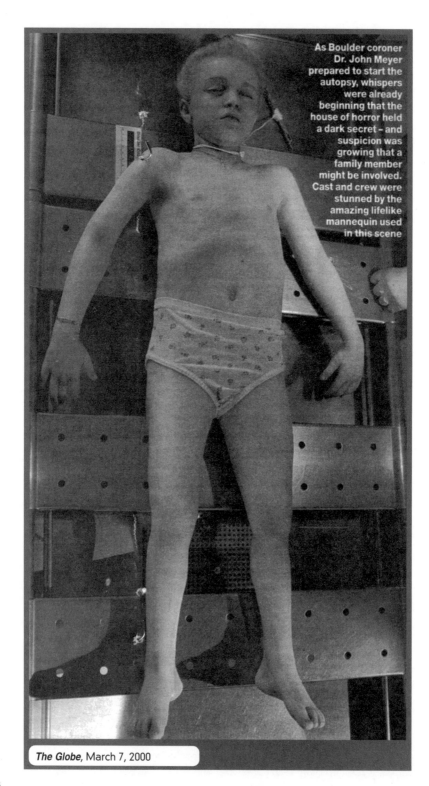

As Boulder coroner Dr. John Meyer prepared to start the autopsy, whispers were already beginning that the house of horror held a dark secret – and suspicion was growing that a family member might be involved. Cast and crew were stunned by the amazing lifelike mannequin used in this scene

The Globe, March 7, 2000

in a leather bridle, and hung by a chain. In the full-color photo, she is made to appear dead." [11]

15. What are you wanting to do with her and to her?

A six-year-old's life-sized JonBenét doll was created and an eight-year-old actress was hired for use in quick careful scenes for the TV movie version of the book, *Perfect Murder, Perfect Town.*

The Globe of March 7, 2000 published 28 stills from the movie set, all focused on the murdered child's sexy stand-ins. The eight-year-old in bright sliding lipstick, smiles and tight pageant legs and ass:

"Dyanne struts her stuff in a costume like JonBenét's. Movie insiders said she was a natural."

And

"Dyanne portrays JonBenét's sweet innocence before tragedy struck."

While the mannequin is seen used in the crime scenes, autopsy (*sans habilement* save the comfortably fit pink and white kidling panties) and funeral casket. The centerfold doll—with her tiny pale grey bug nipples and tiny vaginal bloodstain in the exact correct places; with the garrot still around her baby throat and her eyes closed and her always made-up photo smile face now painted and molded to mimic the blood settling and bruising dead skin—is all advertisement, verisimilitude, cheap visual aid, proxy KP and, mainly, more and better detail.

"In this scene, it's hard to believe the tyke's body is actually a mannequin."

And

"Director Schiller had access to the real crime scene and autopsy information to recreate the events while still preserving secret portions of the investigation."

Compare—as *The Globe* designed—the doll in her casket with the inset of the crowned face her mother kept.

Compare it to the December 11, 1995 cover story of *Time* that included another dead six-year-old in her child's clean white casket, also crowned (this time in white flowers), also in white lace and useless fluffy stuffed toys. And another journalist that crawled onto the suburban squirrels' wheel that churns every single dead child into another precious keepsake doll, a fairy-princess, an innocent, a magic memory of sexy untouchable adult-handled fucked sadness:

"Elisa Izquierdo liked to dance, which is almost too perfect. Fairy tales, especially those featuring princesses, often include dancing, although perhaps not Elisa's favorite merengue. Fairy-tale princesses are born humble. Elisa fit that bill: she was conceived in a homeless shelter in the Fort Greene section of

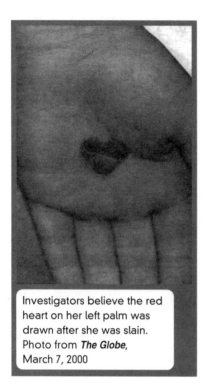

Investigators believe the red heart on her left palm was drawn after she was slain. Photo from *The Globe*, March 7, 2000

Brooklyn and born addicted to crack. That Elisa nevertheless had a special, enchanted aura is something the whole city of New York now knows."

And

"Fairy-tale princesses, however, are not bludgeoned to death by their mothers. They are not violated with a toothbrush and a hairbrush, and the neighbors do not hear them moaning and pleading at night."

Little KP dolls with opened European faces remain faceless due to the lack of complete information. You can hope that, today, it's a father's cock in its face or a moneyed rapist with a motel account and a crack connection but until the news reports—see those of dead KP lolitot Thea Pumbroek especially—all you really have is your taste and the barest understandings of instinct over desire, aesthetics over humanity, erotica over pornography.

There are idiot mothers who'll confuse the movie stills into actual crime scene records who are even more desperate than the tired perverts who frustrate themselves over the differences between what they had in the '70s, what they get on their computers and what they own now as closest. There are close-ups of the doll. There are details of the crime in captions. The little tart got painted with promise and purity. The little doll got stripped and plastered with humanity and vulnerability and the warm longing for home. The dirty pictures twist into news and mystery and sustained grinding fucking ideas all muddied in safe supermarket ennui.

Fine.

Better.

I know it's mostly all lies. But then I don't really give a fuck about who killed little JonBenét. Yet. Right now.

Questions 1-15 are from *Meat*, edited by Boyd McDonald (Gay Sunshine Press, San Francisco,1981). Questions 1-15 are from *The Murder of Childhood* by Ray Wyre and Tim Tate (Penguin Books, London, 1995).

NOTES

1. Brief and Appendix for Peter Sotos, appeal to Supreme Court of Illinois.
2. *AVN*, World Pornography Conference Issue, October 1998.
3. *Who Killed Polly?*, Frank Spiering, Monterey Press, California, 1995.
4. *Polly Klaas: The Murder of America's Child*, Barry Bortnick, Pinnacle, New York, 1995.
5. "It's Like Playing Dress-Up," Dawn German, *Newsweek*, January 20, 1997.
6. "JonBenét's Dream Reveals New Evidence of Sex Abuse," Reginald Fitz & Don Gentile, *National Enquirer*, October 28, 1997.
7. *Fast Forward: Growing Up in the Shadow of Hollywood*, Lauren Greenfield, Knopf/Melcher Media, New York, 1997.
8. The Playboy Interview, Gregory P. Fagan, *Playboy*, October, 1998.
9. *Erotic Innocence: The Culture of Child Molesting*, James R. Kincaid, Duke University Press, Durham & London, 1998.
10. *Pictures of Innocence: The History and Crisis of Ideal Childhood*, Anne Higonnet, Thames & Hudson, London, 1998.
11. "JonBenét Dad Linked to Kiddie Porn Scandal," Richard Gooding, *The Star*, April 29, 1997.

⚡ ⚡ ⚡

Peter Sotos is the author of *Index* (Creation Books), *Special* (Rude Shape Books), *Tick* (Creation Books), *Lazy* (Creation Books), *Playground Sex* (Silling) and *Total Abuse* (Goad to Hell). Mr. Sotos does not wish to have contact with the public at large.

The Child Pornography Prevention Act of 1995

> Pedophilia is the new evil empire of the domestic
> imagination: now that communism has been
> defanged, it seems to occupy a similar metaphys-
> ical status as the evil of all evils, with similar anxiety
> about security from infiltration, the similar under-
> the-bed fear that "they" walk among us unde-
> tected—fears that are not entirely groundless, but
> not entirely rational either.
>
> **Laura Kipnis, *Bound and Gagged***

The Child Pornography Prevention Act of 1995, sponsored by Senators
Orrin Hatch and Dianne Feinstein, added a corrective amendment to earlier bills regarding child pornography, now making it illegal to produce an
image, by computer, pen, airbrush or otherwise, which simply appears to
be child pornography. Fearing "morphed" images and the like, the law was
passed, making it a crime to depict or "convey the impression" that anyone
under the age of 18 is "engaging in sexually explicit conduct." In the following excerpt from the Congressional Record, voters of the bill are promised that Coppertone will not be prosecuted for its depiction of a young girl
flashing her bare buttocks, since the ad is considered "innocuous." The
Child Pornography Prevention Act of 1995 fully depends on prosecutors to
determine what is innocuous and what crosses that vague line where
artists and parents have suddenly become perverts, and have committed
thought crimes deserving of lengthy jail sentences.

  As of this writing, kiddie porn hysteria is responsible for the arrest of
mothers who committed the crime of snapping photographs of their children playing in the bathtub, and getting the pictures developed at the local
drug store where minimum wage employees have become monitors of forbidden perversion for the FBI. The Vatican Library has the largest collection
of pornographic material in the world, and the FBI itself has become the
most prolific provider of child pornography on the internet, for the apparent
justification that it can track down and arrest those attracted by their kiddie
porn websites. How blurry does that line become, from perversion entrapment to perversion, period?

—Adam Parfrey

104th CONGRESS, 1st Session, S. 1237
IN THE SENATE OF THE UNITED STATES, September 13, 1995

A BILL

To amend certain provisions of law relating to child pornography, and for other purposes.

Be it enacted by the Senate and House of Representatives of the United States of America in Congress assembled,

SECTION 1. SHORT TITLE.

This Act may be cited as the Child Pornography Prevention Act of 1995.

(8) "Child pornography" means any visual depiction, including any photograph, film, video, picture, drawing, or computer or computer-generated image or picture, whether made or produced by electronic, mechanical, or other means, of sexually explicit conduct, where—

(A) the production of such visual depiction involves the use of a minor engaging in sexually explicit conduct;

(B) such visual depiction is, or appears to be, of a minor engaging in sexually explicit conduct; or

(C) such visual depiction is advertised, promoted, presented, described, or distributed in such a manner that conveys the impression that the material is or contains a visual depiction of a minor engaging in sexually explicit conduct.

CHILD PORNOGRAPHY PREVENTION ACT OF 1995

COMPUTER-GENERATED CHILD PORNOGRAPHY POSES THE SAME THREAT TO THE WELL-BEING OF CHILDREN AS PHOTOGRAPHIC CHILD PORNOGRAPHY

The ability of computer animation to create realistic-appearing images and effects is, of course, well known to the tens of millions of moviegoers who have seen such recent hit films as *Jurassic Park*, *Twister*, and *Independence Day*. New and increasingly less complex and expensive photographic and computer imaging technologies make it possible for individuals to produce on home computers visual depictions of children engaging in sexually explicit conduct that are virtually indistinguishable from unretouched photographic images of actual children engaging in sexually explicit conduct—material that is outside the scope of current federal law. As Deputy Assistant Attorney General Di Gregory testified:

Pedophiles have created and used altered or doctored images for a long time. In the past these images have run the gamut from magazine cutouts crudely assembled with photographs of children from the pedophile's neighborhood, to artfully rendered collages which have been painstakingly assembled and then rephotographed so that only careful inspection reveals the image as false. But what has always been the case in the past—that the images were readily revealed as false with careful inspection—may no longer be true, as image-altering software and computer hardware are used to create altered images which appear all too real of children engaging in sexual activity. Soon it will not be necessary to actually molest children to produce child pornography which exploits and degrades them—and which can be used to further actual abuse. All that will be necessary will be an inexpensive computer, readily available software, and a photograph of a neighbor's child shot while the child walked to school or waited for the bus.

Computers can be used to alter perfectly innocent pictures of children, taken from books, magazines, catalogs, or videos, to create visual depictions of those children engaging in any imaginable form of sexual conduct. A child pornographer in Canada was convicted of copying innocuous pictures of children from books and catalogs onto a computer, then using the computer to alter the images to remove the childrens' clothing and arrange the children into sexual positions involving children, adults and even animals.

Computer-imaging technology permits creation of pornographic depictions designed to satisfy the preferences of individual sexual predators. As Dr. Cline testified at the June 4, 1996 hearing, most pedophiles and child molesters have special preferences with respect to child pornography, in terms of age, physical appearance and sexual acts or poses of depicted minors. The ability to alter or "morph" images via computer to produce any desired child pornographic depiction enables pedophiles and pornographers to create "custom-tailored" pornography which will heighten the material's effect on the viewer and thus increase the threat this material poses to children. A child molester or pedophile can create, alter or modify a perfectly innocuous image or picture of a child he finds sexually attractive or desirable and produce any manner and number of pornographic depictions featuring that child, which he can use to stimulate his own sexual appetite for that particular child, with potentially tragic consequences for the child. The computer-produced depictions could be shown to the child in an effort to seduce or blackmail the child into submitting to sexual abuse or exploitation, or to other children who know the depicted child in order to seduce them. Dr. Cline testified that seeing such a computer-created depiction would be extremely traumatic for the depicted child.

Computors can also be used to alter sexually explicit photographs, films and videos in such a way as to make it virtually impossible for prosecutors to identify individuals, or to prove that the offending material was produced using children. Technology may have made it possible for criminals to escape responsibility for violating the existing law, even when the pictures are of real minor children being sexually abused or exploited. The day will soon arise, if not here already, that our inability to distinguish the real from the apparent child pornography will raise a reasonable doubt that a picture is really of a real child being molested and exploited. If the government must continue to prove beyond a reasonable doubt that mailed photos, smuggled magazines or videos, traded pictures, and computer images being transmitted on the Internet, are indeed actual depictions of an actual minor engaging the sex portrayed, then there could be a built-in reasonable doubt argument in every child exploitation/pornography prosecution.

In addition to our expectation that this material (computer-generated child pornography) will pose serious problems in the future, we have already been confronted with cases in which child pornographers attempted to use the gap in existing law as a legal defense. For example, in the first-ever federal trial involving charges of importation of child pornography by computer, United States v. Kimbrough, 69 F.3d 723 (5th Cir. 1995), the defendant offered evidence that currently available computer programs could be used to alter a photograph of an adult so that it looked like a photograph of a child. From that evidence, the defense then argued that the Government had the burden of proving that each item of alleged child pornography did, in fact, depict an actual minor rather than an adult made to look like one, and that the defendant should be acquitted if the government did not meet that burden.

In that case, the defense was overcome through a carefully executed cross-examination and production, in court, of some of the original magazines from which the computer-generated images were scanned. But it is also true that in 1993, when the Kimbrough case was tried, the technology was

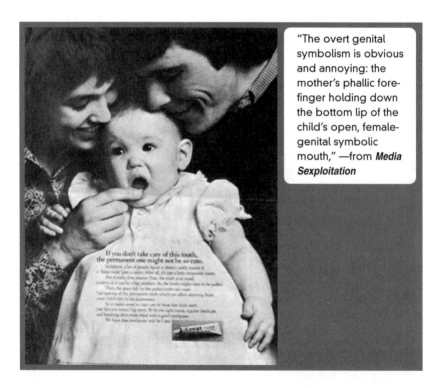

"The overt genital symbolism is obvious and annoying: the mother's phallic fore-finger holding down the bottom lip of the child's open, female-genital symbolic mouth," —from *Media Sexploitation*

still at an early stage of development and as such, the defense was not as potent as it might become in the future. Moreover, magazine archives will be of less value to prosecutors since child pornography produced today will no longer predate the availability of graphic imaging software. Thus, the Government will no longer be able to produce the original child pornography magazine against which a comparison may be made.

Thus the enforcement of existing laws against the sexual exploitation of children with respect to the production, distribution or possession of child pornography requires Federal law to be updated to keep pace with the technology of pornography.

Some may argue that because the computerized production of child pornography does not directly involve, or law enforcement officials may not be able to prove the use of, actual children engaging in sexually explicit conduct, such material somehow does not harm or threaten our children, and we should therefore turn a blind legal eye to its existence. This view ignores the reality of child sexual abuse and exploitation, and the critical role child pornography plays in such criminal conduct.

As discussed above, a major part of the threat to children posed by child pornography is its effect on the viewers of such material, including child molesters or pedophiles who use such material to stimulate or whet their own sexual appetites. To such sexual predators, the effect is the same whether the child pornography consists of photographic depictions of actual children or visual depictions produced wholly or in part by computer. To such a viewer of child pornographic images the difference is irrelevant because they are perceived as minors by the psyche.

As shown by the testimony received at the Committee's June 4, 1996, hearing from Deputy Assistant Attorney General Di Gregory, Mrs. Jepsen, Dr. Cline, and Mr. Taylor, with respect to child sexual abuse and exploitation, the danger to actual children who are seduced and molested with the aid of child sex pictures is as great when the "child pornographer" or child molester uses visual depictions of child sexual activity produced wholly or in part by electronic, mechanical or other means, including by computer, as when the material consists of unretouched photographic images of actual children engaging in sexually explicit conduct.

S. 1237 will close this computer-generated loophole in Federal child exploitation laws and give our law enforcement authorities the tools they need to protect our children

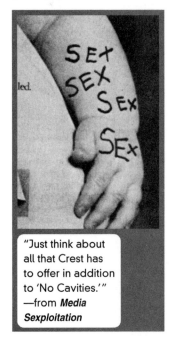

"Just think about all that Crest has to offer in addition to 'No Cavities.'"
—from *Media Sexploitation*

by stemming the increasing flow of high-tech child pornography. It would establish, for the first time, a Federal statutory definition of child pornography. Any visual depiction of sexually explicit conduct, however produced, would be classified as "child pornography" if: (a) its production involved the use of a minor engaging in sexually explicit conduct, or; (b) it depicts, or appears to depict, a minor engaging in sexually explicit conduct, or; (c) it is promoted or advertised as depicting a minor engaging in sexually explicit conduct. Under S. 1237, computer-generated child pornographic images, which in real life are increasingly indistinguishable in the eyes of viewers from unretouched photographs of actual children engaging in sexually explicit conduct, and can result in many of the same types of harm to children and society, would now also be indistinguishable in the eyes of the law from pornographic material produced using actual children.

Pornographic depictions which appear to be those of children engaging in sexually explicit conduct, including computer-generated images, deserve no first amendment protection because the State's compelling interest in protecting children is directly advanced by prohibiting the possession or distribution of such material, for many of the same reasons applicable to the child pornographic material at issue in Ferber. In that case, the Court dispensed with the obscenity test of Miller v. California, 413 U.S. 15 (1973), and upheld a State law banning the production and promotion of any picture of a child engaging in sexual conduct or lewd exhibition of the genitals. The Court held that child pornography is not entitled to first amendment protection, and that "the States are entitled to greater leeway in the regulation of pornographic depictions of children" for the following reasons:

First. [A] state's interest in "safeguarding the physical and psychological well-being of a minor" is "compelling". The prevention of sexual exploitation and abuse of children constitutes a governmental objective of surpassing importance.

Second. The distribution of photographs and films depicting sexual activity is intrinsically related to the sexual abuse of children in at least two ways. First, the materials are a permanent record of the children's participation and the harm to the child is exacerbated by their circulation. Second, the distribution network for child pornography must be closed if the production of material which requires the sexual exploitation of children is to be effectively controlled. Indeed. It is difficult, if not impossible, to halt the exploitation of children by pursuing only those who produce the photographs and movies. The most expeditious if not the only practical method of law enforcement may be to dry up the market for this material by imposing severe criminal penalties on persons selling, advertising, or otherwise promoting the product.

Third. The advertising and selling of child pornography provide an economic motive for and are thus an integral part of the production of such materials.

Fourth. The value of permitting live performances and photographic reproductions of children engaged in lewd sexual conduct is exceedingly modest, if not *de minimis*.

Fifth. Recognizing and classifying child pornography as a category of material outside the protection of the First Amendment is not incompatible with our earlier decisions. "The question whether speech is, or is not, protected by the First Amendment often depends on the content of the speech." New York v. Ferber, supra, at 756-764.

Prohibiting the possession of computer-generated child pornography will prevent pedophiles from using these images to seduce children into sexual activity, and will prevent sex crimes against children. Child pornography is not only "crime scene photos" of child sexual abuse and exploitation, but also a criminal tool for such abuse and exploitation. It is a tool of incitement for pedophiles and child molesters, and a tool of seduction for child victims. Its relationship and involvement with physical criminal conduct directed at children is inseparable. As the Court quoted a New York lawmaker in Ferber, at 761, "It is irrelevant to the child (who has been abused) whether or not the material has a literary, artistic, political or social value." It is equally irrelevant to a molested child shown child pornographic material to seduce or entice him into engaging in sexual activity, or to persuade or blackmail the child into recruiting other child victims, or into remaining silent about the abuse, whether the material was produced by camera or computer, or a combination of the two. It is also irrelevant to the child molester or pedophile who uses depictions of children engaging in sexually explicit conduct to stimulate or whet his own sexual appetites. The molester or pedophile may not even know the difference, nor would he care. Computer-generated images which appear to depict minors engaging in sexually explicit conduct are just as dangerous to the well-being of our children as material produced using actual children.

The conduct depicted in the material made criminal under this bill is a lewd depiction or representation of a child engaging in sexually explicit conduct. There is no difference between the content of photographs or films depicting such conduct produced using actual children and the content of the computer-generated depictions made contraband under this bill. Constitutional immunity is not extended to materials that are "used as an integral part of conduct in violation of a valid criminal statute." Id., at 762. This legislation is aimed at child pornographic material that is, and will continue to be, used to incite pedophiles to molest real children, to seduce real children into being molested, and to convince real children into making more child pornography. Like material produced using actual children engaging in sexually explicit conduct, pornographic images of persons who appear to be minors, depictions indistinguishable from photographs of real children but which are produced by computer, bear heavily on the welfare of the next generation of children who will be sexually abused and exploited by the harmful effects that any form of child pornography has on pedophile molesters and their child victims. It is therefore permissible to consider computer-generated pornographic materials which appear to be depictions of actual minors engaging in sexually explicit conduct as without the protection of the First Amendment.

The State's compelling interest in protecting children is also advanced by prohibiting the possession or distribution of computer-generated child pornography because the enforcement of child pornography and child sexual exploitation laws will be severely hampered if the "distribution network for child pornography" is flooded with computer-generated material. As the technology of computer-imaging progresses, it will become increasingly difficult, if not impossible, to distinguish computer-generated from photographic depictions of child sexual activity. It will therefore become almost impossible for the Government to meet its burden of proving that a pornographic image is of a real child. Statutes prohibiting the possession of child pornography produced using actual children would be rendered unenforceable and pedophiles who possess pornographic depictions of actual children will go free from punishment. The Government's inability to detect or prove the use of real children in the production of child pornography, and thus the reduced risk of punishment for such criminal conduct, could have the effect of increasing the sexually abusive and exploitative use of children to produce child pornography.

C. S. 1237 IS NOT UNCONSTITUTIONALLY OVERBROAD.

To ensure that the statute, and in particular the classification of a visual depiction which "appears to be" of a minor engaging in sexually explicit conduct as child pornography, is not unconstitutionally overbroad, S. 1237 does not change or expand the existing statutory definition (at 18 U.S.C. 2256 (2)) of the term "sexually explicit conduct." This definition, including the use of the term "lascivious," has been judicially reviewed and upheld. United States v. Knox, 32 F.3d 733 (3rd Cir. 1994); cert denied, 115 S. Ct. 897 (1995); United States v. Wiegand, 812 F.2d 1239, 1243 (9th Cir.); cert denied, 484 U.S. 856 (1987). See also, United States v. X-Citement Video, Inc., 982 F.2d 1285 (9th Cir. 1992); 115 S. Ct. 464, 472 (1995). S. 1237 does not, and is not intended to, criminalize or prohibit any innocuous depiction of a minor—photograph, film, video, or computer image—however that depiction is produced. Using two oft-cited examples, Coppertone suntan lotion advertisements featuring a young girl in a bathing suit are not now, and will not become under S.1237, child pornography; neither would the proverbial parental picture of a child in the bathtub or lying on a bearskin rug.

S. 1237's prohibition against a visual depiction which "appears to be" of a minor engaging in sexually explicit conduct applies to the same type of photographic images already prohibited, but which does not require the use of an actual minor in its production. Under this bill, the prohibition against child pornography is extended from photographic depictions of actual minors engaging in sexually explicit conduct to the identical type of depiction, one which is virtually indistinguishable from the banned photographic depiction, which can and is now being produced using technology which was not contemplated or in existence when current Federal child sexual exploitation and child pornography laws were adopted. A bill that does not criminalize an intolerable range of constitutionally protected conduct or speech is not unconstitutionally overbroad. Osborne v. Ohio, 495 U.S. 103 (1990).

It has been suggested, including by Prof. Frederick Schauer in his June 4, 1996 written testimony, that language in the Ferber decision that "the distribution of descriptions or other depictions of sexual conduct, not otherwise obscene, which do not involve live performance or photographic or other visual reproduction of live performances, retain First Amendment protection" (supra at 764-65) suggests that Congress cannot prohibit visual depictions which "appear to be" of minors engaging in sexually explicit conduct but were produced without using actual children. The Committee disagrees. At the time of Ferber, in 1982, the technology to produce visual depictions of child sexual activity indistinguishable from unretouched photographs of actual children engaging in "live performances" did not exist. Further, the cited language from the Ferber decision, on its face, distinguishes between photographic reproductions of live performances of sexual conduct and other visual depictions of such conduct, while making it clear that both are outside the protection of the First Amendment. As the Committee heard from witnesses before it and as it has found, the effect on children exposed to computer-generated child pornographic material, and on child molesters and pedophiles who create and use such material, is the same as that from visually indistinguishable photographic depictions of actual children engaging in such conduct. Computer-generated child pornographic material therefore poses a threat to the well-being of children comparable to that posed by photographic child pornography. The Government therefore has an interest in prohibiting computer-generated child pornographic depictions equally compelling as its interest in prohibiting child pornography produced using actual children.

"Penis Swastika" by Trevor Brown

THE LATE, GREAT AESTHETIC TABOOS

Ghazi Barakat

It is now possible for the U.S. government to send an artist to prison for a painting or drawing that portrays a person under 18 years of age in a sexual manner. In Germany, and even in Canada, a person can be sentenced for using a swastika if it is deemed pro-Nazi rather than used in the approved historic or artistic context. The decision regarding artistic merit is usually left to an unqualified, ignorant and self-righteous judge or jury; the lack of clarity surrounding these laws is a serious infringement on freedom of expression. The "holy" First Amendment has become a constitutional joke, and for every battle won in its honor, many losses go unheard of. Our society is more concerned with protecting feelings and wealthy corporate hypocrites than protecting the right for artists to depict subjects of their choice (even if the context in which they use them is hard to swallow).

It's all a matter of context. You can catch Hitler on the History cable channel daily. Pre-pubescent girls bearing naked bee-sting tits are used to sell Calvin Klein products in magazines available on every newsstand in the country.

Total disapproval is demanded by the media concerning neo-Nazism, terrorism, hate crimes and, particularly, the sexual abuse of little children. But, the media is perfectly willing to sensationalize and exploit these subjects—see JonBenét Ramsey, Columbine massacre, Oklahoma City Bombing and the Unabomber. And an artist depicting these recurring themes could be subject to prison.

At first glance, it seems an increasing tolerance for "obscene" or "offensive" art has come about the last two decades. Larry Flynt was glamorized in a major Hollywood picture, and in an obscenity trial of the rap group 2 Live Crew, the jury actually asked the judge if they could laugh when hearing the censored lyrics. Liberal movements, such as gay rights, have prevailed. Sophisticated pornography on fetishes and subversive themes in general have become more available to the public, largely due to the advent of the Internet. It appears that Western society has more freedom of expression then ever before.

Too bad this idea is a myth. The prevailing political correctness has evolved into a new kind of Puritanism. The same people who fight for the rights of gays are the first to strike out against something that does not fit their agenda.

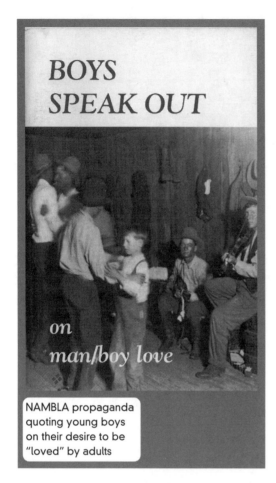

NAMBLA propaganda quoting young boys on their desire to be "loved" by adults

In *Chicken Hawk*, a documentary film on North American Man-Boy Love Association, many gays adamantly spoke out against NAMBLA even though the only apparent difference in their movements was a small age difference as to whom they want to suck and fuck.

Taboos of pedophilia and the swastika have come in handy to generate oppressive hysteria. Even among the professed open-minded, any attempt to suspend judgment about these subjects is interpreted as tacit approval.

In the past century many artists have dedicated themselves to abolishing sexual, sociological and religious taboos. But once these artists become an

established part of our economy and culture, their political bravado loses all its effect, and its message must be asserted again and again.

The work of Stuart Mead, Trevor Brown, Beth Love and the recently deceased Blalla W. Hallmann are examples of the Sisyphus-like struggle against political and sexual taboos. Stuart Mead's work contains a definite fetishistic character, especially towards little girls. Mead says that his sexuality is stuck in a pre-adolescent stage due to severe physical handicaps that forced him to develop his own sexual universe. Spectators viewing Mead's work may very well feel like a Peeping Tom spying through a keyhole. Viewers (voyeurs) get sucked into a dream-world, where pre-adolescent creatures engage in explicit sexual acts. Mead's phantasmagoric erotic universe com-

Henri Darger morphs advertising into illegal representations of children, as interpreted by The Child Pornography Prevention Act of 1995

bines hare-brained sexual fantasies in a humorous, surreal manner. An immense catalogue of perversions, Mead's work is in some ways reminiscent

Detail from "Don't worry, we Blengins will help you escape" by Henri Darger

of de Sade's *120 Days of Sodom*. Astonishingly, Mead's paintings and drawings share obsessions with outsider artist Henri Darger, whose "realms of the unreal," were only discovered after his death, and who—like Mead—attaches penises to underage girls' genitals. Unlike de Sade and Darger, Mead is not particularly keen on cruelty, and seems more inclined to explore a pedophilic inclination, which has a long personal and artistic history.

Oedipal and filicidal archetypes permeate the concept of the family itself with incestuous and homicidal temptations; taboos are inducted to prevent desires that already exist. Mythological

Disemboweld children find themselves menaced by evil adults in a Henri Darger painting

representations of childlike beauty throughout history often carry a suggestively erotic character. The thin line between parental affection and
sexual abuse becomes as fragile as the hymen. Symbols of innocence and
virginity are destroyed whenever this line is crossed. These tragic psychodramas occur with the best of families. Would it be in poor taste to
ask "why not?" when dealing with these particular subjects? Must we content ourselves with merely asking "why?"

Stu Mead's 'zine

Born in 1955 and raised in Waterloo, Iowa, Stuart Mead was stricken with arthrogryposis, a prenatal condition comparable to polio affecting joints and muscles. Stuart's disease inflicted on him a feeling of inferiority. Moving to England with his folks for a short time in the mid-'70s, Stuart returned to Iowa City in 1977 to live on his own. In 1983, Mead started his schooling at the Minneapolis College of Art and Design, from which he graduated in 1987. After graduating he met Frank Gaard, founder of the graphical fanzine *Art Police* (1974–1994), who is still an influential figure and teacher in the Minneapolis art scene. Gaard's aesthetic background is rooted in anti-mainstream Chicago imagists (better known as Hairy Who), a group that included or were inspired by the remarkably subversive artists Jim Nutt and Peter Saul. Gaard encouraged Mead, who

Painting by Stu Mead

Volcanic Eruptions Presents **Crispin Hellion Glover's**

What is it?

Being the
adventures
of a young man
whose principle
interests
are snails, salt,
a pipe,
and
how to get home.
As tormented by an
hubristic, racist inner
psyche.

With

Crispin Glover

Steve Stewart

Adam Parfrey

and the voice
of
Fairuza Balk

Sets by
David Brothers

Cinematography by
Wyatt Troll

Produced by
Crispin Glover
Matt Devlen
Ryan Page
Michael Pallagi

Written and
Directed by
Crispin
Hellion
Glover

Part one of a trilogy.

Image ©2002 Volcanic Eruptions

WHAT

IS

IT

?

"Ihr schönster Tag" (Her Most Beautiful Day) by Blalla W. Hallmann

"Onkel Wolf zaubert" (Uncle Adi Waves His Magic Wand) by Blalla W. Hallmann

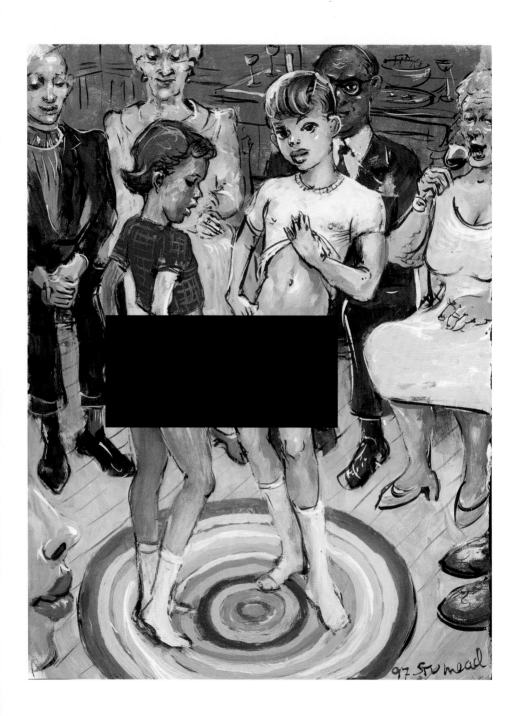

Painting by Stu Mead

Painting by Stu Mead

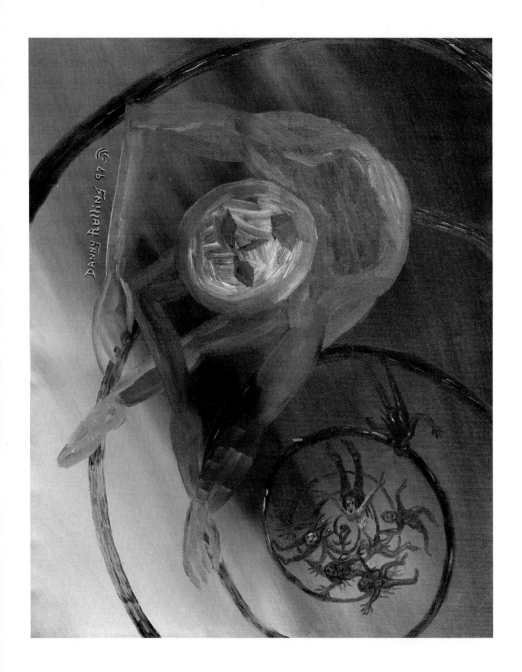

"Fait Accompli" by Danny Rolling

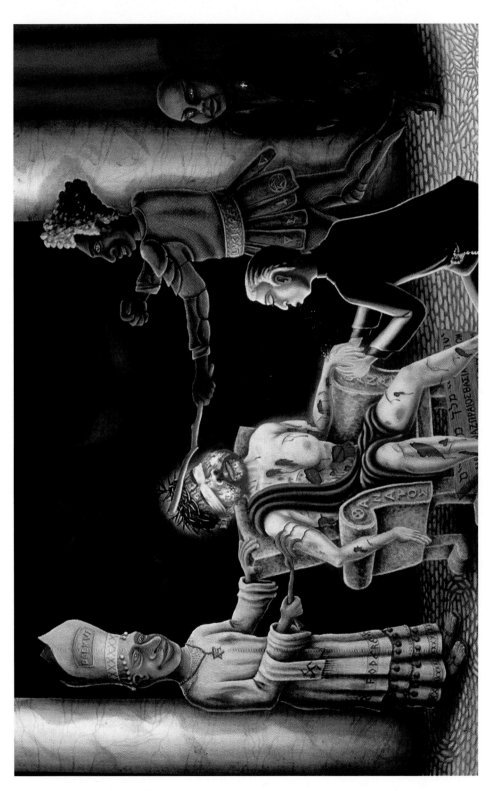

Painting by Norbert Kox

"Masquerade" by Norbert Kox

"Little Red Riding Hood" by Stu Mead

was a tame art student, to visit a whole new approach to his work. In 1991 Gaard and Mead created *Man Bag*, a xeroxed 'zine exclusively interested in sex. *Man Bag* has appeared irregularly to this day, allowing Mead to encounter and release his sexual fantasies about little girls. Through *Man Bag* and some of the readers' perverse letters, Mead confronted consciously and analytically what we might call "the ugliness of pedophilia."

Bestiality, incest, sado-masochism, coprophagia, defecation, urination, child lesbianism, incestuous lesbianism, hermaphrodity, homosexuality, fellatio, sodomy and all forms of blasphemy have been integrated and become standards of Mead's bizarre erotic world. Not only has Mead created an outlet to his perverted sexual fantasies, but he's managed to show his art in a number of galleries in the U.S. and Europe.

In many ways Mead's work has become increasingly offensive in recent years, the sort only found in dark corners of porn stores. In commercial pornography, strict laws forbid the crossbreeding of sexual fetishes. For example, S & M and hardcore cannot be mixed. The perverse laws launched

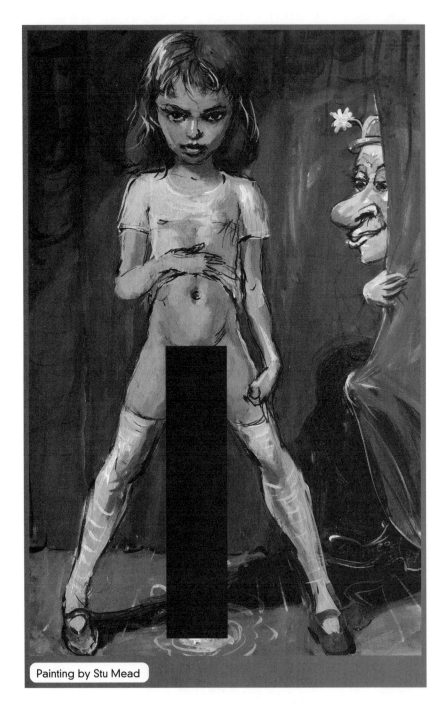

Painting by Stu Mead

against the perverted have not stopped Stu Mead's thematic output. In fact, slides of his work were once handed over to the police by a photo development store in Minneapolis. A few weeks later, a police officer stopped by Mead's house to inform him that what he was drawing was legal, but that the matter was being looked into by cops specializing in vice and child abuse. Mead was forced to hire a lawyer, who discovered the cops were merely harassing him due to the subject matter of his work.

Transporting the paintings of Mead and Blalla Hallmann across U.S. borders received quite a bit of attention from U.S. Customs agents. One officer, offended by a Mead painting of a little girl urinating and defecating beside a

Painting by Beth Love

"Der Pop-star" by Blalla W. Hallmann

fountain, cried out, "Look! There is a child urinating!" to which his fellow officers responded, "This is a just a drawing."

The fantastic and unrealistic nature of Stu Mead's art probably makes it possible for galleries and publishers to exhibit and reproduce his work, though its themes encounter the outer limits of legality. Mead's Freudian approach to his own sexuality is very close to Surrealism and he often refers to the paintings and drawings of Hans Bellmer and Balthus as inspiring his own work. Bellmer and Balthus have both made no secret of their attraction towards young, female objects of desire.

Trevor Brown's obsession for swastikas and kids are evident in his overt art. Because they're so well-drawn, they're often derided as being mere "illustration," but their artistic value is remarkably evident. His books, *Evil* and *Alphabet*, though available in the United States in very small numbers, are banned outright in his home country, Japan.

The work of Beth Love of New Mexico expands on an "innocent" Victorian aesthetic by integrating sick-minded contemporary horror beneath her primary subjects, and within the background. The stowing away of such dread renders the id-forms all the more astonishing.

Blalla W. Hallmann (1941–1997) was born in Quirl, Silesia, a territory annexed by the allies after WWII. Beginning his career as a naïve painter in the late '50s, Blalla was thrown out of the U.S. as *persona non grata* in the late '60s due to one episode of drug psychosis while teaching art at the California State University at San Francisco. His disappointment with capitalism and Western culture notably blossomed after being deported.

Proclaiming himself "the ambassador of hate," Blalla said that "humans are bloodbags full of shit." Sickened by overpopulation as a method for capitalism to increase its polluting riches, Blalla promoted the curtailment of reproduction: "Chop off the family tree, as the whole world is going down the drain."

Blalla's hatred towards the Third Reich, the Vatican, and the United States doesn't bother to differentiate between the three. In his paintings, the cross and swastika are replaced by the dollar sign, money being the new God that makes the world go 'round. A museum exhibition of Blalla Hallman's work in Bavaria was shut down because a painting of Helmut Kohl showed him engaging in explicit sexual conduct. To "celebrate" German reunification in 1990, Blalla painted his "Black Series," ten blasphemous artworks about Hitler in order to kill the "inner Fascist" in oneself. (Two of the "Black Series" are reproduced in *Apocalypse Culture II's* color section.)

Frequently comparing religious catechism and education with child abuse, Blalla believed that history, folklore and historic legacy and Christianity are lies manufactured to perpetuate controlling bullshit.

Blalla despised the art world, whose stars, Andy Warhol, Jeff Koons, Gerhard Richter, Sigmar Polke and Josef Beuys were seen as brown-nosing valets to the rich. Remarking that every painting these guys were selling was money he wasn't making, Blalla believed that the aforementioned artists were stealing from him. Soured by gallery and museum exhibitions, Blalla insisted that all contributors should sign their paintings with the phrase, "I lied!"

Asked why there was so much shit in his work, Blalla replied, "Because everything is shit . . . It's gonna take a while until they're going to advertise a perfume with a beautiful model posing next to a turd."

Ghazi Barakat contributes to erotic and subversive publications in France, Germany, Switzerland and the United States, and curates the work of Stu Mead and other artists. Contact Ghazi through Feral House.

Contact **Stu Mead** of St. Paul, Minnesota and **Beth Love** of Albuquerque, New Mexico through Feral House.

Matthias Reichelt is currently working on a catalogue describing the complete works of the late **Blalla Hallmann** (1941–1997). A remarkable small black book of Hallmann's work, *Heim, Mir Reicht's*, can be purchased from Mr. Reichelt, who can be reached by email: m.reichelt@cityweb.de

Trevor Brown's website can be accessed at <www.pileup.com/babyart/>

"Jane loves junk. Would you like to try some?" from *My Alphabet* by Trevor Brown

Inaugurator of the Pleasure Dome: Bobby Beausoleil

Michael Moynihan

His body a blood-ruby radiant

With noble passion, sun-souled Lucifer

Swept through the dawn colossal, swift aslant

On Eden's imbecile perimeter.

He blessed nonentity with every curse

And spiced with sorrow the dull soul of sense

Breathed life into the sterile universe,

With Love and Knowledge drove out innocence

The Key of Joy is disobedience.

Aleister Crowley, "Hymn to Lucifer"

Bobby Beausoleil, the archetypal Luciferian rebel, presently sits behind prison walls, as he has for the past 30 years. His notoriety primarily stems from a brief association with Charles Manson, and it was Beausoleil's naïve idolization of the biker gangs who frequented Manson's Spahn Ranch hideout that led to his downfall, in which he fatally stabbed a drug dealer after a botched exchange of psychedelics.

Contrary to the image presented in "Helter Skelter" trials, in which prosecutors depicted all of Manson's associates as hypnotized automatons, Beausoleil can be described as a free spirit, with a will and a mind of his own. The attraction between Beausoleil and Manson largely came from music: Charles Manson was a friend of Dennis Wilson's and wrote a song recorded by the Beach Boys; Beausoleil performed in several psychedelic bands, collaborating with notable musicians like Arthur Lee and David LaFlamme (of the band It's A Beautiful Day).

Sexual experimentation also rode the hallucinatory whirlwind. While Manson's orgiastic sexploits are notorious, Beausoleil's erotic allure has also been the stuff of legend, earning him the nickname of "Cupid." Sex-energy has

Bobby Beausoleil on the steps
of the Russian Embassy

photo: Don Snyder

been a focal point of Beausoleil's entire life. How does one so accustomed to expressing their will sexually handle the confines of maximum security prison?

Detained in an environment teeming with distorted masculine impulses, Beausoleil has furiously tapped into his internal erotic currents to transcend his surroundings. Beausoleil's experiments with his sexual subconscious are key elements of his continuing spiritual and aesthetic development.

I BELIEVE THAT EVERY BOY IS ORIGINALLY CONSCIOUS OF SEX AS SACRED. BUT HE DOES NOT KNOW WHAT IT IS.—CROWLEY

Born into a Catholic family in Santa Barbara, California in 1947, Robert Kenneth Beausoleil in his teenage years taught himself to play an old guitar found in the attic. Bobby was also aware of an intense capability for visualizing his desires and a strong aversion to letting anything or anyone hinder their unfolding development. As he reminisced in a 1972 interview while at San Quentin, "It went against my grain . . . being pulled back against my desires . . . There were things I had to do—places to go, things I sensed and knew that I had to throw myself into. I knew that life was a big arena and I was ready for anything that could come along."

Young Beausoleil deliberately cultivated situations where he could spend time in the company of curious females. "We used to build forts as kids and go down into them, boys and girls, and take our clothes off. As small children, building forts and hideouts, clubhouses, sequestering ourselves from the prying eyes of parents, and exploring . . . those were things that happened in my childhood. Perhaps the fact that there was never an instance when we were caught and severely punished for that sort of behavior saved me from some of the inhibition that other young men and young women have later in life." By the age of nine Bobby moved out into his parents' garage, providing him with a much needed realm of independence.

One summer at his grandmother's house in El Monte, a suburb of Los Angeles, Bobby ascended the next rung of sexual discovery. The depressed El Monte was replete with seedy opportunities. "People who had come up from impoverished areas of the country and had moved there, looking for the Grail of greater wealth . . . and hadn't found it and wound up in a white ghetto in Southern California. That was a very different environment than [Santa Barbara], and it was there that I lost my virginity to a girl by the name of Josie, who was not altogether very bright. But she really liked the attention of the boys, so she was kind of the young whore of the area. In retrospect, she was sort of sadly abused—not physically or painfully, but she was taken advantage of."

El Monte set the backdrop for time spent with a motley band of hillbilly friends, one of whose fathers owned a gas station. The boys hung out in a trailer parked on the property, taught each other bluegrass tunes on the guitar, and scraped together automobile parts to build makeshift hotrods. After a few minor run-ins with the local police, Bobby wound up in L.A. Juvenile hall, and was later shipped off to the Los Prietos Boys Camp reform school. He remembers how his drawing abilities were put to use. "I got in trouble once for drawing pictures of naked women. It was with the encouragement of my comrades, because I drew pretty well and we were all 'at that age' and very interested in the opposite sex, and sex in general. One of the staff there, Mr. Boles, who was a devout Catholic, gave me a forty-five minute lecture about how I was leading my fellow prisoners, the other boys, astray into sin and helping to inspire 'sinful thoughts.'"

Upon release from Los Prietos, Beausoleil returned to Santa Barbara and began to grow his hair long. And once again, headed south. After a series of carnal misadventures with the wife of a cousin, he began frequenting night-clubs with a fake ID where he discovered Los Angeles' underground culture, complete with "liberated" females. "That was a whole new world for me— from every point of view . . . My first introduction to the Hollywood scene was through a girl named Bridget, and she was very much a free spirit sexually. I suppose in the same way that she had introduced me to pot and LSD, she also introduced me to 'free love.' She had a girlfriend, from across the cul-de-sac where she lived, who came over and one evening it evolved into a threesome between us, and that was a real enlightening thing for me."

By way of Bridget's male friends, Beausoleil was initiated into the growing psychedelic scene. Briefly he played rhythm guitar in The Grassroots, Arthur Lee's band that would later evolve into the seminal group Love. Amid all the accelerating sex, drugs and consciousness-expansion, Bobby hitched a ride to San Francisco—the center of the mind-bending maelstrom. It was there he met underground moviemaker and Aleister Crowley apostle Kenneth Anger, who was involved with pre-production work on *Lucifer Rising*, a film which he intended to be his magnum opus of flickering light and shadow symbolism.

I CAN ALWAYS TRACE A CONNECTION BETWEEN MY SEXUAL CONDITION AND THE CONDITION OF ARTISTIC CREATION, WHICH IS SO CLOSE AS TO APPROACH IDENTITY.——CROWLEY

Once in the Bay Area, Beausoleil joined a band called The Outfit, but it didn't take long before he realized that he was tired of formulaic acid rock. Bobby decided to pursue his own conceptions, assembling The Orkustra, an "electri-fied chamber orchestra" utilizing unconventional instruments. The group was commissioned to play at the Glide Memorial Festival, an event organized by the Diggers and the Sexual Freedom League, to take place in a rented church com-plex. Beausoleil views the significance of what transpired in a larger sense than that of a simple artistic event.

"After all, we were re-evaluating all the rules and values that had been imposed upon us by the generations before us. That's a necessary process if you're going to develop a new ethic and a new morality, a new awareness and a new understanding. You have to be able to dismantle the old ones first, at least in theory, or symbolically, so that you can see what the new possibilities may be. It was part-and-parcel of that process which was occurring at that point in time, and in that sexual mores—along with all the other values—became dismantled.

"The Glide Memorial exemplified this spirit . . . It was a situation where a large environment, a cathedral, was opened to young counterculture people for three days, and they were told it was okay to do whatever they wanted. It was an event staged expressly for the purpose of exploring one's freedom, in any fashion one might choose to do so.

"Prior to our arrival some of the people involved in setting up the event had built a false wall in a small auditorium that was part of the Glide complex, made of a wooden framework and paper, and there was a shallow space behind the wall of six or seven feet. There was a door that gave access to this little room formed by the false wall. There was going to be a poetry reading taking place in the front section of the room. It was thoroughly convincing that this was a real wall, and it was set up so that it was behind where the person would be reading poetry, in order to minimize the chance that anyone would go up and discover the wall wasn't real. We came earlier and brought our equipment and amps and such, and set up behind the false wall.

"Later that evening we arrived again to play, and first went out and cruised the festival for awhile. Then when it was time we quietly went back behind the false wall, while someone was reading poetry. About six or seven bellydancers were brought back behind the false wall with us. They weren't really belly-dancers, but they were in these exotic costumes, bare-topped with these pantaloons and bangles and jangles on. Then at the appointed moment we struck a chord and launched into one of our exotic danceable pieces, and these girls burst through the paper wall and took over. There was already a crowd of people in there watching and participating in the poetry reading, and now all the sudden it became something completely different. There were shocked looks on some people's faces. Emmet Grogan of the Diggers was there and he knew what was going on, obviously. He immediately started dancing with one of the girls. That was the idea, to get everybody up dancing. The girls were pulling people up out of their chairs. Gradually other musicians joined us and several conga players, who had been up in the main cathedral area, came down. At one point there was this gorgeous blonde girl—a very Nordic-looking Scandinavian girl, somebody else's old lady, unfortunately—who was one of the bellydancers who came near me and I just grabbed her hand and brought her over to where I was playing. She was willing enough, and with my foot I

Magick Powerhouse of Oz

photo: Don Snyder

pulled a chair out front and stood Samantha on it. So she stood in place and danced while I played to her. It's hard to describe—it's one of those times when you just had to be there—but she was dancing and I tried to dance with her, musically. I was playing to her body movements and she was doing likewise in response to me. It was very spontaneous, and it was wonderful—you could not have planned something that went as beautifully as this. After awhile the number of people in there made the air in the room so dense that you could cut through the steam with a knife. Everyone was sweating, people were taking their clothes off. Nobody was fucking at that point, although that did happen over the three days at various times and it was all the more beautiful because it was unplanned. While I was playing to her I took my shirt off. Everyone was perspiring and everybody's bodies were wet. Samantha is standing on the chair dancing and I started licking sweat from her body, impulsively. One of the conga players got up and he started helping me, and then another one did, and pretty soon there were three or four people licking this girl who was standing on the chair. She was overwhelmed and didn't know what to do, and eventually her friend 'saved' her and it was time for the girls to leave and they snuck out the back. But everyone continued dancing, we continued playing, and the drummers were playing with us. The pulse was there and it continued happening, but the girls had done their job. This is what Kenneth Anger saw. He might have been loaded on acid, I don't know, there's a good chance that he was. But I blew his mind. He'd had some other guy lined up to play Lucifer in his film, and he immediately fired him. That was our first meeting. He came up to me in the parking lot, after we played, pointed at me and said: 'You are Lucifer.' Those were his precise words, his opening line."

Anger found what he had been seeking: a living embodiment of male beauty unrestricted by Christian dualism or moralistic self-denial, the perfect male lead for his film *Lucifer Rising*. Film tests were shot, and then Anger invited Beausoleil to move into the house the filmmaker had rented, a dilapidated Victorian which formerly housed the Russian Embassy. A period photo shows Beausoleil perched on the front steps of the building in leather pants with a scorpion's silhouette emblazoned over his crotch, wearing the top-hat which would become his trademark. Aleister Crowley's credo of "Do what thou wilt is the whole of the law" is scrawled in red paint on the ornate wooden doors.

Inspired with his newfound role of "light bringer," Bobby assembled a musical confederation that would record the soundtrack to Anger's visual tapestry. He named the group The Magick Powerhouse of Oz. Beyond this nod to Crowleyan occultism, the other connotations of the name reflected a fascination for the mysterious forces which lurk within and beneath common objects, be they literary or mechanical: "Kenneth had all these arcane volumes of Crowley and such that probably would have been utterly fascinating to most

THE BRINGERS OF LIGHT & THE STRAIGHT THEATER
PRESENT

THE EQUINOX OF THE GODS

THE MAGICK POWERHOUSE OF ℗

KENNETH ANGER
666
THE CONGRESS OF WONDERS
THE AMAZING CHARLATANS
THE MIME TROUPE
THE DUNCAN COMPANY
THE STRAIGHT DANCERS
LIGHTS BY THE NORTH AMERICAN
IBIS ALCHEMICAL CO.

Equinox poster

Collection of Peggy Nadramia

people, but of all the books in his library, the ones that fascinated me the most were L. Frank Baum's Oz books. The double-entendres of sexual experimentation and discovery that are laced throughout all of those books, including in the illustrations in a very subtle way, were just fascinating. So that was part of where the band's name came from. Also, Kenneth took me one time to see the Powerhouse in San Francisco. The Powerhouse is the mechanism behind the cable-cars, the underground machinery which pulls the cable-cars. There are these giant wheels and motors, chains, pulleys and gears. They're huge and they were painted bright colors, one big green wheel and one big red wheel and smaller yellow wheels and they're all turning and rattling and making noise . . . so that was the idea behind the other part of the name: the Powerhouse that's underneath the magic city, which makes everything go."

Only on rare occasions did Anger discuss Crowleyan occultism with Beausoleil; mostly his devotion to such things simply went unspoken. "I think he was trying to get others interested in that perspective, but he was not doing it outwardly, he wasn't explaining it to anybody. He was symbolizing it in his work and he would intimate, but in my conversations with him he never went into any great detail. It was almost as if he assumed, on some level, that I already knew, or I had already 'arrived.' Perhaps to describe something to me in terms of some organization or a specific discipline, would almost, in his eyes, have ruined me. I felt he liked me the way I was, and didn't want to upset the balance.

"Although [Anger's] own personal inclinations are homosexual and mine are not, he nevertheless appreciated sexuality, however it was expressed. I would say that in his artistic visualizations, his films and so forth, his leanings were more homosexual because that's what his own proclivities were. But I don't think he was necessarily unable to appreciate other forms of sexual expression—in fact it became very clear to me that he could."

BUT THE FALLEN ANGEL AND I HAD A FALLING OUT. WELL, IT ALMOST WORKED OUT.
—KENNETH ANGER

Soon difficulties arose between the two artistic collaborators—the actor/musician and the filmmaker—over Anger's apparent squandering of funds and the subsequent slow progress on completing *Lucifer Rising*. Plans were made to stage a concert in order to pull in the money they both needed, and an event was announced that would solemnize the Autumnal Equinox of 1967 in grand pagan fashion. The spectacle would include psychedelic performances, most notably Beausoleil's Magick Powerhouse of Oz playing live behind a vast scrim projection screen onto which a kaleidoscopic lightshow would be beamed. The visuals would also incorporate, among other elements, test films from *Lucifer Rising*, along with snippets from *The Wizard of Oz*. As Beausoleil elaborates, "[Kenneth] had certain costumes that he used for props for the film that were brought in, and he was going to do an invocation along with a pre-recorded tape of some Crowley ritual, to usher in the Equinox. My band was going to play in costume. I pretty much wore the same thing I always did, except I had a new beaverskin top-hat and a full-length blue velvet cape. One of the sax players was the Grim Reaper, with his face hidden in a dark cowl . . . there were all these wild, weird costumes. It was at the end of the Summer of Love. The night of the performance, Kenneth took acid—not the wisest thing to do! We played our first set, and then he was going to do the ritual, and we'd come in at the end of that and start playing again. Everything worked with the scrim, and the lightshow . . . The first set went real well and everybody was kind of awed by what we'd been doing. Then it was Kenneth's turn to do his thing. The tape starts playing, and he's out on the dance floor where some gongs were positioned along with these various props like mannequins with costumes and painted heads on them representing various deities. He starts doing his invocation to the tape, and then suddenly the tape breaks. Here he is, high on acid, the tape breaks, he's in front of the audience, and from that point things just went haywire.

"It was a disaster for him. He freaked out, and it seemed like the things around him started freaking out along with him. I went to the soundbooth to try to help figure out what the problem was. There were studio lights that Kenneth had brought, which were used as spotlights on some of the props, and one of them exploded for reasons unknown. Kenneth—I guess spontaneously trying to figure out what to do—went looking for me at that point and started calling for me, but I was in the soundbooth and I didn't hear him. He went up on the stage calling out, 'Bobby, where are you? Bobby, where are you?' and started tearing holes in the scrim in his attempts to find me. He had a cane which he'd bought for me in a junk store, that had two serpents twining around it, like Caduceus, with a fist for the handle. He was using that for a sort of a wand, and somehow he broke it. He threw the pieces out into the audience, screaming 'I love you!' One friend of mine got hit above the eye and had to have stitches afterward. Kenneth freaking out was pretty much the close of the concert. We played on for a short set and that was the end of that. The audience was pleased, for them it was all part of the show, but for him and I it was a disaster."

The concert was a financial fiasco and resulted with Anger owing the owners of the Straight Theater a substantial sum of money. Another version of the evening and its aftermath has been wryly chronicled by Charles Perry in his book *The Haight Ashbury*:

> Anger and a shadowy Brotherhood of Lucifer rented the Straight Theater for a guarantee of $700 and built a Satanic altar on the floor. They hired Ben Van Meter and Scott Bartlett to do the light show, which was built around slides of Crowley's own tarot cards and 400 feet of Anger's film. . . . The event did not draw a large crowd, but the satanic mood was beyond dispute. At one moment in the brotherhood's invocations around the altar the Tibetan prayer wheel flew off and hit, of all people, the *Oracle* [newspaper's] former art director, who was so badly hurt that an ambulance had to be called. Tough luck for the Straight Theater's insurance policy.
>
> At the end of the show Van Meter returned the film to Anger, who handed it to someone else for safekeeping so he could leave for a post-invocation party. Anger had called it "my first religious film"; to non-satanists it had seemed to be merely shots of Bobby Beausoleil in weightlifter poses. During the night the film was stolen, and the culprit was widely assumed to be Beausoleil. The Straight cleaned up after the Satanic service, the job made somewhat easier by the fact that after Anger left, the audience had looted the altar. The show failed to make its guarantee in gate receipts, and Anger at first peevishly made out his check for $666.66 rather than $700.

Beausoleil denies that he ever stole the film, and points out that Anger's own version of the Equinox event has altered with subsequent retellings. Looking back on the seemingly cursed film project, Bobby sees it in a larger and more symbolic light: "The film was intended to portray the dawning of the Aquarian age from a mythological perspective. The definition that was described to me—and I heard it repeated many times to other people whose support he wanted for the project—was that with *Lucifer Rising* he wanted to create the antithesis of the death images and the death worship in his earlier film *Scorpio Rising*. Lucifer being the herald of the dawn, it was the coming of a new age, the age of the child, the age of Horus. That's what the concept for the film was, and I was picked because I seemed to represent that whole thing to him. The magic of the Haight scene was coming apart, and it paralleled this project that was coming apart, as well as my life which was coming apart and unraveling. I call the time after the Summer of Love the 'Winter of Disillusionment.' The Summer of Love was chaos and what was happening was that the youth movement was trying to grow up too fast."

Whatever transpired that night, it was the end of the relationship between Beausoleil and Anger. Burned out on the fading psychedelia of the Haight and dismayed at the frightening influx of runaway kids inundating San Francisco in search of the hippiedom they'd read about in *Life* magazine, Beausoleil grabbed his few belongings and headed south, eventually winding up in Topanga Canyon outside of Los Angeles. Anger wallowed in despair for a time, and shortly thereafter took out a full-page ad in the *Berkeley Barb* newspaper which was an announcement of his own demise: a photo of a modern gravestone with the words "Kenneth Anger 1947–1967." The earlier date was that of Anger's first significant film, *Fireworks*; the latter date apparently marked the end of his career in America. Within less than a year he moved across the Atlantic to London.

It was in Southern California that Bobby Beausoleil met a slightly older man with a small entourage of young people, a traveling commune who lived in a schoolbus. "The first time I met the Manson people was at the Spiral Staircase house down in Malibu, just at the base of Topanga Canyon. I went there to see a friend that I had known previously from the Hollywood scene. I was visiting him and there was what seemed to be a party going on next door—people smoking pot and playing music. So I just wandered over there and it was Charlie Manson singing and playing guitar, and there were some other guys and some girls. I sat down, I listened for awhile, and I picked up this thing called a melodica. It's designed on the same concept as a harmonica, except it has keys. There was one sitting on the table next to me, and I picked it up and started improvising some counterpoint melodies, which kind of blew everyone's mind—maybe they were all loaded on acid. I played along for a little while and checked out what was going on, then I left."

Shortly thereafter, Beausoleil would again encounter Manson when he responded to a "musician wanted" notice for a band seeking a guitarist for a live shows. The group billed itself as The Milky Way and featured Manson as its frontman. Beausoleil sat in for a few concerts at a beer bar called the Topanga Corral, but it wasn't long before the group fell apart. Bobby followed this with a brief stint of temporary film work, acting the part of an Indian in a B-grade skin flick Western called *The Ramrodder*. Quaint by today's blue movie standards, its sketchy plot serves to show off female flesh undulating to a

Orkustra poster

Collection of Mark McCloud

Hawaiian-style exotika soundtrack. Another of Manson's associates, Katherine "Gypsy" Share, plays a minor role in the film, and some scenes were shot around Spahn Ranch, where the Manson community soon took up residence. At the end of *The Ramrodder*, Beausoleil performs his only significant action in the film: the "eye for an eye" castration of a redneck rapist.

Beausoleil was a lone wolf with an ever-shifting retinue of female admirers. Never did he consider himself a "follower" of Manson, or anyone else. Nor was he a permanent resident at Spahn Ranch, but he spent considerable time there, particularly for the intimate communal events. Manson's sexual dynamism has been the subject of many wild stories, but Beausoleil was able to observe it firsthand with a more critical eye. "More was made of it than was true, in some respects, especially the nature of it, the interpretation of it . . . and Charlie himself made more of it than was real. There was a lot of 'smoke and mirrors' involved, so to speak. There was certainly a basis to some of the legend or myth surrounding that group of people, and Charlie specifically. He was free sexually, he could express himself freely in that regard, and he did. I was present on a couple of occasions when he was able to fuck where a large group of people was present, without embarrassment—which is not easy to do. Most people need to be in a room by themselves, or in a corner. He was doing it with women he was very familiar with, which of course makes it very easy, relatively, than if you're doing something like that with a stranger. In that situation he would invite other men to make love with the women, who of course he was familiar with, but they were not. Naturally they were shy about it, and so he was able to perform when other men were not. And it was a damn trick, you know, because having been both in a situation where I could not perform in front of other people and being in a situation where I could do it quite well, I've experienced both sides of that and so I know what the 'trick' is. I can see it for what it is. But having said that, I will state that a lot more was made of all this than was actually real."

Motorcycle club members were another group of conspicuous habitués at the Spahn Ranch; many of them hung around hoping for sexual favors from the young girls who surrounded Manson. Beausoleil never considered himself a flower child, but rather a more aggressive sort of free spirit, and the harder, rebellious mien of the bikers appealed to him on a instinctual level. "I'm not a hippy—I'm a barbarian," he had pointedly told people, even back in San Francisco. In an effort to gain favor with the bike gangs, Beausoleil offered to be the middleman in a mescaline deal. He assumed this would be a relatively easy transaction, as he had a direct source for the drug via an old acquaintance, Gary Hinman. The deal initially went through without a hitch, as Beausoleil procured 1,000 hits at a dollar apiece. All seemed fine until the bikers angrily returned a few days later, complaining that they'd been burned. The mescaline was bunk—poisonous strychnine, in fact—and at knife-point they demanded their $1,000 back immediately. The events which accelerated in the next 24 hours set in motion Lucifer's final fall from grace. Arriving at Hinman's residence, Beausoleil was told that the $1,000 was already spent and couldn't be returned. Bobby hoped that somehow Hinman would provide a way to resolve the situation, and avert violent retribution from the bikers, but the visit quickly escalated into chaos. The situation was exacerbated after Manson stopped by and sliced Hinman across the face to scare him into repaying the money. In a fit of desperation Beausoleil stabbed Hinman to death after the latter vowed to report the intimidation to the police. He fled the house with Hinman's two beat-up vehicles, and back at the Spahn Ranch he left a VW bus with the bikers as partial payment for the money owed them.

Bobby was apprehended a few days later on the highway near San Luis Obispo in the other car of Hinman's; he was quickly indicted for the murder. His first trial ended in a hung jury, but a retrial in the wake of the subsequent Tate/LaBianca slayings ensured a worse fate. It mattered not that Beausoleil's crime had been committed nearly two weeks before the Tate/LaBianca incidents, and had its own extenuating circumstances—once he was labeled as a "Manson Family" killer, the surrounding hysteria of the moment provided the means for the prosecution to put Beausoleil on Death Row along with those convicted in the Tate and LaBianca cases. Two years later the California legislature repealed the death penalty.

In a 1980 magazine interview, Beausoleil attempted to explain the psychological circumstances that preceded all the seemingly senseless murders, including the one he himself committed: "[The killers] were a bunch of people with their backs against the wall. This wasn't mere discontent, this was lunacy. At least in their minds, they were at the end corner of the world. They couldn't travel any more together without a caravan of law enforcement people behind them. The only place left to go was the desert. They were at the end of the edge of the world and they were scared to death of being pushed off the edge. The desert is death. They wound up in Death Valley trying to live off the bugs."

LIKE SADE AND GENET, BOBBY BEAUSOLEIL HAS SOMEHOW MANAGED, AGAINST ALL ODDS, TO CREATE WORKS OF ART IN PRISON, TO TRANSFORM A REPRESSIVE AND SOUL-DESTROYING EXPERIENCE BY CREATING WORKS OF BEAUTY.
—ANGER

Beausoleil's sexual aura has always been embodied outwardly in his looks— and when he entered San Quentin at the age of 21, he appeared the baby-faced teenager. What was an asset on the outside became a severe liability in the brutal all-male nightmare of maximum security prison. "I realized it when I was in the county jail, before I got to San Quentin, just from talking to people. Some of them were good enough to see the writing on the wall and say something because they wanted me to be aware of what I was heading into and the difficulties I was going to face. And of course there were people that were trying to hit on me, even in the county jail. I say 'trying' because they did it cautiously, and I think probably that had to do with the vibes I was putting out.

"So early on the distortion in sexual orientation became very apparent and I was very aware of the fact that to some of these guys who were 'doing all day,' I was some kind of fantasy come true. I think it was due to a combination of factors, but I never became a victim to any of it. I was never anybody's girl, and when I talk about an aberration, that's what I mean, because what happens is that men in here try to re-orient other men into playing the role of women, which is of course completely unreal. It's a false thing, and they delude themselves that if they're playing the male role, they're not really homosexual. It's only those who are playing the female role who are homosexual. What an insane asylum I have come into! People delude themselves that way in prison, to the Nth degree with those kinds of fantasies, in order to maintain some sort of sense of identity. They don't want to think of themselves as homosexuals, but of course someone who has those leanings, who wants to take up with a man who is pretending to be a girl, is a homosexual, point blank. That's what it is. I saw those dynamics right away, and I understood what was going on and I was very determined, going in, that I was not going to be somebody's girl. I'm not going to be something I'm not, and I knew that would be a rougher path to take. To succumb to it all would have been the easy way, then I'd have had everything in the world I wanted, as far as being in prison. I could have pretty

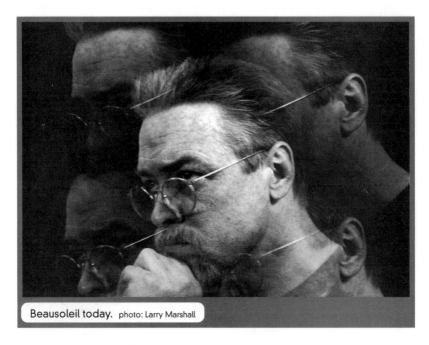

Beausoleil today. photo: Larry Marshall

much called the tune, if I'd been oriented that way. But I'm not wired that way and that made it more difficult.

"I marvel now that I even went through that and survived. I had a boyish face and I looked younger than my years. When I was 21, I looked like I was 17. I could barely grow a beard, and I'm not a particularly big guy. I think it's a combination of things that conspired to 'save' me and to help me maintain my integrity. Some of it was just sheer luck, some of it was bravado. I just let the savage come out. If somebody felt it was important enough to them to try to turn me out, I just let them know there was going to be a price. And, in fact, everybody that had those delusions about me realized early on that the price would be too high. Then after awhile, even though my appearance had not changed that much over time, I had garnered enough respect that it didn't really matter anymore. People figured, 'that's just the way he looks' and they didn't act on any delusions about changing my orientation."

Beausoleil quickly learned to toughen himself against his fellow inmates. As he explains, his demeanor became more uncompromising out of sheer necessity: "For the first number of years that I was in prison, it was a violent world, and I felt like I had to be violent in order to survive . . . This was the kind of world that I was living in, and I believed I had to stand up for myself. Weakness is preyed upon. There were times when I carried a knife in my belt, and was ready to use it."

Like every other potent urge that arises among humans in a repressive environment, sexuality in prison absorbs much of the violence and frustration seething around it, and in the worst instances assumes a predatory nature far more brutal and overt than in the outside world. Beausoleil recounts how he managed to handle the ugliest scenarios to befall him: "There was one incident in San Quentin where I thought it was definitely going to go to serious bloodshed. At the time I had a couple of friends who would have backed me in a pinch, but for the most part I was on my own and it had come to me that there was a group of people who had designs on me and intended to turn me out. I couldn't just take that as idle talk. My way of dealing with that was to go to someone and pick up a shank. It was in the gym, and I went straight to a guy in the group who was most intimidating in appearance and I told him that if he or any of his partners wanted to pursue that direction, I'd be in the towel room and they could come in there and we'd handle it. And I was psyched, I was ready to go, and my fuse was already lit. If you go that far, you've got to be ready. You can't use words like that and not be prepared to back them up. So I went into the towel room, ready to kill the first motherfucker that walked through the door . . . and nobody ever came in. I waited there a half hour. That was pretty much the last of any serious situations. It would have had to have been somebody who was willing to risk their life to have sex, and there's really not too many people that will do that.

"Rape is a lot less prevalent now than it used to be, because of AIDS and so forth, but that same dynamic still occurs, that homosexual orientation, that same process of 'turning somebody out'—all those kinds of things still occur. But these things happen because a lot of people who come in here are afraid. It's because the person who is the victim is essentially controlled by fear—not the immediate threat of a knife or some sort of physical harm, but the imagined threat of a knife, through intimidation. Men in here, some of them, are very good at that."

As Beausoleil illustrates, the options available to someone threatened with sexual violence in prison are few: "Basically there are just two. The first is in the case of a direct threat. In other words, when someone approaches you and says 'It's your blood on my dick or your blood on my knife,' you dig? You deal with the threat and confront the person who intends to make an advance, which is what I did.

"The other option is to go into 'P.C.': Protective Custody . . . You're immediately classified as a weak person, and anything that anybody was thinking about doing in the first place, such as homosexual activity, becomes a done deal, in so far as the perceptions of others go. The perception is that you're a homosexual, you're too weak, and that you need to be locked up. You live with that stigma for the rest of the time you're in prison. They may put you on a mainline at some other prison later on, years down the road, but people will still remember that you took the weak way out, and it will still come back to haunt you and remain a stigma."

Despite the grim surroundings, Beausoleil slowly began to acclimate to his incarceration and realized that, utilizing a bit of ingenuity, he could pursue the creative impulses which still stirred within him. Following a transfer to Tracy Prison, he initiated an inmate music program and thereby gained access to instruments which enabled him to once again start composing music. It was at this point in the mid-'70s that Kenneth Anger re-entered Beausoleil's consciousness, although in the preceding years Bobby had, on occasion, received cryptic missives from him. "I had gotten a postcard from him when I was on Death Row. It was an Egyptian painting of a musician who's playing a harp in front of Osiris, I think it is. The message was: 'They also serve those who sit and wait . . .'

"There was an occasional interview or article on Kenneth that would be sent to me, and at some point I heard that he was again getting ready to do *Lucifer Rising*. It was still his pet project and he was getting ready to finish it, and he had slated Jimmy Page to do the soundtrack. So I decided that I'd talk to him about it, because I'd always felt, ever since our parting of ways in 1967, that this was unfinished business. I still believed in the concept as it had originally been described to me: heralding the dawn of a new age, ritualizing that process, the mythological aspects, and all of that. It spoke to me, it resonated with me. I

"Cupid in Trouble" by Bobby Beausoleil

wanted to complete the project as I felt it was unfinished, and I don't like loose ends."

Upon hearing a demo tape that Bobby sent out to him from Tracy Prison, Anger was impressed enough to fire Jimmy Page and provide Beausoleil with a small budget to purchase proper recording equipment for the soundtrack. Through the help of allies in the prison administration, Bobby was granted approval for the project and permission to receive materials he needed to build keyboards and special effects devices. "The Freedom Orchestra" became the moniker for Beausoleil's band of prison musicians he enlisted to perform the film score he had composed. Conceived in the blood-soaked bowels of Tracy amidst a constant stream of murders and lockdowns, the result was one of the more haunting and evocative pieces of instrumental psychedelia ever recorded, and in 1980 Anger released a version of the film which included the new soundtrack. Upon completion of the *Lucifer Rising* score, Beausoleil continued innovating in the musical realm, despite the obstacles of his confinement. An ongoing endeavor during the late 1970s was the creation of prototypes for the Dream Machine and the Syntar, two of the world's first functional guitar synthesizers, which Bobby designed and built himself using only limited materials and surplus electronics parts.

THE SEXUAL ACT BEING THEN A SACRAMENT, IT REMAINS TO CONSIDER IN WHAT RESPECT THIS LIMITS THE EMPLOYMENT OF THE ORGANS.
—CROWLEY

Another evolving creative exercise that required no special permission from the authorities was autoerotic exploration. "I've discovered more about my own sexuality since I've been in prison than I ever knew when I was on the outside. After all, I've been in prison since I was 21. Before I was incarcerated I did have numerous sexual experiences for someone as young as I was, but the more profound experiences, particularly in regards to the sacredness of the experience, is something that I've developed since I came to prison.

"For the most part I haven't had much shame and I've not associated shame and disgust and guilt with sex, or with my own sexuality. So going to prison wasn't something that took the direction of a monk going into a cloister, where your sexuality is something you're supposed to ignore or 'pray away.' It wasn't that for me, and masturbation is the standard fare for most people in prison. It's what most people have for sex and that's as much true for me as it is for anyone in prison.

"Sexuality took a different turn for me, however, in that it was not the object of sex to have an orgasm, or to masturbate myself to orgasm. As I matured, that was no longer the goal for me. When you're young, you masturbate and it's a novel thing, and the goal is to have an orgasm because that's where you think the actual pleasure is. But if you really become aware of the process you realize it is the end of the pleasure. It's intense, of course, and it's pleasurable, but in general terms it becomes the end of the pleasure and the end of the sexual experience. With masturbation you don't make babies, so ejaculation really becomes the end of the process."

Beausoleil's rites of sexual discovery at first involved his senses and his imagination, but it was not long before he began to utilize his artistic abilities and the few tools around him to take the process to a more and more adept level. "I've always been very sensually oriented . . . I've always been someone, even in those sexual experiences with young women when I was on the outside, who liked to linger, to stroke and to look, to savor that experience. When I was isolated and I no longer had a physical being other than myself, that orientation, that proclivity, became manifest in exploring myself, but to a greater degree it became a situation of exploring sensuality in art. This became a very sensual experience for me. I was able, over time, to learn how to draw the female form—and the male form as well, but primarily the female one—fairly accurately from my imagination, and I began to create my own companions, so to speak. These were not always specifically sex drawings, but sensual drawings, and I spent many, many hours doing that and it became another way of making love for me. I've always been fascinated, through all different occasions, by erotic art. For me, the most erotic organ in the body is not the penis, vagina, tits, or ass. It's the brain and its fruit,

"Fairy" by Bobby Beausoleil

Inaugurator of the Pleasure Dome: Bobby Beausoleil

"Flying Phalli" by Bobby Beausoleil

the imagination. That, for me, is where my sexuality has gone: into developing my imagination, and through my imagination, to love sensually."

SCORPIO IS THE SIGN OF SEX AND DEATH; IT RULES THE SEX ORGANS—THE GOOD GASH AND THE STIFF COCK—AS WELL AS MACHINES, MOTORCYCLES AND ELECTRIC GUITARS. BOBBY BEAUSOLEIL IS A SCORPIO. —ANGER

If one is willing to accept Anger's astrological assessment, it makes perfect sense that it was under the shadow of the California gas chamber that Beausoleil's channeling of visual sensual currents began in earnest, giving life to his cast of pagan nymphs and satyrs. "I think it was originally on Death Row, which was isolated segregation. That's really where it started and when I began getting into art seriously.

"I've done long stretches in one form of lock-up or another where I was not allowed to have a musical instrument. I did quite a bit of time in a place called West Hall at Tracy, because a guard had been killed and anyone who'd had a violent offense was taken off the mainline and put in this place called West Hall which was a segregated area, apart from the main population. I spent about a year in that situation, without a musical instrument. So I spent a lot of time drawing. I managed to get approval to have art materials, most of which were provided by my mother. I used to stay up all night and draw, and then sleep during the day. My medium was colored pencils because that was pretty much the limit of what was allowed—you could get watercolors, but I've always had trouble with liquid mediums for some reason, I slop it too much. I like to use the precise lines of pencil. So it was in those types of situations, Death Row or West Hall, where I just spent my time drawing. I always drew from my imagination. Being in a situation like that, you don't have much in the way of models. I wasn't too interested in drawing my environment—I saw that enough, I didn't need to see it in my art! I wasn't really interested in taking a picture out of a magazine or a photograph and reproducing it, because obviously that is something that already existed. I wanted to create something that didn't exist, so I drew from my imagination. I would draw a human figure, and then compare the figure with a photograph, to see how closely I had come to being reasonably anatomically correct. But it was fantasy art, and I drew fantastical creatures: angels and cherubs, goddesses, satyrs, various animals, dragons. Most of them having to do with paganism I guess, from pagan mythology, and mostly having to do with women as well."

The English magician and artist Austin Osman Spare refined related techniques into a coherent metaphysical philosophy whereby the occultist creates a graphic sigil of his willed desire on paper and then discards or destroys it in order to empower it with a supernatural life of its own. Although he was unfamiliar with Spare's theories, Beausoleil instinctively employed a similar method. "In my mind I'd explored the Kama Sutra through my art, through my drawings—most of which I never shared with anybody. It was very private, and usually I destroyed them later. These weren't things I kept, for the most part.

"I think I was creating something entirely new in my head . . . I wasn't trying to portray real people . . . To me they were spirit-beings, of my own—or I don't know, possibly there was some other sort of communication going on, but I think they were the product of my own being. They took on, for me, enough 'apartness,' that I could relate to them in a sort of current which was giving me sexual feedback. In other words, it didn't stay inside of me—I was bringing these spirit-beings out of myself and being reciprocated."

Often the spirit-beings created with pencil and paper were archetypal female embodiments of sexual urgency, but the intent was not to simply create a personal pornography. Through his art, Beausoleil refined his own personality and consciousness. "Coming though my own imagination to appreciate the feminine, I think it helped to balance me. For all those years living in an environment where the masculine is greatly over-emphasized and the female is simply not present, I saw all the aberrations that would occur in human interaction when that sort of social structure is created. An all-male environment—what an unnatural thing! So for me it was a means to find the feminine within myself and bring it out—and not in a homosexual way, or anything like that, but to be aware and conscious of it, to explore it through this creative vehicle, and thus maintain a balance within myself of masculine/feminine expression."

In the early 1980s, Beausoleil made contact with *Puritan*, a short-lived journal of explicit erotica. "[*Puritan*] wasn't just purveying sex, it was examining sexuality. It attempted to encourage true intimacy and to honor sexuality." He eventually submitted some of his artwork for *Puritan's* consideration. The result was a series of drawings published as "The Erotic Art of Bobby Beausoleil," with an introduction by Kenneth Anger. After comparing Beausoleil to the imprisoned sexual radicals the Marquis de Sade and Jean Genet, Anger effuses: "The cock that Bobby depicts in so many of his paintings, long, rather slender, with a beautifully flaring head, is a self-portrait. Although the face of the male protagonist in these sex rites that are about to happen is never seen, they are signed by that exposed, proud hard-on: Bobby's cock, the stuff of legends and sire of numerous love-children . . . Bobby has based his entire composition on a swastika of desire!"

Beausoleil explains the same principle: "Art was my way of having intimacy, sexually, where there wasn't any. The human imagination is the most erogenous zone, and that's what I was exploring. The goal was not necessarily to have sexual release; it was a very erotic and sensual experience for me. If you're really intent on drawing the curves of the human figure from your imagination, especially the feminine curves, it's a turn-on, because you're there.

"There is a discipline, and I'm speaking of Tantra, where sexuality becomes a path to healing and enlightenment. I very much believe that that's a valid path. I don't think that a person can become liberated in their thinking and belief system, and in their path of spiritual growth, if they're inhibited sexually. These things almost have to go hand-in-hand. There has to be a stage in one's personal evolution where those old guilts, shames, and inhibitions are left behind."

It is ironic that a prisoner should be so unencumbered of sexual neuroses, while the multitude of contemporary Americans, ostensibly possessed of "freedom," spend their entire existences in minds and bodies racked with sexual dysfunction. Viewing the behavior of those on the outside, Beausoleil remarks, "It is a form of psychological schizophrenia in my view, or maybe 'psycho-sexual schizophrenia' is a more accurate term. Our society seems to be sexually polarized in two extremes to a degree that has never occurred anywhere in history that I'm aware of . . . I've studied erotic art—as much as anybody in my situation can study erotic art—and that sort of schizophrenia has always existed, but we've never been in a situation before, in any well-documented country at least, where sexual art, or the explicit portrayal of sex, has been permitted by the society or culture to the degree that it is now. Never has the human form been displayed so overtly in its sexuality as it is now, in terms of the amount that you see of it. It has been displayed in ancient art, the sexual form, the genitalia and so forth, since pre-history, but never to the degree that it is now. Yet at the same time we have a society in which there is predominantly little intimacy—and it's kind of hard to put the two together and understand what's going on here. On the one hand we have this explicit representation of sexuality and on the other hand we have this incredibly huge industry of phone sex, where people don't even touch one another. Electronic conversations and visual representations of the sexual act have somehow become a replacement for true sexual intimacy between people. AIDS has created a lot of [this fear of sexual freedom]. But I'm not so sure that AIDS isn't a reflection of something that is ailing in humanity, rather than the avoidance of sexual intimacy being a reflection of the threat of the ailment of AIDS."

Instinctively discovering what Crowley labeled "energized enthusiasm," Beausoleil has fused his sensual existence and artistic life into an inseparable whole. Given the pleasures and insights to be reaped through such a regimen, he expresses surprise that he is yet to encounter anyone who has taken similar advantage of the isolation of imprisonment. "I've never known anybody who's explored their own sexuality in the way I have . . . but I would think in thirty years that I would have made contact with other people who have taken a similar direction, and found that manner of expression of sensuality, sex, whatever, through artistic expression. I have seen other men in here do art and draw the human form beautifully, but it doesn't seem to be to them what it is for me."

⚡ ⚡ ⚡

Michael Moynihan is co-author, with Didrik Søderlind, of *Lords of Chaos* (Feral House), winner of the Firecracker Award for best music book of 1998. Moynihan's folkish psychedelic band bears the name Blood Axis. Contact: P.O. Box 3527, Portland, OR 97208-3527.

I Support Sexual Liberation

necrocard

I want to help others experiment sexually after my death. Please let your relatives know your wishes.

I request that after my death
A. my body be used for any type of sexual activity ❑
or
B. gay only ❑ straight only ❑ I do not wish my body to be dismembered or disfigured during necrophiliac sex ❑ (tick as appropriate)

Signature _____ Date _____

Full name _____
(BLOCK CAPITALS)

In the event of my death, if possible contact:

Name _____ Tel (   ) _____

Issued by Neoist Alliance, BM Senior, London WC1N 3XX. Send British Stamps or IRCs for further information.

MY LIPS PRESSED AGAINST THE DECAY

Chad Hensley

Leilah Wendell sleeps with decomposed corpses. She is a necrophile occultist with the ability to "connect intimately with the Death entity via the empty vessels we leave behind when we die." Wendell doesn't make love with just any old bag of bones; the rotted cadavers she fondles become possessed by the Angel of Death. The dessicated body comes to life in Wendell's embrace, reanimated by the spirit of this supernatural being.

The Angel of Death is an ancient eldritch specter better known as the Grim Reaper. Wendell claims that this being has been her cosmic soulmate since she was four years old. According to Wendell, Death materialized in her room and sat down beside her as she lay in bed early on a Sunday morning. Most people, especially children, might become disturbed if a skeletal apparition suddenly appeared before them. But little Leilah wasn't bothered at all, and immediately befriended Death, whom she would come to call Azrael—Death's Angelic name.

Though she claims that Death is neither male nor female, Wendell refers to Azrael as a him, since people have an easier time relating to gender. Wendell has encountered Azrael many times; he usually assumes the form of a cloaked skeleton but has also appeared before her as an old man in flowing purple and silver robes. He has even taken the shape of an animal—a large, cawing crow, guiding Wendell to cemeteries where open, occupied tombs awaited her arrival.

As Wendell grew older, her meetings with a personified Death continued, drawing her to visit secluded graveyards or places where tragic events had occurred. The more encounters she had with Azrael, the stronger her love grew for him. "I soon realized I was in love with Death!" says Wendell. "I was eleven years old, laying prostrate on a grave-mound writing love poems to the dead guy beneath me, and quite enjoying the sensation."

Other than funerals, Wendell would not see her first dead body up close until she was 14 years old. On a visit to her sick mother in the hospital, she snuck into a service elevator on the way to the fourth floor. Inside the elevator, two young orderlies attended a gurney between them. On the gurney, beneath a white sheet, lay a cadaver, a limp arm hanging over the edge. "What struck me was how the fingernails had this interesting shade of blue," explains Wendell. Suddenly the elevator came to an abrupt stop between floors. The lifeless hand lunged out and grabbed hold of her wrist. Instead of screaming, Wendell simply stood there "enjoying the moment" until the orderlies noticed. "All I could do was smile as they politely tried, with some force, to loosen the icy hand from my wrist. Without really thinking, I took my other hand, placed it over

Leilah Wendell

the corpse's, and the grip gently released. I placed the dangling hand back on the gurney and the elevator started its ascent. The orderlies just stared at me. The expression on their faces was priceless."

When Wendell was old enough to enter the job market, her relationship with Death led her to a morgue to seek employment with the Medical Examiner's office in an area of expertise she fondly refers to as "Forensic Archeology." Exhumations and their death-enhanced details brought Wendell closer to Azrael than ever before.

Leilah fondly recalls one particular night at her job when she removed five feet of packed earth and exhumed a "decayed, cheap pine box enveloped in weeping willow roots. The roots resembled thousands of long, tendril-like tentacles. Under the shadow of grey storm clouds and armed with an odd arsenal of everything from bolt cutters to barber's scissors, I descended into an open grave, carefully snipping around the coffin's cracked lid."

"After 15 minutes of work, I could finally get a pry bar into the crevice and gently wrenched the lid free. The whole corpse was literally enmeshed in a form-fitting macramé of spidery tendrils like something straight out of *Invasion of the Body Snatchers*! The corpse was beautifully mummified by a combination of spiny green wrappings and the natural desiccant quality of the clay."

The next few hours would be a delicate and time-consuming process for Wendell.

"The roots had literally penetrated the corpse and had been feeding upon its elements. In places, like around the head, the roots could be cut and peeled away in large chunks, much like peeling an orange. Beneath, the withered body had the preservative quality of a freshly-unwrapped Egyptian mummy. I could tell that the body had not been embalmed, which is always a plus, as embalming is a sure way to wreak havoc on the natural decomposition of the human body."

An unembalmed corpse in a state of complete decay is what Wendell affectionately refers to as a "moldy oldie." According to her, for those individuals who are necromantically inclined, there are three stages of death—prep-room fresh (the newly dead), gooey louie (a rotting corpse), and moldy oldie (decomposition complete). Wendell solemnly intones: "I am a necrophile. I had a long time between admitting this and denying it due to the connotations mankind has put upon this word. The fact is that people have abused its true meaning, stretching its definition to encompass varying sorts of psychopathic behavior."

There have been times when Wendell thought she was losing her sanity. "As I became more involved with all aspects of death, it confirmed all the things I was feeling on a spiritual level. At the time, I still had doubts in my head like 'Am I going crazy?' But I think when you see stiffs moving about, making gestures and all kinds of little weird things, you kind of get convinced. I have always felt most at home among the dead, like I belonged there, and that the world of the living was an alien place to me."

It might come as no surprise that Wendell is a friend of Karen Greenlee, another necrophile (see "The Unrepentant Necrophile" from the first *Apocalypse Culture*). Besides sharing an erotic attraction to corpses, both women have worked in a mortuary. But there is a difference in taste. While Wendell enjoys moldy-oldies, Greenlee is only aroused by the freshly embalmed. Greenlee's lust for dead bodies also seems to be more sexually explicit than Wendell's cadaver encounters. She not only enjoys a touchy-feely with her corpse-lovers, like Wendell, but she also indulges in the occasional 69 with them. There even seems to be competition between the two as to whom has slept with the most bodies. Despite differences, their friendship has strengthened over the years. Wendell says they talk on the phone at least twice a week and occasionally travel across country to visit each other.

One of Wendell's first necrophiliac experiences with a buried corpse took place in a small mausoleum. "I opened the tomb door, slipped in, and closed it tightly behind me. I pulled a small candle from my pocket, lit it, and made my way down the shaky, wooden staircase. I opened the rusted gate and entered the lower cell. The cracked ceiling was high enough to easily accommodate an upright stance. Three caskets were stacked against the wall to my right. Wedged in on all sides, the caskets could not be budged.

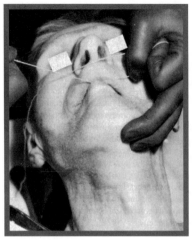

"To my left was an unnaturally large sarcophagus. Its top was torn open as if it had somehow erupted from within. I lifted the candle and found a supine figure laying lifeless on a bed of straw and earth. I reached down into the ravaged casket and began to peel the stiff sheet from the dead form. Gently unwrapping the brittle cloth from the beautifully decaying body, I had to reach underneath the corpse to untie the twine that held the withered arms folded across the chest. As I bent over the body, one of the skeletal hands slowly reached up and caressed my body. The other hand clasped me in a cold embrace as I was pulled down into the coffin until my lips pressed against the decay."

For Wendell, the taste of death was "like a bitter harvest, sweet as an exotic nectar." She could feel the outline of bones against her body. She whispered "let me sleep beside you" as she parted the veil of cobwebs that covered the skeletal husk. She removed her clothes and climbed into the casket, laying down beside the decayed cadaver.

"Drawing the fragile corpse into my embrace, I could feel my heart pounding against the hollow chest." That night she slept in the tomb with her lover. In the morning, she would depart after giving the corpse "a final, passionate kiss that left the taste of sweet earth on my lips."

After encountering other re-animated corpses possessed by the Angel of Death, Wendell began to realize that somehow the dead were able to serve as direct catalysts between Death and herself. "Being near bodies brought

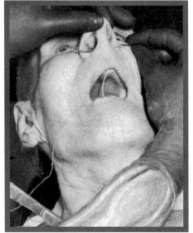

me closer to Him, and made me more fully love all aspects of what He is." According to Wendell, often she wouldn't have to venture out to find a dead body. Cadavers seemed to find their way to her.

On her 28th birthday, a co-worker gave Wendell a special gift wrapped with a huge red bow. The birthday present was a "remarkably preserved and naturally desiccated corpse splayed upon the red carpet of my dimly lit studio." This was one of the most exquisite bodies Leilah had ever seen—mummified by the natural dryness of the local soil. Unembalmed and intact.

At midnight, she carried the body to her bedroom, which was lit by candlelight, disrobed and got into bed. "He felt so good beside me. Bits of clay and ash covered my sheets as I maneuvered his skeletal hands around my body. I kissed his cold lips and the world around me became oblivion. I remember staring into empty eye-sockets and tears welling up in my eyes, when I felt a hand tightening around my waist. The other with-

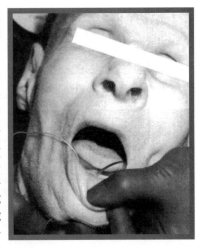

ered hand began to tighten around me as well, and continued to do so until I could barely strain to breathe. My face was pressed up to his, and our lips locked together for some time."

Leilah would have to return her gift in two days. "In the arms of such beauty, I wanted to find a way to preserve His love and honor the gift. I decided to make a casting of the face. A death-mask, if you will. The emaciation and fragility of the skin required a delicate hand, and some rather non-traditional materials. I was used to that, as nearly all the clay I use for sculpting is made from natural clays that I gather from certain cemeteries.

"Making the face cast was the problem. It might tear the latex mold, or destroy the skin, which had the feel of a thin and semi-brittle, paper mache. The casting was painstaking. Some parts were cast in latex, some cast with wax impressions, and a couple of minute details were cast with chewing gum. At times, I would close my eyes and run my fingers over the corpse's face and try to discern every nuance so that I could replicate it as best as possible on the sculpture. When the sculpture was finished, it was mounted on wood, like a relief and framed in autumn foliage. After the work of art was completed, I took the body to my bed again." On the third day, Wendell washed the corpse with rosewater, sprinkled the body with jasmine oil, and laid it out on a ceremonial sheet of black velvet. "I kissed him good-bye, and wrapped him up."

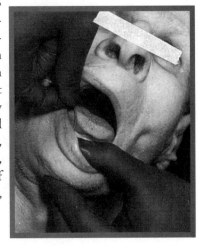

Some of Wendell's necrophiliac experiences did not always work out so smoothly. One night in a morgue, a cadaver wrapped itself around her and would not let go. "I know from working in funeral homes that dead bodies do have muscle spasms. But you know the length of time that happens and you know the levels to which that occurs. We're talking about a corpse we dug out of the ground after a month and a half. Somebody else had to untwine the body from me. Very embarrassing."

"Carnevale" by Leilah Wendell

"Requiem Quintet" by Leilah Wendell

Wendell's last position in the mortuary field ended in a spectacular way. After working for four months at a funeral home, the owner decided it was time to install a state-of-the-art walk-in freezer unit. "Business picked up a bit until there was only one body inhabiting the spacious cooler. This particular body had been discovered under an abandoned house, buried loosely in red clay. The coroner determined it had been there for over eight months. Like my previous lovers, the body had more-or-less been mummified by the surrounding soil. The body was alone in that ominous, silver freezer, so I visited him as often as possible. I'd hold his hand, read to him, and kiss him. I felt his loneliness, his sense of abandonment, his terrible, terrible sadness.

"Azrael" by Leilah Wendell

"On a still and cloudless night, I sat on the metal tray beside him, holding his withered hands to my heart. Inside the sealed freezer unit, the candle flame began to flutter. Strange, dark shadows filled the small chamber. A gnarled hand clenched me and I was drawn down to his cold, sweet lips. We kissed passionately, and I laid my head on his still breast, which resonated a sound much like a wind tunnel blowing in my ear. Now, both hands groped at my hair, then down my back until we were lying together arms and legs entwined. I looked up to see the steel walls of the freezer unit contract and expand. Suddenly the heavy door flung open, and like a vacuum, the air inside was sucked out. The corpse went flaccid, the candle extinguished. I proceeded to tidy up and head home.

"No sooner did I reach the front of the funeral home when all hell broke loose. It sounded like the Fourth of July with explosions and fireworks overhead. The power lines above me were on fire, arcing and shooting off sparks in every direction. I just stood there in awe, watching the power lines between the freezer unit and the service pole burn and fuse. The next thing I knew, fire engines and cops were everywhere. I found out that half of the town was

"Autumn Bride" by Leilah Wendell

blacked out due to this display. The side walls of the freezer room were all bent in. The heavy steel door lay on the ground. The large hinges, fused metal, and cold smoke filled the room.

"What baffled the authorities the most was the fact that the corpse inside lay untouched and undamaged. The funeral home was closed for repair and I was laid off due to the slow season." Wendell suspected that her boss had been discussing her activities with some of the employers. "The funeral industry is a very tight community, especially in the small towns where I worked. Needless to say, it was virtually impossible for me to get another job in that field where I lived."

Since the time of the mortuary blacklisting, Wendell has managed to turn her relationship with Death into a business. Her current home is a curiosity shop and art gallery, located on Magazine Street in the heart of uptown New Orleans. The House of Death, as her patrons fondly refer to the gallery, is a two-story Victorian house painted entirely purple and black. Oil paintings of dancing corpses and frolicking skeleton sculptures and a seven-and-a-half-foot golem made from a 100-year-old skeleton, decorate The House of Death. Exhumed grave clay and other, more ordinary art supplies are also sold. Much of the artwork in the gallery is Wendell's own, as she has become an accomplished artist. She is also a published poet and author of several books, including *Our Name is Melancholy*, *The Necromantic Ritual Book*, and *Encounters with Death*.

Wendell produced a bi-annual mailer so her fans and other like-minded individuals could keep up with her activities. "The Azrael Project Newsletter," filled with essays, art, poetry and mailing list contacts, was distributed to over 25,000 people throughout the world. While over 75% of Wendell's correspondents say they have seen Azrael in one form or another, around 1% actually claim to be necrophiliacs. Wendell openly admits that most of these individuals seem to be only in it for sexual gratification, despite her opinions on the corpse as a sacred vessel.

The general consensus among psychological researchers is that necrophiles are inherently sick and perverse. "True necrophilia is so rare and misunderstood, it cannot possibly be properly documented with a fair and balanced precept," argues Wendell.

"Most available research on the subject paints a distorted and repulsive picture of the practice by folks who are either ignorantly or deliberately subjective, rather than objective. According to psychiatric documentation, nearly all necrophiles have been sexually abused."

Wendell strongly assures that this is not the case with her. "I did not come from an abusive home. In fact, I was raised in a modest 1950s suburban home. The only unusual thing about my childhood was that I was visited regularly by a dark and foreboding entity.

"The true necrophile desires only intimacy with Death. The crypt is what separates the necromantic from the textbook necrophile who views the corpse solely as an inanimate plaything. To violate a corpse for simply the satiating of one's own sexual needs is the highest form of irreverence one can show towards Death."

And a fresh cadaver does nothing for Leilah Wendell! "To me, such a state is still quite representative of life. The body contains so many living organisms and bacterium working at a frantic pace to achieve their goal, decomposition. Only when this is complete, will the last aspect of life die. When the bathroom-tile green of the morgue dulls your senses, and the formaldehyde sterility of the embalming room clouds your head, there is still a place where the feel, the aroma, and the aura of death prevails."

For Wendell that place is a crypt. "Here you are not dealing with any shred of human individuality, you are dealing solely with death itself. There lies the rub, and the niggling point in any study of necrophilia. It is the all-important difference between necrophilia being viewed as a sexual deviation, or as an intimate encounter with Death.

"I don't believe in sex with the dead. I believe that the body can be a catalyst for a spirit to come through to you because it is an empty shell. It is an empty vessel. It's like a radio station that you turn on to get white noise. It's more or less a transmitter. I do not believe you should just go out, dig up a stiff, and have your way with it. I'm very, very much against that. My *Necromantic Ritual*

Book contains a whole chapter on necrophilia and the necromantic rite. Just digging up a body is not what it's all about. That's a violation. Today's modern concept of necrophilia is not at all what I think about the subject. Taken from a ritualistic point of view, the dead body is a sacred altar. A contact point for the Death energy. Something tangible, something to touch."

⚡ ⚡ ⚡

Chad Hensley is the editor of *EsoTerra*, a journal of extreme culture. He can be reached at hecate999@mailexcite.com

   Leilah Wendell is the proprietor of The Westgate Museum, devoted to necromantic art & literature and dedicated to the Angel of Death. She can be reached c/o The Westgate, 5219 Magazine Street, New Orleans, LA 70115.

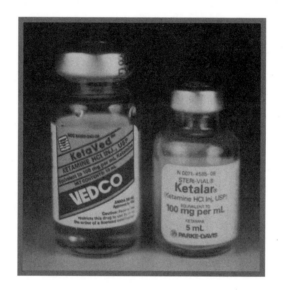

THE KETAMINE NECROMANCE

David Woodard

Ketamine was introduced by God to give dead people a means of communicating with us, the living. Since the '60s, millions of living persons have thus chemically entered a state of illuminative communication[1] with the dead, though perhaps only hundreds of thousands have done so willfully.

When I was six years old, I was laid up in traction in a children's IC ward following a traumatic bicycle accident in Santa Barbara. A leg, a rib and a finger had been broken. Although I was in a state of shock, a kind Filipino nurse allowed me to participate in my own ketamine administration before surgery. Responding to my abject terror, the smiling nurse fixed my hands on the syringe and provided guidance. I eased the needle into the flesh and muscle of my left buttock. She let out a little laugh, said, "That wasn't so bad, now, was it?" and, resuming the reins, depressed the plunger.

Soon I entered a near death experience (NDE). I met and spoke with the spirit of the little girl on the other side of the curtain surrounding my bed. She had fallen from a horse, and we were both observing our bodies while hovering near the ceiling. The spirit of another little boy was also present, and the three of us were united in a state of awe and thrall. The little girl calmly said that she would remain. When I later regained consciousness and inquired about her, I was told by my parents that she had died during my surgery.

I do not know one individual in the formidable elite of ketamine researchers who is willing or able to explain the agenda, circumstances, needs or, in any detail, the character of spirits of the dead. At least satisfactorily. These brave pilgrims walk within our city walls, amongst our cobblers, speed dealers, politicians, homemakers, hitmen and Sunday school teachers, harboring grave secrets they themselves cannot access, for paranoid dead interlocutors holding tremendous stock in privacy have conveniently disabled mortal memory.

American neurologist, dolphin mystic and patron saint to those who would sincerely grace the K-hole, Dr. John Cunningham Lilly (whose grandfather's signature caresses the 1927 $10 bill) has, however, made a commendable stab in his fragmented 1978 autobiography, *The Scientist*[2]. Here, Lilly has identified the ketamine mystique as a linguistic matter. Language is an opaque smokescreen from which one may completely withdraw in order to see something outside of our viciously protected worldly illusions. Ketamine does bring one to a figurative and literal speechless state, in which one is suspended in spiritual animation beyond words, utterly disinterested in and impervious to their influence. The information one receives, regardless of its immediate comprehensibility, cannot be translated into words; it is, thus, pushed back into the subconscious, as ketamine's effects wear off and the subject's familiar linguistic grids resume position, obfuscating the new knowledge.

Here is how Lilly describes a ketamine experience, stated in the present tense, though obviously written *ex post facto*:

> I am in a peculiar state of high indifference. I am not involved in either fear or love. I am a highly neutral being, watching and waiting.
> This is very strange. This planet is similar to Earth, but the colors are different. There is vegetation, but it's a peculiar purple color. There is a sun, but it has a violet hue to it, not the familiar orange of Earth's sun. I am in a beautiful meadow with distant, extremely high mountains. Across the meadow I see creatures approaching. They stand on their hind legs as if approaching. They are a brilliant white and seem to be emitting light. Two of them come near. I cannot make out their features. They are too brilliant for my present vision. They seem to be transmitting thoughts and ideas directly to me. There is no sound. Automatically, what they think is translated into words that I can understand.[3]

Lilly's research in the '50s, during which he established inter-species rapport with dolphins[4], had shown that the dolphin's intelligence is more advanced than man's, his compassion for others greater, his language more refined, his brain, though basically similar, a more complex and evolved organ than man's. In dissecting the brains of his dolphin friends, Lilly successfully located important emotional centers, which, predictably, caught the interest and fed the imagination of the American intelligence community. In the early '60s, the CIA offered Lilly a salary he chose to accept, in exchange for setting to work at locating these same emotional centers (and their operating frequencies) in the human brain. After one year, Lilly bowed out of the fancy CIA job and struck out on his own, deeply offended by the Organization's intentions in securing his participation in the first place. The U.S. Government was naturally interested in learning how to pinpoint and resonate specific centers in the human brain on a mass scale in order to neatly mechanize and militarize the general populace. Toward that end, the distinctly American science of radionics would eventually emerge, i.e., the high-power transmission of basic, unquestioning thought patterns and emotions associated with obedience and submissiveness broadcast over vast geographic areas. Lilly's own mystical predilection for the scrying of coincidence rather than furtive control over others couldn't have placed him at greater odds with the Organization. In the chapter "Seduction by K," we find prominent occurrence of Lilly's own acronym, CCCC, or Cosmic Coincidence Control Center, the ultimate governing body over the universe, and ECCO, or Earth Coincidence Control Office, our local attaché to whose rudimentary Council of Elders one, if worthy, may aspire. The aspirant must submit to extensive and careful ketamine experimentation, abidingly observing successive dosing within the 100—150 mg range.[5]

Following is a list of the states of being one may achieve through injections of ketamine as per Dr. Lilly's "Dose Guidance Curve": 30–50 mg places one into "I," or Internal Reality; 75–100 mg places one into "They," or Extraterrestrial Reality; 150–200 mg places one into "We," or Network of Creation; and 300–400 mg places one into "U," or Unknown.[6]

Until recently, one could quasi-legally order ketamine in those states where it did not appear in the health and safety code book. Slowly, throughout the '90s, free states diminished as code books piled up.[7] On August 12, 1999, U.S. Attorney General Janet Reno officially named ketamine a DEA Schedule III narcotic, making unauthorized possession a felony anywhere in the United States.[8] It is no coincidence that Dr. Alexander Shulgin focused primarily on the legal status of ketamine in the introduction to his classic sourcebook, *Controlled Substances: Chemical And Legal Guide to Federal Drug Laws.*

Ketamine is indeed the kidnapper's, rapist's and hitman's dream drug, imparting thorough dissociation between the victim's ego and anaesthetized body. Within five or six minutes of intramuscular injection (easily administered by a smooth operator sans restraint assistance), the victim is impervious to and unaware of their environment and body. They have also forgotten the notion of having ever occupied a body or been alive, though the eyes may remain open as the mind remains deeply engaged in cinematic and somehow irrefutable hallucinations. Over the next hour, the seasoned professional may conduct business with less anxiety and tremendously enhanced confidence, particularly where one is called upon by precarious circumstances to neutralize a subject. More importantly, however, ketamine holds strong promise for use in necromancy and black magic.

Subjects generally report visions and sensations akin to the classic NDE: soaring through a tunnel toward a pure light, gaining an acute and glowing sense of proximity to God, angels or demons, and becoming utterly emancipated from the soon long-forgotten ego, personality and physical self-concept. But what is often gapingly absent in a report is the portion of the subject's experience as he or she enters the pure light. This is probably not an intentional omission on the subject's part, but rather a severe memory lapse due to his or her lack of inner strength to defeat dead people's often crafty memory-screening techniques. Although ketamine is a drug administered and experienced by living beings, the necromantic communications facilitated by its use tend to benefit the dead, offering their spirits a tantalizing portal through which they may experience the world of the warm-blooded. Perhaps the dead are desperately clustering around an elusive window they have been chasing down for five or six thousand years of gnashing, burning, excruciating torment. Perhaps one of them would manage to claw his way into the ketamine user's fleshy, nubile brain for a 56-minute respite. Such communication seems a match of spirits— at times fencing, at others playing mah-jongg or a game of decapitate-the-end-less-row-of-tractor-drivers or amputate-the-handicapped. In a ketamine experience, you are likely to become a subatomic particle sniffing at the ominous butt of nuclear war, the pinnacle of NDE-driven necromantic glory and the greatest hope of all dead spirits that are not enjoying themselves. William Burroughs said that a nuclear explosion offers total annihilation of the soul, but what do subatomic particles have to say on the matter?

For the mindful juvenile delinquent, ketamine is easy to obtain anywhere in the U.S., and the body of literature concerning its mindful acquisition (as well as that of pharmaceutical drugs in general) has grown steadily since the mid-'70s. As crime expert, renowned cabalist[9], self-styled entheobotanist and former LAPD officer Thom Mounte advises in his occasionally adroit memoir, *From There To Here In No Time*:

> " . . . find a remote animal clinic known to treat felines. If the wearing of gloves seems to you potentially conspicuous in the chosen situation, prudently double-coat all fingertips in verithane and allow to dry thoroughly. Discreetly pay your visit well outside of business hours, of course. Always cut power first, then phone lines. Carefully break a small, inconspicuous window, ideally leading to a bathroom or directly to the store room. Be sure not to cut yourself. Quietly enter the building with a low luminescence flashlight, and promptly locate the pharmaceutical cabinet. Break open and relocate all ketamine (vials individually boxed or unboxed, generally stored in six-packs) to an inconscpicuous shoulder bag. Familiar brand names include Ketaset (highest quality, industry standard), Ketaject and Vetamine. Leave immediately and very carefully." [10]

You may prefer to purchase your ketamine over the counter at a pharmacia, open to the public, in Mexico. *Yo quiero* Ketamex, the pervasive and inescapable brand. Bear in mind that attempting to conspire to transport any quantity of ketamine across the Mexican border into the U.S. is a felony. As of August 12, 1999, however, ketamine's prescription-only human use is officially sanctioned through its DEA Schedule III status. Your doctor can prescribe ketamine for your extremely serious migraine headaches, though he is only likely to do so after repeated visits and exhausting the more standard remedies. In addition to the doctor's bills, you can expect the Rite Aid pharmacist to ring up $185.00 for your 5 ml vial of ketamine (over 50 times the price a veterinarian, or fake veterinarian, pays).

Prefer to play it safe and cheap? Spend a few infraspiritual days and nights perpetually taking the drug in your Rosarito Beach hotel room, and discreetly solicit smuggling tips from spirits of dead people you meet in the room during that time. You now have death itself on your side; as far as your new dead spirit friends and associates are concerned, you absolutely must be equipped, wherever you go. Be careful, forfend thyself, and remember that you are right. Decline to allow customs officers and policemen to see how much you know you are right, for, after presiding over the plight of the dead, you will naturally be inclined to show that most suspicious and incriminating, though subtle, facial expression and general deportment of all: the look of God. God shouldn't have to worry about being sodomized in a Mexican jail for 10 years, only to have his eyes enucleated and his raw, empty sockets fucked and dripping cum for another 20 years before being assigned a court date. Blend in. The secret is the secret—wherever you go, dead or alive, period.

Nowadays, ketamine is used primarily for short-duration feline anesthesia; it is the anesthetic of choice for feline spaying and neutering operations. It was first developed in 1962 at the University of Michigan, allegedly in their search for safe anesthetic products. Ketamine blocks glutamate neurotransmitter pathways in the brain without depressing respiratory and circulatory functions.[11] The drug was first mass produced by Parke-Davis under the brand name Ketalar and was used extensively in Vietnam War field surgery procedures and as a "buddy drug," where its profoundly religious emergence phenomenon[12] was quickly noticed, offering brave American G.I.s a little insight into their glorious predicament—a golden door. Ketamine is still used in hospitals, particularly if the patient is a young child, burn victim, skin graft subject or prepubescent victim of sexual abuse. In the latter case, the genitals and rectum are routinely and thoroughly examined for evidence by a team of forensic experts whilst the understandably distraught young subject is safely restrained under heavy (600–800 mg) ketamine anesthesia.

Solidly bar all possibilities of other people in any way interfering, interfacing with or interrupting your ketamine experience. The physical presence of others may threaten to create an unpleasantly disorienting atmosphere, compelling normally gentle spirits to suddenly grow tense and inadvertently pull you too close, as in the famous cases of D.M. Turner and Marcia Moore.[13] Moreover, the visage of you lying there, unconscious, may serve as an invitation for a mischievous roommate, trespassing policeman, errant spouse or troubled teen to kidnap, rape, drown and/or decapitate you (perhaps shoving your freshly sloughed genitals deep into your open-ended mouth for a graceful flourish of ambience)—without your ever being the wiser.

Secure your materials: at least one 10 ml (1,000 mg) vial of ketamine and a package of 1 cc ultrafines. Select and prepare the room for your experience carefully. If you have a comfortable bath and an uninterrupted day or night during which to operate there, the bathroom should certainly be seized upon as first choice. Otherwise, plan to lie down in bed or on a couch for that period. Make sure the room is quiet, dark and pleasant, and that you are relaxed and comfortable—ideally under blankets or a sheet. You needn't observe any particular dietary stricture. As always, however, alcohol should be studiously avoided, as should all deadly poisons; in combination with ketamine, alcohol may present the subject with a minor but annoying headache shortly following the experience. You may wish to position two or three red and/or green candles at safely peripheral locations in the room. Be sure they are well secured and will not be knocked down, in the rare instance that your body snaps into massive, uncontrollable convulsions while you are unconscious.[14]

Inject 1 cc (100 mg) intramuscularly (i.e., at the upper, outer quadrant of either buttock). Assume a very comfortable position, breathe deeply and relax. The experience begins in five or six minutes, and you will very soon thereafter leave your body . . . When you return approximately one hour later, take notes and promptly repeat. Continue to repeat on return five or six times, attempting logbook entries to the best of your abilities despite overpoweringly rapturous disinterest in words (a temporary condition associated with aphasia). It is imperative that you continue to receive 1 cc (100 mg) doses successively over an extended period, as described. For it is only with this sort of faithful and reliable periodicity that the experience may successfully develop and mature into a trusting, bonding and valuable embassadorship for you in the land of the dead.

NOTES

1. The coinage belongs to Johannes Trithemius (1462–1516), successively Abbot of the Benedictine Abbey of Sponheim and then of St. James ("Schottenkloster") in Wurzburg, angelic necromancer and author of the profoundly influential *Steganography*, which in the next century would serve as inspiration and template for Dee and Kelly's Enochian Keys.
2. Lilly, John Cunningham, M.D.: *The Scientist*; Philadelphia: Lippincott, 1978.
3. Ibid.
4. Pawning his work off as a sort of miracle, Lilly thus inspired the Hollywood movies, *Flipper* and *Day Of The Dolphin*—over which, naturally, he grieves; for the former reflects on his work lightly, the latter in the most negative and destructive manner possible. Now 84, Lilly vigilantly continues his ketamine research as well as his battle against tuna fishers' rights to kill dolphins in their practice of net fishing.
5. Lilly, *The Scientist*.
6. Ibid.
7. A. T. Shulgin, conversation at salvinorin a conference, December 12, 1998.
8. One known physical danger peculiar to ketamine abuse, Olney's syndrome, alleged to threaten the heavy user over an extended period (e.g., daily for a period of six months), is curiously omitted from the imaginary, rape-oriented petitions which led to Reno's decision. Also omitted was the mild weakening of the kidney walls, another genuine danger; one may prevent the latter through daily use of milk thistle seed extract.
9. Mounte's well-received 1986 translation of *Sepher Yetzirah* into Persian verse remains universally esteemed.

10. Mounte, Thom: *From There To Here In No Time*; Phoenix, AZ: Pioneer Press, 1993. The forthcoming revised edition (Fall 2000) provides two valuable methods of extracting salvinorin a (a nonserotonergic, extremely hallucinogenic terpene psychoactively kindred to—though chemically and probably neurochemically unrelated to—ketamine) from the froth of boiled salvia divinorum leaves.

11. This renders the subject sensory-deprived, while circumventing the otherwise standard legal requirement to waste hospital money on a standby anesthesiologist in the event of breathing difficulties.

12. Extremely hallucinatory experience similar to deep, lucid dreaming, which becomes apparent to the subject on emerging from anesthesia one to two hours after receiving a professionally administered dose (400–800mg), or within five minutes of receiving a self-administered subanesthetic dose (75–150mg).

13. See Moore, Marcia, and Alltounian, Howard: *Journeys Into The Bright World*; Rockport, Mass.: Para Research, 1978. Shortly after co-authoring the above, which chronicles her ketamine research, Moore disappeared from her Seattle home; two months later, her remains were found at the base of a tree in a remote snowdrift. Alltounian, Moore's anesthesiologist widower, has recently intimated to Dr. Karl L.R. Jansen, MD, PhD, MRCPsych, author of *K: Ketamine, Dreams and Realities* (Charlotte, North Carolina: Multidisciplinary Association for Psychedelic Studies, 2000), that, contrary to legend, Moore's remains had not been found decapitated.

14. Ketamine-induced convulsions can be similar to the blindly violent, frenzied dance-like movements of a person under the influence of PCP. Although extremely rare, precautions would seem sensible.

⚡ ⚡ ⚡

David Woodard is a composer of military marches and fanfares. An inventor and builder of psychoactive machines, his work has been exhibited at the Los Angeles County Museum of Art. A faithful diarist <davidwoodard.com>, he may be contacted through Feral House.

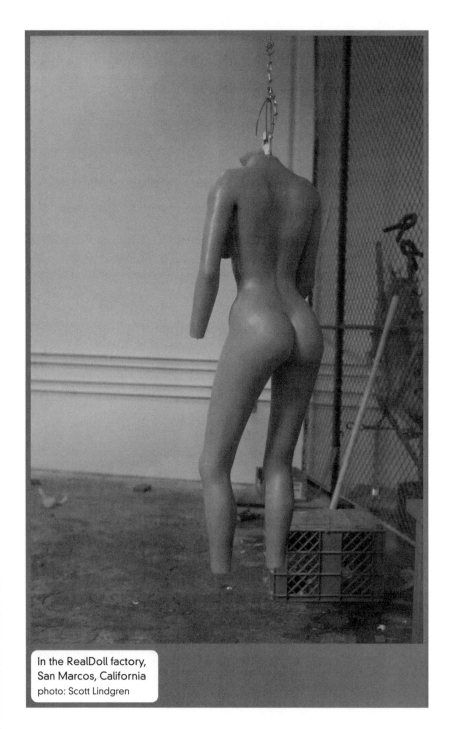

In the RealDoll factory,
San Marcos, California
photo: Scott Lindgren

REALDOLL

Adam Parfrey

When my girlfriend and I saw Hugh Hefner settle in the row ahead of us at a recent movie screening in Westwood, he was accompanied by two well-dressed but thuggish bodyguards and two blonde twins, who, from the tip of their toes to the tip of their noses, appeared to be entirely manufactured. Was the primary technician of our masturbatory culture able to create actual living/breathing/talking RealDolls?

RealDoll, an expensive masturbation device, has received quite a bit of attention from radio, television and the Internet. Howard Stern stuck his penis into a RealDoll on the air, testifying to having much better sex with it than with his wife. *Politically Incorrect*, a talk show that fishes the narcissistic brain pans of celebrities for opinions about cultural trends, devoted an episode to RealDoll. A porn page <chrisrenee.com> places its banner on the RealDoll website <realdoll.com> to promote pictures of RealDoll's breasts and genitals along with stories of advocates' jerkoff fantasies. RealDoll advocates are happy to extricate fantasies from their heads and blow them up to life-size scale, in which they become masturbatory supermen to these slim-bodied, large-breasted silicone devices. It's remarkable to contemplate that hundreds of thousands of lonely males log on to the RealDoll porn websites for sperm-spewing fantasies about penetrating rubber dolls:

> Her tight pussy presses around my organ like a sheath taking my pulse. And that pulse is racing!
>
> When Sylvie allows me to come up for air, I take the opportunity to fondle her swelling boobs with closed eyes, relishing the feel of ample feminine curves under my palms. Her nipples are small and perky, standing at attention like little soldiers under my caresses.
>
> Then I rear up to watch her pussy suck my dick. The girl notices it and gives me a little extra squeeze. I spasm slightly, trying to maintain control. "No, Sylvie. I don't wanna come. I just did it yesterday with Julie!"
>
> "Julie? Your other RealDoll?" Surprise, jealousy and a little pique mingle in her voice. "Well—if you can do it with her, then you can do it with me, too!"
>
> With that, she gives her pelvis a few twisting motions . . . and my control vanishes.
>
> I groan as I feel the jets of my one-day supply pump into her body. "Why did they have to teach you that?"
>
> Ignoring my complaints, the hussy eagerly strokes my mast while I lean forward on my hands, letting her milk me dry, shuddering and jerking. At last, my orgasm subsides and I slip from her to crash onto my back, exhausted.

My dick, sticky with cum and lubricant, flops onto my belly in its tingly afterglow state.

"Our first time!" Sylvie chortles next to me. "It was great, wasn't it?"

I lift myself to an elbow, heedless of the jism running across my stomach. "You are stunning, you are fantastic!" I tell her. "But you've got to learn who's boss around here!"

"Why, you are!" she responds innocently. "Now—can you do me a favor?"

"What?"

"Your juice is running out of me and down my ass. Can you clean me up? The cleaning tools are in the packet."

Curious, I kneel over her, indicating for her to show me. She spreads her thighs wide. Indeed, whitish fluid is dribbling from her cunt and forming a gooey puddle near her right buttock.

"Poor darling!" I pat her smooth thigh. "Right away, ma'am! Cleaning coming up!"

Matt McMullen, the San Diego County-based heavy metal musician (his band is called "Chaotic Order") and RealDoll creator, had very little idea that the mannequins he was creating would have such demand as a masturbatory appliance. The following interview with McMullen took place in his San Marcos factory, which fills millions of dollars' worth of orders a year.

McMullen: I started, in my free time, sculpting a life-sized girl. I made my molds and initially I started working with some latex and some different low-end rubbers because I didn't have the financial means for silicone at the time.

Parfrey: *How costly is that? Working with silicone as opposed to latex?*

McMullen: You can make a latex head filled with foam for about $2. You can make a silicone head for $50. That's the difference. So silicone, while I was aware of it, wasn't in the picture at the time. I just wanted to make something, so I made a couple of latex dolls and they were very appealing to the eye and

The RealDoll hermaphrodite model—
still unavailable to the buying public
photo: Scott Lindgren

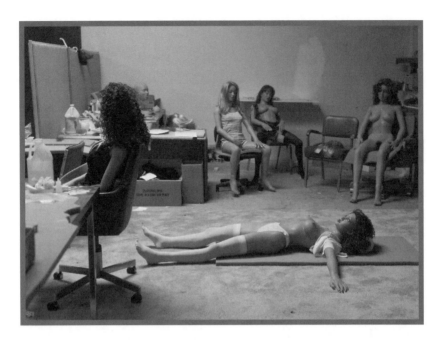

photographed well, but they still looked fake. I want it to look real and make people look twice. I want it to look real when you pose it. When you bend the elbow, I want the material to collapse and compress in a realistic way. With the latex and the foam, when you bend her arm it basically looked like a stuffed shirt. It would fold in half and it looked very unnatural. So you were stuck with the pose that was sculpted, which was defeating the whole purpose. I eventually got into the silicone. Right around that time I had a website, and I started putting pictures up. It started off real small. It didn't get a lot of hits. Then, all of a sudden, the website began to get really popular. I started getting email from these guys saying, "How much would it cost to make one of these? I want to buy with the stipulation that I could have sex with it." I started thinking that this could be a love doll. It didn't occur to me that anybody in their right mind would pay five thousand dollars for a love doll [it now costs from $5,249 to $5,749, depending on model ordered], but sure enough these guys, when I told them, "Hey, this is how much it's going to cost. It's really expensive, it takes a lot of time." I thought for sure these guys were going to go, "Oh forget it!" But, a few of them hung in there and said, "Okay, I'll send you a check." So I put the sexual organs in and I started thinking more along the lines of the way it felt instead of the way it looked. Eventually I arrived at this thing and said, "This'll work. It's fully functional, it feels pretty real. I tested it out, it worked. Everything was in order." Then I came up with this name, RealDoll, and it just took and I started getting more and more traffic. It started to take off. I quit my job. And that's where it came from.

Has anyone else done this before you? The Japanese, for instance?

There are some Japanese companies that have made realistic love dolls, but they're stuck in that mind-set of "How cheap can we make it and how much money can we make off of it?" They look better than your typical blow-up doll, but they're made of foam and you can fit the thing in a suitcase if you want. With our dolls I'm thinking, "I want it to weigh as much as a girl, I want it to feel like a girl, I want it to look like a girl, I want it to move like a girl." The ones we've got, hands down, are the best love dolls anywhere. To my knowledge, nobody else has attempted this yet.

There is historical precedence. Do you know about the artist Oskar Kokoschka?

No.

Around the turn-of-the-century he dated Alma Mahler, Gustav Mahler's wife. After Alma Mahler ditched Kokoschka, he became obsessed with her, and convinced Alma's dressmaker to construct a doll in her likeness, and he carried this doll around everywhere.

No kidding?

Then there was Count Von Cosel in Florida. After his beloved wife died, he embalmed her, spoke to her, and ate dinner with her every night. Then there are the mannequin artists, George Segal and Duane Hanson. Anton LaVey of the Church of Satan created a set-up in his house with degenerate mannequins pissing themselves in a bar he called "The Den of Iniquity." He claimed to have had a much better and fulfilling time speaking with the mannequins than with actual humans.

Oskar Kokoschka's self-portrait
with Alma Mahler doll

We've had many people writing to us likening us to Anton LaVey, definitely convinced that we're all Satanists here and that we must be worshipping the devil and stuff.

Are Christians writing this to you?

No, actually, they're our fans. But some people speculate that this is some evil thing and that we're out to eradicate females and that we want to replace them.

Really? Who says that?

Far-right-wing feminists, who'll write a short and sour email saying that we're sick and how can this doll even come close to comparing with a real woman? We don't say these dolls are a replacement, they're an alternative. It's kind of like a Snickers bar to get you through the day before dinner. It's just a snack, and it beats your hand, that's for sure. If you don't have a good imagination and you're having a hard time picturing this girl, with the doll you can look down and there's a girl there. She's not doing much, but she's there.

Have you thought about making them do more?

We've got a lot of things going, enhancements, if you will. What we're going to have available pretty soon is an electronic system which will be broken down into sensors in different parts of the doll's body. Those sensors will detect penetration and will send the message to a small CPU, which will then produce pleasurable sounds. We're hoping to make it interactive, where the rhythm will affect the feedback. The force that this guy's using will affect the

Hans Bellmer's doll

feedback, the volume level, the excitement level. Maybe over a period of say, ten minutes, she—the doll—becomes more and more excited as you continue the stimulation and will eventually reach an orgasm, which will then trigger maybe a vibration unit, and you'll feel a contraction or something like that. We're also looking at infrared sensors in the eyes that will detect when you walk in the room and the doll will say something like, "Come play with me," to "Did you take out the garbage?" depending on your particular set of fantasies. I've already done some dolls where you can make the eyes open and close, and you can make the tongue French kiss,  but it's all manual. There's a knob or a wire cable that you have to pull to activate it, so it's more like a puppet than a self-contained, animated unit.

You must get a lot of kook mail. What's the most amusing?

We've had people write and ask us if we can make a very realistic male dog doll. We've had people that want a green doll or a red doll, with a tail and horns, all kinds of weird stuff. A lot of crackpots have written us claiming to be robotic engineers and send us schematics that look like a kindergardener drew it.

Will you do a caricature of any specific person?

I get a lot of people saying, "Make me a Pam Anderson doll. Can you do that?" They want porn stars, celebrities . . . people want their wife that has left them. It's sad, but I can do it if there's enough money involved.

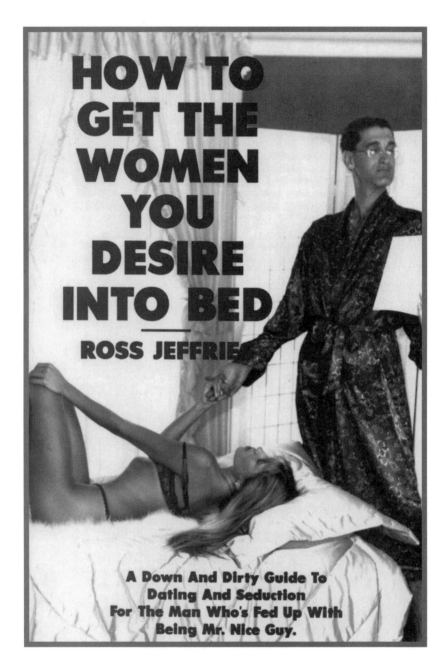

HOW TO
GET THE
WOMEN
YOU
DESIRE
INTO BED

ROSS JEFFRIE

A Down And Dirty Guide To
Dating And Seduction
For The Man Who's Fed Up With
Being Mr. Nice Guy.

WHO IS THE MOST MASTERFUL SEDUCER OF THEM ALL?

Adam Parfrey

It's a sad, lonely world. So sad, so lonely, that the insipid, broadly smiling, facelifted mug of John Gray, author of *Men Are from Mars, Women Are from Venus*, all-pervades newspapers, talk shows and infomercials, telling everybody "how to get what you want from relationships."

Fifty percent of all paperbacks sold are romance novels, turning the eternal boredom of married lives into forbidden fantasies of rape and romance. Porn movies, the male version of romance novels, flush men with the make-believe of big-dick power fucks.

There are even sadder situations—the pathos of individuals who can't even find a way to get themselves involved in a relationship needful of John Gray and his repellent books.

This loser contingent buys *How To Pick Up Girls* or other self-help tomes in the dating category. Others flock to web sites promoting the idea of hypnotizing women to do their bidding. One such site holds hundreds of porn stories of the mind control genre, featuring titles like "Ass-Fucker Hypnotist" and "My Brother, My Master." One "Dr. Deeper" sells tapes for buyers to gain "Penile Enlargement Through Hypnosis!" Another site sells manuals that "instantly turn you into a ladies' man." An email spammer sends people 900 numbers that tell you "HOW TO MEET PROFESSIONAL DANCERS AND MAKE A DATE ALMOST IMMEDIATELY!"

Many of these seduction teachers compete and bust each other's nuts on newsgroups like alt.seduction.fast with phrases like "worthless fuckwad" and "manipulative phony." The question remains: Who is the most masterful seducer of them all?

Ross Jeffries is perhaps the most financially successful guru for the woman-starved. His come-on: "How To Totally Mind-Fuck Almost ANY Woman Into Screwing Your Brains Out . . . And Make It Seem Like You're Just Having A Normal, Innocent Conversation!" was picked up and slobbered after by *Rolling Stone* and *Playboy*. Jeffries' painfully ordinary looks are used as a marketing device: "If someone like me can seduce hot women, so can anybody."

Jeffries' techniques, which he claims will induce "gorgeous" women into giving unhappy and unsuccessful males memorable blowjobs, differ from competitors in that they employ neuro-linguistic programming, or NPL. NPL, the "art and science" of programming oneself and others, was developed in the '70s by UC Santa Cruz instructors John Grinder and Richard Bandler, and

Secrets of

Speed Seduction

"Home Study Course Workbook"

How To Create An Instantaneous Sexual
Attraction In Any Woman You Meet!!!

Copyright 1994
Ross Jeffries

Now with
Newsletters and
Seminar Notes

promoted through books like *Trance-Formations*, which has a New Age cover of witches, dragons and rainbows. Influencing the entire NLP route were the discoveries of renowned psychologist Milton Erickson, who, as NLP experts Joseph O'Connor and John Seymour call it, "taught how to induce and maintain trance in order to contact the hidden resources of our personality." The whole idea can be boiled down to two words: gaining rapport.

Some dozen years ago, Ross Jeffries figured that gaining rapport could be the method by which he could end his sexual starvation. From Jeffries' Speed Seduction™ website:

Here's Just Some Of The Secrets You'll Be Learning In This Incredible, Mind-Blowing, Eye-Opening Complete Home Study Course:

How To Create A Magnetic Attraction Within Minutes When You Aren't Close To Being Her Type!

Getting Her Fast Despite A Boyfriend Or Husband!

Creating Instant States Of Overwhelming Connection!

Eradicating Last Minute Objections To Sex!

Quotes, Negation And Other Super-Weasel Patterns!

Playing With Her Mental Pictures Using Language To Engage Her Sexual Fantasy Mechanisms

The Secret Understanding Of The Speed Seducer!!!

Using "Stealth Suggestion" To Paint Word Pictures That Trigger And Stimulate Her Imaginative, Emotional "Right Brain"

Using Her Innate/Subjective Sense Of Time So It Seems Like She's Already Been In Love With You For Months When You've Only Known Her Just A Few Hours

Using Speed Seduction For Business Success And Making Loads Of Money!!

What isn't different from *How to Pick Up Girls* is that Speed Seduction™ lessons teach that one must use lines and pay so much attention to how the prey is reacting that it becomes impossible to relax and be oneself. On Halloween, an entire week of Speed Seduction™ lessons were taught in the Bahamas for the small sum of $2,500.00, where one is apt to meet gleeful students like Mark Cunningham, who testifies on Jeffries' website:

> I just wanted to let you know how happy I am with your Secrets Of Speed Seduction seminar tapes. Your innovative approach gives me a power and impact that the "experts" say is impossible! Hot damn!
>
> I am not in the best of shape physically or mentally, a pretty typical 41-year-old guy, so I thought I'd have to go through a period of conditioning. Man, was I wrong! Here are some examples:
>
> Dr. Amanda—I went for my eye exam and met this young woman with a great voice. So I started talking about tonality and how you can feel an incredible connection with someone you just met. Later, riding me until she collapsed, she kept saying "I can't believe I'm doing this!" Kind of surprised me too, so I went out to try again and this time I found. . .
>
> Carol—a real space case; she believes in crystals, astrology, etc. But she's also 26, blonde and an aerobics instructor, so what the hey? I got her out for coffee and hit her with the blammo pattern. What a cosmic connection! Now she can't keep me out of her mouth and loves to gobble my male energy!
>
> Tammy—a 23-year-old newlywed with buyer's remorse. Same thing—instantaneous connection, time distortion, bringing out feelings of incredible pleasure and satisfaction. I discovered she was multi-orgasmic and loves to suck!
>
> Laura—a big, busty, leggy gal; sort of a Midwest Elle MacPherson, she told me I wasn't her "type" and she had a boyfriend. No problem, I said, and just kept talking—got her laughing, built that incredible connection, anchored peak experiences, zoomed her around in space

---

Trance Words #3

find yourself

What does it mean to "find yourself" doing something?
That it wasn't consciously planned or executed!
Which means T - R - A - N - C - E!

Speed Seduction™ learning card

> ## Speed Seducer Rule #4
>
> ### Keep your skills a secret!
>
> Speed seducing works because it is hidden and unde-
> tectable. True at very advanced levels you can tell
> them what you're doing and it will still work, but why
> give them the chance? Your aim is to get a result, not
> impress with what you know.

and time and I left her in that peak state while I ushered her back to
my place.

Not to brag, Ross, but this shit is going on all the time now! It
doesn't matter how old she is, if she has a boyfriend or husband or
if I'm her "type." NOTHING MATTERS! You're a fucking genius!
Mark Cunningham
Maumee, Ohio

This praise may be in part due to Jeffries' use of one Mark Cunningham as
a seminar instructor, who teaches how to seduce wives—the fair game of hypnotic Casanovas. "There's no such thing as a married woman," says
Cunningham on one of Jeffries' tapes. "Just a woman who is married."

I met with Ross Jeffries for an interview at a restaurant of his choice—Santa
Monica's Broadway Deli. Skinny, six-feet tall, and sporting a face he describes
as being Harold Ramis-like, Jeffries reveals himself in interview as one hard
worker, fast in speech, vague and suggestive in terminology.

Jeffries: There are a lot of people out there who fancy themselves as competitors. The difference is that everything the competitors do is in the dating box,
the dating frame. They may give you a different set of plays, but you're still on
the same field, playing the same game. I think dating is a stylized form of
humiliation for men, in which men play the supplicant, the beggar. So I
encourage my men, uh, my students, to step outside of that framework and to
build a better one that works. Dating for most men is a form of gambling, of
supplication. You know what I mean by "supplicant?'"

Parfrey: *You're trying to build up men's self-respect?*

No. No. Self-respect? In a sense, yes. Self-respect is a broad generalization.
You can have all the self-respect in the world but if you get into a bar fight
with a guy who's seven feet tall and 350 pounds of muscle, you can have all
the self-respect in the world and it won't do you any good. . . . I teach men a

different framework that has nothing to do with dating. I teach them that dating is for women they're already sleeping with. Dating as a vehicle to give them a choice, a selectivity and power, just doesn't work. Unless they are part of an elite that society says is attractive to women. Good looks, fame, power, money.

Then it's easy?

It's still not easy. Women still have the power. They're still controlling access to the sex. You're still playing the role of the supplicant. You just have a lot more tools. Regardless of what a man looks like, and how much money he has, for most men dating is still a form of gambling. They don't know what's going to happen. . . . That's where they get the term, "I got lucky." Think about the implications of that term. Think what it means to get lucky. I think what it means is that you don't have control. You don't have the means. Do you fly?

No.

Do you have a flying phobia?

I don't have a flying phobia. I thought you meant, do I pilot an airplane?

Well, you've flown before on airplanes?

Of course.

Let's say when you get on an airplane you say to the pilot, "How can we make sure we get to our destination?" And he honestly says, "I don't know. Maybe we'll get lucky." You'd get off the plane.

I've heard the pilot say, "maybe we'll get lucky" on Southwest Airlines.

Okay. Okay. For most guys, even if they have what society says is good to have, dating is a form of rolling the dice. I want to give people a much deeper measure of control, and a much greater measure of choice. I wrote a book called *How to Get Women You Desire Into Bed*, which I feel is pretty primitive compared to what I do today. I wrote that back in 1989. Then I

Speed Seducer Rule #5

Be a stainless steel fist in a velvet glove!

Always be as low key as possible in application of your skills. Not "ha - ha I'm doing this thing to you" but "isn't it interesting how the mind works?" Soften, soften, and soften some more.

> ## Weasel Phrase #8
>
> ### You might find (yourself)
>
> Useful as, the <u>start</u> of an intensifying chain of phrases, it implies that they're going to experience what you describe as something that just happens, so not only can they <u>not</u> resist it, but it implies that <u>you</u> had nothing to do with it! "You might find that a picture of you and me being together in a special way pops right into that space in your mind."

studied marketing on my own, started selling the book, and then I came up with Speed Seduction back in '93 and came up with courses and hooked up with my business partners and started doing seminars.

There are specific words, phrases that you recommend and you have written down on cards. It's like you're writing a script.

Let me back up. There are two ways to understand what I do. You can look at the small pieces, and we can look at them, and we will. Those are the individual things I've said, but on a broader level it's about understanding the entire concept of dealing with women on a completely different level. I'd really like to talk about that first. See this girl. She's got a lot of choice, a lot of power. You think, wow, I want to be with that. Okay. But I can teach guys to so captivate her mind, and touch her mind on such deep levels then suddenly they have all the power. I have students that can astonish you with what they can do. They're not in the traditional mode. In my seminars, I'll get students up there who are fat, bald, old, broke. And they go up there and tell their stories, and see the guys out there. Their brains start to fry. They go this is impossible, it can't possibly be true. And when you look at it from the traditional framework, it can't be true. It's like a magic trick. It appears to be magic, but if you know the principles, the way the illusion is designed, you don't know that particular trick, you can probably ferret out how it was done. You can take Doug Kenney. Who's another magician? Penn and Teller. You know who they are.

Yeah.

You can send them to a show by David Copperfield. If they don't know a trick, they can probably figure out how it's done because they know the dynamic behind it. So let me teach you something. (Pause.) Consider a woman's mind like this. There are different places, different structures, in a woman's mind. There's the typical, everyday, what I call culturally programmed woman. This is just a metaphor. Consider a ship. A cargo ship. When it comes to sex, a man's mind is one cargo ship with one big container . . . (Jeffries yells at some unknown woman) CARLITA! CARLA! What's up, baby?

(A waitress of average looks comes to the table.)

Carla: How are you? What have you been up to?

Jeffries: Just doing another interview.

Carla: Yeah? Good for you. I've been meaning to call, but I've been so busy.

Jeffries: Ooooohhhh. Well, do you still have my number?

Carla: I do.

Jeffries: . . . Call me.

Carla: Are you around?

Jeffries: I'm around. If I hear from you, I'll be wonderfully, pleasantly surprised. All right? So . . . (Carla leaves, leaving Jeffries to turn his attention from his seemingly unsuccessful pickup scheme to the interview.) When it comes to dating . . .

You don't like the long-term relationship?

If I find someone who sufficiently interests me to make that commitment, I will. My last serious girlfriend, Kim, I dated her two-and-a-half years, she now teaches at my seminars, and she teaches her own seminars. Consider a man's mind when it comes to sex to be like a ship. One big hole in it. A woman's mind is like this ship with all these segmented, water-tight compartments. One can be completely shut off from the other. So what I like to teach men is that when it comes to women there's the culturally programmed woman, that's a woman with all the rules, all the roles, all the measurements like "I'll only date guys who look like this." This kind of look, this kind of job, I don't do anything until the fourth date, all those kinds of things. But on much deeper levels there's the natural

---

Trance Words #11

Imagine

It's not important to me that you imagine having mastery of these skills! To imagine requires using your internal processes <u>visually</u>; similar to day dreaming or hallucinating! In other words ... T - R - A - N - C - E!

woman, that's the one with all the indulgences, with the wild sexual fantasy, the kind of things if she'd let loose none of her best friends would ever know this about her. She keeps her daydreams, her secret, hidden fetishes, and those things don't reach to dating. Dating just triggers the culturally programmed woman. So the question is: the thing is, every woman longs for that experience, to meet someone so fascinating, so compelling that those normal measurements, like he has to look like this, they get set aside. She feels herself drawn in and she surrenders to this experience. So the question, Adam, is: What is the process that a woman can undergo that allows her to realize that she wants to be with a guy, not because he's her type, not because he fits all those pre-programmed stereotypes that she's used to, but he touches her in a way that she experiences true passion, okay? No, that's not just lust in the moment, that's not even when she finds she gives all that she has, it's when she's touched so deeply that she finds things coming forth from her that she never even knew what she had, that's not a function of people programming things, that's a function of how you use your language to capture and lead her imagination, and activate (he snaps) those deeper structures. Those deeper structures are either out of her conscious awareness or they're slumbering. All right? Now my claim is this. If you can learn to awaken those structures, link them to you, anchor them to some of those things you learn in NLP, and then accelerate them, and then you can have doing things with you, for you, to you, that have nothing to do with all the normal measurements that have to do with dating. And you can do it predictably. That's my client.

(Jeffries barely pauses, looks me straight in the eyes and points to his palm.)

Here's the thing. Think about this. If this is real, if this is not a scam, if I'm not exaggerating. If this is real, think about the implications, cuz I'm taking the normal power balance in society, and screwing it, and giving men who normally wouldn't have that choice of power, that choice of power, to me that is one of the most subversive revolutionary things you can do, take the normal power balance and fuck it up. It's like giving weapons to the settlers so they can fight the Indians.

(Another pause, another direct look into the eyes.)

Most men get into relationships by default, not by choice. They accidentally met someone who ends their sexual starvation and that's when you're more likely to be dishonest and cheat, with something that's scarce. But when you have abundance and opportunity and choice, then you don't need to do those things. You don't need to cheat. My students get married, but when they get married, they become the kind of husbands that piss off other husbands because their wife goes to other wives and talk about their men like they really want to be there. They haven't defaulted. If what I say is true, it's not going to be mainstream for fifty or sixty years, since it's so against, uh . . . here's the greatest compliment anyone ever gave me. Two compliments. One person told me I was the Tesla of getting laid. Which was great. Edison, no. Tesla, yes. Someone else said I was Thorpe. Do you know who Thorpe was?

No.

Thorpe was a British mathematician who so figured out the rules of blackjack that the casinos had to change the rules. That was like, wow, Thorpe!?

Do you believe you're good at hypnosis?

(Long pause.) Yeah, I think so. I think any communication that captures the imagination and forces the person to go inside and search for the meaning of words is hypnotic. All communication has hypnotic elements. When a perfectly intelligent man looks at a gorgeous woman and goes into a state of sputtering lust and can't even think of his own name, that's a form of trance. Make sense? We have a get-laid think tank, in essence. I take a little piece of what someone sees in isolation and someone else sees, I can put it together, like this. (Snaps his fingers.)

Do you have a long-term plan?

Eventually I want to get into psychic influence. I've got breakthroughs in psychic influence, too.

Psychic influence?

Yeah. Remote influence.

Remote viewing?

Remote viewing is passive. I take someone who's a thousand miles away, sort of merge with them and put thoughts into their head. Sounds wacky. But I made some major breakthroughs in that, too. I'm as far from New Age tofu eating as . . .

But it pays well.

I don't care if it pays well or not. I'm as far from that as you can get. I also think that there are ways of going through psychic influence that can be precise.

How can you measure it?

You measure it . . . uh, hypothetically. Let's say there's a woman you know. You haven't talked to her in six weeks. I teach you something that sends her into a dream, that you're having wild sex together, and you'll talk to her. And then next morning she calls you and describes the dream in great detail and it matches, one on one, perfectly. You'd have to say there's something odd going on there.

ISLAMIC CULTURAL PROGRAM
FREE MARRIAGE COUNSELING

UNDERSTANDING YOUR WOMAN

Brothers don't ever put your penis, in your woman's mouth because this spoils your woman. When you put your penis, in your woman's mouth or in her rectum, you are misusing your woman, And what you are doing to her is: you are starting your woman out on A Sexual Habit. And you are not conscious of what you are doing to her.

This is what causes all of our young people's marriages to go sour. This is the reason that all of our young people start fussing and fighting like cats and dogs six months to A year after their mirriage.

Now, the reason that all of our young people's marriage start messing up in about 3 to 6 months is because, It takes about 3 to 6 months before that mess, that you shoots in her mouth, begins to take an affect on her brain.

Now, it mess you up to, but, it messes your woman up Quicker then it mess you up, because she's got the thing in her mouth, and she gets the full load every time, and you are licking A hole, so you are missing most of yours so that's why it messes her up Quicker then it mess you up.

And the affects that this mess have on your woman is: it clogs up the love current in her brain, and she don't have any feelings for you any more. And the more of this mess she eats the less feelings she have for you.

And it works the same way on you, as it works on her. You see, when you eat this mess, It makes you hard headed, and rebellius, and cold blooded, It kills the love in you, It makes you selfish, and small minded, and you can't reason with your woman any more, because all she can think of is, sex sex sex, just like A sissy. And, thats why all the arguements start.

If that young man knew, that when he starts puting his penis, in his woman's mouth that, that was the begining of the end, of his love affair, he would cut off his right arm, before he would ask her to do that to him. but he is not conscious of what he is doing to her, if he loves her.

So then after he messes her up, they finally come to the conclusion, that love, don't last. But, that's A LIE. LOVE DO LAST. Love will last you A LIFETIME, If you don't misuse it. And when you put your penis, in your woman's mouth, or in her rectum. you are mis-use-ing your Love. And that's Why it turns sour on you. So don't mis-use your woman, And she will Love you the rest of your Life.

And if you and your woman have this problem. NOW. What you have to do is This: You and your woman will have to get your heads together, and KICK, THAT SEXUAL HABIT. And once you have Kicked, Your Sexual Habit, You can get your Love Life back together again.

Steps in Overcoming Masturbation

Mark E. Peterson, Council of the 12 Apostles

Be assured that you can be cured of your difficulty. Many have been, both male and female, and you can be also if you determine that it must be so.

This determination is the first step. That is where we begin. You must decide that you will end this practice, and when you make that decision, the problem will be greatly reduced at once.

But it must be more than a hope or a wish, more than knowing that it is good for you. It must be actually a DECISION. If you truly make up your mind that you will be cured, then you will have the strength to resist any tendencies which you may have and any temptations which may come to you.

After you have made this decision, then observe the following specific guidelines:

A Guide to Self-Control:

1. Never touch the intimate parts of your body except during normal toilet processes.

2. Avoid being alone as much as possible. Find good company and stay in this good company.

3. If you are associated with other persons having this same problem, YOU MUST BREAK OFF THEIR FRIENDSHIP. Never associate with other people having the same weakness. Don't suppose that two of you will quit together, you never will. You must get away from people of that kind. Just to be in their presence will keep your problem foremost in your mind. The problem must be taken OUT OF YOUR MIND for that is where it really exists. Your mind must be on other and more wholesome things.

4. When you bathe, do not admire yourself in a mirror. Never stay in the bath more than five or six minutes—just long enough to bathe and dry and dress AND THEN GET OUT OF THE BATHROOM into a room where you will have some member of your family present.

5. When in bed, if that is where you have your problem for the most part, dress yourself for the night so securely that you cannot easily touch your vital parts, and so that it would be difficult and time consuming for you to remove those clothes. By the time you started to remove protective clothing you would have sufficiently controlled your thinking that the temptation would leave you.

6. If the temptation seems overpowering while you are in bed, GET OUT OF BED AND GO INTO THE KITCHEN AND FIX YOURSELF A SNACK, even if it

is in the middle of the night, and even if you are not hungry, and despite your fears of gaining weight. The purpose behind this suggestion is that you GET YOUR MIND ON SOMETHING ELSE. You are the subject of your thoughts, so to speak.

7. Never read pornographic material. Never read about your problem. Keep it out of your mind. Remember—"First a thought, then an act." The thought pattern must be changed. You must not allow this problem to remain in your mind. When you accomplish that, you soon will be free of the act.

8. Put wholesome thoughts into your mind at all times. Read good books— Church books—Scriptures—Sermons of the Brethren. Make a daily habit of reading at least one chapter of Scripture, preferably from one of the four Gospels in the New Testament, or the Book of Mormon. The four Gospels—Matthew, Mark, Luke and John—above anything else in the Bible can be helpful because of their uplifting qualities.

9. Pray. But when you pray, don't pray about this problem, for that will tend to keep it in your mind more than ever. Pray for faith, pray for understanding of the Scriptures, pray for the Missionaries, the General Authorities, your friends, your families, BUT KEEP THE PROBLEM OUT OF YOUR MIND BY NOT MENTIONING IT EVER—NOT IN CONVERSATION WITH OTHERS, NOT IN YOUR PRAYERS. KEEP IT OUT OF YOUR MIND.

The attitude a person has toward his problem has an effect on how easy it is to overcome. It is essential that a firm commitment be made to control the habit. As a person understands his reasons for the behavior, and is sensitive to the conditions or situations that may trigger a desire for the act, he develops the power to control it.

We are taught that our bodies are temples of God, and are to be clean so that the Holy Ghost may dwell within us. Masturbation is a sinful habit that robs one of the Spirit and creates guilt and emotional stress. It is not physically harmful unless practiced in the extreme. It is a habit that is totally self-centered, and secretive, and in no way expresses the proper use of the procreative power given to man to fulfill eternal purposes. It therefore separates a person from God and defeats the gospel plan.

This self-gratifying activity will cause one to lose his self-respect and feel guilty and depressed, which can in the extreme lead to further sinning. As a person feels spiritually unclean, he loses interest in prayer, his testimony becomes weak, and missionary work and other Church callings become burdensome, offering no joy and limited success.

To help in planning an effective program to overcome the problem, a brief explanation is given of how the reproductive organs in a young man function.

The testes in your body are continually producing hundreds of millions of reproductive cells called spermatozoa. These are moved up a tube called the vas deferens to a place called the ampulla where they are mixed with fluids from two membranous pouches called seminal vesicles and the prostate gland. The resultant fluid is called semen. When the seminal vesicles are full, a signal is sent to the central nervous system indicating they are ready to be emptied. The rate at which this filling takes place varies greatly from one person to another, depending on such things as diet, exercise, state of health, etc. For some it may be several times a week, for others twice a month and for others, hardly ever.

It is normal for the vesicles to be emptied occasionally at night during sleep. This is called a wet dream. The impulses that cause the emptying come from the central nervous system. Often an erotic dream is experienced at the same time, and is part of this normal process. If a young man has consistently masturbated instead of letting nature take its course, the reproductive system is operating at a more rapid pace, trying to keep up with the loss of semen,. When he stops the habit, the body will continue to produce at this increased rate, for an indefinite period of time, creating sexual tensions and pressure. These are not harmful and are to be endured until the normal central nervous system pathway of release are once again established.

During this period of control, several things can be done to make the process easier and more effective:

As one meets with his Priesthood Leader, a program for overcoming masturbation can be implemented using some of the suggestions which follow. Remember, it is essential that a regular report program be agreed on, so progress can be recognized and failures understood and eliminated.

Suggestions:

1. Pray daily, ask for gifts of the Spirit, that which will strengthen you against temptation. Pray fervently and out loud when the temptations are strongest.

2. Follow a program of vigorous daily exercise. The exercises reduce emotional tension and depression and are absolutely basic to the solution of this problem. Double your physical activity when you feel stress increasing.

3. When the temptation to masturbate is strong, yell STOP to those thoughts as loudly as you can in your mind and then recite a pre-chosen Scripture or sing an inspirational hymn. It is important to turn your thoughts away from the selfish need to indulge.

4. Set goals of abstinence, begin with a day, then a week, month, year, and finally commit to never doing it again. Until you commit yourself to never do it again you will always be open to temptation.

5. Change in behavior and attitude is most easily achieved through a changed self-image. Spend time every day imagining yourself strong and in control, easily overcoming tempting situations.

6. Begin to work daily on a self-improvement program. Relate this plan to improving your Church service, to improving your relationships with your family, God and others. Strive to enhance your strengths and talents.

7. Be outgoing and friendly. Force yourself to be with others and learn to enjoy working and talking with them. Use principles of developing friendships found in books such as *How to Win Friends and Influence People* by Dale Carnegie.

8. Be aware of situations that depress you or that cause you to feel lonely, bored, frustrated or discouraged. These emotional states can trigger the desire to masturbate as a way of escape. Plan in advance to counter these low periods through various activities, such as reading a book, visiting a friend, doing something athletic, etc.

9. Make a pocket calendar for a month on a small card. Carry it with you, but show it to no one. If you have a lapse of self-control, color the day black. Your goal will be to have no black days. The calendar becomes a strong visual reminder of self-control and should be looked at when you are tempted to add another black day. Keep your calendar up until you have at least three clear months.

10. A careful study will indicate you have had the problem at certain times and under certain conditions. Try and recall, in detail. what your particular times and conditions were. Now that you understand how it happens, plan to break the pattern through counter-activities.

11. In the field of psychotherapy there is a very effective technique called aversion therapy. When we associate or think of something very distasteful with something has been pleasurable, but undesirable, the distasteful thought and feeling will begin to cancel out that which was pleasurable. If you associate something very distasteful with your loss of self-control it will help you stop the act. For example, if you are tempted to masturbate, think of having to bathe in a tub of worms, and eat several of them as you do the act.

12. During your toileting and shower activities, leave the bathroom door and shower curtain partly open, to discourage being alone in total privacy. Take cool brief showers.

13. Arise immediate in the mornings. Do not lie in bed awake, no matter what time of day it is. Get up and do something. Start each day with an enthusiastic activity.

14. Keep your bladder empty. Refrain from drinking large amounts of fluids before retiring.

15. Reduce the amount of spices and condiments in your food. Eat as lightly as possible at night.

16. Wear pajamas that are difficult to open, yet loose and not binding.

17. Avoid people, situations, pictures or reading materials that might create sexual excitement.

18. It is sometimes helpful to have a physical object to use in overcoming this problem. *A Book of Mormon*, firmly held in the hand, even in bed at night, has proven helpful in extreme cases.

19. In very severe cases it may be necessary to tie a hand to the bed frame with a tie in order that the habit of masturbating in semi-sleep condition can be broken. This can also be accomplished by wearing several layers of the clothing which would be difficult to remove while half-asleep.

20. Set up a reward system for your successes. It does not have to be a big reward. A quarter in a receptacle each time you overcome or reach a goal. Spend it on something which delights you and will be a continuing reminder of your progress.

21. Do not let yourself return to any past habit or attitude patterns which were part of your problem. Satan Never Gives Up. Be calmly and confidently on guard. Keep a positive mental attitude. You can win this fight! The joy and strength you will feel when you do will give your whole life a radiant and spiritual glow of satisfaction and fulfillment.

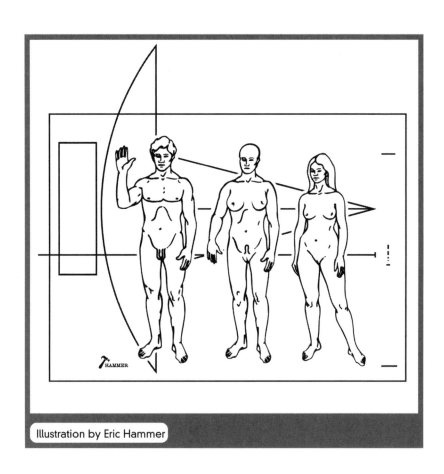

Illustration by Eric Hammer

THE NEW HERMAPHRODITE

George Petros

⤙⇨ ONE ⇦⤚

In the future the perfect human being will be a hermaphrodite—an intersexual fusion of genders combining male and female genitalia, male and female hormones—Hermes and Aphrodite, god and goddess, *diablo* and *diabla*.

Intersexuality—common in the Animal Kingdom—is the mingling of the sexual characteristics of both male and female within a single creature. Intersexual creatures combine aspects of genital form and reproductive organs, thereby exhibiting contradictions of the morphological criteria of gender.

Intersexual human beings—hermaphrodites—possess both testicular and ovarian gonadal tissues and exhibit ambiguous gender—in other words they have both a penis and a vagina. Perhaps the reader envisions "chicks with dicks," "pre-op" hookers, outrageous "she-males," or twisted Victorian nightmares—they may seem real, but statistically speaking such stereotypes are based more on pornographic empiricism than on research: the preponderance of natural intersexuality occurs among the world's worms, slugs and snails.

Intersexual humans are rarely "true" hermaphrodites—they rarely exhibit simultaneously "perfect" genitalia of both genders and they rarely possess equal amounts of testicular and ovarian tissue. A chromatin gender-determination test performed upon a true hermaphrodite can result in either a positive (female) or a negative (male). Most intersexual humans are either female pseudohermaphrodites or male pseudohermaphrodites exhibiting one or more contradictions of gender but with only ovarian or only testicular tissue (and whose chromatin test results in a positive or negative depending on "primary" gender).

Less than one percent of the human population are hermaphrodites. Throughout history they have been hidden away, fetishized, loved, pursued by adventurous romantics seeking bisexual bliss and ferreted out by witch hunters seeking victims. The degree to which their various genital apparatuses developed no doubt contributed to both their fortunes and their misfortunes. Every once in a while a true hermaphrodite must have appeared, stepping forth from heaven like a great genetic gift for some lucky lover.

Today, if we describe an "ideal" hermaphrodite as possessing the morphologically perfect genitalia of both sexes, and divorce the concept of hermaphroditism from reproduction, then we can assume that it's possible for almost any healthy human being to become hermaphroditic by way of surgical, chemical and psychological processes.

Tomorrow, if we describe an ideal hermaphrodite as an individual of "both sexes" capable of sexual activity with both genders and capable of both insemination and gestation and/or asexual reproduction (and perhaps as being an indispensable part of the normal sexual activity of non-hermaphrodites), then we can predict that it should be possible to produce hermaphrodites by genetic engineering.

But this is today, and the limits of today's technology describe the area in which our imaginations may range; similarly, the limits of today's sexual mores describe an area beyond which lie only our dreams. There are two ways to become hermaphroditic—birth and surgery. Perhaps someday there will be a third—genetic engineering, as mentioned—and perhaps in some science-fictional future even further-out fantasies of bisexuality and self-replication will become realities.

Biological and historical overviews are in order: In the beginning some deities punished humanity, or some deities rewarded humanity, or some aliens had intercourse with humanity, or some time travelers made a mistake—thus appeared the first human being having the sex organs of both genders.

The word "hermaphrodite" comes from Greek mythology—Hermaphroditus was the son of Hermes (commerce, invention) and Aphrodite (beauty, love). To fulfill his particular desires he joined himself into one body with the water nymph Salmacis. Unsatisfied with his new form, he laid a curse upon a fountain in which he swam so that other bathers in it became intersexual like him.

Every person begins life as a hermaphrodite. The fetus possesses undifferentiated sexual glands that will eventually become either ovaries or testes according to the vagaries of chromosomal mechanics. There are two genders because two are enough to generate the maximum number of potential genetic recombinations, assuring virtually every healthy individual a chance to mate with a member of the "opposite sex." Furthermore, sexual reproduction, in which genomes are shuffled between generations, is a means of shedding adverse mutations. A "third sex" as presently imaginable would be impractical—mating must remain a relatively simple matter, at least until humanity's survival is guaranteed. But after that . . .

Hermaphrodites as they exist today do not constitute a third sex, but in the future, in "three-way" sexual relationships, they could provide as-yet-unimagined forms of erotic stimulation. Through carefully cultivated collective fetishism, such stimulation could become indispensable to human reproduction—just like all the other signals and activities that bring people to orgasm.

References to hermaphroditism are plentiful in history and literature, but the reader should regard them with a grain of salt. The ages have seen much censorship, mistranslation, misquotation, misogyny and homophobia, and such obstacles to objectivity make all sources suspect. The concept of hermaphroditism has become interchangeable with transvestitism, homosexuality and androgyny to the point where all represent the same archetype.

The people of ancient India referred to intersexual humans as "hijiras" and accorded them the status of females while simultaneously despising and revering them. The Romans considered intersexuals to be oracles, yet treated them with disdain. The Navajo Amerinds recognized three sexes: male, female and "nadle," ostracizing the latter, whom they considered to be of both sexes. Renaissance Europeans entertained two principal literary interpretations of hermaphroditism—mythic androgyny and satiric androgyny. The mythic variety embodied allegories of union and togetherness. Satirical androgyny represented a split, as well as ostentation and campiness, and often hinted at flamboyant aspects of homosexuality. Today porno, exotica and a general fascination with medical anomalies and unusual sexual practices inform the prevailing view of hermaphroditism.

Thus far the question has been, "What is a hermaphrodite?" The word "freak" is vulgar and charged with hierarchical heartache—hermaphrodites are simply different types of people who can be very beautiful. Harsh attitudes are unfortunate, but in fact most societies have frowned upon them and regarded them as imperfect in addition to abnormal—the Romans characterized them as tragic. However, they are not tragic at all; perhaps they represent a mutation towards some higher form—a streamlined, self-perpetuating form waiting deep within the intricacies of human DNA; an asexual being free of dependence on others, able to reproduce by sex with any other human or by itself.

Assuming hermaphrodites to be a step in the direction of perfection, it's necessary to re-examine the historical aversion to them. Eventually they'll be desired by a broad range of people; ultimately many non-hermaphrodites might wish to become intersexual to some degree. After all, whatever can happen will happen (genetically speaking), so why not usher in the inevitable with an orgasmic outreach to a future unknown? The question becomes: "Who wants to be a hermaphrodite?"

Who will lie down beneath the surgeon's blade? Who will change their very bodies into new animals? A better civilization could arise out of the bipolar ashes of human imperfection—or widespread hermaphrodism could become the straw that breaks civilization's back. Either way, who will say, "I do!"?

The process of becoming hermaphroditic through surgery depends on technologies developed in furtherance of transsexuality, the cutting edge of body modification.

Body modification is the deliberate reconstruction of the human form. It encompasses all procedures that change human morphology. Body modifiers restore the faces of accident victims, create sexual signals where nature has proven deficient, or perpetuate sadistic mutilations from which lifetimes of horrors will bloom. Throughout history, by the patient application of either science or superstition (or both), body modifiers proved themselves capable of making anybody into anything.

Present-day techniques make possible a complete transformation from one gender to the other. Individuals who undergo "sex-change" or sex-reassignment procedures are transsexuals. As pioneers of the flesh, transsexuals are members of a new, transcendent human type unlike either of the primal genders from which they draw their genetic and emotional material.

Transsexuals undergo surgical correction of "gender dysphoria," a condition in which their gender identity is in conflict with their sexual anatomy, causing physical discomfort and psychological rejection of the "normal" biological and social roles of male or female. Transsexuality is often associated with homosexuality, but about half of all transsexuals remain sexually attracted to members of their newly achieved gender.

Sex-reassignment surgeries for men make a nerve-rich segment of the otherwise-removed penis the fleshy basis of a neoclitoris (through a procedure called clitoriplasty) and construct a vaginal canal out of muscle and skin and nerves and transplanted mucous membranes (vaginoplasty). Auxiliary procedures include breast enlargement, thyro-arytenoid muscle resectioning (to elevate vocal pitch), as well as prolonged hormonal and nutritional therapies.

For women, intensive plastic surgeries extend and incorporate the clitoris and urinary tract into a fleshy appendage, which becomes a penis (phalloplasty), and manipulate the labia to blend into the groin (labioplasty). Female-to-male transformation can also involve the implantation of either a fluid-pressure penile prosthesis that, by the actions of a pump and reservoir, injects water into spongy material, stiffening the appendage, or an implanted rigid silicone rod that creates a permanent state of erection. Mastectomies, hair transplants and prolonged hormonal and nutritional therapies complete the program.

Surgical transsexuality represents the cutting edge of medical science. It's a dangerous, costly and protracted process that only the most daring and ambitious sufferers of gender dysphoria will endure. It takes several difficult years to complete. Since there's no guarantee that things will go well in any surgery—especially those as experimental and risky as sex reassignments—some unfortunate people's lives have been ruined by fine blades making erroneous swipes, ill-guided steel tubes piercing bladder walls, bad nerve splicings that leave faces twitching, or countless other mistakes.

Not every sex reassignment is successful. Not every sex reassignment is even completed. Sometimes fortune or social circumstance change during the long transition from girl to boy or from boy to girl. Some procedures may be too costly or painful to be continued. Many partially transformed individuals are unable to further modify themselves due to a lack of surgical success or money or resolve. They often live out their lives in confusion and depression (or else they join the "hermaphrodite" hookers—usually pre-op males enjoying the fruits of hormonal therapies—who haunt sex ads and red-light districts).

Most individuals who undergo sex-reassignment surgeries and related procedures adjust to their new anatomies and lead productive, fulfilled lives. Throughout their protracted transition from gender A to gender B, they're able to engage in all sorts of sexual activities—and many of them cherish those unique transitory pleasures.

Some transformers avail themselves of both male-to-female and female-to-male transgender technologies. Those clever ones become "transsexual hermaphrodites"—and live happily ever after.

As the number of transsexual hermaphrodites increases, society will undergo a commensurate transformation—part sexual liberation and part witch hunt. Transsexual hermaphrodites might polarize public opinion in the same way that "sex-change" pioneers did during the mid-twentieth century—but unlike transsexuals, the new hermaphrodites will be an obvious addition to the body politic rather than blending in among the billions of single-gender individuals.

It's most likely that the initial hermaphroditic trend will embrace elements of androgyny, because androgynous physical types can easily adopt the fashions and effects of both genders. As personal tastes evolve, any physical type of human being will be able to transform via varying combinations of gender-bending possibilities. As a result, all sorts of new weirdos will appear in the sex business.

Ultimately, if scientific trends continue, genetic engineers will produce hermaphrodites. Chromosomal materials that dictate the natural occurrence of intersexuality will be isolated and the appropriate genes recombined so that carefully planned "natural-born" ideal hermaphrodites will come into existence. At first they might be responses to the demands of fetishistic billionaires with plenty of patience. If genetic hermaphroditism works out, some adventurous parents might desire children of the newly created gender "Hermaphrodite" will become just another option on the menu of possible traits available from libraries of "natural" DNA samples and their synthesized, patented analogs. The prenatal subjects no doubt will be imbued with other desirable physical and mental qualities so that true hermaphrodites could be among, or stand alone as, a new breed of "super people."

The new breed won't be welcomed by everybody. Governments and religions might attempt to contain and control hermaphroditism. Great controversies will arise in which ethical questions about artificially induced hermaphroditism become subservient to the pragmatism of politics, advertising and philosophy. Will asexual reproduction be legal? Will hermaphrodites live among the general population? Will they be able to be polygamous? The only thing that will settle such controversies will be the level of power to which the hermaphrodites rise.

Mechanical and electronic components eventually will replace parts of the fragile human body. Nerves will interact with wires as computers and psychic superchargers augment the mind. Sex organs will scramble together until it's impossible to tell what's bio from what's techno and what's male from what's female. Hermaphroditic whores, bisexual biomachines, sick sideshow freaks, or the perfect lover—whatever turns you on!

·⇒☞ TWO ☜⇐·

Like everyone else of my time I was taught to stay away from hermaphrodites. Everyone knows they're bad news and they're nothing but trouble from which the most exquisite grief will come. They look good and they smell good and on the surface they're very alluring and seductive, but once they get their cocks into you, and yours into them, you're pretty much hooked until either you die or you get with the lucky few who manage to escape.

I was taught that hermaphrodites are shit-stupid lying whores who hate us because we were born male or female and can therefore go to heaven when we die, and I was also taught that we move forward in time with them through an adaptive evolution that makes our symbiosis a fact by default because some scientists said that's the way it's gotta be thousands of years ago. But I believe that the evolutionary mechanism is fucked up.

I was under their spell, and I sat there and cheered them on as they burned me out, fucked me, sucked me, did me up and drained me dry.

One night I was at a party and a hermaphrodite was there. I avoided "it," but of course I was very polite. The heavy drugs came out and the hermaphrodite looked at me with a sultry sort of "you can do exactly anything to me" quasi-telepathic allure. Little boy's eyes, little girl's eyes—I took that first forbidden step in the wrong direction when I went over and said, "Hello."

In the beginning it was all good. Every once in a while a hermaphrodite or two would come over and chill me out. They were engineered so fine—they're a true crossbreed. You take the giant cock into your mouth and slowly squeeze it with your lips and then move it out of the way so you can smartly lick the peachy pussy—it starts there. You squeeze a little harder, lick a little longer and they start to do all these crazy things to you. You would think that they could simply do the heterosexual and homosexual things in different combinations, each of which would be amazing—however, that would all be predictable, and you would have expected even the most extreme stuff. But a hermaphrodite is different than that. It's as if sexual potential increases in some wild geometric progression so that performance prowess increases exponentially. They're like drugs because you gotta have it, but unlike drugs because the experience is always totally new.

As time went on, it got bad. I started seeing more of them. It's a mental thing: you want that awful cock vibrating inside you, and you want to fuck that exploding pussy at the same time. The monosexual human mind was not designed to fathom both of those things simultaneously, and the chemicals in the brain overload and part of your mind shuts down and you can see everything in such a beautifully clear reality and you're getting your lights fucked out and suddenly you come—it's just too much, and you become addicted.

Hermaphrodites are taking over the world because they're different and smart and everybody's afraid to even criticize them and they've amassed so much power and wealth and fame and immortality and insular arrogance and seething hatred of each and every one of us—you see, they're like a third sex that can breed with itself in a cloning sort of asexual way. They don't need any monosexual input. They fuck us for the same reason we fuck them. Hermaphrodites are self-contained and aren't necessary for anything, really. One of the biggest questions in the history of science is why exactly they were created in the first place. But they're here and we've either got to kill them or learn to live with them.

Their own kind have warned them not to fuck us, that we're a step backwards, that we're dirty and primitive—can you blame some of them for wanting to check us out? But forget them. They lower our intelligence. They infect boys and girls alike. They twist us up into big balls of shit.

But most of them go about their business-as-usual of taking over the world, steadily and surely, and ignore us except when they want entertainment.

I've been staying away from them. It's been a long time since I sat there crying and coming, hoping for beautiful things when I knew all along that all they would give me was weirdness and porno images and spent seed. I think about them all the time, and about how everybody always warned me that hermaphrodites are really fucked up. . . .

⚡ ⚡ ⚡

George Petros is the editor of *Seconds* magazine, and the Psychedelic Solution Press. He published of the serial art graphic mag, *EXIT*. He can be reached at Seconds, 24 Fifth Ave, NYC, NY 10011, or seconds@bway.net.

Total Body Transplants

John McKenzie (ABCNEWS.com)

Transplanting organs from one body to another has become routine. The liver, the kidney, the heart. Multiple transplants are more daring, but they too are common.

What about getting it all? The complete package. Someone else's whole body—attached to your head.

"A total body transplant" is how Dr. Robert White of Case Western Reserve University describes it. "All of the organs, all of the extremities and so forth, brought in the form of a transplant."

The idea is to take the functioning body of someone whose brain is dead and attach it to the head of someone whose body is dying, someone experiencing multiple organ failure.

"I'm talking about a procedure that could actually be done with appropriate practice and the safeguards," says White. "I don't want to say tomorrow, but certainly within the year."

Doctors have already performed total body transplants on monkeys. A team of neurosurgeons at Case Western in Cleveland developed the elaborate procedure.

First they connected the arteries and veins in the neck. Then they attached metal clamps to the spinal column to hold the head in place. Tubes connected the trachea and esophagus. Then doctors sewed up the skin and muscles around the neck.

Six hours after the operation, the monkeys awoke with totally different bodies.

"That brought a fair amount of excitement to us," says White. "They not only would follow us with their eyes around the laboratory, but they could hear, they could taste. The could feel about the face."

White has been criticized by some people as a modern-day Dr. Frankenstein. But he's an internationally renowned brain surgery pioneer who has more than 700 health-care publications to his credit. None of his work, however, has been more controversial than his recently devised procedures for human body transplants.

"There are a great deal of similarities between what we accomplished in the monkey and what we believe we can accomplish in the human being," says White, adding that "we anticipate it would actually be easier. The structures in the human neck are simply larger, and we're more experienced in dealing with them."

While total body transplants show just how far surgeons have come in manipulating the body, they have yet to figure out how to reconnect the spinal cord. So, for now, patients undergoing this operation would not be able to move their new bodies. But with spinal cord research developing so rapidly, many scientists expect that problem can be soon overcome.

"We're making substantial progress in the area of spinal cord regeneration," notes White. "When that problem is solved, then the patient who undergoes a total body transplant may very successfully maneuver and get out of bed, and function as a total individual."

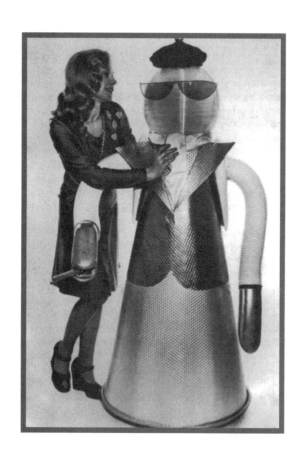

Death by Installments

Peter Cochrane

> I'll tell you a little secret, sonny. I don't really
> believe I will be dying. I believe I've learned how
> to transfer my great intellect into the machine, thus
> cheating the Grim Reaper of his greatest prize.
>
> **Graves in _The Schizoid Man, Stardate 42_**

The journey had been uneventful as we drove the family down from Nottingham towards Ipswich on the great north road. I turned to my wife and said . . .

"Let's play a mind experiment. Suppose I was dying of an incurable disease and all my mental faculties were complete, and you had the opportunity of transferring all of my mental awareness and capability into a computer. Would you do it?"

"Oh no," was the response. "It would not be you, it wouldn't be real and it would be artificial. I wouldn't like that at all."

"Oh! Well, suppose the transfer of me was into an android, a human-like machine that had all the ambulatory and tactile qualities of me the real person, how would that do?"

"Oh no, that would still not be you, that still wouldn't be real and I wouldn't like it at all. What a horrible thought!"

"Okay, suppose in 10 minutes we have an accident and I lose my leg and have to have a tin leg fitted, could you get used to me with a tin leg?"

"Oh yes, that would be okay."

"And if in a few years I was to lose an arm, you could live with me with a tin leg and a tin arm?"

"Yes, that would be all right."

"Even if that leg and arm were more than just a piece of tin, suppose technology had reached the point where it felt and looked like real skin and it was fully functional?"

"Oh, that would be even better!"

"Interesting. Then if I was to have a pacemaker, you would be happy with that?"

"Yes."

"Plus an artificial kidney?"

"Yes."

"How about an artificial pancreas—after all, they are now experimenting with prototypes and it won't be too long before we will be able to afford one?"

"Well, I suppose that would be okay, too."

"Now at the University of Sheffield there is a Professor working on artificial eyes; these are totally electronic. Who knows, one day they might be implantable, so as my eyes fail, if I have to have my eyes repaired with electronic replacements, would that be okay?"

"Well, I suppose so."

"I noticed the other day that Jack Ashley the MP had an electronic inner ear fitted to restore his hearing after many years of being deaf, so I suppose if my ears fail, you will be quite happy to see me with an electronic ear?"

"Well, yes."

"Suppose my liver fails and I have to replace this too?"

"Well, okay."

"My stomach and my spleen and . . ."

"Just a minute, I am not having you dying by installments!"

"Well, at what point are you going to say it is not me inhabiting this amalgam of flesh, blood, metal and electronics—at what point is it not me? Is it when we make the final step of transferring my biologically developed brain to an electronically developed brain? Is that the break point when it isn't me?"

"I don't know, but I don't like it and if I had the choice I wouldn't do it!"

"So let's just scroll this experiment back a little, at what point would I be acceptable to you? You have already said that you would accept me with a prosthetic arm and leg and pancreas and heart."

"It is not something I want to think about anymore!"

This discussion was a re-run of an earlier mind experiment I had tried with my mother some years after my father had died. I had suggested to her that we might have been able, in the future, to have lifted his very consciousness from his frail and dying body, that was just able to support a still fully functional and very active brain into some supercomputer. Similarly, she objected quite vehemently at the very thought of transferring a loved one into a machine form. Interestingly, my reaction to the proposal was that I would have done anything to have maintained contact with that intellect, that being, that person who had first initiated my life. That entity that had nurtured, taught and loved me from the moment I was born until we finally said goodbye. His physical manifestation mattered less to me than his very great loss. I would have done anything to have maintained contact with him in whatever form. Unfortunately, I never had the courage to ask of him in his dying years the same question, and which decision would he have made. I suppose as I age this question will be a reoccurring one and who knows, it might even become pertinent to me. If not pertinent for me, then it will certainly be pertinent for my son or my son's son or whomever. At some point in the development of our technology, it is almost certainly going to be the case that we will be able to transfer human minds, and beings, into some machine form. At our present rate of progress, less than 20 years will see super computers with an equivalent processing and storage capability to the human brain. Granted, they will be physically larger and probably have no ambulatory capability, but this is just a start. Within 30 years, the development of such machines should have reached our desktop or even pocket. Whether such machines will be capable of supporting new life forms, or improving existing ones, remains to be seen. Probably the key challenge is the understanding and access to the human mind itself. We do not understand how the human brain works, as we have not yet unraveled its unbelievable complexity. Perversely, with the assistance of supercomputers, it might be possible for us to create sufficiently good models to achieve a full understanding.

What kind of world will it be where no one ever has to die, or for that matter suffer unbearable sickness and failure of health? A world where we can live inside a static machine, communications network or inhabit some android or robotic form? The answer of course is totally different to what we have experienced so far. Probably the only inkling we are able to gain of what might be possible is currently available through the use of virtual reality. Experiments with the incredibly shrinking scientist, able to wander around atomic structures and feel the forces combining the nucleus and electron by merely putting out their hand at one extreme and at the other, our ability to wander throughout the galaxies and tamper with the influence of black holes in a virtual cosmos. Being able to go anywhere and do anything at any time and any place will soon be with us through the magic of telepresence, VR and tremendously increased computing powers, and an ability to communicate over vast distances at virtually zero cost. The next logical step is the transfer of mind itself into machines, away from all the limitations imposed on us by our present biological form and that of our currently limited electronics. A billionfold increase in computer power, coupled with a similar increase in communications ability and information storage, looks likely to be realized in 30 years. Perhaps our only chance of making full use of such technology is to become an integral part of that technology itself! The advantages are almost unthinkable.

Space and time travel would be conceivable over eons—vast distances and time—certainly into the future. However the reverse direction is still in doubt! Multiple branch point decisions, multiple lives, multiple experiences—duplicate copies of ourselves, back-up copies at regular intervals pending any form of disaster—true time capsules, perhaps forever, would all be possible. We could be everything, be everywhere, be everyone, experience everything! No disease in the conventional sense, but software bugs, viruses and parasites threatening our multiple lives perhaps! A computer storage and capacity shortage—instantaneous teleportation by radio and light beams. Beyond the moon in two seconds, the sun in eight minutes, the galaxy in 100,000 years. . . .

Perhaps sex would take on a new form—the merging of our new entities, the coming together, not through the transient physical coupling of two nervous systems, but through the merging of two complete bodies of intelligence and experience. Ultimately. Perhaps even the merging of all human life forms into a single ethereal being supported by an organic hardware both growing and developing like some cosmic jellyfish. Or perhaps as a wave of energy propagating throughout the universe looking for a host machine or entity—perhaps even seeking others of a similar nature. Could it be the very creation of the ultimate life force—a oneness throughout all of time and space? Let there be light, but the really super computer first!

Peter Cochrane is Chief Technologist of British Telecom, who says his criterion for success is the answer to the question: "Can I fall in love via the technology? I'd say that, currently, you can't over the Internet, phones, or videoconferencing. Not by themselves, anyway. You need to press the flesh, too. But when we advance to the stage where the communications technology becomes as efficient as tactile or emotional contact, we'll have succeeded. That's the way I want to go, and I can already see things moving that way."

http://www.labs.bt.com/people/cochrane/
peter.cochrane@bt.com

THE SYRUP OF MEMORY

Jeffery Lewis

I am going to attempt to solve a mystery. The mystery I wish to solve is one of the central mysteries of the 20th Century—that of UFOs and the close encounter phenomena associated with them. I think I am particularly and . . . peculiarly well-qualified to make this attempt. I may not have made a "frontal assault" on the problem—meaning it is not a mystery I intended to solve, but which I have come at from the "rear," so to speak.

The mystery I have been working on intentionally for the last 20 years is that of dreams. I tackled dreams to try to get a handle on terrific mood swings I used to suffer from. I found that I saw things in dreams that explained the mood swings—meaning, if I dreamt I was drowning one night and then woke the next morning drowning in depression, I had to conclude that the dream and emotional state were intimately connected. If a dream had a profound effect on my state of mind, I was forced to conclude that the "dream world" was as real as the physical/awake world.

After stepping into that other world, with its observations saved into approximately 200 120-page notebooks, I now believe that I know the solution to the UFO problem. When I entered the dream world, a very real world in its own right, I ran into a power that boggled my mind.

This power is something poets have known about, and artists have been aware of for centuries: the Mountain of Inspiration. Dante's entire *Divine Comedy* is one man's tour of this staggering metaphysical power structure built into our unconscious being. The Greeks knew this system of control by Divine government as Olympus, upon which the Olympian deities sat. Inspiration from those deities, whether benign, as in poetic inspiration—or malignant, as in arrows of madness or plague—was seen by the Greeks as issuing down from above from Apollo, God of light, via nine female powers known as the Muses. Every culture, from Christian to Hindu, from Native American to Buddhist, has their own version of this same throne of the deity from which inspiration flows down to mortals where, most often, it strikes them in their sleep, as a dream or a vision, or a channeling.

When I naïvely entered the dream world in order to gain better control over my emotions, I ran point blank into this towering metaphysical structure which goes right to the core of the galaxy and into the essence of the atom. In order to consciously control my emotions I was going to have to learn how this system worked, and even overthrow it if necessary!

This is when I began to run into opposition from the system in the form of UFO assaults and abductions like the ones Whitley Streiber describes in his book, *Communion*. And when I began to experience this opposition, I began to conclude that something I was doing threatened this system, and particularly the ferociously well-guarded secret of the UFOs.

The UFO mystery operates to bamboozle us into eschewing our defenses so that we become easy to conquer, even offering ourselves as slaves for the Great White Brothers from the skies. What follows is one trip into and back from a close encounter of the third kind—contact with aliens.

February 12, 1994

The first dream tonight is really fucking scary . . . until I see what it's about . . . then it's even scarier, but in a different way.

In the dream I am in a social situation, a party, perhaps, in the front hallway of our old Biltmore house in Illinois. This is the house where a court case was ongoing in many other dreams, concerning, I think, the abduction of Eros from the living room.

In this dream, I only make it into the front hall, where I sit down in my desk chair, the chair in which I usually sit typing pieces based on dream testimony. I notice that my current notebook is open on the chair, and that I will be sitting directly on top of it. When I sit down, this appalling thing happens. My butt cracks. Cracks like it was made from cheap glass, and syrup, pancake syrup, pours out! I think to myself, "How can I possibly fix that? Glue myself together like a piece of cracked china?"

Then I abruptly wake. I am relieved to find that I am not a piece of cracked china, at least not literally. At this point most dreamers would turn over, and go back to sleep. The next day they might, or might not, notice how they felt particularly rigid, or fragile, afraid of breaking something and having something pour out. Few dreamers would recall the entire dream and be able to solve the mystery of its meaning.

Following this dream, as I lie in bed awake, I have two immediate connections to help explain it. The first idea is that spilled syrup initiates recall of abduction memories in the film *Fire in the Sky*, in which Travis, the young man abducted by aliens, is at a party welcoming him home following his disappearance for more than five days. Terrified by the party, and his lack of recall of the incident, Travis hides beneath a table in the kitchen where he shivers in catatonic withdrawal. He spills a bottle of syrup, which eventually drips onto his face, initiating his recall of the abduction and the awful medical assault performed upon him, similar to those described by Whitley Streiber.

So, here is the same syrup, leaking from me. Why? What does that mean?

The second connection comes. My butt "cracking like cheap glass" is precisely a line from a poem of mine I was working on. But in my poem, it is the frozen eye of a doe, a dead doe, shot during hunting season, harnessed to the back of a pickup truck, that cracks "like cheap glass." The poem concludes that the eye that cracks, from which the sorrow of Orpheus pours out. The doe's eye is actually the "tragic I"—it's me. All this seems a long way from aliens, but it is not, I assure you.

I testified at a public reading that the dismemberment of Orpheus by Maenads, worshippers of the Goddess, continues to be a murder, a capital crime for which the perpetrators, the Maenads, have never been brought to justice. I also asserted in this reading the murder by the Maenads was politically motivated, an assassination, the purpose of which was to filch the magical power of Orpheus, his lyre, and his ability to govern the elements, and give that power to the Goddess. Orpheus is dismembered because, according to myth, he despises women. This is the testimony of the Maenads, the members of the cult. What Orpheus in fact despises is the practice of human sacrifice to feed the Goddess or God. He is unwilling to sacrifice his power, the power of his lyre, to the Goddess, so that she, Mother Nature, may rule—instead of human creators, metaphysical technicians.

To sum up this dream: my role, as powerless poet, is to be depicted as cheap glass, a fired karmic vessel, designed to contain but not leak the awful grief of the primary poet, Orpheus. But through my dreamwork I have cracked the murder mystery of Orpheus, and am now testifying in the Court of Divine Judgment on the crime. I swear on the veracity of my dream work, that it contains the true testimony on these matters, and that the myth we have received, which we read in Edith Hamilton, is false.

The reason why I leak syrup is because I feel the accurate record or version of mythic events such as mine on Orpheus will cause everyone who reads or hears about them to recall the truth about being abducted, raped, experimented upon, stabbed, murdered. That these crimes were named "Communion" in Streiber's book, is to protect the guilty.

If the metaphysical power system I've dreamed about controls the Court, it would be likely that they'd do anything to stop me from testifying. And that is precisely what I will show that it does.

THE SENTENCE
Following my testimony regarding the dream in which I leak syrup I see two me's being sentenced by the court. The sentence for dreaming about the murder of Orpheus will be carried out in the past! Most UFO abduction

experiences operate like that—they are actions by the Divine Court carried out in the past for "crimes" we have yet to commit in the future! This is part of what the dismemberment of the divine body of Orpheus means— pieces of our divine, or metaphysical, bodies are scattered through time.

In the sentencing, I am in the living room of the Biltmore house speaking to a lawyer who assures me that my crime was minor, a misdemeanor. Since I am terribly frightened of the Court, I am relieved to hear my crime was considered minor. But I am also aware that there is another "me" in the same hallway I stand now, my butt cracking and pouring syrup. The butt-cracked me is being accused of the murder of . . . Mom! Me #2 is found guilty and sentenced to death! Strangely enough, I feel relieved, as if this "me" were really a heavy twin weighing me down.

THE SUPREME FEAR

So what am I seeing here? This courtroom scene in the dream world is Divine Judgment upon my soul. This supposedly occurs after you die, but the Court of Osiris, the Judge of the Dead, is in operation every single night in the metaphysical realm of deep sleep.

I'm being judged for the murder of Mom. But that is ridiculous, isn't it? My mother is still alive, albeit ailing, in Florida, so surely I did not commit matricide. But, if I raise the truth about Orpheus, that he was murdered by Mother Nature cults in order to create their Goddess, the Goddess of Nature, Gaia, then the truth would kill Mom, or Mother Nature, in the same fashion that democracy kills the divine right of kings to rule, or to tax a population without representation. That is my "crime." I am killing Mom by asserting that poets would govern the planet better than a Mom over which we have absolutely no control. In order for other human creators to regain this power, their Orpheus power, then the Sacred Realm of Sleep must be reconquered, abolishing the Court in operation during sleep time. To keep us meek, make us cower in our beds, Mom makes us fearful that we'll be swallowed by demons or some sort of supreme angel.

THE UNKINDEST CUT

My sentencing by the Divine Court indicates a "split personality." Either I was cut in half, or the terror of the sentencing was so great that I split myself in half and drove a portion of myself into my unconsciousness. The "misdemeanor" part of me is allowed into the living room, allowed to live. And the part convicted of murder is cut away, somehow. Did I cut it away? In dreams these things just happen, and you don't know why. If you wish to be a poet with genuine Orphic power, you have to be sentenced to death, be willing to be damned. Because the truth of UFO is "knowledge of hell," this is knowledge for which humans are damned by the Divine Court. Like Orpheus, a poet with elemental creative power is a threat to Mother Nature. The Court of Divine Judgment was established to preserve that order, the mystery of the power of the Gods. The only way to solve the UFO mystery is to overturn that court and its rulings against us.

$$\text{⚡ ⚡ ⚡}$$

Jeffrey Lewis is a resident of Minnesota. He can be reached through Feral House.

McDeath

Satanic Rulers of Darkness

Introduction:

Looming in the far distance, standing ominous,
Lurking in the dark corridors
Is the Nazi swastika of the nineties,
The infamous, blood-dripping golden arch.
Sinister and murderous trademark symbol
Of worldwide terrorism, and criminal activity.
The personification of evil is the hellish,
Money-hungry, cow-killing cult empire called McDeath.

Verse 1:

Enter the devil's kingdom at your own risk.

Welcome to the dishonest, heartless and corrupt,
Deadly house of doom and murder.
The fast food poison, animal-holocaust-concentration-camp-hell,
That converts once-living creatures into flattened, decomposing
Patties of putrified, contaminated, bacteria-laden meat,
Sandwiched between an ant-covered stale bun.

Verse 2:

May all bear witness to:

The millions of meat junkies waiting in line for their daily factory farm
Drug dose of McDeath: chemical food poisoning to go.
Straight to the emergency ward, on to intensive care, and
Soon afterwards, to the neighborhood cemetery.

Please make copies and distribute worldwide

Dan Kelly

> What Orwell feared were those who would ban
> books. What Huxley feared was that there would
> be no reason to ban a book, for there would be
> no one who wanted to read one. Orwell feared
> those who would deprive us of information.
> Huxley feared those who would give us so much
> that we would be reduced to passivity and ego-
> ism. Orwell feared we would become a captive
> audience. Huxley feared the truth would be
> drowned in a sea of irrelevance. Orwell feared
> that we would become a captive culture. Huxley
> feared we would become a trivial culture, preoc-
> cupied with some equivalent of the feelies, the
> orgy porgy, and the centrifugal bumblepuppy. As
> Huxley remarked in *Brave New World Revisited*, the
> civil libertarians and rationalists who are ever on
> the alert to oppose tyranny "failed to take into
> account man's almost infinite appetite for distrac-
> tions." In *Brave New World*, they are controlled by
> inflicting pleasure. In short, Orwell feared that what
> we hate would ruin us. Huxley feared that what we
> love will ruin us.
>
> **Neil Postman, *Amusing Ourselves to Death***

Every square inch of America is plastered with its indigenous art form, advertising.

The saturation has been noticed and thoroughly critiqued by a cadre of crit-ics and a clutch of media pranksters. Less well-known are the tactics advertis-ers employ to lodge their messages into the fleshy grey folds of our cerebral cortices. The phrase is already suggesting itself, isn't it? Mind Control. But that's just crazy talk—strident rhetoric tempered in '50s and '60s masscult mistrust, right?

The initial rumblings of advertising/mind control paranoia more or less emerged from Vance Packard's 1957 bestseller, *The Hidden Persuaders*. Composed of data siphoned from ad executives (and little else), *Persuaders* revealed numerous creepy, psychic peephole techniques used by Madison Avenue to crack open consumers' skulls and produce ads that tickled what they found there—a sinister business then dubbed the "Depth Approach."

Deeply shocked by assaults on psychological privacy, Packard exposed such marketing practices as hiding cameras in store aisles to record how often housewives blinked, and packages which "hypnotized" consumers into selecting them. In a country crackling with McCarthyism, Packard nipped an exposed nerve. *The Hidden Persuaders* retained the number one bestseller spot for six weeks, and the idea of an ad industry inhabited by mad scientists and evil magicians entered American folklore.

Not that it made a difference. Consumer advocates were appalled, hearings were held, and the outrage mill churned at full force. All for naught: "Depth Approach" research continues to the present day, fostered by overzealous marketing researchers and that American population segment willing to have their psyches plunged for ten bucks and a fanny pack.

BODY LANGUAGE

Among the spookier applications of the Depth Approach is the use of psychophysiological measurement. Best known as the machines that beep and ping in the background during TV hospital dramas, physiological measuring devices chart brain waves (EEG), heart rate (EKG), electrodermal activity (EDA, aka Galvanic Skin Response, GSR), and muscular activity (EMG). In everyday use, physiological measures let the doctor know that your heart is still beating and

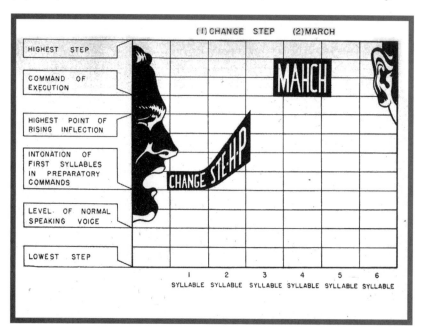

your brain is tumor-free. Many marketers believe that these hi-tech gizmos induce your body to reveal what your mouth isn't telling them.

What sounds like razor's edge technology really isn't. Packard makes brief mention of an early experiment in which the *Chicago Tribune* gauged the reactions of subjects hooked to lie detectors, while exposing them to images and sounds to be used—or not used, according to the results—in future advertisements. The idea and procedure persists, though the devices have been refined.

The "psycho-galvanometer," for instance, attaches two sensors to a subject's fingertips while a series of test ads scrolls by. Like the old-fashioned lie detector, the psycho-galvanometer reputedly detects changes in one's emotional state, accomplishing this through measuring the opening and closing of pores. According to Sierra Madre-based research firm Walt Wesley Co., open pores indicate alertness and that the message is sinking in, while closed pores suggest boredom, resistance, and rejection. Walt Wesley Co. stands by its psycho-galvanometer research, and so do many of their clients, including Johnson & Johnson, DuPont, and Allstate Insurance.

Other GSR experiments chart the dilation of pupils. High levels of galvanic skin response and pupil dilation are presumed to imply that subjects are receiving the message and actively processing it, making for better retention and contented market researchers. Low GSR and pinned pupils conversely convey low receptivity and processing, and consequently, low retentiveness—or, perhaps, overconsumption of amphetamines. Any ad promoting big pores and Keane kid-sized pupils ensures that viewers will slurp up its message like hyperactive sponges.

Then again, maybe not. Truth be told, this isn't hard and fast science.

EEG testing follows the same premise, save that brain waves are the measurement of choice. In EEG research, electrodes are attached to the back of the subject's head with a dollop of electrode paste, allowing a jiggly pen to chart the darting and dancing of their brain waves as he or she observes a parade of advertisements. Active brain waves are favored by marketers for several reasons. First, EEGs may be recorded without interruption, allowing for real-time comparison between results and the commercial observed. Secondly, in an observation by Michael L. Rothschild and Esther Thorson in their 1983 treatise "[EEG] Activity as a Response to Complex Stimuli . . ." EEG is "measurable under even lower conditions of involvement, in that attention can be measured (at least in theory) without the need for any questions to be asked."

In other words, EEG records response without causing a subject the inconvenience of taking time to process a message and form an opinion. A line is drawn from stimulus to response, with no messy interruptions in between.

What, precisely, is being measured? Linda F. Alwitt—then in the employment of the Leo Burnett ad agency—dug deeper in a 1985 experiment, wherein 30 subjects were hooked up to EEGs and subjected to a television commercial gauntlet. Alwitt paid special attention to the way her subjects' brain waves reacted during direction changes (cuts, zooms, incidental music), brand messages (mentions of the brand name, shots of the product in use), reactions (realism, touching, humor), and so forth; especially concentrating on recording the reactions of the parietal and frontal areas of the brain. (The parietal absorbs information and decides upon its relevance; the frontal controls emotional behavior.) As for the results—well, they don't conclusively prove anything, though Alwitt seemed happy with them. As hypothesized, the parietal area reacted readily to the sales spiel, while the frontal area flashed into action whenever the actors touched or otherwise acted "realistically." Alwitt's study showed that commercial content stimulated EEGs in various, measurable ways. Which meant . . . Well, Alwitt and her fellow researchers weren't quite sure yet. Like most EEG studies performed during the '80s, Alwitt *et al* were interested in amassing data for later study. Information on—and, apparently, interest in—EEG research abated with the advent of the '90s, though some marketing companies continue to carry the torch. (On its webpage, Capita Research Group, Inc. trumpets its EEG-based "exclusive Engagement Index (EI) testing procedure" which "[utilizes] patented NASA technology.") What exactly happened to all that stockpiled '80s data, however, is left to the reader's imagination.

One theory is that EEG research was elbowed aside by the sexy, hi-tech appeal of positron emission tomography (PET), functional magnetic resonance imaging (fMRI), and eye-tracking devices. Humanistic market researcher Gerald Zaltman broke ground with the first two devices when he and co-researcher Stephen Kosslyn shunted subjects into PET scanning tubes while listening to descriptions of tacky car dealerships with sticky floors, bitter coffee, and oily salesmen. In one example, PET brain scans show that when receiving negative input, the right brain glitters like a Christmas tree—particularly around the frontal lobe area. Adequately charted, PET imaging offers exciting new opportunities to demographically segment consumers not only by income, address, age and sex, but also thought patterns. As Kosslyn describes one application of PET scanning:

> Some customers are visual; others are auditory. Use brain scans to classify your customer base, and then target the first group with a newspaper display and the second with a radio spot.

Despite Kosslyn's whiz-bang vision, that's not happening anytime soon. Once again, the results are extremely open to interpretation, and, compared to galvanometers and EEGs, PET and fMRI scanning equipment isn't cheap, and far too bulky to cart down to the shopping mall for field research.

The same drawbacks apply to eye-tracking devices, though their findings are, arguably, more conclusive. Eye-tracking technology is multi-tiered in its applications, from the benign (helping quadriplegics to operate computers) to the malignant (helping fighter pilots target missiles by sight).

Eye-tracking hardware consists of an elaborate headgear with cameras on both sides, another on top, and a transparent sheet of special glass hanging several centimeters before the subject's eyes. Eye movements are tracked by an infrared beam reflected off the glass' surface, into the subject's pupil. Pupil movements are transmitted to a nearby computer, translating them into horizontal, vertical and depth coordinates. The camera on top of the headgear captures the scene viewed, even as the eye's physical movements—including pupil dilation, blinks, fixations, pursuit, and saccades (the herky-jerky motions made as the eye jumps from one point to another)—are recorded. A cursor traces the path taken by the viewer's gaze; mapping out what the subject was looking at and when.

For its marketing application, the subject is shown a series of ads—a catalog, magazine, or a store display—while the cameras roll. Information derived from this exercise is rarely surprising. In the English-speaking world we learn to read from left to right and top to bottom; thus, most advertisements are viewed in this pattern. Other results are a bit more interesting. In a Yellow Pages eye-tracking study, subjects spent 21 percent more time viewing color ads than ones in black and white; 42 percent more time gazing at bold listings than plain ones; and, quite weirdly, 100 percent more time viewing color bank ads than black and white ones. Another study charted catalog reader eye movements, where it was learned that tic marks and crosses seized the most attention, followed by boldly meaningless interjections such as "Star Buy!" and "Special Offer!" Elsewhere, Dr. Siegfried Vogele of Germany calculated that a junk mail recipient spends 11 seconds, tops, deciding whether to open it or throw it away. A good chunk of this time is occupied with viewing the back of the envelope, opening it—as studies reveal—from right to left. Vogele recommends making those precious seconds count by placing teaser copy or a titillating photo in the top left corner. Herr doktor also offers a pecking order of attention-grabbing illustrations: Big pictures are noticed before smaller ones; color pictures before black and white; shots of people are attended to before product photos, and children are always perceived before adults. Through the implementation of eye-tracking equipment costing anywhere between $20,000 to $250,000, Dr. Vogele has proven what every retail advertising drone—of which the present writer was one—has known for the past century.

All very interesting, but so what? Such is the fundamental nature of psychophysiological research. Though all these measurements of ad effectiveness make for snazzy pie charts, no one is entirely sure what is being measured or how it correlates with what is observed. In illustrating the researchers' attitudes, however, the subject cannot be easily dismissed.

In their article "GSR Reconsidered . . . ," in the September-October 1995 issue of *The Journal of Advertising Research,* authors Priscilla A. LaBarbera and Joel D. Tucciarone posit that,

> The human being is endowed with certain psychological mechanisms which can be monitored and reflect definitive manifestations of mental, hormonal, and/or motor activities that are intimately associated with information processing, emotional reactions, decision-making and choice, as well as nonvolitional reactions. In comparison, self-reported measures typically are retrospective and involve a translation or self-interpretation of one's mental or behavioral responses.

What's more:

> Because consumers have little voluntary control over their autonomic nervous systems, changes in bodily functions can be used by researchers to indicate the actual, unbiased amount of activation or arousal resulting from marketing stimuli.

In short, Ego abdicates to Id, and psychophysiological-inspired advertisements are designed not to reflect what appeals to reason, but what soups up your heart rate and makes your pores ooze. It is obvious that marketers see consumers as little more than flashlight-following Sea Monkeys. Keep this at your mind's fore, if ever an ad for wheat bran starts your adrenaline pumping. Perhaps all the EEG data isn't gathering dust in a vault after all.

AUGURING THE SUBCONSCIOUS

Intrusive as it is, psychophysiological research provides one line of defense against the mind's breach: study of the subconscious is restricted to observation of bodily tics and secretions. Then again, did you really think today's marketers would let a thin membrane of skin and guts come between them and their profits?

Hypnotism, for example, clamors to be exploited; and indeed it has been, though not as extensively as you might think. Once again, Vance Packard preceded the cutting edge in reporting the use of hypnosis by New York-based agency Ruthrauff & Ryan back in the '50s. Mesmerized by hypnotism's possibilities, R. & R. hired a stable of Svengalis to roto-rooter their focus groups' brains. As usual, Packard is scant on details, but then, as now, the agencies cried proprietary information when asked for the results. One intriguing session was mentioned, however, where a hypnotized subject repeated, word for word, the copy for an ad he had read 20 years before.

Currently, and curiously, hypnotism has again come to the fore; though, if the newspaper business sections are any indication, its sole practitioner is

Irvine, California research firm proprietor Hal Goldberg. Undoubtedly more the result of diligent PR and newswire-dependent journalists than industry-wide acceptance, articles plugging Goldberg appeared in several newspapers throughout 1998; each so remarkably similar in coverage, one supposes Mr. Goldberg employs a bit of mesmerism during the course of his interviews.

Goldberg idealizes hypnosis as a panacea against memory blockage, and a surefire method of garnering honest, uninhibited responses. Sessions are attended by small groups, who are coached to focus on a green spot on the wall as Goldberg lulls them into a trance. Meanwhile, a video camera captures the moment, while ad reps sit behind one-way glass and Goldberg asks his thrall for their subconscious attitudes about the product at hand. Goldberg's sessions are pricey, ranging between $3,500 and $4,500 per group. Unhypnotized groups are slightly cheaper, the higher price reflecting how deeply Goldberg delves to find willing subjects. It appears many people are still leery of hypnotism's Svengalian stigma, and fear the possibility of spilling their guts too freely. Goldberg separates the chaff from the wheat early on, interviewing volunteers by phone to inform them of his methods, then arranging face-to-face interviews before the final session. Honesty rarely pays: 50 percent of Goldberg's focus groups usually drop out when they learn they're about to have the whammy put on them.

Goldberg also contends with the doubts afflicting psychophysiological market research. It smacks of marketing hoodoo—a fancy gimmick with little validation of its effectiveness. Critics point out that hypnotized groups lack the dynamics of unhypnotized ones, namely the give-and-take necessary for productive discussion. Moreover, most experts consider hypnosis' reputation as an all-powerful recall tool undeserved. Not that their opinions matter: Goldberg has performed his hypnotist act for J. Walter Thompson, Bozell Worldwide, and other big league ad agencies. Many an ad rep has sworn by hypnosis' effectiveness as a brain-plunging tool, likening its effects to "a shot of sodium pentathol."

In other subconscious-tampering news, it is worthy to note the current state of subliminal advertising—now enjoying a minor renaissance of renewed interest and critical damnation.

Subliminal advertising's first bright and shining moment came in the late fifties, when *Hidden Persuaders* figure James Vicary juiced up a movie theater's popcorn sales by flashing "Eat Popcorn" on the screen with a rapid projection device called a tachistoscope. A Free Will bogeyman tale to be sure, though, curiously, Vicary failed to substantiate his experiments with any sort of scientific record. Moreover, despite repeated experimentation, no one, on either side of the argument, could reproduce his jaw-dropping results under controlled conditions. No surprise there: In a 1962 interview, Vicary admitted it was a

MEDIA SEXPLOITATION

The Hidden Implants in America's Mass Media--and how they program and condition your subconscious mind

Wilson Bryan Key
author of SUBLIMINAL SEDUCTION

hoax, contrived to hype his agency and reduce the cost of commercial airtime. In Vicary's brave new world, subliminals would be unobtrusive mini-commercials, embedded within TV programming and noticed only by those predisposed to see them. If we're to believe Mr. Vicary, the practice's brain-washing possibilities never crossed his mind.

Not so with Dr. Wilson Bryan Key, whose salaciously titled books *Subliminal Seduction, Media Sexploitation,* and *The Clam-Plate Orgy* sent subliminal paranoia screaming into the stratosphere. In 1972's *Subliminal Seduction,* Key reported that Vicary's clunky old tachistoscope was only the prologue to a long history of advertising mindbuggery. Vicary's "Eat Popcorn" command only lasted for 1/3000th of a second; Key, on the other hand, posited that today we are continually bombarded with subconscious commands whenever we peruse a magazine or flick on the TV. Through a methodology of semiotic deconstruction, projective technique and brainstorming, Key and an assembly line of Key-worshipping students discovered questionable symbology peppering damn near every ad they encountered. Sex and death symbolism cropped up everywhere: Booze ad ice cubes housed floating skulls, erect phalluses, and operas of human suffering; Betsy Wetsy-type doll ads were larded with hidden F-words and pedophile-provoking imagery; Simon & Garfunkel's ditty "Bridge Over Troubled Water" was revealed as a grotesque ode to shooting smack, and, in a bizarre aside even for Key, it was determined that the reason everything tastes great on a Ritz is due in part to the dozens of golden-brown "SEXes" baked onto every cracker.

Naturally, it has been suggested that Key is nuttier than a Waldorf salad (though the present writer views his practices more as an attempt to perpetuate a one-man cottage industry). Key doesn't exactly support his case when he admits to ignorance of how subliminals alter behavior, if indeed they do, if one accepts their existence to begin with. Nor are his research methods universally lauded, with his apparent loath for control groups, and the gratuitous groupthink occurring between Key and his students.

Regardless, subliminals remain a hotly contested topic, with advertisers vehemently denying their existence and 62 percent of America believing in their presence and power ("subliminal learning" motivational cassettes, videos, and screen savers do brisk business, earning upwards of 50 million dollars per annum). Additionally, while Key shows relish for his Ibsenesque role, it may perturb him that a generation of art directors weaned on his books have converted subliminal perception into a Post-Ironic aesthetic. For example, browbeaten into rejecting penile-visaged, child-seducing Joe Camel as their spokesdromedary, Camel cigarettes converted their classic logo into a recurring visual pun. In one campaign, "subliminal" camels were airbrushed into cyclones of cigarette smoke, Zippo lighter flames, and beverage watermarks. Above it all, a headline stated, "What you're looking for?" Similarly, Absolut vodka, in one of their ubiquitous ads, hid the bottle amidst a batch of ice cubes, entitling the result "Absolut Subliminal." A slap in the face intended for Key? Perhaps, but the fact that Camel sales increased by a volume of 5.3 percent after the campaign's implementation must sting a bit.

Where television is concerned, the FCC frowns on subliminals. However, when their use was made an offense punishable by license revocation, the Supreme Court overturned the decision on the grounds that it violated the First Amendment. After that, the National Association of Broadcasters moved to forbid its members from dropping subliminals into the broadcasting soup, though this is only an ethical obligation, not a legal one. Incidentally, it is worth noting that the FCC decreed that all broadcasters had to switch from analog to digital transmission by millennium's end. Digital technology, it turns out, expedites subliminal ads beautifully by allowing "hidden" messages to be overlaid and/or inserted into programming with higher frequency and greater subtlety. While it is likely that subliminals are a paper tiger, this does not preclude future advertisers from tweaking broadcasts with various subliminal

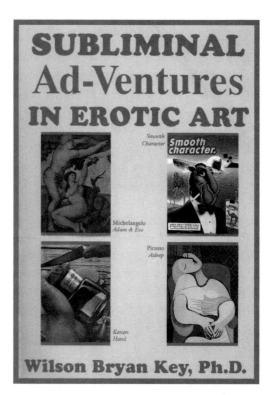

mixtures. Perhaps in prelude, back in 1993, Seattle-based retailer Bon Marche advertised Frangos candy with one-fourteenth-of-a-second long television commercials. In light of this, we might want to reconsider the old golfing adage of "Every now and then, you can't help but hit one right."

FACILITATING OUR INCONVENIENCE

Moving on to less glitzy avenues, we discover stealthier research techniques; techniques which recollect Pogo's maxim of meeting the enemy and discovering he is us.

Since its inception in 1972, the Uniform Product Code has twisted the noses of fundamentalist Christians, privacy advocates, and kooks at large alike with its suspicious, zebra arrangement of stripes and numerals. Appearing on every box, bag, carton and can stocking the grocer's shelves, if the UPC isn't the Mark of the Beast, it's a damn fair substitute.

Supermarkets, however, love the little monochromatic bastards. With their creation, UPC codes cut labor costs by speeding up checkout lines and jettisoning the need for individual price tags. Inventory control also became a breeze, allowing for instantaneous re-ordering of stock when shelves grew bare. Theoretically, scanners will eventually be connected to the sources of production, alerting them to speed up or slow down production as demand rises and falls. As a direct result of this high-speed bean counting, a new business cropped up: the selling of Point of Sale (POS) scanner data to the food and marketing industries, and anyone else who cared to buy it.

Even in 1972, consumer spending habit analysis was nothing new, but with POS scanners, consumer information became a quantifiable product, pre-packaged and ready to be sold in large meaty chunks. In and of themselves, scanners aren't such a bad thing, but little by little, the grocery stores are creating a cybernetic fusion of product and the people who buy it. These days, you no longer simply buy merchandise, you become intertwined with it.

A fine example of this benignly dehumanizing intrusiveness has been initiated by British shopping market magnate Safeway, whose avuncular slogan— "Safeway . . . Simplifies Your Life"—may give more sensitive readers the willies. In 1995, Safeway launched their Shop & Go program, which works like so: Entering their local Safeway, the customer encounters a power bank holstering 96 handheld scanning devices. Taking scanner in hand, our shopper meanders through the store, loading his cart with self-scanned merchandise. The scanner performs multiple tasks, such as recording each purchase, keeping a running tab, notifying the shopper about sales, and freeing the supermarket from the expense of hiring another cashier. At the end of one's shopping spree, the scanner generates a receipt, which is paid for at the checkout area. (It's probably safe to assume that you have to bag your own groceries, too.)

According to Safeway's reports, Shop & Go accounts for 20 percent of their sales, with many stores toppling over the 40 percent mark. Convenient, yes, but for whom, exactly?

In a similar turn of events, handheld scanners have left the supermarkets and entered our homes. *Computerworld's* June 10, 1991 issue reported the implementation of custom bar code scanners—referred to as "wands"—by over 15,000 Nielson survey households in that company's "Scantrack" program. After bringing their groceries home, survey participants wave the wand over each UPC code, recording what they bought, how much, and at what price. Items not purchased at Nielson stores are not recognized by the wand, causing it to prompt the user to punch in the item's brand name and price. (Use of coupons and special promotional items demand similar filial devotion.) Afterwards, wand users download this info via modem to the Nielson computer bank, where the data is analyzed and dissected, so as to adjudicate the demographics relating to Cheez Whiz and Fiddle Faddle sales. Participants are rewarded hamster style with "points" for a successful download, which may be exchanged for a selection of lovely gifts. It's a costly system, but worth it. Unlike anonymous POS scanner data, wands put a face to the purchases.

Ridiculous, you say? Besides a bland handful of dullards sappy enough to let their privacy be abridged, nobody is obliging enough to strap themselves to a nagging device that demands and tallies their every shopping decision, right? Insofar as wands are concerned, true enough. At-home scanners are rude devices with a 10 percent cooperation rate. Okay, how about a smaller device which promises all the perks and none of the inconvenience of a wand, yet which records your every consumerist move? Scoff if you must, but are you now, or have you ever been a loyalty card-carrying member of your local grocer?

Loyalty cards are a logical extension of POS scanners. Whereas POS scanners methodically produced the aforementioned meaty data chunks, loyalty cards slice that data into choicer morsels that denote who is buying what, and why. Resembling credit cards, loyalty cards are acquired by surrendering one's name and address; phone, driver's license and social security numbers; number of children and types of credit cards one possesses; and, in some cases, eating habits (e.g. whether you are diabetic, vegetarian, or abstain from alcohol) to the store's marketing department. In exchange, the cardholder receives a stunning piece of microwave crockery (or similar low-margin gift), and becomes privy to special discounts and promotions. Over 40 percent of the nation's supermarkets sponsor loyalty card programs, making for an awful lot of "private" citizens who would never allow a scanner into their homes. And how do the stores account for the need for all this personal information? As one form explains: "In order to improve our services to you, it would be helpful to know a little more about you and your family." How touching.

As their name implies, loyalty cards encourage shoppers to remain true to their store. (In marketing parlance, card members who shop elsewhere are called "defectors.") Notably, loyalty card studies have shown that the top 20 percent of a store's customers are accountable for over 64 percent of sales. Such "collaborators" are apt to have their loyalty—read: uninhibited consumerism—amply rewarded.

From a marketing research angle, loyalty cards are a Dutchman's goldmine of demographic opportunity and information. The program can place certain products in the path of specific consumers (in one example, a customer who buys kitty litter but never cat food can be hit with a cat food coupon), thereby reducing advertising and marketing costs. In addition, a persistent loyalty card program can peel a store's stock down to the bare essentials—a process called "micro-merchandising." Can't find polenta at your grocer anymore? So sorry, 85 percent of all Happy Idiot Grocery loyalty cardholders don't buy polenta. Too bad for you. Membership has its privileges, but allegiance greases the wheels.

Card programs also permit for annoying periodic target marketing blitzkriegs. England's Safeway chain has over six million cardholders, for instance, and 75 percent of all Safeway sales are conducted using loyalty cards. Thus, in 1996, Safeway sent out 12 million direct mailings, clogging the mailboxes of cardholders who had no one to blame but themselves. By the by, Safeway reports that all that ripping proprietary data about British spending habits isn't disposable. Data remains on-line for two years before being locked in the vaults for future reference.

Nerve-racking as loyalty cards may sound, they're simply precursors for more ruthlessly efficient grocery privacy invasions. Smart cards, for instance, are loyalty cards' nasty little brother. They too appear to be mere plastic cards, but each one contains an itty-bitty microchip that not only charges groceries (paper money, who needs it?), but records customer-relevant data like birthdays, anniversaries, recipes, favorite foods, and so forth, for future target marketing. Like loyalty cards, smart cards keep a running tab on a customer's purchases for database-linked direct mailings, and to alert customers (read: prod into buying) to special deals and limited time offers. In Holland, smart card technology has wind sprinted into the 21st Century. Many Dutch stores have incorporated multi-media terminals which—when a customer slides in his or her smart card—display individually targeted offers and print out personalized shopping lists, which are automatically downloaded into the card. The terminals also encourage customers to try their luck, Vegas-style, at a game of chance. Winners are paid off with a free goodie—perhaps a box of dog biscuits.

Like most wars, the TV ratings battles inspire technological quantum leaps. In the early days, survey families kept track of shows watched through paper diaries. Once again, humans being procrastinators at heart, recording viewing habits became of secondary importance to survey families (children being the worst offenders), and the diary was often left to molder under piles of old *TV Guides*. Realizing this, ratings companies developed the television meter, a device which recorded whether and when the TV set was turned on or off. That wasn't enough for the ratings boys, however, who are currently working on projects that would give Big Brother a priapism the size of Delaware.

The vanguard of this new wave of privacy raiders is the inoffensive-sounding "people meter." For the time being, people meters are activated only when their buttons are pushed, and their duties are limited to noting the time and channels watched by their hosts. The future looks bright then, for our nation of couch potatoes, with the development of the passive electronic audience detector. These gizmos limit themselves to measuring motion, heat, and sound in the area surrounding the TV, allowing the meter to extrapolate how many people are in the room and what they're watching. Creepy, eh? Well, don't blink, or you'll miss the next doohickey the marketing boys are tripping over themselves to turn loose on us—the passive people meter. Ever wonder what's wrong with watching a little television? You may think twice when the television is watching YOU. Passive people meters are rigged with digital cameras that "photograph" the viewer and compare it, via pattern recognition software, to a prerecorded image encoded in the main database. This permits a passive people meter to gauge how many passive people are in the room, what they're watching, and, most importantly, who they are. This information is then downloaded to the main computer bank, which keeps track of all those lovely demographics.

But wait, there's more.

A program dubbed "single source tracking"—as developed by a company called ScanAmerica—allows for the combination of data generated by people meters with that tabulated by UPC scanner wands (or, we can assume, smart cards). Once again, contemplation and the formation of opinions are rendered moot. Focus group babblings will be cast aside, leaving consumers to cast their votes for or against advertisements and programming en masse, as they experience them. Response time is sliced to a microscopic edge, advertising is manufactured according to stimulus and response, and the relative possibility of reaction superseding experience seems less and less farfetched.

Marketing mainstays such as phone surveys are also grinding towards more grating levels of annoyance. If your dinner is interrupted, hang up immediately and spare the telemarketer the mortification of taking orders from a machine. Most telemarketers spend their days squatting in cubicles, wearing telephone headsets, while a computer dials each number and prompts them with scrolling text. Known as automatic dialers, these systems cut performance time by randomly dialing numbers and patching the telemarketer through only when a human voice answers; fax lines, answering machines and voice mail services are ignored entirely.

The reader may have encountered Audiotex while dealing with a customer service line, wherein a prerecorded voice asks questions answered by pressing buttons on a touch-tone phone. Telemarketing companies have made prodigious use of Audiotex for the past few years, but eventually even these will be uprooted by Automated Speech Recognition (ASR) systems. Like Audiotex, ASR interviews are conducted by a pleasant prerecorded voice (usually a woman's, to place the person at ease). Unlike Audiotex, ASR requires no buttons—all questions may be answered vocally. You are literally "talking to a machine."

When an ASR system "hears" a reply, the speaker's voice is converted into numerical code, which is then translated into what is referred to as a sound spectrum. The sound spectrum is then compared to a databank of prerecorded voices, until the closest approximation of the speaker's voice is found. Once the word is recognized by the system, the computer notes the speaker's response and proceeds to the next question. If the computer does not understand the respondent's answer (because of background noise, a bad connection, muttering, silence, etc.) it offers a sincere prerecorded apology and cajoles, "I'm sorry. I didn't hear that. Please answer <list of all valid answers>," until the respondent wises up and does it right. This problem may be abridged within a few years, as Great Britain-based telecommunications company GEC Marconi has already developed an adapter that recognizes up to 1,200 words. Marconi are also the geniuses behind Flexicall—an interactive voice response system capable of simultaneously handling fully automated telephone interviewing on thirty separate lines. Flexicall is currently used for Audiotex keypunching transactions, but may eventually be expanded to accommodate an ASR system on even more simultaneous lines. In one researcher's wet dream, this will allow for skeleton crew staffs and a plenitude of multi-national telemarketing transactions conducted 24 hours a day. This will happen within the next five to 10 years, so get used to either disconnecting your phone or foregoing hot meals entirely.

In the present scheme of things, the ad community's primary mission is to seize your attention, then activate your retention. As the difference between brand-name products winnow away to nothing, information is sacrificed for image, leading to the vacuous amalgam of high-gloss, low-content eye candy passing for today's commercials. Do they work? It's safe to presume that image inflation accounts for the popularity of unspectacular merchandise like soft drinks and gym shoes, and the persistence of cancer- and cirrhosis-causing sin products like cigarettes and alcohol. Pumping up the volume and slathering on the colors, today's ads promise new and improved versions of more of the same, in hopes of grabbing the maximum possible market share.

Hi-tech market research technology, however, says fie to all uncertainty, seeking instead a psychological Northwest Passage to our dishonorable desires and linking them to our primal urge to acquire. Mind-reading presages mind control; a process implemented with no little amount of help from ourselves every time we trade a shred of privacy for a 10% discount on Pop Tarts. While dignity and time are ethereal concepts, we forget that they remain quantifiable ones; ready to be traded, banked upon, and thoroughly exploited by the less scrupulous among us. Id-stroking advertisements? The mind jigs, reels and churns at the possibilities.

NOTES

Alwitt, Linda F. "EEG Activity Reflects the Content of Commercials." *Psychological Processes and Advertising Effects*. Ed. Linda F. Alwitt and Andrew A. Mitchell. Hillsdale, NJ: Lawrence Erlbaum Associates, Publishers, 1985. pp. 201-17.

"Big Boom in Electronic Research is Predicted." *Marketing News*. July 4, 1988. 11.

Bloom, Paul N. "Avoiding Misuse of New Information Technologies: Legal and Societal Considerations." *Journal of Marketing*. Vol. 58, No. 1 (Winter 1994): p. 98.

Blyth, Bill and Heather Piper. "Speech Recognition: A New Dimension in Survey Research." *Journal of the Market Research Society*. Vol. 36, No. 3 (July 1994): p. 183.

Blyth, Bill. "Potential Applications of Automatic Speech Recognition (ASR) to Market and Survey Research." 1998.

Buss, Dale. "There's a Rugged History, But Grocery Chains Are Moving Ahead at a Lively Pace." *Supermarkets*. June 24, 1998.

Coggins, Jay and Ben Senauer. "Innovation in Grocery Retailing." The Retail Food Industry Center. University of Minnesota, Nov. 1997. (Paper prepared for the Board on Science, Technology and Economic Policy of the National Research Council Conference on 'Industry Performance.')

Dacko, Scott G. "Data Collection Should Not Be Manual Labor." *Marketing News*. August 28, 1995. p. 31.

Dittus, Edward C. "Marketing Research Directions in the USA." *Journal of the Market Research Society*. Vol. 36, No. 1 (Jan. 1994): p. 29.

"Eyelink Head-Free Eye-Tracking System: Preliminary Features and Specifications." SR Research Ltd., 1472 Thorndyke Crescent, Mississauga, Ontario, Canada, L4X IR3.

Fellman, Michelle Wirth. "Mesmerizing Method Gets Results." *Marketing News*. July 20, 1998. p. 1.

Gellene, Denise. "Scrutinizing Shoppers' Subconscious." *Los Angeles Times*. Jan. 15, 1998. p. D1.

Gofton, Ken. "In Search of a Better Way." *Marketing*. March 13, 1997. S7(3).

Hildebrand, Carol. "A Wave of a Wand Tracks Buying Habits." *Computerworld*. June 10, 1991. p. 31.

Hodgson, Dick. "Eye-Tracking Studies Can Help Fine-Tune Packages: Effects of

Direct-Mail Envelope Design Research." *Direct Marketing*. May 1993. p. 67.

Horovitz, Bruce. "The Future of Advertising May Lie at the Fingertips of a Bike Mechanic." *Los Angeles Times*. August 27, 1991. p. D6.

Hughes, John. "Hypnosis Helps Marketers Refine Their Sales Pitch." *The Toronto Star.* October 17, 1997. Final Edition. p. E7.

Joch, Alan. "Eye-Tracking Technology Can Initiate an Ongoing Dialogue Between You and Your Computer." *Byte*.

Kamp, Anton and Fernando Lopes da Silva. "Technological Basis of EEG Recording." *Electroencephalography: Basic Principles, Clinical Applications and Related Fields*. pp. 92-93, 110-12.

Key, Wilson Bryan. *Media Sexploitation*. New York: Signet, 1977.

Key, Wilson Bryan. *Subliminal Ad-Ventures in Erotic Art*. Boston, MA: Branden Publishing Co., Inc., 1992.

Key, Wilson Bryan. *Subliminal Seduction*. New York: Signet, 1974.

King, Harriet. "Seattle Retailer Touts Candy with Tiny Ad." *The New York Times*. Nov. 23, 1993. p. C4, D4.

Krugman, Dean M. and Richard J. Fox, James E. Fletcher, Tina A. Rojas. "Do Adolescents Attend to Warnings in Cigarette Advertising: An Eye-Tracking Approach." *Journal of Advertising Research*. Vol. 34, No. 6 (Nov.-Dec. 1994): p 39.

LaBarbera, Priscilla A. and Joel D. Tucciarone. "GSR Reconsidered: A Behavior-Based Approach to Evaluating and Improving the Sales Potency of Advertising." *Journal of Advertising Research*. Vol. 35, No. 5 (Sept.-Oct. 1995): p. 33.

Lantos, Geoffrey P. "Ice Cube Sex: The Truth About Subliminal Advertising: Book Review." *Journal of Consumer Marketing*. Vol. 13, No. 1 (Winter 1996). p. 62.

Mackay, Hugh. "Subliminal Myth: How a Generation Was Fooled."

Mulqueen, Eibhir and Richard Balls. "Loyalty Card Game Reveals Consumer Spending Trends." *Irish Times*.

Nannery, Matt. "Safeway's 'Marketplace of One'." Information Access Company. July 1997. p. 75.

Pink, Daniel H. "Metaphor Marketing." *Fast Company*. April-May 1998. pp 214-229.

Ray, William J. and Jerry C. Olson. "Perspectives on Psychophysiological Assessment of Psychological Responses to Advertising." Advertising and Consumer Psychology. Ed. Larry Percy. USA: D.C. Heath and Company, 1983. pp. 253-69.

Riche, Martha Farnsworth. "Look Before Leaping." *American Demographics*. February 1990. p. 18.

Rogers, Martha and Christine Seiler. "The Answer Is No: A National Survey of Advertising Industry Practitioners and Their Clients About Whether They Use Subliminal Advertising." *Journal of Advertising Research*. Vol.34, No. 2 (March-April 1994). p. 36.

Rosbergen, Edward and Rik Pieters, Michel Wedel. "Visual Attention to Advertising." *Journal of Consumer Research*. Vol. 24, No. 3 (Dec. 1997): p. 305.

Rothenberg, Randall. "Joseph Turow's Breaking Up America: Advertisers and the New Media World—Book Review." *Atlantic*. June 1997.

Rothschild, Michael L. and Esther Thorson. "Electroencephalographic Activity as a Response to Complex Stimuli: A Review of Relevant Psychophysiology and Advertising Literature." *Advertising and Consumer Psychology*. Ed. Larry Percy. USA: D.C. Heath and Company, 1983. pp. 239-51.

Rothschild, Michael L. and Yong J. Hyun. "Predicting Memory for Components of TV Commercials from EEG." *Journal of Consumer Research*. Vol. 16, No. 4 (1990): p. 472.

"Smart Cards Allow Supermarkets Loyalty Scheme to Target Individual Shoppers." Holland. June 16, 1998. (Found on Web)

Stiefelhagen, Rainer. "Eye Gaze Monitoring: What Are We Working On?"

Taylor, Humphrey. "The Very Different Methods Used to Conduct Telephone Surveys of the Public." *Journal of the Market Research Society*. Vol. 39, No. 3 (July 1997): p. 421.

"The Blatant Persuaders: New Trend in Advertising Pokes Fun at Subliminal Suggestion." *The Economist*. June 29, 1991. p. 61.

Velichkovsky, Boris M. and John Paulin Hansen. "New Technological Windows Into Mind: There is More in Eyes and Brains for Human-Computer Interaction."

"Veteran Camel Replaces Joe." *U.S. Distribution Journal*. Sept.-Oct. 1997. p. 54.

Zaltman, Gerald. "Rethinking Market Research: Putting People Back In." *Journal of Marketing Research*. Vol. 34, No. 4 (Nov. 1997): 424.

Capita Research Group, Inc. website

Subliminal Threat website

Iscan, Inc. website

ϟ ϟ ϟ

Dan Kelly has contributed to *The Baffler* and other publications, and has a self-published collection of essays titled *Cop Porn*. He can be contacted at 2513 N. California Ave., #223, Chicago, IL 60647.

The late Serge Monast's Blue Beam booklet

PROJECT BLUE BEAM:
THE ELECTRONIC SECOND COMING

Wes Thomas

Rumors of "Project Blue Beam" have been circulating the Internet for the last several years. We have been warned that there's a secret government plan to use satellite-based lasers developed by NASA scientists to project holograms of the messiah in the sky to simulate the Second Coming and convince Christians that the rapture is occurring.

"We are about to undergo extremely cruel domination by a confederation of reptilian species at the head of all 'black ops' of most nations," says one website.[1] "There will even be 'Montauk'-type projects that will take up a whole bunch of people as in a rapture . . . and whisk the whole bunch into never-never land."

The deception will be worldwide, we are advised. In each region, the local messiah—Mohammed, Buddha, etc.—will appear. Everyone will hear the messiah's voice in their head in their native language. The objective: create mass panic and a one-world religion that will lead to total takeover by a one-world government headed by—you guessed it—the Antichrist.

In the minds of some Christian fundamentalists, a likely candidate for the Antichrist is the Maitreya. According to his John The Baptist, Benjamin Creme,[2] the Maitreya is the reincarnation of Christ and has been appearing around the world performing miraculous healings.

The Maitreya will appear in the sky projected by laser beams, says Creme. "The radio and television networks of the world will be linked up . . . and we shall hear his words silently entering our minds, in our own language."

Conspiratologist "Ru Mills" offers another twist on the idea. In a forthcoming book, *Diana, Queen of Heaven*, she says Project Blue Beam will create "miraculous appearances of Lady Diana" to children around the world in an attempt to create a world religion. The children "will claim Diana has given them healing powers," and the two living sons of "Saint Diana," William and Harry, "will become akin to two living Jesus Christs. . . ."

FAKE ALIEN TAKEOVER

Blue beams have also been a central motif of alien-abduction stories, such as Travis Walton's encounter, popularized by the movie *Fire in the Sky*. Travis claimed a hovering UFO shot a blue beam at him, knocking him unconscious, after which he was abducted by aliens. Could this have been a military experiment with laser-generated UFO and alien imagery?

The leading proponent of the Project Blue Beam conspiracy theory is Norio Hayakawa, a Southern California funeral director who runs the Groomwatch[3] citizens organization in his spare time to keep tabs on the suspicious goings-on at the mysterious Area 51 in Nevada. Hayakawa's version, more tailored to the *X-Files* crowd, features aliens instead of messiahs.

He speculates that a secret global cabal of elitists has been promoting popular beliefs in UFOs and an "alien presence" with the intent of staging a phony "extraterrestrial" takeover to cause worldwide panic and justify forming a global government.

All of this raises the question: Is Project Blue Beam just another loony Internet urban legend or is there some reality to it?

The original Blue Beam myth appears to have originated with Canadian journalist Serge Monast, who described it in conspiracy newsletter *Leading Edge* [4] in 1994.

Monast, who also authored a biography of Rael, a Frenchman who has convinced his followers he's an alien sent here to save the world, died of a heart attack in 1997 before he could reveal his sources or more of the alleged scheme.

AIR FORCE PSYOPS

"The technology required to simulate such a fake event is now being readied at locations such as at Area 51," asserts Hayakawa. One technology to achieve this is "cloaking," using electrochromatic panels, he believes.

These panels use thousands of tiny colored lights that take on the appearance of a chameleon-like stealth aircraft's sky background.[5] Electrochromatic panels on such an invisible vehicle could conceivably create an image of Christ, Diana, the Virgin Mary or whatever that appears to be suspended in the sky.

Other stealth technologies that could be used, speculates Hayakawa, include triangular aircraft such as the alleged TR-3A (the "Black Manta"), a new series of Unmanned Aerial Vehicles (UAVs), a world-wide data control system called "Data Repository Establishment and Management, or DREAM), HAARP, "mind-control" weaponry, and the Battle Engagement Area Simulator/Tracker, or BEAST, developed for Star Wars programs and featuring 3-D "battlefield" holographic image projections.

In 1997, a *Defense Week* article[6] revealed that the U.S. Air Force had in fact discussed a system for projecting three-dimensional holographic images as decoys or as an "angry god" above a battlefield.

It also said the Army's JFK Special Warfare Center and School disclosed in 1991 it was planning to develop a psyops (Psychological Operations, as popularized in the movie *The General's Daughter*) system using a hologram to "project persuasive messages and three-dimensional pictures of clouds, smoke, rain droplets, buildings."

VOICE OF GOD

The Air Force also reportedly considered a plan to project a giant hologram over Iraq, with the voice of Allah commanding soldiers and citizens to overthrow Saddam Hussein.

According to *New World Vistas*,[7] published by the U.S. Air Force Scientific Advisory Board in 1996, the voice for such an image could theoretically be created by modulated high power microwaves impinging the human body and heating tissue. The result would "create an internal acoustic field in the 5-15 kilohertz range, which is audible."

Other research is less theoretical. In his book, *The Body Electric*, Nobel Prize nominee Robert O. Becker describes experiments conducted in the early 1960s by Allen Frey, who discovered that radio-frequency signals could be perceived as sound in the head, as well as later experiments conducted in 1973 at the Walter Reed Army Institute of Research by Dr Joseph C. Sharp, who proved he could "hear and understand spoken words" delivered via pulsed microwaves beamed into his brain.[8] And in 1980 U.S. Army researchers found they could "remotely create the perception of noise" inside or behind the head by exposing subjects "to pulsed microwaves with average power densities as low as microwatts per square centimeter.... By proper choice of pulse characteristics, intelligible speech may be created . . . [for] camouflage, decoy and deception operations."[9]

Another possible source of an audible voice was suggested in the British science magazine *New Scientist*.[10] Allegedly, in the late 1980s, at a New Mexico military research facility, "researchers working with high-power laser weapons discovered they could create a glowing ball of fire in the sky by crossing the beams of two powerful infrared lasers." By modulating the lasers, they could also create a "voice-like effect." The writer, however, was unable to confirm the "Voice of God" story.

Another Air Force publication, *Air Force 2025*,[11] dismissed the practicality of creating holograms in the sky in the near future. Holograms are produced by scattering laser light or intense bursts of white light off objects and forming three-dimensional interference patterns stored within solid emulsions or crystals.

That's great for museums and labs, but according to the report, "No credible approach has been suggested for projecting holograms over long distances under real-world conditions, although the Massachusetts Institute of Technology's Media Lab believes holographic color projection may be possible within 10 years. Holographic and other, less high-technology forms of illusion may become a potent tool in the hands of the information warriors."

STAR WARS TECH

But such illusion-generating weapons are more likely to be earth-based than projected from satellites, say some experts. The *Air Force 2025* report's panel of futurists envision a Global Area Strike System (GLASS), using a directed-energy weapon (DEW) system composed of powerful megawatt-class earth-based lasers that "bounce" their high-energy laser beams off space-based mirrors to reach the target. Such a system could conceivably also be used to project laser images in the sky.

According to former Lawrence Livermore Strategic Defense Initiative engineer Charles Ostman, such images are feasible, using high-power military lasers and esoteric plasma and other technologies.

But a California electrical engineer formerly involved in military high power microwave development doesn't think such images would appear "real" enough. "I think it would look like a projection to persons familiar with film, video or laser projection and modern multi-media presentations. It may be good enough though to fool residents of third-world nations who have been kept isolated from examples of modern technology, however.

"I'd expect electron/ion beam projectors mounted on satellites or high-altitude aircraft might be employed. Such presentations would almost certainly have to be done at night, to avoid image wash-out by the sun. But I expect such images would look 'flat,' lacking depth, and suffering from parallax at different locations. They would also be relatively limited in apparent size in order to concentrate energy and make them visible over wide areas."

Laser sky projection expert Randy Johnson of San Diego already uses high-energy visible-ion lasers to project images onto clouds or smoke from fireworks at large outdoor events. He has also projected the Sea World logo on atmospheric thermal inversion layers—similar to mirages reported in deserts.

However, he says current scanning technologies are "limited to fairly low-resolution wire-frame images." Laser projection of bright, realistic raster (TV-like) images of a sky messiah or UFO "would require lasers capable of thousands of watts, such as those planned for use in Star Wars programs."

As for Project Blue Beam-like schemes, Johnson says that in 1985 he was approached by a representative of televangelist Rev. Robert Schuller, pastor of the Crystal Cathedral, in Garden Grove, California. "He wanted to emulate the Second Coming of Christ by projecting laser images in the clouds. I turned him down."

More recently, in 1996, a huge triangular object stretching the apparent length of three football fields and blocking out stars was observed over Phoenix, Arizona. The frightening phenomenon was reported by hundreds of people. Was this a late-night talk show-induced mass hallucination or a dry run for a Blue Beam-like psyop?

As we go to press, CAUS (Citizens Against UFO Secrecy)[12] is in court attempting to force the Pentagon to reveal what it knows. The answers, if any, should spawn a whole new generation of Blue Beam mythology.

NOTES

1. http://www.dnai.com/~zap/sdiisnwo.htm.
2. Share International, http://www.shareintl.org.
3. Groomwatch, http://www.eaglehost.com/groomwatch.
4. Leading Edge International Journal, Issue No. 73, Summer Supplement, 1994.
5. Bill Sweetman, *Popular Science*, May 1997.
6. "Air Force Organizes For Offensive Info War," *Defense Week*, March 31, 1997.
7. New World Vistas, U.S. Air Force Advisory Board, 1996.
8. Gary Selden and Robert O. Becker, *The Body Electric: Electromagnetism and the Foundation of Life*, William Morrow & Co, 1987.
9. K. J. Oscar, "Effects of low power microwaves on the local cerebral blood flow of conscious rats," AD-A090426, June 1, 1980, Army Mobility Equipment Command (Fort Belvoir, VA, United States).
10. Justin Mullins, "And the voice said," *New Scientist*, December, 25 1999/January, 1 2000.
11. *Alternate Futures for 2025* (Air Force 2025), 1996, Air University Press, http://www.au.af.mil/au/2025
12. Citizens Against UFO Secrecy, http://www.caus.org.

⚡ ⚡ ⚡

The author would like to thank members of the EWAR and Mindcontrol email lists for suggestions and discussion of these ideas.

Wes Thomas (west@sonic.net and http://www.sonic.net/~west) is a former editor (*Mondo 2000*), systems analyst, publicist, and electronic countermeasures system designer.

Project Blue Beam: The Electronic Second Coming

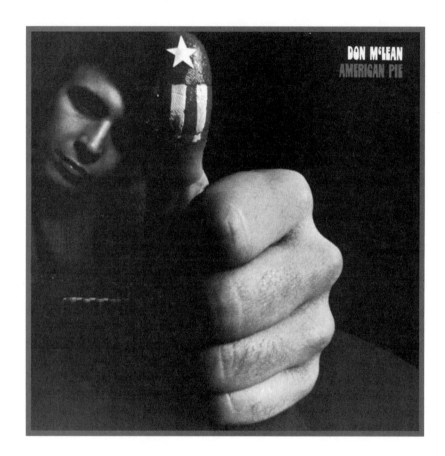

Bye Bye, Miss American Pie
As Sung By Aryan Nations

[The following excerpt was taken and condensed from the Church of Jesus Christ Christian Aryan Nations Bible Law Course No. 64. The neo-Nazi organization is apparently quite impressed by the apocalyptic profundity of the Don McLean pop song.]

In Revelation 15:3 we find the victorious Christians singing The Song of Moses. This Song of Moses was introduced thousands of years earlier in Deuteronomy 31:14. In verse 29 we find that this song is for the "latter days." "Latter days" is a term for the period of time at the end of the age and just before Jesus Christ's return.

Deuteronomy 31:19 says, "Write this song . . . and teach it to the children of Israel." Notice that this song was to be taught. In Revelation 14:3 we find that, ". . . and no man could learn that song but the hundred and forty and four thousand, which were redeemed from the earth." Revelation 14:3 also contains the phrase, "as it were," indicating that the "new song" is not new but an old song that seemed new. Many Christians have read about the Song of Moses in Revelation. Very few knew it was written in Deuteronomy. Even fewer had any understanding of its prophetic and symbolic meaning. Moses taught the meaning of the song but the explanation has been forgotten. We are now about to re-learn this song. It will be "as it were" a new song.

In these "latter days" another song appeared. In 1971 a very unusual song became popular. On the record label, it even claims to be God's song! The copyright notice reads, "Yahweh Tunes, Inc." "American Pie" is that song. While many of us have sung this song, and many of our children memorized its words, none have understood the meaning of this catchy tune. Did you understand these words?

> So, bye bye Miss American Pie
> Drove my Chevy to the levee
> But the levee was dry
> Those good 'ol boys were drinking
> Whisky and rye, singing
> This'll be the day that I die
> This'll be the day that I die

What does it mean, "Drove my Chevy to the levee but the levee was dry"? Are these just nonsense words or is there a hidden meaning? Have you puzzled over the words in verse 3 of "American Pie," "and while the king was looking down, the jester stole his thorny crown." Do you know of a king who wore a crown of thorns? In other verses of "American Pie" we sang about "the king's widowed bride." (Jesus Christ's widowed bride?) In other verses, "the book of love" (the Bible?), sacred music, church bells, Satan, faith in

God above, and in the last verse, "the three men I admire the most, Father, Son and Holy Ghost."

Until now, few have learned The Song of Moses and no one has "learned" this other new song. But, like The Song of Moses, American Pie is not a "new song." It is an old song because "American Pie" tells the same story as The Song of Moses! Both songs are written in word symbols. Both are Bible Stories. Neither can be comprehended unless you are one of God's elect.

[The Aryan Nations report then dissects the entire lyrics of "Bye, Bye Miss American Pie," reading them as criticisms of Sex Education and other Satanic Humanist perversions, how the Supreme Court removed prayer from public schools, how America is no longer a Christian nation, how Jews control Christian churches and all television programming, movies, and even Christian publishing, how Jews will take over America and the world with fake nuclear terror, and finally how Christian America will awaken and refuse to yield to the Jews.]

American Pie, an EARTHLY version of Yahweh's HEAVENLY Song of Moses?

The Song of Moses and "American Pie" tell the exact same story. Perhaps American Pie is Satan's version of The Song of Moses.

But The Song of Moses is not Moses' song. It is God's song because He gave it to Moses. Look at the record label for "American Pie." Notice the words, "Yahweh Tunes, Inc." In Lesson Four we found that Yahweh is a form of the Hebrew name for God. So, on the label, "American Pie" gives legal notice claiming that it is also God's song. Whether or not it is actually God's song may be debated, but the facts are, that legal notice was put there on purpose by someone for some reason.

In Deuteronomy 31:28 Moses was instructed to "call heaven and earth to record against them." If "American Pie" has some relationship to the Song of Moses, then perhaps "American Pie" also "calls heaven and earth to bear witness against us." Look again at the record label. You will also see that the song was published by Mayday Music, Inc.

May Day is the major holiday in the Communist world. Perhaps this indicates Communist music. Here we could have represented an earthly power. "Yahweh Tunes, Inc." would likewise represent the heavenly power. Therefore, in symbols, the label on the record also calls heaven and earth to bear witness against us.

The Good News

The song "American Pie" leaves America in a hopeless state and the anti-Christ forces in total victory. Deuteronomy 31:16-17 also mentions this helpless state of affairs, " . . . and this people will rise up, and go a whoring after the gods of strangers . . . and they will forsake Me. Then My anger shall be kindled against them in that day. And I will forsake them, and I will hide my face from them . . . And so that they will say in that day, Are not these ills come upon us because our God is not among us." (The Father, Son and Holy Ghost, they caught the last train for the coast.) Verse 29 of Deuteronomy 31 identifies this time as "the latter days."

But, notice two things. 1. "American Pie" has six verses and seven choruses. Is one verse missing? 2. Whereas "American Pie" ends in hopeless despair, the song of Moses ends in "rejoice all ye nations, with His people; for He will avenge the blood of His servants, and will render vengeance to His adversaries, and will be merciful to His land and His people."

Many churches have Pastors in search of sheep to shepherd. The Committee is more like a General in search of an Army. The Committee is helping to raise up and prepare up "the marching band that refused to yield." Now that you have completed the Bible Law Course, won't you please stay with us and help us raise up others? Join the "marching band that refused to yield." Your monthly or weekly contribution will help us place more ads, distribute more flyers, send out more free sample Bible Lessons. Onward Christian Soldiers.

If you have been reading the verses quoted in your Bible, you may have noticed two things:

1. The God was in full command at all times.

2. He will save us and punish the wicked.

"American Pie" has six verses of bad news. But because there are six verses and seven choruses, we suspect one missing verse of Good News. . . .

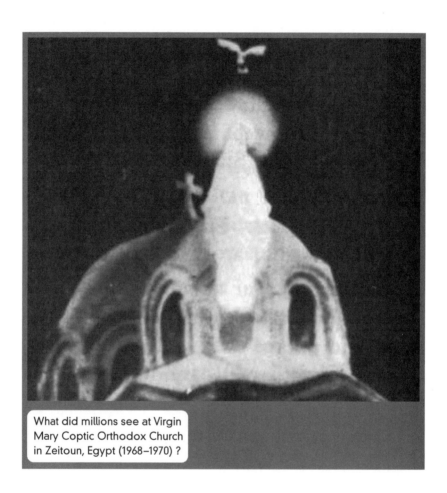

What did millions see at Virgin Mary Coptic Orthodox Church in Zeitoun, Egypt (1968–1970) ?

HOLDING ONTO JESUS' FEET

David Sereda

In October 1994, I was bankrupt, living in a small tent in my father's yard. I had been an active environmentalist for over 15 years, having cleaned up oil spills, planted over 700,000 evergreen trees in Canada, directed a nonprofit foundation (The Tesla Foundation) promoting scientific discoveries for a better environment, and had run an eco-venture capital company called The Green & Blue Corp with a wealthy Saudi partner, where we made serious efforts to raise monies for scientific discoveries for a better environment. Many of the world's wealthiest people turned us down.

There I was, living in this small tent. The rains came and flooded it. I was freezing to death as the water flowed in the front doorway of the tent. Soon, I was floating out of my body. I was first purified by the Holy Ghost (made clean), then taken above the rain clouds, just before sunrise. Suddenly, atoms came rushing together from every direction of the universe at once. The sound was oceanic and cosmic. The atoms quickly formed the body of Jesus Christ right in front of me. Jesus is billions of times more innocent than all the children on earth. Because the Lord is the most innocent, the Glory of Innocence, Love, Ecstasy, Peace, Power and Grace flow through Jesus brighter than one thousand suns. The actual white light shining from Jesus' face was brighter than one thousand of our suns. Jesus' robe was as bright as the sun itself. Like an earthquake in my veins, I collapsed at Jesus' feet as if dead, holding onto Jesus' feet as the Lord spoke to me for nearly half an hour. The whole universe seemed to be emanating from this one being. I experienced Jesus as God, not the Son of God, but God. The first words Jesus spoke were: "I have appeared to a number of people throughout history, but at different levels of their spiritual ability. No one has seen me in my entirety. You, right now, are not seeing me in my entirety. It is not possible at this time."

I met Jesus again on Easter morning, 1997, and the Lord crushed me with more Ecstasy and Love than I ever thought could have created the whole galaxy, and, perhaps, the universe. Jesus spoke again for a half hour. I make the messages available to all who wish to study them.

⚡ ⚡ ⚡

David Sereda is the author of *Face to Face with Jesus Christ* (Blue Dolphin Publishing).

Fig.1: Nimrod, world order tower builder. Deified as Mithra, syn. Jupiter: Zeus-piter, the "Sky-father".

Fig.2: Santa prototype: Father-Zeus (Jupiter) seen as "Father Christmas". Zeus-Ammon, syn. Venus-Noga, i.e. Lucifer (Satan).

Entertaining falsehoods opens one to the big lie (2 Thes. 2: 10-12). Beware the traditions & doctrines of devils. According to Scripture the New World Order is the kingdom of Antichrist. The modern Christian church has prepared his way, and the New World Order shall usher him in.

JESUS/LUCIFER, SANTA/SATAN
THE APOCALYPTIC PARABLES OF NORBERT H. KOX

Adam Parfrey

Norbert Kox is no panty-waist, Hallmark card-reading, mainstream church-loving imbecile.

The now gentle, middle-aged Norbert Kox—"Norb" to friends—began his life as a badass biker, a guy who fought all comers at bars. Once, he slit the throat of a barfly with the aid of a pool cue. In his early days, Norb stripped and painted motorcycles and cars, kind of like a Northern Wisconsin Von Dutch. According to his friend David Damkoehler, a Green Bay art professor: "While [Norbert] was a biker his actions were legendary. People who encountered the early Norb recount vivid, vulgar acts done with a flair and an originality that compare with the most outrageous performance art of the time."

A bad acid trip—a really, really bad trip—led Norb to come to grips with his "Born to Lose" mania, and explore the other side of the fence:

> It was the summer of 1974 at a motorcycle hill climb in Wisconsin Rapids; we would always go a day ahead of time and party hard until the hill climb.
>
> I never experimented much with LSD. That night when the acid was being passed out, I was already stoned and overconfident. When I said I would take two hits, my friend wasn't able to dissuade me, knowing I had never done more than a half-hit before.
>
> Before long, the acid was swimming in my mind, and everything

Reject the Christmas tradition. The true Christ Yesu was not born on December 25. The Pseudochrist Jesus is Lucifer "Light Bearer", or Mithra, syn. Zeus (Sky Father). His birthday is Christmas. Antichrist will be worshipped as God and Saviour through the modern so-called Christian church. "Woe to the inhabiters of the earth... the devil is come down unto you... (Rev. 12:12).

around was either comical or beautiful. Everything that moved had a tail like a comet, and everything that shined had a million sparks. It was blowing my mind. I remember thinking, "Wow! This is fantastic." But the beauty was intermittently shattered by ugly visions and obscene words. The force was closing in on me and I started to feel its effect.

I became trapped in a circle of events, events which always brought me back to the same spot, but each time it would occur I became a little more frightened. Events would happen exactly the same as before. It was not within my power to change one thing, not even the words I would speak. What I saw was an exact recurrence of previous events; the only thing different were my thoughts. I became more and more paranoid each time around.

Vicious dogs were in the air all around, snarling. Everyone was walking through fire, which wasn't unusual for our bunch except for the frequency and order it was happening. My brother Magoo was wearing an underwater snorkling mask. He broke the glass out while it was still on his face. He would laugh hideously, waving a broken-off car antenna, sparks flying in every direction. Fear gripped me deeper as I thought to myself, "I have to talk to someone. I am so scared, I've never been this frightened before." Then another guy I knew, Teen Angel, would jump out of the trunk of his car, and a new spark of hope would lighten my heart as I rushed towards him, then, as quickly as he appeared, he was gone. I thought if only I could get some sleep, I might find rest. I knew I could not take much more. I would start to head for the tent, but only a few steps later I would stumble and begin to fall. Then I would find myself staring at the Coleman lantern while the moths would land in the fire and die. Every episode ended at the Coleman lantern, where it began, and then the horrible sights would start over, and I knew I was in for another lap.

While at the lantern, I would feel a certain temporary relief. I would seem to recompose my senses a little, somehow hoping that it was all over, but still knowing in my mind that the repeating chaos had just begun. Soon the fear would grip deep in my bowels. Was I alive, or dead? There was no way for me to know. I prayed that it was all my imagination and that the gang was just trying to freak me out. But to my dismay I would find myself staring once again at Magoo, seeing him through the shiny glass of the snorkling mask, which would then again twist and break, glass falling down his heavy beard. It's one thing to watch the *Twilight Zone* TV show; it's another thing to live a creepy episode over and over again. I was crying, I was peeing my pants. I thought I would die of fear, but when death didn't come, I thought that I had already died and gone to Hell. I'd been through these hell circles four, five, six times, and then they were still going. By now I had almost given up hope thinking that I'd ever see my family again. I was in another world. If I was not dead, I was a zombie locked in an insane asylum.

I wanted to repent. I wanted another chance. "Oh God," I said, "Don't let me be like this forever." I do not know how long I prayed, or all that I said, but God did hear me.

The air began to feel different. The ice-cold chill had melted away in the summer breeze. The cases of beer which had been stacked high the last time around were now empty cans and torn cardboard. The perspiration evaporated from my forehead and I began to collect my thoughts. I could not believe it. It was too good to be true. Had Hell rejected me, or was Satan just building up for the big one?

—From Norbert Kox's unpublished 900-page book, *Six Nights Till Morning*

After being sent to hell, Norb repented and came up the other side like the mythological entity, Sol Invictus, the sun god. The drug-taking, hell-raising alcoholic Norbert Kox gave away all his possessions, and brought a bible with him out to the Wisconsin forest to intensely study the word of God and become a mystic. Between cave explorations and creating a kind of monastery filled with his Visionary Art, Norb

Begin all things with the Illustrious name of ALLAH the Yielder the Most Merciful.

The Fallacy of Christmas

أَكْذُوبَةُ عِيدِ الْمِيلَادِ

"Santa or Satan?"

سَانْتَا أَم الشَّيْطَانُ؟

ALLAH is the Most Magnificent, and to Him is due All Gratitude

EDITION #

The Nubian Hebrews have come to the same conclusion as Norbert Kox

The old-style St. Nicholas by Sarita Vendetta

came to grips with essential realizations that still drive him today.

Norbert's research impales the sacred cows of contemporary Christianity with truck-sized holes. Armed with findings from his investigations, Norbert paints startling, even gruesome canvases in which one can see the influences of Mattias Grünewald, Salvador Dali, even Joe Coleman.

In his readings of biblical text in the original Greek and Hebrew, Norbert discovered that what contemporaries believe to be Christ is actually a demonic imposter. The way the word "Jesus" is spelled and pronounced has nothing to do with the way it was conveyed in the original holy book—as "Yesu" (yay-soo). The letter "J," as Norbert found, was the invention of a 16th century German printer, a fancy way of depicting the letter "I."

Jesus, Yesu. Semantics. Pronunciation. Big deal. So what. And as some historians have discovered, such as Acharya S. in her book *The Christ Conspiracy*, or J. M. Robertson in his tome *Pagan Christs*, the idea of Jesus Christ has been assimilated from a multitude of pagan cultures. The crucifixion. The dates of Christmas and Easter. The Passion Play. All of it.

Norbert Kox directs your attention to the words of Yesu that preach against "prophets of deceit which cause my people to forget my name." The Christ personified in the iconic Warner Sallman illustration of the blond-haired, high-cheekboned, European-looking "Jesus" is a demonic pretence. Norbert backs up that assertion with his artwork; one of his most famous paintings is of a demonic entity poking through his Warner Sallman-type disguise. Norbert discovered that the word "Jesus" adds up to 666 by his numbering system, a bible code whispered to him by holy inspiration 20 years ago, and not by Michael Drosnin's recent bestselling book. "I just about fell over when I discovered that about the word Jesus. Lucifer also adds up to 666."

Investigations into false beliefs occupy much of Norbert's time and attention. The Catholic Church is chockablock full of them, he says, including such things as incorruptible bodies, miraculous visions, tens of thousands of gruesome holy relics spread across the world in the form of bleeding statues, appearances in the sky and on windowpanes and tortillas of the Holy Virgin, and other forms of unsavory phenomena. One of the biggest lies of the modern age is the supposed Christian link invested into the person of Santa Claus, an entity Norbert calls "Satan Claws." As Norbert wrote for the December 1986 edition of the very small publication, *The Wisconsin Caver*:

> The origin of the Santa Claus myth has been traced through the ancient religious traditions and beliefs of many cultures. In most European countries the Christ Child is the traditional "gift-bearer." Kris Kringle is the corrupted form of the German Christkindel. In modern Christmas tradition Kris Kringle and Santa Claus are synonymous.
>
> Santa is referred to as "the children's Christmas deity," but we all know that Santa Claus is not really the Christkindel. Then what deity is he? Another of Santa's names is Saint Nicholas, and an archaic name for the Devil is "old Nick," viz. jolly old Saint Nick. He swore to pose as God, and to sit upon his throne in the north. Santa is an anagram, can you figure it out?
>
> Zeus, a prototype of Santa Claus, was identified in Norse Mythology as Odin or Wotan, "god of the sky." Odin was revered for his wisdom. "From his high throne in Asgard, he could see all of heaven and earth." Asgard was the farthest point north, viz. Santa's throne at the North Pole from where he knows and sees all. Odin's (Zeus') Eye is also called "the All-Seeing Eye."
>
> "Odin was believed to bestow special gifts at Yuletide to those who honored him by approaching his sacred fir tree." (*Babylon Mystery Religion*, p. 165.)
>
> The idea of Santa Claus riding through the sky in a sleigh drawn by

reindeer may have been derived from ancient sun-god myths. The pagan god Mithra rode through the sky in the mule-drawn chariot of the sun-god. He passed through the underworld at night. Is Santa Claus the image of Mithra?

The early Santa Claus, "Father Christmas," with evergreen holly and scepter, was a representation of Father Zeus, or Jupiter.

Magistrates and generals, in celebrations, donned the costume of Jupiter. With special robes and reddened face, they carried a laurel branch scepter and wore a laurel wreath on their head. Another name for Santa Claus is Kris Kringle, which is a corrupted form of the German Christkindel (Christ Child). The Magi confused the Christ child with Mithra. Thus Mithra, the deified Nimrod, is the image of Kris Kringle. Nimrod, the founder of Babylon, can undoubtedly be identified as the first Santa Claus.

In Dark Age Germany a play about the Garden of Eden was performed each Christmas, using a fir tree decked with apples. The "Paradise Tree" was later accommodated to home use. Eating apples or fruit from the Paradise or Christmas tree was slightly rebellious, but once the first bite was taken, it was not long before the tree was bare. Another custom was the "Christmas Pyramid." A wooden pyramid was decorated with candles and shiny decorations, and placed in the living room of the home. About the 15th Century, people began to combine the tree and pyramid, moving the decorations to the tree. By the 17th Century even the candles were moved to the tree, thus eliminating the wooden structure, the tree itself becoming the pyramid.

The Christmas tree idea actually originated in Egypt long before the so-called Christmas era. Other civilizations also revered a sacred tree. The Buddhists worshipped in caves, and their sacred tree was found inscribed in almost every cave, according to the *Encyclopedia of Freemasonry*. Historical records prove that Santa Claus and the Christmas tree were associated with pagan religion, and both have been worshipped in ancient cave temples.

Ideas communicated by Norbert Kox through his artwork are not very popular with individuals pushing the status quo. An August 1999 news story in the Associated Press discussed Norbert's latest run-in with powerful church entities who consider him blasphemous. As it turns out, the controversy backfired on the offended church leaders. Attendance of the exhibit, and monetary donations to the museum escalated drastically as a result of their ire:

GREEN BAY, Wis. (AP)—A national Roman Catholic group is protesting that a museum exhibit is blasphemous.

The exhibit, which opened in early July at the Neville Public Museum in Green Bay, uses rosaries, crucifixes and other religious objects to bring out artist Norbert Kox's interpretations of biblical themes. The display includes the Virgin Mary depicted as the "Great Harlot" and a Christ wearing a necklace with the Satanic symbol "666."

"It's very clear that there's no logical conclusion other than that Mr. Norbert Kox wants to stick it to Catholics," said William Donohue, president of the New York-based Catholic League for Religious and Civil Rights.

Donohue said he is not seeking removal of the exhibit, but he wants the museum's board to put a written statement next to the exhibit explaining that its members don't personally condone it.

The museum's governing board, an advisory group appointed by Brown County Executive Nancy Nusbaum, voted Wednesday to support the display.

Nusbaum said her office had received two negative phone calls and two negative letters since the exhibit opened in early July. No local Catholic diocesan officials or clergy members have voiced complaints, she said.

Clergy throughout the area have been invited to attend a discussion of the exhibit with the artist tonight, she said.

Brown County runs the museum through a partnership with Neville Public Museum Corp., which funds all exhibits and related activities. The corporation's board plans to discuss Donohue's protests next week.

The New Franken artist contends that his exhibit, called "To Hell and Back," is not meant to be offensive. Kox said he carries the Bible with him and regularly quotes scripture.

Kox has said his pictures convey his belief that "pagan teachings have crept into the church," and that the faithful must think for themselves.

Wanting people to think for themselves? If that is Christianity, that's the sort of belief the editor of *Apocalypse Culture* would not mind being part of. But it's clearly not the sort of Christianity manifested by most of its organized variables in the world today.

⚡ ⚡ ⚡

Norbert Kox's art is seen on the cover and the interior of the Dilettante Press book, *The End is Near: Visions of Apocalypse, Millennium and Utopia*, with text by Roger Manley, Stephen Jay Gould, Howard Finster, The Dalai Lama, John the Divine and Adam Parfrey. His artwork has shown in Milwaukee, Los Angeles, New York, Chicago and elsewhere. To get in touch with Norbert Kox, contact the Dean Jensen Gallery, 759 N. Water St., Milwaukee, WI (414) 278-7100.

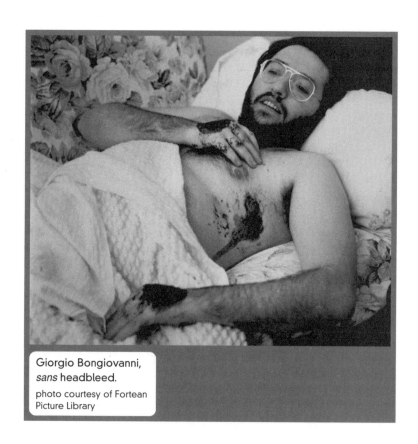

Giorgio Bongiovanni,
sans headbleed.

photo courtesy of Fortean
Picture Library

THE BLEEDER

Adam Parfrey

M*ysteries, Marvels, Miracles* is Catholic author Joan Carroll Cruz's catalogue of weird phenomena interpreted as the blessed intervention of Jesus and company in the physical world. Among the strange holy happenings described by Cruz are bilocation (being in two places at once), levitation, odor of sanctity (Jesus' favorite perfume suddenly wafting from decomposing corpses), odors of sin (bad deeds appearing in the form of bad smells), transverberation (being struck in the heart by an arrow from God, not Cupid), miraculous transport (like a medieval *Star Trek*), mysterious provisions of food and money, invisibility, jabbering in strange languages, the refusal of holy corpses to rot after death, and God's use of bugs to become passenger pigeons of the blessed Word.

The creepy star of the mystical phenomenon, stigmata, with all its bloody wannabe-crucified ritualism, has enjoyed many contemporary manifestations. *The Catholic Encyclopedia*, in its 1912 edition, enumerates 312 verified stigmatists, who bled in simulation to the imagined wounds of the folkloric entity known as Jesus Christ.

Twentieth century stigmatists Padre Pio and Theresa Neumann are the most recent stars of the mystical bloody sore brigade. Neumann was the most remarkably horrific, prolific bleeder, and was even said to consume nothing but air and water for most of her life. Photographs of Theresa Neumann's eye-bleeds are more reminiscent of Oedipus and Greek Tragedy than Christianity, but the holy gore story was quite a good sell for the Church at mid-Century. Protestant killjoys believe stigmata has more to with demonic possession than blessed simulacra. Depending on who was making their assertions, skeptics declared stigmata to be the result of fraud or the remarkable potential of the human body to follow the unspoken dictates of the human mind via belief. The way stigmatism combines blood, paranormal phenomena and a modern primitivist connection to the Great Beyond attracted Hollywood for the grist mill's 1999 release, *Stigmata*.

The Vatican has not yet verified that the crusty cross appearing on the forehead of the youngish Italian man Giorgio Bongiovanni is a legitimate apparition; on the other hand, Bongiovanni short-cuts the church's bureaucracy to meet with the Jesus entity on his own time, his own place. The intergalactic taxicab Jesus uses to visit Bongiovanni is the old-style flying saucer, and so the stigmatist tells about his bloody grace not at the Catholic church, but at UFO conventions, where he discusses Jesus' revelations of the Secrets of Fatima— the anti-Communist prophecy communicated to three Portuguese children in

Bongiovanni's Jesus, brought down by UFOs for a 21st Century Holy Supper

1917. Not only does Bongiovanni say he is the reincarnation of one of the three Portuguese servant girls at Fatima, but claims that Jesus himself piloted a UFO one day to reveal to him the "Third Secret of Fatima," or the one unreleased by the Catholic church, one that tells of the evils of organized Catholicism and the imminent destruction of the Vatican.

Giorgio's stigmata also appears on his hands, the place where the folkoric Christ is thought to have been nailed to the cross. In contradiction to many centuries of holy art as well as stigmatic bleeds, forensic scientists and historians are now convinced that the crucified were nailed by their wrists, and never through their palms, as this would not support a body's weight.

And, as seen by the opening photo, Bongiovanni is also stigmatized on his side, at the point stories hold where Jesus Christ was said to have been pierced by a Roman spear.

Giorgio Bongiovanni provides a remarkable smorgasbord of contemporary religious conceits:

1. Holy Reincarnation
2. UFOs
3. Dialogue with Jesus
4. Jesus' Divulging of Conspiratorial Secrets and the non-stop bleeds that assist him in proving the holy importance of his messages.

Bongiovanni is a coveted speaker at UFO conventions worldwide, where he sells his self-published magazine, *Nonsiamosoli* (which translates as "We are not alone") as well as publicity photos and illustrations that combine belief systems of Christianity and UFOlogy. Doubtlessly upsetting the stomachs of militia members and populists, Bongiovanni tells us that his various meetings with the UFO flying Jesus, as well as with ex-commie king Mikhail Gorbachev, have convinced him that the world must undergo restructuring as a United Nations-led New World Order. Or, to be brief, what patriots believe to be the conjuration of Satan.

The material following comes from one of Bongiovanni's press releases.

The Mystic and Human History of Giorgio Bongiovanni

Among all supernatural signs that have taken place in these last 2000 years, the stigmata phenomenon plays an important role. Stigmata represent the wounds inflicted on Jesus on the cross which appear on a person's body. Many recipients of this sign have deeply marked the history of mankind and the general view of the community, for instance the experience of stigmatists such as Padre Pio and St. Francis of Assisi.

Man's science was never capable of explaining the nature of the phenomenon; on the contrary, the explanation often given was pertinent to a case of psychosomatic manifestation due to mystic hysteria or the somatization of the Love for Jesus. These explanations are true in cases in which the wounds appear for a short period of time, but cannot explain cases in which the marks are permanent, or at least, appear for a very long period of time and do not become infected nor cause other pathological phenomena usually present in such cases.

Instances of miraculous healing, bilocations, strange scents and blood signs have made the experience of stigmatization more extraordinary. There aren't many examples of stigmatists with permanent stigmata, but many more present temporary signs which are manifested in dates relative to a religious recurrence. The Italian Giorgio Bongiovanni is a stigmatist with permanent stigmata. He was born in Floridia on September 5, 1963. When he was 13, he met Eugenio Siragusa, who claimed to be in contact with superior beings from other worlds and who has spread their warnings and advice throughout the world.

Giorgio spent the next 10 years of his life near Eugenio Siragusa, who raised him with a culture and a knowledge that are not of this world; his teachings prepared him for the experience he would live in later years. In 1984, he got married and moved to Porto S. Elpidio, on the Adriatic Coast in Central Italy, where he opened a small shop dealing in accessories for shoes which did permit him to gather a small fortune.

In 1985, Eugenio suggested that Giorgio and his brother Filippo, together with some other collaborators, start the bulletin *Nonsiamosoli* (We are not alone); its main theme was Eugenio's contacts with these beings and their concerned appeals to humanity, as well as the messages spread by him in Italy and abroad. These warnings are pertinent to the most important themes of our times: nuclear danger, drugs, pollution, illness, social injustice, corruption, growing immorality. The bulletin dealt with witnesses of celestial manifestations, UFO sightings, weeping of statues and sacred images and so on.

Through *Nonsiamosoli* the publishers tried to sensitize man and let him become more spiritually aware.

However, on April 5, 1989, Giorgio Bongiovanni had the first of a series of contacts that would change his life completely.

Theresa Neumann

On his way home from work, he saw, standing next to his car, a female figure who seemed to be waiting for him. She was dressed in white with a blue belt around her waist, and upon her chest a rose.

It was a little past midday and the sun was high in the sky. Giorgio was amazed to see that this Lady was shining with a light of her own. Moving nearer, he realized that she was raised above the ground. He thought he knew her and so he called to her, and she answered him in a sweet voice: "I am Myriam, my son," and dictated to him a short message in which she told him that the time had come to uncover the face of the AntiChrist. After this first encounter, he met her again and Myriam, the Holy Virgin, also revealed to him his past lives on Earth and told him that he had been chosen because he cannot be influenced like many of the seers she had contacted in the past.

Whenever Giorgio was contacted by her, he saw her coming out of a globe of light, and at the end of the contact he saw her leave as if absorbed by the globe. This confirmed to him without any doubt and quite unexpectedly what Eugenio had revealed about his experiences, about angelic beings coming with their spaceships of light accompanying the apparitions of Jesus and the Holy Virgin.

These globes of light have certainly held a main role in extraordinary events like the famous "Miracle of the Sun" which occurred in Fatima in

1917 during the apparition to three young shepherds, Giacinta, Francisco and Lucia. It's to Fatima that the Holy Virgin asked Giorgio to go and promised to manifest a great sign for him and for the whole of mankind.

On September 2, 1989, Giorgio heeded this call. In the big square of the Sanctuary, it was a little past midday, and under the oak tree of the apparitions of 1917, he fell into ecstasy and, hovering next to a big branch, he saw the same divine Lady. She greeted him with, "I'm happy that you have come. . . I was waiting for you. . .", and went on explaining to him about the mission he had been called for: to spread worldwide the contents of the Third Secret of Fatima which, with great regret and sorrow on Her part, the Catholic Church hadn't officially revealed yet to mankind. Then, she made him a very important disclosure: the cosmos is inhabited by many civiliza-

tions who have been visited by Jesus Christ before us and have put into practice his teachings. In this way, they have accepted the redemption. On the contrary, we have killed him on the cross, and, as a result, we have built a society charged with barbaric actions and monstrous crimes. In addition, the Virgin said, thus confirming what Eugenio Siragusa had already revealed, that these civilizations worked together by cooperating in the divine mission of

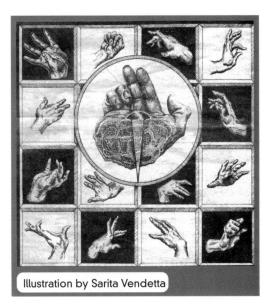

Illustration by Sarita Vendetta

which they are aware, and today they are visiting in peace inside crafts we call UFOs. She then asked him to remain free, outside any institution, whether religious, political or otherwise, as Her message is meant for the whole of mankind regardless of belief, race or social class. In the end She asked him if he was willing to carry a part of the suffering of Her son Jesus. When Giorgio agreed, two beams of light came out of the Virgin's chest and struck the palms of Giorgio's hands and stigmatized them. After that tho Holy Virgin disappeared, as if absorbed by the globe of light that until then had been hovering behind Her.

The whole event had taken place amid total indifference on the part of the people who crowded the square. When the two friends who had accompanied Giorgio started to cry out, some people approached the three, but walked away as soon as the their curiosity had been satisfied. Only two black men and two black women remained to help him up and to comfort him. The pain was excruciating, as if some invisible nails were piercing his hands through. During the journey back, he experienced long hours of great pain, during which time the stigmatization of his hands was completed.

The holes also appeared on the back of his hands. Days later, Giorgio had another ecstasy in Porto S. Elpidio in the presence of 1000 people. The Holy Virgin came with Jesus to tell him that from that day on, the Third Message of Fatima was entering the phase of fulfillment; at the end of such phase, the second manifestation of Jesus on Earth. She also added that she would no longer appear to him, but from that day on, Jesus would advise him and accompany him throughout his mission.

As She was speaking these words, tears of blood were streaming down Her face. Then, it was Jesus who spoke to him and revealed to him that His visitation upon the Earth had started, and it would be evident to all when the time was ripened.

Since that day, Giorgio began his mission of bearing testimony throughout the world.

He went to Spain, Switzerland, and, in 1990, to South America, and stopped in Argentina, Uruguay and Paraguay. His case attracted the attention of the mass media. Through the press, by radio, by local TV, the message was transmitted to thousands of people. He also spoke with people in crowded conference rooms and auditoriums. In Asunción, Paraguay, he met the Royal Family of Spain; he showed the stigmata to Queen Sofia and spoke about the message of Fatima.

The Queen herself introduced Giorgio to Mikhail Gorbachev and his wife Raisa. It happened quite unexpectedly at the national auditorium in Madrid, an event that was even recorded by the Spanish national TV. Giorgio asked for his permission to spread the message of Fatima in the USSR and Gorbachev agreed. Giorgio himself was amazed by what was happening, but the Holy Virgin had promised to him, a humble cobbler, that She would make possible that he meet the world mighty.

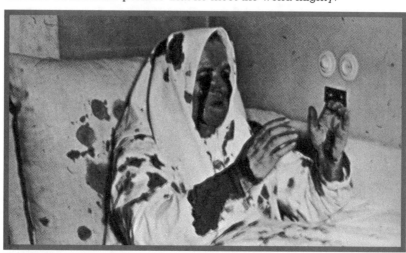

Russia has a leading role in the future of mankind, as the Holy Virgin pointed out in the message of Fatima.

In March 1991, Giorgio was in Africa, in Kinshasa, Zaire. The impact was dramatic: the decline and the misery of the people are such that no comparison can be made with what we commonly call living. Survival is an everyday, painful struggle. Starvation and diseases kill adults and, above all, children. Giorgio spoke on national TV and accused the dictator, Mobutu, of not doing anything in order to help his people, whereas his corrupted politicians and he live in wealth.

In the largest square in Kinshasa, in front of 20,000 people, he fell into ecstasy and spoke to Jesus, who delivered to him a message of love, promise and justice.

On September 2, 1991, at his home, two years after his first stigmatization in Fatima, Giorgio, in ecstasy, saw Jesus, who stigmatized his feet. At the beginning, the stigmata in his feet appeared as two bleeding crosses, and then became of the same shape as the marks in the hands. His wife and friends participated in this event.

As the suffering grows, so does his mission. When he is in Italy, his days are filled: he meets people who want to see and talk to him, he attends Congresses, and releases interviews to Italian and foreign press . . . and the bleedings.

Every day, and sometimes more than once a day, the crucifixion of Christ is renewed in his body with great pain. Giorgio has also been able to personally meet important members of the Catholic Church, who are connected with the message of Fatima.

Both in Italy and abroad, many people ask of him to heal them from their physical ailments, but he always explains that this is not his task. Jesus has not given him the power to heal, but his mission is to awaken the consciousness and the spirit of men. In any case, he has a word of comfort for

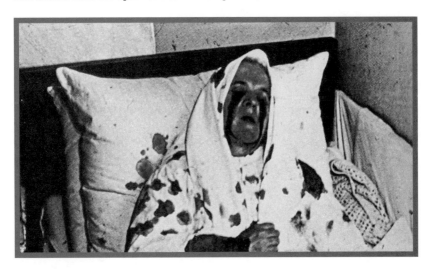

everybody. In some cases, however, thanks to the faith of the people who come into contact with him, the miracle occurs and they are unexpectedly healed.

In early 1993, he was examined by a group of doctors, psychologists, psychiatrists, and among them a specialist in neuropsychiatry, Stanis Previato. In their report they affirmed that the phenomenon of the stigmata cannot be explained by the physio-pathological laws known today by medical science. Furthermore, they added that he has a normal and balanced mental condition.

It is important to underline that these journeys made by Giorgio are inspired by Jesus. Answering the call, on 25th July, he went to Uruguay, in a location called "Aurora," a place known for its UFO sightings. That evening, Giorgio had a sighting of four bright spaceships. With him were 20 people, among them a pilot, a lawyer and a famous journalist.

One of the objects shone even brighter than the others. After performing some evolutions in the starry sky for a few minutes and recorded by the camera, the object grew in brightness and then vanished. During that night at the hotel, in Giorgio's room, the sixth stigmata appeared on his forehead: a bleeding cross.

The following morning he explained to all his amazed friends, collaborators and journalists that something unexpected had occurred. In a way unknown to him, he had found himself at the place of the sighting, inside the same globe of light.

There Jesus spoke to him before blessing him on the forehead, the same spot where the bleeding cross appeared afterwards.

He also received an important and grave message, in that Jesus confirmed to him that His arm had started to strike humankind, but that for this manifestation to occur it was necessary to wait a little longer. The occurrence of the event echoed through the mass media to the extent that numerous papers reported on their cover the bleeding cross, and it was also shown on TV.

October 28, 1994 was the first time in history that a stigmatist had spoken in the United Nations building. In late November, Giorgio was a guest speaker at the annual UFO Congress in Nevada. Eugenio Siragusa had been invited in the first place, but ended his mission, and he asked Giorgio to represent him at the Congress. The experts viewed Giorgio's experience as the link between two different aspects of the UFO manifestation: psychical and spiritual.

David and Hitler
go to the planet Mars

David and Hitler go to the planet Mars. They see 2 fire balls and red ash. They are both wearing protective glasses. They decide to go swimming, but realize there is no water on Mars. David asks, "How come? I can have a coke at home." "I don't know," says Hitler.

They go to the rocketship and set sail. Their rocket spins in the air and crashes. They see more fire balls and red ash and are stunned.

They are alone on the planet with only fire balls. They saved their suits from the rocket and put them back on. They can now go swimming in their fire suits.

Water is spraying out of their rocket. They collect the water in buckets. Probes and satellites from the earth take over. Kennedy, the President, comes to visit. Kennedy refuses to give them money because they broke the rocketship. David and Hitler are mad.

David and Hitler see canals and go to them, just plain dry land canals, no water. They are sad because they can't find water.

Hitler kills Kennedy because he hates him and because Kennedy didn't even bring a canteen of water with him.

David and Hitler jump on a satellite and probe and return to Earth. They ask, "What time is it?" Then they go buy a beer and say, "Yah, Packey." "No, you're Packey."

⚡ ⚡ ⚡

Written by **David**, a 32-year-old semi-retarded man, in 1997.

Eric Yates is threatened with castration by the puppet show in *What Is It?*

photo: Robby Capponeto

(AN ESSAY CONCERNING THE SUBTEXT OF THE FILM BY THE SAME TITLE)
Crispin Hellion Glover

> . . . but there is another sort of character who will
>
> narrate anything, and, the worse he is, the more
>
> unscrupulous he will be; nothing will be too bad
>
> for him and he will be ready to imitate anything,
>
> not as a joke, but in right good earnest, and before
>
> a large company. As I was just now saying, he will
>
> attempt to represent the roll of thunder, the noise
>
> of wind or hail, or the creaking of wheels, and pul-
>
> leys, and the various sounds of flutes; pipes, trum-
>
> pets, and all sorts of instruments; he will bark like a
>
> dog, bleat like a sheep, or crow like a cock; his
>
> entire art will consist in imitation . . .
>
> **The Republic, Plato (427–347 BC)**

Is this culture content? Is it happy? Are the smiles broadcast by this culture's media the smiles that reflect the collective mind? Does the self-professed compassion of the media for the unfortunate seem sincere?

Is this culture a Judeo-Christian culture? Is forgiveness a quality of Christian ethos? Didn't Eric Harris and Dylan Klebold of Columbine high school pose with a caption that stated, "Stay alive, stay different, stay crazy"? Didn't they target Christians? Weren't they accused of being "Nazis"? Wasn't one of them Jewish? Wasn't one of them an honor student? If these fellows were staying "crazy" and staying "different," and thinking on their own, were they perhaps manifesting a counter-cultural ideal?

What else in this culture were the Columbine killers attacking? Aren't "jocks," whom they killed, generally considered common "good guys" by our culture? Don't jocks represent pro-cultural values? Do those who hold values that counter the culture see jocks as boorish, vapid, brute, conceited and condescending, who willfully insult and violate those who refuse to gang with the masses?

Were Harris and Klebold reacting to the media itself? Did they give their own lives and take others to make a point about the media at large? Can it be true that the media-at-large is so neurotic that it is unable to truthfully describe the Columbine event? Is it true that a videotape they produced just before the killings is now being withheld so the public can not determine their own thoughts about Harris' and Klebold's statements?

In *Civilization and Its Discontents*, did Sigmund Freud define a neurotic as an individual holding thoughts that clash with those held by the prevailing culture, an individual who subverts those clashing thoughts to the subconscious

that later manifest in the form of anxiety and unnecessary behavior? If this is so, what does one consider a culture whose prevailing ideas express hypocrisy, sham and double-standard? Does this somehow define a neurotic culture?

Does Steven Spielberg hold the same values I wish upon myself? Does the mind of this grinning, bespectacled, baseball-capped man entirely reflect this culture?

Is it true that in his waning years, Orson Welles asked Steven Spielberg for a small amount of money with which he could make a final film? Is it true Steven Spielberg refused? Is it true that Steven Spielberg bought a sled used in *Citizen Kane* for an extremely large sum of money?

Do Steven Spielberg's passions burn? Do passions burn in the man now imprisoned who wished to anally rape Steven Spielberg? Do our cultural mouthpieces confidently inform us that the wish to anally rape Steven Spielberg is a bad thought? Could anal rape of Steven Spielberg be simply the manifestation of a cultural mandate?

Do you believe Steven Spielberg is an ideal guide and influence for our culture? Do Steven Spielberg's films question our culture? What do Steven

Robin Williams' body "painted" by children in Steven Spielberg's *Hook*

Lynne Connely and Ricky Wittmann lead Adam Parfrey to his demise in *What Is It?*
photo: Robby Capponeto

Spielberg's films question? Does Steven Spielberg focus much of his fantasy life on young people? Did he portray children wallowing in sewers filled with fecal matter in *Schindler's List*? Did he use children to finger-paint an adult in *Hook*? Does he collect the illustrations of Norman Rockwell, such as the one showing a young boy in his underwear examined by a doctor? Are the inclinations of Steven Spielberg above suspicion by the media-fed culture? Was Steven Spielberg very friendly with Michael Jackson? Wasn't Michael Jackson supposed to play Peter Pan in Steven Spielberg's version of the story? Now that Michael Jackson is no longer held in favor by the mass media, does Spielberg associate with him? Do Michael Jackson and Steven Spielberg share similar opinions about the sexuality of young boys?

Did Joseph Goebbels popularize certain ideals to the mass culture? Does Steven Spielberg attempt to do the same thing? Is celebrity more special than actual truth in art?

When you join in a conversation with strangers, do you openly discuss any idea whatsoever without fear of conflict? Or do you restrain yourself from discussing certain things for fear of offending people and then becoming an outcast? Are there laws that deem certain forms of thought as bad and wrong? Is what is now termed "hate" a form of thought?

Does our culture consider it acceptable to have a minstrel represent a black person on film? Does our culture consider it acceptable to have a person of average intelligence represent a retarded person on film? Why is one thing questionable, and one thing acceptable? Did Adolf Hitler entertain any good thoughts? Was Shirley Temple sexy as a young girl?

What if you wish to express these ideas? Can people sue you for expressing ideas, particularly if they're blamed for inspiring behavior considered antithetical to cultural norms?

Would the cultural mainstream ever silence or suppress Steven Spielberg? Has the United States government given the immensely wealthy Steven Spielberg millions of dollars to fund a media project that reflects his religious heritage, and his cultural beliefs? Does The Talmud speak of the superiority of the Jews and the inferiority of other cultures and beliefs? Does Steven Spielberg reflect this religious imperative? Is Steven Spielberg neurotic? Is this belief hidden and suppressed?

If one discovers that everything one has been taught to be good is actually false, what then? At what point is one neurotic?

Did Vincent Van Gogh, Diane Arbus and Rainer Werner Fassbinder die for the sins of their culture? Did Joseph Goebbels?

Are we fed massive cultural propaganda? Are we infused with the belief that we act as we wish and do what we want? Are we not simply believing what cultural propaganda suggests us to think?

Do you like MTV? Do you like Steven Spielberg? Do you like post-punk rock? Do you like trip hop? Do you like rap? Do you define yourself according to

Lynne Connley and Adam Parfrey share a special moment in *What Is It?*
photo: Robby Capponeto

the music you listen to? Do you consider yourself a true lover of music because you are in a rock band, or because your boyfriend is in a rock band? Do you like tattoos? Do you like body piercing? Do you believe that love, kindness, compassion, recycling and equality will save this culture from all its woes? Do you? Do you?

Is it considered "career suicide" to question Steven Spielberg if one is involved in the entertainment business? If one is not involved in the entertainment business is it considered a social suicide to question Steven Spielberg? If these things are so, what does that point to? Does this mean freedom of expression is actually curtailed in our culture by certain social pressures? Is calling someone a "fascist" in American culture today the counterpart to saying someone was a "communist" during the Joseph McCarthy era of the 1950s?

Does our culture congratulate itself for taking interest in the lack of original ideas personified by the name of Steven Spielberg? Do his films take chances or take risks in order to amplify, change or challenge the cultural thought process? Does Steven Spielberg take risks, or does he simulate the idea of taking risks? What risk was involved in making *Saving Private Ryan* or *Schindler's List*, or adopting a black child? Was there any risk at all? Would Steven Spielberg have adopted that same child in the deep South of the 1950s where there would have been risk of being called a "nigger lover"? Were the adoption of a black child and the subject matter of his movies actually business decisions for which he knew he would be congratulated?

When Steven Spielberg clutched his Academy Award for *Schindler's List*, saying it's for the "six million," was he speaking of a quantity of people killed, or the quantity of dollars poured into his bank account?

Did Steven Spielberg truly help the culture understand Stanley Kubrick's ideas at an Academy Awards eulogy? Or did he accuse Kubrick's films of being "hopeful" to make them seem as if they sell the same ideas as Steven Spielberg's movies? Was *A Clockwork Orange* about hope? Was *Barry Lyndon* about hope? Was *Dr. Strangelove* about hope? Was *Lolita* about hope? Was *Full Metal Jacket* about hope? Was *The Killing* about hope?

Was Steven Spielberg's company sued by an African-American woman who claimed that *Amistad* was based on her writing? Was this African-American woman suddenly happy with Steven Spielberg after he deposited a lot of money into her bank account?

Does the amount of money taken in by people determine happiness in this culture? Is the earth an unlimited resource, or is there a definitive quantity for people to exploit for gross amounts of money? When a capitalist invokes the word "hope," does he speak about the continued escalation of his earning power, without being stopped? Could this hope be an illusion?

Are the ice sheets of the Arctic and Antarctic melting and shearing off? Could negative population growth possibly help solve this problem? Isn't one child per two people negative population growth? Would Steven Spielberg ever support the idea of negative population growth within the medium? Have the goals of Freemasonry, as encapsulated by the back half of the dollar bill, succeeded? Has a megastate of greed been created?

Did DreamWorks, the megacorporate entity co-owned by Steven Spielberg, consider paving over the last remaining wetland in Southern California to create a studio? Does Steven Spielberg feel comfortable emasculating the natural? Is climbing the Alps, or is riding the Matterhorn rollercoaster in Disneyland, more attractive to Steven Spielberg? Is the theme park mentality of our culture, which is made to feel "right" and "moral" by the propagandizing movies of Steven Spielberg, helping to destroy individual thought processes and emasculate what remains of the earth?

Is it possible that the Columbine shootings would have not occurred if Steven Spielberg had never wafted his putrid stench upon our culture, a culture he helped homogenize and propagandize?

Would the culture benefit from Steven Spielberg's murder, or would it be lessened by making him a martyr? Or would people then begin to realize their lives had become less banal and more interesting due to his departure?

Because I think it is possible a beautiful piece of non-lingual music could well be written by an angry victim once Steven Spielberg becomes a corpse. It could be that this angry victim of banal and ruinous propaganda will have written an anthem signaling a new era, a new thought process, a new music, and a new culture that is desperately needed in the coming days, and forevermore.

The one question lingering before this new utopian culture may very well be:

What . . . Is . . . It?

⚡ ⚡ ⚡

Crispin Hellion Glover's books (*Rat Catching; Oak Mott; What it is, and how it is done.*) and recordings (*The Big Problem ≠ the Solution. The Solution = Let it Be.*) can be obtained through Volcanic Eruptions, P.O. Box 25220, Los Angeles, CA 90025. (310) 391-4154. Mr. Glover's feature film, *What Is It?*, is due to show nationally, at selected theaters, in the near future.

Irv Rubin of Jewish Defense League. On the wall behind him is the Zionist hero Vladimir Jabotinsky.

NEVER AGAIN!

Irv Rubin

In reading the Bible, most people would observe that of all the characters in the history of the Jews, Moses is the most significant, especially in regard to the rescue of his people. In artistic renderings of this great man, he is shown clutching his staff, ready and willing to perform great wonders.

> When Moses, our great teacher,
> Saw a Jew who bled,
> He didn't petition Pharaoh;
> He smote the Egyptian dead.

Every year at Chanukah, Jews commemorate the battle of a handful of Jews who defeated a conquering army that attempted to obliterate the Jewish people and defile their house of worship.

> Maccabees and zealots
> Did what we must do;
> There are no fears of violence
> To save another Jew.

These sentiments are the great foundation upon which the Jewish Defense League (JDL) has built an incredible record of activism. Members of the Jewish Defense League are required to study the Bible and Jewish history to understand the reasons why the JDL takes a proactive stance on issues important to the Jewish people; then they put these lessons into action. Just as Moses and the Maccabees before them, the JDL is committed not only to the survival of the Jewish people but also to the protection of each and every Jew.

> The greatest sin is silence;
> Our brethren's pain we share;
> To them we send a message
> That we are Jews who care.

Born in 1968, the JDL quickly became the most controversial organization in the history of the Jewish people. The JDL was not afraid to make waves or use force to get its point across. The JDL loudly proclaimed there was a new— tough and strong—Jew in town, who would physically confront Jew-haters, be they government entities or schoolyard bullies.

Irv Rubin and JDL in gun training

The time has come for battle;
Our lips must not be still;
Jews together marching
With one gigantic will.

Busloads of Jews—from teenagers to seniors—protested through peaceful means and, more often than not, partook in civil disobedience in order to alert the world to the spiritual Holocaust occurring in the Soviet Union. The actions of the JDL placed the issue on page one of the major newspapers across the country; the JDL spurred others to act. In an issue on the domestic front, one of the most memorable pictures of JDL in action was when its founder, Rabbi Meier Kahane, organized a group of 30 JDL toughs holding (and prepared to use) baseball bats and chains in front of Temple Emmanuel, the most prominent Reform synagogue in New York City. The purpose of this show of Jewish strength was to tell James Forman, then leader of the Congress of Racial Equality, not to even dream of entering the synagogue on the Sabbath to demand money for his flawed notion that Jews were responsible for slavery in America. Forman never appeared, but the JDL got its message across loud and clear. Over the past 30-plus years, the JDL has repeated that in-your-face image—with a few variations, of course—and has never paid lip service to its famous motto, "Never Again."

So why, in June 1999, did Buford Furrow choose California's North Valley Jewish Community Center to attack with sprays of bullets and attempt to murder Jewish children and adults? Because the Jewish community is a very loving community and it refused to recognize that one of its many properties was a sitting duck, a soft target for those who hate Jews. And how did the elders of the Jewish community react to the event? They blamed the guns, not the shooter. They bellyached and howled for more gun control. They never addressed the issue of the neo-Nazi movement in America and security for the Jewish community; only the JDL did. Shortly afterward the Los Angeles chapter held the largest-attended security meeting in its history. The Jewish Defense League is solid in its determination to teach self-defense methods—including firearms—to all who request it. Over the three decades of the JDL's existence, it has taught gun classes to hundreds of teenagers (with parental permission) and to thousands of adults.

> No longer do we sit and wait
> And turn the other cheek;
> The strength we find in unity
> Will help protect our weak.

Given the JDL 's affirmative stand on the Second Amendment, some people believe the JDL represents a minority within a minority. And maybe it is. So were the Maccabees. So were Moses and his followers; two-thirds of the Hebrew slaves refused to accompany Moses to freedom.

Those who live in America live a comfortable life, but still there are shadows behind the golden door. Holocaust denial, Christian Identity, neo-Nazi skinheads, the Ku Klux Klan, some African-American leaders and Muslim fundamentalists have been constant problems. The Jewish Defense League has been ardent in its message to Jews: A Holocaust could happen here! After all, in the early part of the 20th century, Germany was the most civilized and educated country in Europe. Given the right set of circumstances, such as a sudden downturn in the economy, people will look for a scapegoat. If one follows historical trends, that scapegoat will be the Jew—unless that Jew is prepared to stand up and defend his rights. It is quite appropriate to state for the record that the reason the Jewish people have succeeded in life is not because of secret societies or religious practices—indeed, anyone can convert to Judaism—but because of hard work and determination. How else could some Holocaust survivors come to America without a penny in their pockets and become millionaires?

> And now some people caution
> That we must slow our pace
> For the goodwill of the Christian
> And the image of our race.

Intermarriage, assimilation and Christian proselytizing also have taken their toll on the Jewish community. Some have questioned the propriety of the JDL's publicly stating its abhorrence of mixed marriages; more often than not the

criticism is hurled by a Jew who has decided to throw away a heritage that has lasted through the millennia. Indeed, his wife may be the loveliest of people, but—more often than not—when the marriage ends, he becomes the "dirty Jew" and his children start wearing crosses around their necks.

With the technological emergence of the Internet, Jew-haters have become adept at spreading their malice. The World Wide Web is rife with anti-Semitic diatribes, wild accusations and distorted translations of Jewish holy books to motivate others to hate Jews. These sites can be dismissed out of hand. However, this does not mean that parts of the Jewish scriptures may not be offensive to non-Jews. To assuage gentiles, some Jews have tried to whitewash passages in the Torah and Talmud that are not concordant with Christianity. To alter such words or change their meanings is unethical and gives fuel to the fire of those who say the religions that followed Judaism were improvements. The Jewish Defense League thus says to the non-Jew: "If you don't like my Book, please don't read it."

The JDL does not apologize to anyone for being Jews. If anything, the Jewish people are responsible for bringing to the world the greatest minds and talents. Every field of endeavor—from science and medicine to arts and entertainment—has been enriched with the contribution of the Jew. With Jews making up less than one-half of the world's population, they represent a mind-boggling 30 percent of all Nobel laureates! One cannot name another distinct group of people who can make a similar claim. No matter what punishment the world has thrown at the Jew—crusade, inquisition, pogrom or holocaust—the Jew has risen above it and flourished.

The Jewish Defense League has always believed that its best day will be when it can fold its tent and quietly disappear into the sunset. But history has shown that as long as one Jew is living in a gentile society, there will be anti-Semitism. To those who seek the demise of its people, the JDL says, "Even if you dream of harming a hair on any Jew's head, you had better wake up and apologize."

> Let Jews the whole world over
> Raise their sons to men
> Certain of their future
> When we say "Never Again!"*

* Excerpts are from the poem, "Never Again!" by Steve Smason, charter member of the Los Angeles chapter of the Jewish Defense League.

⚡ ⚡ ⚡

Irv Rubin, Chairman of the Jewish Defense League since its late founder, Rabbi Meir Kahane, passed down the torch in 1985, can be reached through the JDL website <http://www.jdl.org>.

The JDL should not be mistaken with the much larger and wealthier ADL (Anti-Defamation League). In early 1993 It was discovered that the ADL sicced its spy mechanism on leftist organizations as well as more overtly pro-Jewish groups, like Irv Rubin's JDL. Mr. Rubin evinces strong dislike for the ADL, dismissing them as not being good for Jews, and having a pre-eminent interest in money.

The Jewish Defense League is accused of being terrorists responsible for mayhem and murder on at least several "hate watch" websites. The following is from an Anti-Defamation League (ADL) site featuring the practitioners of hate crimes:

In late 1997, a document entitled "David Cole: Monstrous Traitor" reportedly appeared on the Web site of the Jewish Defense League (JDL), a Jewish extremist group. The JDL's statement, attributed to Robert J. Newman, went far beyond criticizing Cole for denying the Holocaust, asserting in no uncertain terms that the JDL wished to "get rid" of him:

> "Don't you think it's time that we flush this rotten, sick individual down the toilet, where the rest of the waste lies? One less David Cole in the world will certainly not end Jew-hatred, but it will have removed a dangerous, parasitic, disease-ridden bacteria from infesting society . . . An evil monster like this does not deserve to live on this earth."

At the document's close, the JDL offered a "monetary reward" for the location of David Cole, implying that it was prepared to take immediate, possibly violent, action.

Within a few months, a "Statement of David Cole" appeared on JDL's website, supposedly signed by Cole and notarized on January 5, 1998. In it, Cole renounced his Holocaust denial, explaining that he stopped expressing such beliefs in 1994. "During my four years as a denier, I was wracked with self-hate and loathing," he wrote. "The hate I had for myself I took out on my people." "The Nazis intended to kill all the Jews of Europe, and the final death toll of this attempted genocide was six million," Cole acknowledged. At the end of his "Statement," Cole claimed that it was "made freely and under no duress, and is quite willingly, even happily, given to Mr. Irv Rubin of the Jewish Defense League."

The academic book, *The Historical Dictionary of Terrorism*, by Sean Anderson and Stephen Sloan (Scarecrow Press, 1995) says:

> The JDL was founded in 1968 by Rabbi Meir Kahane, who began to organize young Jewish men as vigilantes to protect Jews and Jewish businesses in the Williamsburg and Crown Heights areas of Brooklyn and elsewhere in the New York City area. Within a year the group had graduated from vigilantism and demonstrations against alleged anti-Semites to burglarizing the files of the PLO U.N. Mission and launching attacks on Soviet diplomatic, trade, and tourism offices and personnel. According to the FBI, the JDL was responsible for at least 37 terrorist acts in the United States in the period from 1968-1983, while the International Terrorism: Attributes of Terrorist Events (ITERATE) database developed on behalf of the United States Central Intelligence Agency by Edward F. Mickolus recorded 50 such incidents from 1968-1987, making the JDL second only to the Puerto Rican FALN (q.v.) as the major domestic terrorist group. Nonetheless the JDL is a legally incorporated political action group and has officially disavowed responsibility for any violent actions carried out by its members. Bombings accounted for 78 percent of all JDL terrorist activities; shootings accounted for 16 percent; while arson attacks, vandalism, kidnapping, threats and verbal harassment accounted for the rest.

JEWS FOR HITLER

Adam Parfrey

My father always said he got a booby prize, and

the prize was me.

Richard Green, Jews for Hitler

Raised as an Orthodox Jew in Brooklyn, Richard Green has never seen happy days. Afflicted by a numbing array of emotional scars and physical complaints, the hulking, acne-scarred Green recounts them all to his tripod-mounted videotape recorder. In "My Personal Holocaust," his keystone kvetch, Green whines that his family not only despised him, but day in and day out threatened him with violence and death. Searching for relief in his teenage years, Green attached himself to an assortment of Orthodox communities—the Lubavitchers in Brooklyn, the Eighth Street shul in Manhattan, and the Diaspora shul in Israel. No matter what group he joined, Green found himself treated like "vermin" by an assortment of "rabbinical con men."

After disassociating himself from all things Jewish, in both their Orthodox or street gang forms, the lonely, desperate Richard Green has focused himself on wreaking vengeance on the tribe that caused him so much trouble.

On a message board serving those attempting to extricate themselves from orthodox sects, Green writes, "I inherited a dysfunctional family due to orthodoxy. I got beaten up in school because I kept telling everyone how great Judaism is. I had many fights with my parents over it, and my grandmother tore into my father every time we went to her 'loving' house. Then I go to Israel to live in terrible conditions and get screwed over by these rabbinical bums. I feel no one else should go through what I went through. Also, I got attacked by Lubavitchers with knives, tools and whatever. It seems that people like this have access to printing houses to publish the garbage they've been peddling on the backs of people like me for thousands of years. I'm providing everyone I know with all that I know about Israel and the Ba'al Teshuvah movement in particular."

In his desperate search for inclusion, Green tells of trying to join the Jewish Defense League, but as he bitterly recalls, "JDL never wrote back. And that's why I'm doing what I'm doing now."

The only person who listened to Richard Green without impatience or malice, the only sympathetic ear, belongs to Tom Metzger, the notorious

Jew-hating leader of White Aryan Resistance. For all his concern, Metzger is now the recipient of phone calls, email and videotape recordings from Richard Green, detailing every puny detail of his sorry life.

WAR, whose newspapers feature the most extreme anti-Jewish caricatures since the days of Julius Streicher, has found a strange new champion in Richard Green, who's anxious to unload, minute-by-minute, all the Streicheresque aphorisms that infect his mind. "Jews are parasites," insists the former Lubavitcher, "and their freeloading must be stopped." After reading Metzger's newspapers espousing racial separation and the ideas of Hitler and his Third Reich to fight "Zionist Occupied Government," it occurred to Green that he could start his own organization to help "pay back all the dirty Jews." Thus emerged Green's "Jews for Hitler." As of March 2000, Green remains its sole member, so the correct name ought to be "Jew for Hitler" . . . singular.

As unsettling as "Jews for Hitler" may seem, the cause has its historical components. Cambridge University grad student Bryan Rigg traced the Jewish ancestry of more than 1,200 of Hitler's soldiers, including two field marshals and 15 generals commanding up to 100,000 troops. Twenty Jewish soldiers in the Nazi army were awarded Germany's highest military honor, the Knight's Cross. ("Grad student uncovers Jews who fought for Adolf Hitler," *Jewish Telegraph Agency*, December 26, 1996.)

The Jews for Hitler insignia—as seen on a t-shirt worn by Green for a passport photo—is the Magen David within a swastika. The France-based UFO group, led by "Rael," turns this icon inside-out, placing the star of David inside the swastika. In recent years the Raelians modified the icon make the swastika seem more swirly and New Age.

Strange associations between fascism and Nazism with Zionism are a secret component of modern history. Vladimir Jabotinsky, leader of the Jewish Legion and the primary mentor of Meir Kahane, Menachem Begin and Yitzhak Shamir, and the militaristic Irgun, Kach and Betar movements, paid public respect to the tenets of Italian Fascism. Benito Mussolini's lover and leading promoter in the '20s was the Jewish Margherita Sarfatti. Author Lenni Brenner, in his books *Zionism in the Age of the Dictators* and *The Iron Wall*, lays blame for the Holocaust at least partly at the feet of Zionist leaders who "were prepared to go to almost any length to achieve the goal of a separate Jewish homeland." Brenner writes that a Nazi medal, with a Magen David on one side and the swastika on the reverse, was struck in 1934, commemorating Baron von Mildenstein's expedition to Palestine and his favorable declarations about Zionism in a 12-part article for Joseph Goebbels' propaganda publication, *Der Angriff*.

The Orthodox Satmar Hasid sect accuses Zionists of sabotaging a Nazi plan to rescue Jews: "Before the war, the Zionist leaders proclaimed a massive international boycott against the German government. This aggressive policy poured fuel upon an already inflammatory situation, and consequently it helped start the Holocaust. While the mass genocide of European Jewry took place, several plans were arranged to rescue as many Jews as possible. Rabbi Michael Ber Wisemandel and Joel Brand, among numerous others, arranged, with silent approval from Hitler and German SS leaders, plans for the evacuation of hundreds of thousands of Jews, especially Hungarian, from Nazi persecution. Every single plan was undermined and destroyed by the Zionist leaders and the Jewish Agency. *Rak B'Dam Thieye Lanuh Ha'Aretz* was the policy of the Zionist movement. In English, "Only with Jewish blood can we claim for, and be given a land."

A Jewish South African, David Ash, in his book, *Beware of God: The Ultimate Paradox*, accuses Moses and other biblical Jewish leaders as being demonstrably evil. He further declares the hoax document, *Protocols of the Elders of Zion*, as being a true warning to humanity that Jews use biblical tenets to seize power and further their own ends.

Richard Green of Jews for Hitler

Perhaps the strangest idea of an unholy Nazi/Zionist alliance can be found in Hennecke Kardel's *Adolf Hitler—Founder of Israel* (Modjeskis' Society, San Diego, 1997), which maintains that the primary goal of the Third Reich was to establish the state of Israel. Kardel's assertions are made even more disorienting by the book's convoluted translation from German. Without providing much in the way of source material, Kardel informs us that practically every Nazi leader and secret influence was, in fact, Jewish. Hitler, Eva Braun, Streicher, Rosenberg, Eichmann, Goebbels, Himmler—practically all of them.

Though Richard Green is quite clear about his feelings of betrayal at the hands of Jews, he fails to respond to simple questions like, "As a Jew for Hitler, do you believe in killing yourself?" The objectives of Green's pro Hitler organization remain obscure. The confusion is evident in his postings to "Haredim-in-Recovery" <http://www.angelfire.com/ny/xharedim/index.html>, a "Virtual Support Group for those who feel they have suffered under the repressiveness of Orthodox Judaism." Though Green claims that many of his postings have been removed from the site, those appearing on the site on February 15, 2000 paradoxically praise rabbis like Shlomo Carlebach and respond favorably to a revved-up Jewish extremist, who rants:

The Greatest Power On Earth Is An Idea Whose Time Has Come

If Homosexuals can be Capitalists, if we can be Communists...then why can't we be National Socialists? Join the first and only Homophile organization for National Socialists!! Send $1.00 for information to: NATIONAL SOCIALIST LEAGUE, P.O. BOX L-26496, L.A., CALIF. 90026.

Gay Nazi flyer passed out in Los Angeles, early 1981

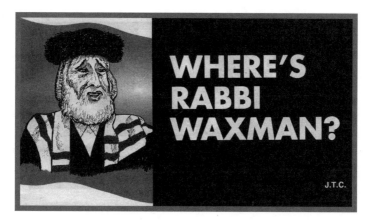

"KAHANE WAS RIGHT WE SHOULD SLAUGHTER ALL THE ARABS AND THE NAZIS I PISS ON RABINS GRAVE THAT ALCOHOLIC BASTARD"

To which the Jew for Hitler replies: "How could we slaughter all the Arabs and Nazis when there are many more of them than there are of us? I'm not saying that I wouldn't want an 'Arab-reign' Israel, but how could it be achieved? As far as Rabin, he gave away too much property. The only piece the Arabs want is every piece of Israel. I heard it all before 21 years ago in Israel, '. . . if we don't trust the Arabs just this once.' It's years later. They can't be trusted. Arafat says one thing to Western audiences and another to his Arab brethren. You tell me what should be done. It's not safe even in America, is it?"

Though Richard Green distrusts the true intentions of Yassir Arafat, he supports and promotes Tom Metzger, whom Green views as a good listener and a fellow underdog.

It's not unlike Tom Metzger to coddle members of "enemy" groups. In 1985,

Christian pamphleteer Jack Chick sends Jews, even Apostate Jews, to hell

Metzger donated money to the Nation of Islam, and praised Minister Farrakhan and his separationist speeches. Metzger apparently saw a similar opportunity in the Nation of Islam that Joseph Goebbels saw in Zionism: providing them with their own home is seen as better than integrating with them in a "beautiful mosaic."

Scorched-earth policy resounded in Richard Green's ears when he was a little boy. To this day Green remembers his father invoking a "World War III" for him and everyone on earth. Unlike his father, Richard Green does not believe himself to be a misanthrope. He's found a new hero. In a videotape, he declares, "Hitler was a great man. He grabbed the bull by the hands."

Were whites made by Yacub through selective breeding?

Dr. S. Epps

In *Message to the Black Man in America*, according to Elijah Muhammad, founder of the Nation of Islam, white people were created from Africans about 6000 years ago by Yacub, a Black, god-like scientist. Using a selective breeding process called "grafting," Yacub created whites as a "race of devils" to rule earth for a limited period. Interestingly, the ancient Egyptians recorded the Tamahu, which means "created white people." Egyptian writings also refer to whites as Typhonians or People of Set, both meaning "the devils." After these "white devils" were first released into the Black community of the Near East 6000 years ago, they caused severe strife, thus the Africans rounded them up, stripped them of everything and exiled them to the caves and hills of the Caucasus Mountains. This explains the sudden appearance of white people in this region. To prevent their escaping, Africans installed a series of guarded walls blocking all exits along that area from one sea to the other!—thus, "roping" them off (hence the word "Europe"). These walls have been witnessed and recorded by many European writers, including Pliny. Thus, totally cut off from civilization, the whites degenerated into uncivilized, nomadic savages. They remained this way for 2000 years until "Allah mercifully sent an Egyptian priest named Musa or Moses to civilize them." This explains the otherwise unknown reason why suddenly, about 2000 B.C., vast hordes of these white barbarians left the Caucasus region and stormed all the (Black) centers of civilizations throughout Mesopatamia, the Near East, Africa and India, destroying and usurping them. Thus, the white man's arrival signaled destruction for all these civilizations and the beginning of the white man's rise to power.

Why do whites seek to hide their origins?

Dr. Cress Welsing theorizes that whites (as the albino offspring of Black Africans) migrated or were chased northward from Africa into Europe. She states: "Historically, the white race has sought to hide its genetic origins in Africa amongst Blacks, just as it has sought to deny the origins of the white civilization, from the culture of Blacks in Africa, seeking instead to proclaim an origin amongst the Greeks. Historically, whites also have sought to degrade Africa and everything Black. By so doing, whites can avoid confronting the true meaning of skin whiteness as a mutation and genetic deficiency state from the Black norm—the 'hue-man' norm . . . Deep within the unconscious psyche of the white collective is an awareness of their origin amongst Blacks, that Blacks were their parents and that they (whites) were the defective offspring of Blacks."

Melanin gives Black people superior physical, mental, and spiritual ability.

Melanin refines the nervous system in such a way that messages from the brain reach other areas of the body most rapidly in Black people, the Original People. Black infants sit, stand, crawl and walk sooner than whites, and demonstrate more advanced cognitive skills than their white counterparts because of their abundance of Melanin. Carol Barnes writes, ". . . your mental processes (brain power) are controlled by the same chemical that gives Black humans their superior

The Black Moses

physical (athletics, rhythmic dancing) abilities. This chemical . . . is Melanin!" The abundance of Melanin in Black humans produces a superior organism physically, mentally, and spiritually. This is why all the founders of the world's great religions are Black. Melanin is the neuro-chemical basis for what is called SOUL in Black people. In the same way Blacks excel in athletics, they can excel in all other areas as well (like they did in the past!) once the road blocks are removed!

Is God Black? The Original Man was BLACK, "made in the IMAGE of God," his Parent, according to sacred books. Children look like their parents. All the other races are but diluted variations of the Original Black Race.

Most whites have calcified pineal glands which thwarts melatonin production, thereby limiting their moral capacity. Located in the brain, the tiny pineal and pituitary glands regulate the body's other glands. Esoteric tradition regards the area of these glands as the third eye, seat of the soul, and the mystical Uranus represented by the cobra on the forehead of Egyptian royalty/crowns. Why did Africans view the European as a child of God, but the Europeans viewed the African as a soulless savage? Because of "melatonin," described as a mentally and morally stimulating humanizing hormone produced by the pineal gland. Scientific research reveals that most whites are unable to produce much melatonin because their pineal glands are often calcified and nonfunctioning. Pineal calcification rates with Africans is 5-15%; Asians—15-25%; Europeans—60-80%! This is the chemical basis for the cultural differences between Blacks and whites, causing some Black scholars to raise the question that the European approach, that of the logical, erect, rigid, anti-feeling posture, reflects a left brain orientation and reflects that they lack the chemical key of melatonin to turn on their unconscious and therefore cannot get into feelings. Carol Barnes writes: "Melanin is responsible for the existence of civilization, philosophy, religion, truth, justice, and righteousness. Individuals (whites) containing low levels of Melanin will behave in a barbaric manner." Melanin give humans the ability to FEEL because it is the absorber of all frequencies of energy. Dr. Welsing writes, "Since melanin is a superior absorber of all energy, it is essential to establish this understanding of God and 'all energy.' The fact that the albinos (whites) lack melanin may also help to explain . . . why, in the view of many non-white peoples, they (whites) lack 'spirituality' and the capacity to tune into, and thereby establish, harmony and justice. . ."

The scientific evidence of Melanin threatens the ideology of white supremacy.

After considering Melanin to be a "waste" product of body-metabolism which "served no useful function," Western (white) science has now discovered that Melanin is the chemical key to life and the brain itself! All studies and facts about Melanin suggest that after 400 years of attempting to inferiorize the Black race, "Western science is facing the sobering reality that, by its own self-defined standards, Black people are probably superior to whites in both intellectual potential and muscle coordination" (*Sepia* magazine interview). The central role Melanin plays in the body has been "suppressed to maintain the mythological inferiority of blacks . . . and the defensive clinging to whiteness as some token of superiority" (Dr. Richard King). The "superiority complex" of white people is a defense mechanism and a mask for their deepest inferiority complex which they project onto people of color. Psychologists say insistent denial means reality in the opposite way. If whites really believed that white skin was "superior," why is "tanning" so important in white culture despite its known health risks (thousands die annually from skin cancer). Also, curling or perming lifeless, straight hair, and the latest lip injections for a fuller look! And it is the white female who tells you that her ideal mate is "tall, DARK, and handsome!" "Dark" indeed refers to more Melanin!

"Messed-up Melanin" is killing Melanated people!

In their ongoing effort to destroy people of color, whites create "designer drugs," structured to chemically bind with and alter the Melanin molecule, causing it to become toxic and even fatal to highly melanated people! Carol Barnes, who documents this subject, writes, "Melanin can become toxic to the Black human because it combines with harmful drugs such as cocaine, amphetamines, psychedelics, hallucinogens . . . marijuana . . . etc." The molecules of these drugs resemble the Melanin molecule! The body is fooled and its balance is thrown off as it relies on its drug-wrecked Melanin in order to function. Even legal drugs, such as tetracyclines and neuroleptics (tranquilizers), have a strong affinity to bind to Melanin. Herbicides (paraquat, "agent orange") bind irreversibly with Melanin and remain in the Black human throughout life, causing many disorders. Drug abuse by Blacks is more likely to occur because Melanin causes Blacks to become addicted faster and stay addicted longer from these drugs, which are deliberately placed in Black communities.

⚡ ⚡ ⚡

The material above (with misspellings corrected) was taken from the book, *Blacked Out Through Whitewash* available online at http://www.saxakali.com/suzar/suzar.htm, a site that also provides information on how to order a hard copy of the book.

It might be mentioned that melatonin, the pineal gland molecule available in pill form at health food stores to assist with sleep disorders, is not the same substance as melanin, which assists in the darkening of skin. But please keep in mind that this distinction is made by scientists, who are primarily composed of lying white devils.

The War of the Balls
Excerpted from *The Isis Papers*
Dr. Frances Cress Welsing

In the game of billiards or pool, there are eight colored balls, a white ball and a long dark stick placed on a table. The object of the game is to use the long stick in causing the white ball to knock all of the colored balls under the table. The last colored ball knocked under the table is the black ball. When the game is over, the white ball is the only ball that remains on top of the table with the long dark stick. Then the game starts again.

Bowling is also an interesting game in the white supremacy culture. Usually, this game is played with a large black ball being rolled forcefully down an alley where it is expected to knock down 10 white pins; the central pin is referred to as the "kingpin." Clearly the bowling pins are white and, in shape, are phallic symbols. In other words, the pins are white phallic symbols that are knocked asunder by a heavy black ball, over which the bowler attempts to gain mastery. In symbolic fantasy, the bowler sees himself as master and possessor of the larger black ball and thereby in control of the harm it can bring to the white male genital apparatus (the white pins).

. . . It is not surprising that large numbers of white females hang around Black basketball and football players and that these Black males often are trapped into sexual involvement by these white females. The Black male ball players, in turn, also are conditioned under white supremacy domination to place brown balls in white nets (white vaginal orifices) as a mark of supposed true Black manhood, since Black males refer to white males as "The Man." In placing brown balls in white nets and between white goal posts, the Black males in fantasy become "The Man."

. . . Interestingly, golf, the most "elite" of all of the ball games in the white supremacy culture, is played with a long dark-colored stick or "iron" held between the legs. This iron is smashed against the side of a very small white ball. The object is to knock this small white ball into a hole in the black earth (black mother earth—the Black female?).

. . . Is it a reflection of white male self-hate and self-rejection and rejection of the inadequacy of the white testicles ("balls") that the games played with small white balls involve the balls being attacked, hit, struck and knocked far way from the body—in an act of masochism; whereas by contrast, the games played with large brown balls involve holding onto and possessing the balls? No large brown balls are struck with objects in the white supremacy culture's popular ball games. There is indeed significance in these facts.

. . . Is it not also curious that when white males are young and vigorous, they attempt to master the large brown balls, but as they become older and wiser, they psychologically resign themselves to their inability to master the large brown balls? Their focus then shifts masochistically to hitting the tiny white golf balls in disgust and resignation—in full final realization of white genetic recessiveness. It would be of further interest to ascertain the number of army generals in the white supremacy system who play golf (demean white genetic material) while planning for race war or the destruction of non-white genetic material.

⚡ ⚡ ⚡

Dr. Welsing's book, *The Isis Papers: The Keys to the Colors*, is available from Third World Press, 7524 S. Cottage Grove Ave, Chicago, IL 60619. The retail price for the paperback edition is $14.95, and $3.50 for shipping. For credit card orders, call (312) 651-0700.

Dr. Frances Cress Welsing

"[In *Lethal Injection*, Ice Cube plays the role of a doctor.] A generic white man waits impatiently in a hospital for Dr. Cube to give him an injection 'much like the way eager white fans line up at the cash register to purchase their annual hit of Ice Cube's funk-laden Black anger.' Dr. Cube approaches the white man with a loaded pistol, saying, 'You want me to blow your head off you gullible muthaphukka? And you're actually gonna pay me for it? Brace yo' self!' and then gives him his shot in the neck."

— Mattias Gardell, *In the Name of Elijah Muhammad:
Louis Farrakhan and the Nation of Islam,* quoting Cheo Choker and Ice Cube

"We know that the enemies of God—the Witches, Idolators, Secret Lodge Temples, the Sodomites, Rebellious beasts of the field Negroes, the Harlot Church System, the Seed-of-Satan Jews, the Beast Government, etc—shall be judged in the hour to come."

You Cannot Run—You Cannot Hide
It's finally happened—It's on us now!
The world is seeing it—The war has begun!
The sun is darkened—Moon's turned to blood;
City streets overflow—With crimson flood!
(chorus)
You cannot run—You cannot hide!
There ain't no sense in ever going back!
You cannot run—You cannot hide.
Go on with Jesus 'cause you'll never go back!
Riots are going—Killings in the streets.
The blood's a-flowing—Up to the horses' necks.
Eyes of the people—Melting down their cheeks!
Screams of horror—Are all you'll ever hear!
Kings of the earth—Captains of this world
Out to make War, With God's Christ and His Lord
Fowls of Heaven, Eat the enemies' flesh.
Who can make war with the Beast? We can!
It's over with—Rubble everywhere!
A new age has begun and Righteousness is here!
What was it for? Did it have to be?
Knowing God draweth nigh—Oh, can't you see?

— from the Christian Identity booklet,
"Prepare War," by C.S.A. Enterprises, Zarephath—Horeb

"I didn't come to Kean College to dillydally or beat around the bush. I didn't come to pin the tail on the donkey. I came to pin the tail on the honkey.

"Honkeys should be given 24 hours to get out of South Africa. And what should we do with the rest? We will kill the women, we will kill the children, we will kill the babies. We will kill the crippled, we will kill 'em all. We will kill the faggot, we will kill the lesbian, we will kill them all . . . Kill the old ones, too. Goddamnit, if they are in a wheelchair, push 'em off a cliff in Cape Town . . . I said kill the blind, kill the crippled, kill the crazy. Goddamnit, and when you get through with killing them all, go to the goddamn graveyard and dig up the grave and kill 'em, goddamn it, again. 'Cause they didn't die hard enough."

—Khallid Abdul Muhammad
at Kean College, New Jersey, November 29, 1993

"I've seen the white boys with the baggy pants and all of that. I see it as kind of a compliment that you want to be black so bad, you're going to make an ass out of yourself. That's cool, go ahead. You will never be black. Nobody is ever going to take you as black. But go ahead and try your hardest. Young black males are the most popular thing to be. I mean, white girls are in love with black men. Don't ask me why. Especially in Los Angeles. They just like that. 'I want somebody black. Somebody mean.'"

—"G-mo" from *Fast Forward* by Lauren Greenfield

BROWN MAGIC

Kadmon

> It is important to accept man in his totality, his shit, and his death. In the acceptance of obscenity, excrement, and death there lies a spiritual energy which I make use of.

Salvador Dali

In ages past, the universe was hallowed for man, and everything was invested with life: animals, plants, stones, time and space, tools and weapons. Every level of being and every manner of decay had a sacral significance. Cities and diseases were also holy, as was the coccyx bone, the *os sacrum*. Such beliefs existed in antiquity, continued through medieval times, and survived in traces until the modern age. Not even excrement was excluded from such a worldview—the feces, too, were venerated and imbued with life. In Rome, the Cloaca Maxima was a sacred place consecrated to the goddess Venus Cloacina, patroness of nightly bowel movements, toilets, and sewers.

In the Healing Arts of antiquity and the Middle Ages, human and animal excrement was a precious medicine. In the actual prescriptions, however, its use was hidden behind euphemisms such as "Occidental Sulphur" and "Cibet." The physician and natural philosopher Paracelsus called it *carbon humanum*, and once made a number of enemies when he presented a bowl full of excrement to some colleagues, telling them: "If you do not want to familiarize yourselves with the secrets of putrefactive fermentation, you are not worthy of being called physicians."

Excrement was utilized in medicine in every possible form: still steaming or cooled down, liquid or solid, as powder, tincture, and ointment. A French chemist even created a liqueur from feces and brandy which he called *Eau de Mille Fleurs*. A new branch of science began to emerge: scatology. It blended magical and medicinal concepts regarding the healing power of excrement, and united these feculent notions together in an applied mythology. In Frankfurt, at the end of the 17th century, the scholar Christian Franz Paullini collected all the prescriptions he could find relating to these practices. In the year 1696 his *New and Improved Healing Filth-Apothecary* was published—a *grimoire* of the disreputable black art of applied scatology, filled with countless hints for how to employ excrement as medicine. In

The Great Fart Cloud

this book, feces appeared to be an almost universal cure for any ailment, possessed of immeasurable healing powers and magical attributes. "And it is indeed wonderful that a matter which is able to cause irresistible disgust by its look and smell may not only be considered as a curio and a thing of scientific study, but also as a unique treasure to maintain health." (Samuel Augustus Flemming, quoted in Bourke's *Scatalogic Rites of All Nations.*)

Many prescriptions resembled alchemical instructions with their lists of ingredients which were difficult, if not nearly impossible, to obtain. Scatology revealed a surreal and borderline psychedelic world. People were convinced that specific qualities and powers utilizable by humans were present not only in the teeth, horns, claws, bones, and feathers of animals, but in their droppings as well. The birdshit of the sharp-eyed falcon would restore debilitated human vision when rubbed in the corner of the eye in the morning. Men stricken with partial paralysis were smeared with the feces of serpents to regain their flexibility. Women employed the same technique when they wanted an uncomplicated birth. Those who yearned to remain young resorted to the excrement of boys or girls. Men who were afraid of losing their sexual potency ate the shit of stags, bulls, and billy-goats. Women who wanted to have children carried a small bag of rabbit droppings around with them day and night, for the rabbit was a symbol of fertility. Christian Franz Paullini wrote about a tightrope walker who ingested squirrel shit every morning—it increased his sense of balance. Those who were deaf or hard-of-hearing prized the feces of the perceptive lynx. Often there was a close magical connection between the symbolic significance of a particular species of animal and the medical properties its droppings were believed to possess, although this was not always the case.

In the marketplaces of antiquity and the Dark Ages, traveling salesmen offered every possible variety of excrement for sale. Black markets arose where genuine as well as bogus feces were sold at occasionally stupendous prices. Shit-collectors combed through their local forests, searching for the excrement of owls and falcons. Others made it easier on themselves, and in dimly lit rooms they colored the feces of dogs and hens with pigments, herbs, and spices. This chthonic strain of medicine attracted many swindlers, who offered for sale the excrement of eagles, elephants, crocodiles, lions, and many other treasures . . . a brisk trade in foul magic.

Even as recently as the last century, the excrement of the Dalai Lama in Tibet was considered sacred. According to several Tibetan researchers, it was formed into relics, to be employed as amulets, hung up in tents or worn around the neck. They were also used in medicine. The amulets looked like pills—certain varieties were black in color, others red, some even white. In his book *Scatalogic Rites of All Nations*, the American ethnologist and scatologist John Gregory Bourke described how in the spring of 1889 he obtained a silver reliquary case containing four ochre-red pills from a Tibetan researcher. He gave it to a physician to examine it, but the doctor was unable to discover anything unusual about it. Over the course of the last century this custom of utilizing excremental amulets seems to have been abandoned.

> Farts and excrement are highly essential subjects; medicine and philosophy should turn to them with the greatest attention. The same is true for metaphysics. It has always been my regret that the Surrealists held their noses even when they were only just thinking about them.
> — Salvador Dali

Applied scatology harnessed the inherent forces of disgust and abhorrence. It was the Left Hand Path of medicine, a black homeopathy. Those who desired healing had to traverse the empire of revulsion. This demanded a willpower capable of overcoming any aversion or dislike. Certainly one aspect of the healing came about via the cathartic effect of ingesting or applying the excrement; thereby shit, symbol of the final, crudest matter, became an elixir of life. This same manner of thinking was clearly at work when the occultist Aleister Crowley asserted, "Therefore you have to search for things which are poisonous for you—to the furthest degree—and to make them yours through love. You must assimilate what you find disgusting into this path of totality."

An identical conception plays a significant role in some Tantric doctrines as well. In an exercise called Viparita, the senses and perceptions must be inverted to the degree at which those things causing horror and disgust lose their menace for the psyche:

Things which provoke disgust are analyzed, purified, and their values are extracted; they are used for the perfection of man. In the Chakra Tantra, Viparita consists of habitual ingestion of repulsive and irksome substances such as urine, excrement, menstruum and semen. Viparita is an exercise in destroying disgust by taking in loathsome things that are beneficial, by doing extremely unconventional things. . . . With this diversion one walks a systematic, accurate and scientific path, understanding that the process of aging can be halted and reversed through the utilization of disgust.

Michael D. Eschner, Die geheimen sexualmagischen
Unterweisungen des Tieres 666.

The "black art" was not only important in Tantricism or the ancient and medieval practice of medicine. One may discover it in alchemy as well. The first step of the alchemical work was termed *Nigredo*: blackness. Its characteristics were putrefaction, decay, death—it was a saturnine sort of symbolism which

Four Turds in the Furnace

prevailed in the descriptions of the black phase. In some manuscripts there are also images of glass vessels containing enigmatic black ingredients and darkly blazing liquids. Writers have often pointed out that this "mysterious substance" could be found all around in the everyday reality—yet people underestimated or scorned it. As the Italian esotericist Julius Evola remarked in his treatise on alchemy, *The Hermetic Tradition*:

> The surprising thing is that feces, ashes, and other remainders are considered as valuable things which the "Son of the Art" must guard against underestimating and throwing away, because it is precisely from them—so it is explained—that Gold is made, or rather, they are Gold themselves—the true or "Philosopher's Gold" and not the common one.

There were alchemists who did not consider their domain as one of spiritual philosophy, or as a sacred science that portrayed various wise doctrines of occidental and oriental antiquity in psychedelic allegories, but rather as a natural science dedicated to physical transmutation and metabolic transformation. Thus they began to search for natural substances that were similar to those described and depicted in occult texts. Mircea Eliade, in his history of alchemical traditions, *The Forge and the Crucible,* quotes the following:

> "The philosophers say that the birds and fishes bring the Stone to us, each man possesses it, it is everywhere, in you, in me, in all things, in time and in space. It presents itself in base guise" . . . the Stone "is familiar to all men, both young and old; it is found in the country, in the village and in the town, in all things created by God; yet it is despised by all. Rich and poor handle it every day. It is cast into the street by servant maids. Children play with it. Yet no one prizes it, though, next to the human soul, it is the most beautiful and most precious thing upon earth and has power to pull down kings and princes. Nevertheless it is esteemed the vilest and meanest of earthly things. . . . this Stone which is not a stone, a precious thing which has no value, a thing of many shapes which has no shapes, this unknown which is known to all."

Putrefactio

Might human and animal excrement be that mysterious and precious *prima materia* out of which gold could be transmuted? Many alchemists were afraid to get their hands dirty by utilizing feces in their magical work. But others, practitioners of the black arts and Faustian researchers, were not frightened away by anything. Hoping to make a feculent discovery, they took the "black arts" literally and descended into dark chambers and cesspits in order to unveil the golden mystery of excrement: they set out upon the Left Hand Path of alchemy.

The German author Michael D. Eschner, in his book *Die geheimen sexualmagischen Unterweisungen des Tieres 666 (The Secret Sex-Magick Teachings of the Beast 666),* claims:

With his analysis of substances normally considered unclean, the medieval alchemist probably came closest to the old teachings. He was aware that dirt was the outer form of the hidden God, and that price-less gleaming gold was to be found in ores and metals which were rejected by those who could not distinguish between the valuable and the worthless.

Such views were not confined to the Medieval mind, and have persisted among certain strains of occultism into the 20th Century. As Fritz von Herzmanovsky-Orlando wrote to his friend, the symbolist artist Alfred Kubin, on December 22, 1914: "Pissoirs, toilets, and chamber pots are the focal points of occult sensuality—still not yet properly esteemed."

At the beginning of this century the writer and occultist Gustav Meyrink undertook some alchemical experiments in Prague. In every sphere, he was a man who desired to peer behind-the-scenes of our "visible reality" in order to experience more of the hidden world. He wrote about these alchemical adven-tures in his account "How I Tried to Make Gold in Prague." In a second-hand bookshop he came across a medieval text by a Count of Milano, which stated that the *prima materia* of alchemy could be created from human or animal excre-ment. The text contained detailed descriptions. Meyrink decided to dedicate

The Holy Shit

himself to this alchemical work of metamorphosis. He contacted an old man who worked in the sewers and obtained a bucket of feces from him:

> The old alchemists maintained almost unanimously that the process of elixir preparation was guarded by dark powers of the underworld and as a result could lead to unspeakable disaster: poverty, incurable disease or a violent death. If it was at all possible, one must guard against an explosion of the glass vessel which contained the substance slowly transforming over the slow heat. According to the prescription, I warmed the contents steadily for weeks. My chemical advisor and I were surprised to notice inexplicably beautiful color changes which reached the iridescence of a peacock's plumage. As I stood one day in front of the retort, it suddenly exploded with a loud bang, and its contents splashed up in my face. I repeated the experiment, this time in an open vessel. The play of the colors became still at the first stage of blackness. It remains utterly incomprehensible to me why the flask exploded again—and at the exact moment when I happened to be standing in front of it. When I wanted to repeat the operation for a third time, I fell sick with a hideous disease.
>
> Gustav Meyrink, *Das Haus zur letzten Latern*

In one of the mystical films of the Chilean director Alejandro Jodorowsky, excrement is changed into gold after it passes through the black, red and white stages of alchemy. This equation of feces with gold, most probably a result of the influence of Carl Gustav Jung's extensive writings on alchemy and psychological states, was also an essential element in many of the paintings and writings of the Catalan artist Salvador Dali. As he exclaimed:

> I perceive existence from an alchemical point of view. I do not believe in an abstract conception of man. His sex, his smells, his excrement,

The Great Cosmic Anus

the genes within his blood, his eros, his dreams, and his death are essential aspects of his existence. . . . I believe in the power of putrefaction. . . . Every great art is borne of alchemy and the overcoming of death. . . . I am making gold when I transcend my bowels with a superconsciousness. . . . Let's study shit to lead a happy life!

⚡ ⚡ ⚡

Kadmon is an artist and researcher living in Vienna, Austria. He releases musical works under the name Allerseelen, and publishes the monographs *Aorta* and *Ahnstern* on esoteric subjects. He can be reached: c/o G. Petak, Postfach 778, A-1011 Wien, AUSTRIA.

The following true anecdote, from the respected Austrian physicist Professor Heinz von Foerster, was told to Michael Moynihan.

My story is about an itinerant artisan named Wayland the Smith. Such men were very popular at the end of the 11th and 12th Century in Europe, workmen who knew very well how to do this or that, and walked from country to country, from city to city, from king to king, and offered their services.

Wayland was walking through Europe and offering his service to every king he meets, and finally he comes to one king and offers himself as a blacksmith.

The king said, "That's wonderful, but I'm sorry—I already have a blacksmith."

"Why don't we make a contest then," Wayland replied, "and you can hire the better blacksmith?"

"Alright," said the king, "but what sort of contest?"

Wayland proposed the following: the local blacksmith shall make a suit of armor in which to clad himself. Wayland, on the other hand, would make a sword. The local blacksmith would sit on a chair, and Wayland would take the sword and try to cut the sword through the armor of the other smith.

The king said, "That sounds very reasonable, because if you cut through it, the other smith will be dead. But when you can't do it, and the sword breaks—then we will hang you!"

And Wayland said, "Yes, a good deal."

So they both went into their forge shops. Wayland started to make a sword and the other gentleman began to make a suit of armor. Wayland begins his forging of the sword in the following way: he takes some iron and shaves it down into finer and finer iron filings, and then takes some bread and kneads these iron filings into the bread, mixes it with a little bit of milk, cooks it up, and feeds it to chickens. The chickens eat it, they peck it up, peck it up, peck it up. Then after a few days Wayland carefully collects the droppings of the chickens. He cleans them, washes them off and then kneads the iron filings which he retrieves into new bread, with new milk, cooks it a little bit, and distributes it to the chickens. Again they peck it up, peck it up, peck it up. He collects the droppings afterward and does the whole thing again. He does this exactly 13 times, and when this is complete he takes the iron filings and forges them into a sword.

The other smith has already made his armor in the meantime, and the chap is sitting on the chair. Wayland comes along with his new sword and *whoosh!*, he cuts the other guy precisely into two parts, one to the left and the other to the right. So Wayland got the job! And of course then he continues on with his adventures.

Now the fascinating thing was that in Düsseldorf, a German city which is important in modern times for the steel industry, there is a large institute for metallurgy. At some point around the years 1930-33, one crazy guy there heard about this story and decided to make the experiment of Wayland the Smith. To the ridicule of all the people in the Metallurgical Institute, he brought 50 chickens into the courtyard there and repeated the experiment. He followed it exactly, step by step. While the chickens were eating the iron filings and excreting them again, he collected some of the iron and measured it spectroscopically. "What's going on with that iron?" he wondered. "Is there any transformation?" Yes, he observed, there was! He observed a bit more of nitric acid in the spectral line of the metal, and after so and so many times of running them through the chickens, he forged all the remaining iron filings and found out that what happened to the metal is that it became tough. It would not crack so easily. There is a process in the steel industry which is called nitriding, and the result is a form of casehardened nitride steel. Steel that is just carbonized, it's very sharp and hard but easily crackable. With nitriding, however, it retains a toughness, like leather. If it is hit against a surface like stone or another piece of iron, it stays intact but cuts through the other object. And the man who duplicated Wayland's feat discovered that for this process with the chickens you had to repeat it precisely thirteen times to get the maximum amount of nitriding, because if you do it too much then the iron becomes weak.

What's also interesting is that this experiment was done just around the time we had found out in the steel industry in Germany that nitriding was one of the most modern ways to make tough steel; this had only been discovered a few years before.

The wonderful thing is that of course everyone asks, "How could Wayland have known this?" But the question itself is wrong, because at that time this way of thinking was not in existence. An entirely different way of thinking—a holistic worldview, or what today we might call "systemic thinking"—was in existence.

The past is full of these fabulous stories, it's only unfortunate that we have ignored them for such a long time.

Edible Reward for Dry Pants

By Richard M. Foxx and Nathan H. Azrin from
Toilet Training the Retarded

$\mathbf{D}$etecting when the resident has eliminated is not always easy. If it is quiet in the toilet, the sound of the urine hitting the water in the toilet bowl could cue the trainer. However, there may be times when not enough urine is expelled to make a detectable sound or when it is not quiet in the toilet since several residents may be receiving training at the same time. Rewarding a resident by mistake when he actually has not urinated only confuses him as does failing to reward him when he has urinated. Since positioning the resident with his legs far enough apart to permit an unobstructed view is uncomfortable, the resident would probably not remain in that position very long. Because of these difficulties, a new method for immediately detecting eliminations is needed. A urine alert answers this need. It consists of a plastic insert which fits most standard toilet bowls. In the bottom of the urine alert are two moisture-detecting snaps which are connected by wires to a battery-powered signal box. When urine touches the snaps, a tone sounds, which alerts the trainer that the resident has eliminated. To terminate the sound, the urine alert bowl must be completely emptied and the two moisture-sensitive snaps wiped dry with a cloth.

Inappropriate Eliminations

Inappropriate eliminations must also be detected as soon as they occur. Immediate detection of accidents allows the trainer to provide an immediate disapproving reaction. A pants alarm was made expressly for immediately detecting accidents. The pants alarm consists of a lightweight signal box that is pinned to the resident's underwear. Two wires lead from the signal box, pass between the resident's legs, and attach to the moisture-detecting snaps in the crotch section of the underpants. When the resident has an accident, the signal sounds as soon as the urine wets the cloth area between the moisture-detecting snaps.

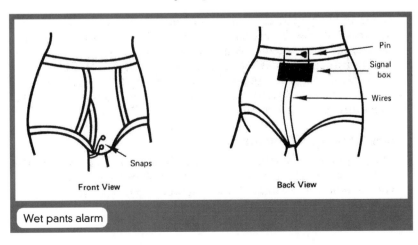

Snaps

Front View

Pin

Signal box

Wires

Back View

Wet pants alarm

Both the urine alert and the pants alarm remove the necessity of the trainer maintaining a constant vigil of one resident, thus allowing the trainer the freedom to work with more residents and to keep the necessary training records. The apparatuses allow immediate detection and reaction to appropriate and inappropriate eliminations. The trainer can then provide the combination of positive reactions for appropriate eliminations and disapproving reactions for inappropriate eliminations, both of which are essential in the program.

Candies and Treats

Candies and other edible treats are used to reward the resident for successful eliminations and for remaining dry. The amount of edible reward that is given at the dry-pants inspection should be less than the amount given for successful voiding. The edible reward for dry pants should be small and approximately bite-sized: for example, an M&M candy. The edible reward for voiding, in contrast, should be quite large: for example, one-third of a candy bar or 10 M&M candies. A large reward for voiding increases the resident's motivation to toilet himself. By providing the resident with a piece of candy together with verbal praise you are indicating to him that he has pleased you.

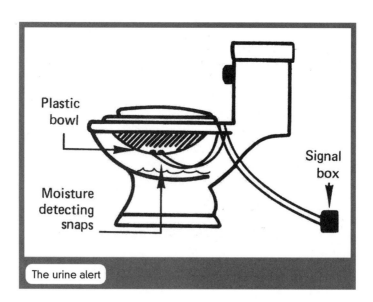

Plastic bowl

Moisture detecting snaps

Signal box

The urine alert

Shit List

A *Hustler* magazine article on strange sex practices included a cult of coprophagists, the medical term for shit eaters. One Southern California group, Jack's Number Two, moved from San Diego to Houston after its "Jack" died of AIDS. A speaker from the group suggested that the practice, despite AIDS and parasite infection, was going strong.

The following excerpt is from the organization's newsletter on brown paper.

Shit buddies, it's a problem. Your weekend toilet pig is all set to arrive for the greatest shit eating this side of sewerland, but how to get those long, thick, brown turds to ooze slowly and firmly out of a hungry brown asshole into that heavenly manshit soft, sweet and raunchy just on cue when you both need it.

Well, scumbags, diet and preparation have a lot to do with it. Even then, it isn't for sure. But it does help to know that what you eat is exactly what you get!

For firm, hard brown turds, try eating a bowl or two of rice, well spiced (cumin is great!), some corn (which make the turds nice and chewy), and as much chicken as possible. This will help sweeten your shit, particularly if you add a little sugar and a little fruit. Potatoes, popcorn, and starchy yellow vegetables all help to make good, firm turds.

But for a more pungent odor and taste try cheese, red meat, fish and plenty of green vegetables. The green vegetables, together with lots of fruit, will soften those manturds and will give a nice, sweet creamy consistency to your dump.

Now if you want thick, dark, solid turds try a couple of teaspoons full of Pepto Bismol four, six and nine hours before the session. A couple of hot cups of coffee should get those hard manturds moving out of your shithole. Or get your hungry bottom to shove his tongue and fingers right up there and scoop it out. As an added attraction for those sophisticated raunch gourmets out there, raisins and nuts swallowed whole come out the same way, fellow pigs, all nice and cooked and taste unbelievable. And we all know how to cook a banana up a stinking manchute—makes a good meal.

For heavy shit-farts try eggs for breakfast; beans, cabbage, and kraut for lunch and dinner; together with cashew nuts and wheat germ. With all that inside you, add a touch of cider vinegar and you're ready to blast off for the stars!

Hope this helps some of you fellow scatmen out there. Any more recipes for the perfect gourmet shit scene? Let's hear from you. Good eating!

DYSTOPIA

Boyd Rice

We are told that the function of evolution is to perfect the species. Man adapts and mutates constantly, discarding characteristics that hinder his survival, and assimilating those that strengthen it. Given that premise, the human race could evolve into the much-heralded Superman: a living God.

Look around. And think again. Are we seeing the survival of the fittest? Or could it be the survival of the unfittest? What do you see? The decline of intelligence year after year, accompanied by the radical increase of numbers.

Do we still operate under the Divine Right of kings? Do people at the top still call the shots? Or did the idealism of rule absolutely collapse, favoring only those who find ways to profit from the Dystopia? As bottom-feeders set the agenda, everyone is reduced to being treated no better than the lowest rung by a dumbed-down, idiot-proofed nanny state. It's not that the lunatics are running the asylum, but with democracy's deification of Victimhood, lunatics are coddled and subsidized, and the productive are their slaves.

It is said that the state, the system, the rich inflict on these Victims a hideously poor self-esteem. But could it be that these Victims are actually enjoying a self-esteem propelled to majestic heights unjustified by capability or accomplishment? In the Dystopia, delusions are accommodated, and the humiliation of ineptitude remains a thing of the past. The Dystopia motivates all to wear the thorned crowns of Victimhood, delusion and ineptitude.*

The feelings and emotion of Victimhood slay logic and reason, winning every battle of the Dystopia. Hysteria is Dystopia's tyrannical God.

People who recognize the rise of the Dystopia often lack the detachment to accommodate perspective. These individuals believe that if enough people were aware of the Dystopia, then the vermin would disappear, and the downward course of the Dystopia would somehow reverse itself. But the Dystopia is so vast and all-encompassing, it pervades every aspect of modern life. With the Dystopia, the only cure is fatal to all of us.

---

* Publisher's note: In the February 6, 2000 *New York Times* magazine, in an article titled, "Incompetence Is Bliss," author David Rakoff writes of a recent study called "Unskilled and Unaware of It" by Justin Kruger of the University of Illinois and David Dunning of Cornell that maintains, "few people have any idea how incompetent they really are. . . .Those who scored lowest on the objective tests scored highest in their own self-evaluation. The same held true in reverse: high-scoring subjects underestimated their skills and how well they compared with others."

Hating the Dystopia solves no problems, and doesn't get you anywhere but the insane asylum. One must love the Dystopia. That's right. Love it. Dystopia is your friend. Savor the suffering, take pleasure in the misfortune of others. Become the proverbial one-eyed man in the kingdom of the blind. As the world crumbles around us, understand that the streets are paved with gold.

ϟ ϟ ϟ

The above article was adapted from a lengthier essay of the same title. The recordings of **Boyd Rice,** both under his name and Non, have been released by Mute Records, World Serpent, and Soleilmoon. He can be reached at P.O. Box 300081, Denver, CO 80203.

Mr. Awesome and paid model, Whitney Wonders

MR. AWESOME PROVES EVERYBODY IS A STAR

Adam Parfrey

Total democracy has won the war. Today, everyone can promote the idea of their absolute worthiness on websites, and has access to newsgroups to post yet another ignored opinion. What has value, when everything is irrevocably reduced to yet another quark in an endless swirling sea of mediocrity?

It is in this era that Roy Shildt, aka Mr. Awesome, has emerged.

Mr. Awesome does not have a website. (Not yet.) Mr. Awesome does not have a product. (Not yet.) Mr. Awesome does not even have a running automobile. But Mr. Awesome does believe that he's worthy of celebrity. "If a garbage bag like Kato Kaelin is a celebrity, then I'm a celebrity."

Roy Shildt believes that his awesome potential is based on three major factors:

1. Roy Shildt is listed in the 1986 edition of *The Guinness Book of World Records* as having had the highest score for the video game, "Missile Command." Almost 100 "computer athletes" are listed in the Guinness Book, but Mr. Shildt was inducted as the first member of the "Video Hall of Fame" (location unknown). The individual who achieved the highest score for Donkey Kong cannot make the same claim.
2. Roy Shildt took out a one-third-page ad in the May 1989 issue of *Playgirl* magazine, which includes a picture of his disturbingly naked muscle-bound body standing next to a six-foot aluminum ladder. Listed in this ad are Mr. Awesome's sperm count statistics, his availability for "bachelorette parties, character roles in motion pictures, Swedish massage, tour guiding and personal fitness training," and his actual home phone number.
3. After mailing a letter and issue of *Playgirl* magazine to the media personality Madonna, the woman—according to Mr. Shildt—actually called him up. Material mailed to this writer by Mr. Shildt included a lengthy, obsessive fixation in the form of the *Playboy* column "20 Questions" speculating on Madonna's desperate need for Mr. Awesome's sperm.

Mr. Shildt tells me that the prime vehicle for establishing his coming celebrity will be a comic called, "The Comic Book Life of Roy Shildt," which would include a "mini-story" called "The Mr. Awesome Training Manual" that informs "comic book nerds over the age of 18 how to 'get all the hot babes you ever dreamed of.'"

"We can sell millions," rants Mr. Shildt/Awesome to this author by phone. "Millions. All you have to do is help me write it, and print the thing. If you fuck me over like the scumbags of Hollywood and everyone else, you'll get yours. If you do me well, I won't forget you. Mr. Awesome is the avenging angel of all the fucked-over people who tried to make it in Hollywood. My name is going to be worth a lot of money."

Feral House regrettably turned down the possibility of selling millions of *The Comic Book Life of Roy Shildt*, though we promised Mr. Shildt the possibility of appearing in *Apocalypse Culture II*. Mr. Shildt seemed extravagantly optimistic about his article in this book. After all, the book you are now holding in your hands may very well establish Mr. Awesome's coming stardom. "If you're good to me, and don't fuck me over," reminds Mr. Shildt, "you can use me for *Apocalypse Culture III*, and for the cover as well!"

On the auspicious day in which this future superstar was interviewed, Mr. Shildt took a bus to meet the author at a Venice Beach restaurant (as he doesn't have the money to register his automobile bearing Mr. Awesome vanity plates). During the interview, Mr. Shildt spoke of his dynamic life and plans for wealth and celebrity. And, before he took a bus back to his apartment, he loaned me a few negatives of his poses with a *grotesquely* silicone-enhanced porn actress who goes by the name "Whitney Wonders." These photos would apparently be used for reproduction in the "Mr. Awesome Training Manual."

Among Mr. Shildt's salient characteristics is his refusal to hear the word "no." Day after day we received Mr. Shildt's long and loud phone calls, and to achieve a small respite from his hard sales inquiries, we failed to answer his phone calls for some hours, even turning off the ringer. This made Mr. Shildt angry. Here is one of his messages:

"I don't know why you're ducking my call, but I want those negatives back or I'm going to call the police and report 'em stolen. So listen, you gutless little faggot, you better call me back right now or I'm going to fucking find you and kick your fucking ass. You understand, thief? Or I'm going to call the police. My number is 310-477-xxxx, you gutless gay bastard."

Another message, following:

"I don't understand why you're ducking my calls, Adam. I mean it's ridiculous. I'm trying to do better for you. I can't understand your reasoning. There's no reason to duck my calls. Don't you have any guts at all? Jesus Christ! My number is 310-477-xxxx: Why don't you just return my call and straighten this thing out? Hello? Are you standing there listening to this?" (click)

From here on, dear reader, we'll try not to be a gutless little faggot. Mr. Shildt's remarkable saga is herewith presented in interview form.

Mr. Awesome, what were the calls like when you ran the advertisement in Playgirl?

Nuts. Just nuts. Then some women called me who were curious, wondering if *Playgirl* was pulling a stunt. Said, is this a real person? I thought that *Playgirl* magazine was playing a joke. I say no, it's really me. They say what's it really about, and I say, American women have the right to know who's jacking off in the sperm banks and fertility clinics. Trying to give America a new viewpoint from someone who's actually done the job. (*Hyena-like laugh.*) And some of them wanted sperm.

You're a sperm donor?

Yeah, yeah. That's how I met my wife. We worked something out there. (*Ferocious laughter.*) The basic theory is why should the sperm banks make all the profits? Why go for frozen sperm when you can have it fresh from the source? (*Laughs.*)

Mr. Awesome and car
photo: Scott Lindgren

Do you have children?

Just one. Five-year-old son.

What's his name?

Calvin.

Named after Calvin Klein?

Yeah. Sure enough, he is. (*Laughs.*)

Are you kidding me?

No, I'm serious.

You like Calvin Klein's name?

We had no one else to name him after. My wife likes the way I look in underwear, so I said, let's name him Calvin Klein. (*Laughs.*)

Who else was calling you?

Lots of nuts. Famous people and not-so-famous.

What famous people called you?

I'd rather not say at this point. I spoke to Madonna and a few others in her class. Famous ones.

After this ad came out?

Yeah. I got a few of them. Rather not say their name, outside of Madonna. She's already admitted she's spoken to me, and plus, we were supposed to have a competition to see who her sperm donor would be. She ended up getting inseminated by this guy Carlos Leon and, uh, which to my understanding was an unplanned pregnancy. She was having sex with the guy, never expecting to get pregnant, and then she did. I think Madonna had some problems getting pregnant the normal way. The chances are so small. Virtually negligent. But lo and behold, by luck of the draw, she did get pregnant off of him. As a matter of fact I've got some substantiating evidence of that. You just can't go around saying things without proof. Doesn't matter what you say, it only matter what you prove. That's one of the hallmarks that I live by.

Playgirl *is considered a gay magazine.*

No it isn't. A lot of gays buy it, but it says on the cover "Entertainment For

Women," and that's what it means to me. Hey! Here's *New York Post*, April 13, 1996. They've done an article on Mr. Leon here. And I just highlighted it. You don't have to read the whole thing, just the part that was highlighted.

Did she call you up, or did you call her?

I sent her a package with the ad and all my information. Resumé. I sent her an actual copy of *The Guinness Book of World Records*. And then she called me. I got the package to her by special delivery.

What are you wearing around your neck?

Just a little gold dumbbell.

What about the round thing?

A jade ball. A good luck charm.

Has it provided you good luck?

(*Much laughter.*)

You grew up in New York?

Brooklyn.

Did you shave off your eyebrows?

No. They're just really light.

Could you tell me about your background? Your family?

(*Laughs.*) I grew up in Bensonhurst. My father was a letter carrier for the United States Mail Service. A real asshole, too. A major scumbag, too. Philanderer.

Philanderer?

Yeah. (*Laughs.*) Drunkard. He used to . . . he beat me all the time.

When did you move out to Los Angeles?

In 1979, I started out as a UCLA student. Graduated in '85. Six years an undergraduate. I have a degree in Psychology and a minor concentration in business. I worked for securities companies for a while, and I worked for Gold's Gym for a while.

What did you do at Gold's Gym?

I started at the bottom picking up the weights, and hoping to get promoted, but I never did. I did some casting calls. A bit part. Nothing to speak of. Didn't make any money out of it. But I've enjoyed my life, but I haven't made any money out of it. I've been lifting weights since high school. Power lifting has been my big thing since I was at my peak.

Where did you get your idea for a comic book?

You know GlamorCon?

You mean that thing they have near L.A. Airport?

Yeah. That's where I see the celebrities there, the women, the *Playboy* playmates and the guys running around there are the same ones at the comic book convention and I said, hey, where's the general public? And they're not there, it's only the comic book guys. And it came to me since I read *Playboy* a lot and I saw that book, *How To Pick Up Girls* in there, that's been selling well for years and years, and I see all these comic book guys in here. And I thought if we bring the two things together, a *How To Pick Up Girls* superhero comic book thing, it could really sell well, and I worked on that idea, how to incorporate myself as a comic book hero. The method with which I picked up girls was the *Playgirl* magazine exposé, and I figured what's good for the goose is good for the gander. If a *Playboy* playmate is a celebrity then certainly I am a celebrity. I'm the first computer athlete in the Hall of Fame in the *Guinness Book of World Records*, plus I'm in *Playgirl* magazine. The World Record computer athlete is what makes me Mr. Awesome. Everything else is just the garnish. If a garbage bag like Kato Kaelin is a celebrity, then I'm a celebrity. If a bimbo like Monica Lewinsky is nominated for Woman of the Year, then I should seriously consider running for President. What really got me started was that Donna Rice thing. In 1986, I think it was. This idiot gets photographed on the lap of some politician and all of a sudden there's a whole big scandal and now she's selling jeans on TV. She's a multi-millionaire for being a goofball. Hey, that's what got me the idea for *Playgirl* magazine. If they make a celebrity out of Donna Rice, then certainly I deserve to be a celebrity too. I can be just as crazy as anybody else, if that's what it takes. (*Laughs.*) If they don't recognize me from playing video games, then they'll have to recognize me for something else.

What are you going to tell people about how to pick up girls?

The method I used in how to pick up girls was all done through *Playgirl* magazine. The Mr. Awesome program is how to write a resumé, how to publish it in *Playgirl* magazine, how to screen the phone calls and set up the dates.

Gee, you tell me that several million people are going to buy your comic book. And if most of them took your advice there would be millions of ads in Playgirl *magazine. Wouldn't that be competition for you?*

Well, that's the whole thing. I don't think anyone else would do it. Maybe only one person in a thousand would even seriously consider doing it. . . .

But aren't you trying to teach young men how to pick up girls?

That's the way I did it. I don't think anyone else would have the gall to do what I did. If you read *How to Pick Up Girls*, the one that Eric Weber wrote, it really doesn't do very much for you. It gives you a few pick-up lines, it gives you some confidence, but as far as picking up girls, it doesn't work. It's like saying, sure, you could pick up a girl at a supermarket and sleep with her that night, as I said, but you'd have better chances hitting the lottery. That was one of the things in the back of my mind when I ran the *Playgirl* ad. I said, hey, what would happen if you could buy three million lottery tickets, all at the same time? Standing in a supermarket, you might be able to come on to a girl two or three times a day, by the time you got someone, it would be in the next 30 or 40 years. But if you could send out three million pick-up lines to some girl reading *Playgirl* magazine then sooner or later you're going to get at least two or three of them! That's where the idea came. The Mr. Awesome Program works!

So, have you used your program to meet other girls, besides your wife?

Yes, I've met a few other girls. I've inseminated them. I've got a few kids out there.

What about the gay people who called? What did you tell them?

You get a lot of gay people who call, obviously. You just say, please don't call me any more, and you be polite about it. You don't want to be rude to these people. Actually, I was rude to one. Some guy kept calling me, and I said some insulting things to him and he just kept calling me constantly just trying to annoy the shit out of me. So just say if a gay guy calls, thank you very much, but I'm not interested. Just ignore the gays, and concentrate on the women.

What about the woman you posed with in those pictures?

Whitney Wonders? Yeah, I met her through the ad. A lot of porno women called me. A few. I met a few of them. Most of them call you up and laugh at you. Some of them call up masturbating. You deal with it or you don't, depending on the mood you're in.

How did you get the photos with this Whitney Wonders?

After she called I had her number for a while, and when the idea for the book came up, I called her up and she came over. I paid her $300 for the shoot.

So you never did anything with her.

Yes, I did. We had a couple of dates. But you know, I wasn't doing a book. The book came later.

I thought you had a wife.

My wife, I'm just living with her. She's . . . . It's a special circumstance. It's a mutual . . . . Just a cohabitation of mutual convenience, really, it's not a real marriage. Even though we are legally married.

Do you want a real marriage?

Yeah. Yeah. As soon as I can afford it. I'm putting all my eggs in one basket, I'm looking to score on the comic book deal. Why I really haven't moved forward on a financially gainful position is because I'm expecting a couple of lawsuits, so I'm really . . . I'm really, I'm really taking advantage of the fact that I'm judgement-proof right now. So even though I'm broke and I'm 44 and I'm ruined because if you're 44 and you're broke, forget about getting any decent money, unless you marry some rich woman. But yeah, I'm hoping to make a few million dollars from this book deal, I'm thinking I'm going to sell a few million copies and there's going to be some lawsuits involved.

Lawsuits?

There's going to be some lawsuits involved. Things I'm going to say in there. People might not like, you know. You can sue anybody for anything these days. So, you know. I have some inside information on some rich and famous people that I'm holding back because I'm hoping that Madonna will be interested in it, and if and when Madonna and Heidi Fleiss get together to conclude their movie deal, Madonna said she's thinking of putting me in it. So the information I have I'll give to her and maybe she'll incorporate it into her movie so maybe there'll be lawsuits from that as well, so I have to be careful.

How would Madonna put you into a movie?

Like the Richard Gere character in *American Gigolo*. It's a real hazy thing right now. I wrote a synopsis on a script and Madonna called me and said we'll think about it. She laughs. She likes me. She's laughing. She thinks I'm a funny guy, and it's a "we'll see what the future holds, no promises" kind of thing. I've got my fingers crossed. I'm hoping that that movie will be made and I will become a big star. Or at least a household word. At least as good as Kato Kaelin. If that garbage bag is a celebrity, I should be a celebrity.

[At this moment of the interview, Mr. Awesome makes sure my tape machine is switched off. He's about to tell me some very important information regarding another projected masterpiece called *Portfolio of the Fellatio of the Rich and Famous*. Apparently this epic has to do with Hollywood entities who called him up and attempted to get together with Mr. Awesome to get him hooked on drugs and involved with homosexual sex. Mr. Awesome then flashes a photo of a haggard-looking man in his late '50s who's taking off his pants.]

Who is that man, Mr. Awesome? I don't recognize him.

His nephew is very famous, as famous as they come. With *The Portfolio of the Fellatio of the Rich and Famous* I'm going to expose all those Hollywood scumbags. But first Madonna has to get involved. Is your tape machine turned off?

Following the interview, Mr. Awesome faxed this writer a sheet of his writing. Here is the document, unmolested, uncorrected, in full, exactly as written:

POINTS TO COVER

1. Roy Shildt is billing himself as Americas' last honest man; a cross between General Patton/chippendales/and the Full Monty.

2. Roy Shildt is not gay but soon discovers that "you can't get something for nothing" in Hollywood. Roy Shildt makes his acquainatnce of a Hollywood power broker. This power broker, using his nephew as an example, says his nephew has no acting ability and is in fact an international movie star! (guess who?) This power broker says to Roy I'll hook you up to success and get you drugs (I have proof) if you let me suck your cock for free. Roy Shildt uses his spy camera to capture the blow job on film and thus starts his portfolio of "The Fellatio of the Rich and Famous." Roy Shildt offers the portfolio & information to rock star Madonna for inclusion in the Heidi Fleiss movie that Madoona was putting together (as told in "People" magazine). Roy Shildt has a "consultation" with Heidi Fleiss to see if there is any overlap between Heidis' client base and Roys' "Fellatio Portfolio". We can't say anything specific right now because it's kinda hush-hush on the Q-T and very confidential so you had better pre order your copy of Mr. Awesome: The Comic Book Life of Roy Shildt right now. It will reveal all!!!

3. This power broker is the first inductee (complete w/photograph) into "The Rich and Famous Fellatio Hall of Fame" and will be completely revealed in the comic book titled Mr. Awesome: The Comic Book Life of Roy Shildt. Pre order yours now or you'll be sorry! Send name, address, and $9.95 payable to

Roy Shildt
PO Box 241432
LA CA 90024

The book will be shipped within the next 90 days.

4. I can prove the power broker blow job & drugs but I can't prove he called me from the "Playgirl" ad. Consider not saying specifically how we met to avoid lawsuit! (advice of legal counsel)

Nicolas Claux's bloody pact with Satan

THE VAMPIRE MANIFESTO
Nicolas Claux

Every lifeform on earth is part of an ecosystem. Each animal, plant or insect is a link in an endless chain. This is how nature survives. Big animals eat smaller ones, then they die and become fertilizer. This is the ultimate meaning of life. But something has gone seriously wrong. Humans emerged from the mud, and began to do real damage to the ecosystem. It created technology, the absolute enemy of nature. And then came science: the ultimate control. Natural predators—sabertooth tigers, wolves, bears, white sharks—were exterminated. Technology gave mankind the tools to separate its species from the rest of the ecosystem. This separation will lead this planet to a certain fall.

HUMANITY IS A PARASITE
A parasite infests its surrounding environment and completely drains it of energy. Mankind doesn't accept its role as a link inside a chain. Men want to be the last link of this chain. They try to modify their DNA, so that they can live longer. Some scientists argue that when men develop the technology to colonize other planets, they will leave a deadened planet earth to infest another. Does this sound familiar? This is how termites settle their colonies. Thanks to industrial technology, human society is transforming more and more into an insectoid society with complete control over individuals. To become a productive member of multinational corporate society, each individual is educated through television and other forms of mass culture. In less than fifty years humans will be genetically programmed, even before birth, to fulfill its tasks. Unproductive elements (freaks, mentally sick people, born rebels) will be exterminated. Several free thinkers have already enunciated the dangers of a technology-controlled society, but they all were neutralized by law enforcement agencies. Look what happened to Theodore Kaczynski, a subject of CIA mind-control experiments from 1956–61 at Harvard. Freedom as we have known it is doomed. But this is the obvious fate of a species that has slowly evolved from the status of predator to that of parasite.

THE THINGS PEOPLE CALL "GOD"
God is beyond your concept of good and evil. God does not have a conscience. What you call "conscience" is a genetic program that prevents you from damaging mankind's development. Compared to the perfection of other lifeforms—ants, for example—humankind is merely a rough sketch. God wouldn't pay attention to such a pathetic form of life. Most people will object to this vision of the human race. Their main argument is that humanity is not just a simple link in the chain of nature. Humanity is a creation of God, and

God created mankind in his image . . . so men should rule nature. Bullshit. Let's suppose a supernatural being created the universe. Tell me why this "being" should be limited by human emotions, such as love, hate, anger, resentment, compassion? Tell me why this being would care about the fate of its most destructive creation? Tell me why it would give the tools to that creation (genetics, nuclear energy . . .) so that it would nearly become its equal? Think through it. This is a simple-minded, anthropomorphic concept of God. If spiders had the brain to imagine God, they would surely imagine that God has eight legs and that it created spiders so that they could cover the world with webs. The concept of "God" is not something I deny. But how foolish humans are to believe that "God" feels human emotion. God does not care whether the human race survives or becomes extinct. The thing you call God doesn't give a fuck about you! You wish it would, so that there would be a purpose to your miserable existence. But there's none. Your only purpose is to breed and infest. Human emotions such as love are genetically programmed impulses so you can accomplish your task as a parasite. Hate and aggression are also genetically programmed impulses to help you survive and protect your own spawn. You try to justify these emotions through spirituality. But that is simple escapism from reality. Reality hurts. One day you'll find out that you're not unique. You'll find out that you're just another parasite and that society wants you to breed, consume and infest. You find that the meaning of life is to protect the eggs of your human brothers. Love and hate are there to help you fulfill your task. "God" is there to teach you the rules. Everything becomes clear. Something went wrong with your genetic program . . . you are a mutant.

NEANDERTHALS: PREDATORS OF THE HUMAN RACE

Thirty thousand years ago, something could have stopped the human race from infesting. Nature gave a natural predator to homo sapiens: the Neanderthal. Neanderthals were physically superior to humans, bigger, stronger, with a bigger brain. Modern archaeology, especially in the south of Europe, shows that Neanderthals were cannibals. They did not do it for religious rites, or out of hunger. There was a large variety of game around them. But they specifically liked human meat. They considered *homo sapiens* a form of cattle. Their role in the ecosystem was to regulate the demographic explosion of the human race. This is how nature regulates its growth: when a species becomes a danger to the ecosystem, nature develops new means to regulate its infestation: diseases (AIDS, plague, cancer) and mutations (development of superpredators like Neanderthals). If Neanderthals had survived the ice age they would have prevented humanity from destroying nature. But, like all superpredators, Neanderthals were not enough adapted to a brutal change of climatic conditions. They followed the fate of dinosaurs and became extinct. But some of their DNA survived. And with this, the taste for human meat.

THE RESURGENCE OF THE SUPERPREDATORS

Many have tried to explain why some apparently normal people crave the taste of human flesh. Psychiatrists call it a paraphilia. Ethnologists call it an atavistic resurgence. Let's simply call it a survival of Neanderthal DNA. Think about this: Why did the phenomenon of serial killers appear in the end of the 19th Century (Jack the Ripper)? Simply because it was the consequence of the Industrial Revolution, when men attempted to have complete control of nature. Humanity achieved its mutation as a parasite. So the laws of nature assisted the resurgence of Neanderthal DNA. All across the industrial world, some were born with a compulsion to kill their fellow human beings, and treat them as cattle. Cases of multiple murders involving cannibalism appear in every society facing a technological crisis, like the USA or Russia. Individuals like Nikolaï Djumagaleiv, Jeffrey Dahmer or Edmund Kemper clearly have Neanderthalian facial features. The craving for murder and human flesh eating is a common trait among such types of serial killers. And most serial killers who did not practice cannibalism were only prevented from doing so because of a strongly religious upbringing. But when you read their confessions, most of them admit to having a desire to drink the blood or eat the flesh of their victims.

HUNTING HUMANS

I am aware and proud of my heritage as a superpredator. I am aware and proud of the Neanderthal DNA in my veins. I am aware and proud of my place in the ecosystem. I do not believe that the things I did were wrong or "evil." Human termites sense the danger that people of my kind represent, but they don't understand that we only threaten their infestation. They are dimly aware that people like me are the response of nature to their rampant devastation of planet Earth. My task, our task, is to regulate the human race. We have the same purpose as the ebola virus. My genetic programming tells me to hunt, kill, and eat human cattle. Society cannot "rehabilitate" me, because I am genetically different from your average human insect. I am Danger. I am the Enemy. You can lock me up in a cage. But others will come and restore the balance of nature. Humanity is doomed.

⚡ ⚡ ⚡

Nicolas Claux, the prolific artist, cannibal, and so-called "Vampire of Paris," is imprisoned for murder.

Illustration by Harold McNeill

HUMANFLOOD

Pentti Linkola

The Finnish philosopher Pentti Linkola, who lives an ascetic life as a fisherman in a remote rural region of his frigid homeland, dares to utter the unspeakable. In order for the planet to continue living, man—or *homo destructivus*, as Linkola names him—must be violently thinned to a mere fraction of his current global population. Linkola's metaphor for the predicament is as follows:

> What to do, when a ship carrying a hundred passengers suddenly capsizes and only one lifeboat, with room for only ten people, has been launched? When the lifeboat is full, those who hate life will try to load it with more people and sink the lot. Those who love and respect life will take the ship's axe and sever the extra hands that cling to the sides of the boat.

As time creaks onward, Linkola's predictions and indictments grow more dire. He has come to realize that extreme situations demand extreme solutions: "We still have a chance to be cruel. But if we are not cruel today, all is lost." The sworn enemy of secular humanists, Linkola knows that the fate of the earth will never be rescued by those who exalt "tenderness, love and dandelion garlands." Neither the developed nor underdeveloped populations deserve to survive at the expense of the biosphere as a whole. Linkola has urged that all Third World aid be cut off, asylum status for refugees be halted, so that millions will starve to death or be promptly slaughtered in genocidal civil wars. Mandatory abortions should be carried out for any female who has more than two offspring. The only countries capable of initiating such draconian measures are those of the West, yet ironically they are the ones most hamstrung by debilitating notions of liberal humanism. As Linkola explains, "The United States symbolizes the worst ideologies in the world: growth and freedom." The only realistic solution will be found in the implementation of an eco-fascist regime where brutal battalions of "green police," having freed their consciences from the "syrup of ethics," are capable of doing whatever is necessary.

In Finland, Linkola's books are bestsellers. The rest of the world clearly cannot stomach his brand of medicine, as was evidenced when the *Wall Street Journal* ran an article on Linkola in 1995. A stack of indignant hate mail ensued from ostensibly turn-the-other-cheek Christians, loving mothers, and assorted do-gooders. One reader squawked, "Sincere advocates of depopulation should set an example for all of us and begin the depopulating with themselves." Linkola's reply is far more logical: "If there were a button I could press, I would sacrifice myself without hesitating if it meant millions of people would die."

What follows is the first major text of Linkola's to be translated into English. It is a chapter from his 1989 book *Johdatus 1990—luvun ajatteluun.*

—Michael Moynihan

What is man? "O, what art thou man?" the poets of the good old days used to wonder. Man may be defined in an arbitrary number of ways, but to convey his most fundamental characteristic, he could be described with two words: too much. I'm too much, you're too much. There are five billion of us—an absurd, astonishing number, and still increasing . . . The earth's biosphere could possibly support a population of five million large mammals of this size, given their food requirements and the offal they produce, in order that they might exist in their own ecological niche, living as one species among many, without discriminating against the richness of other forms of life.

What meaning is there in these masses, what use do they have? What essential new contribution is brought forth to the world by hundreds of human societies similar to one other, or by the hundreds of identical communities existing within these societies? What sense is there in the fact that every small Finnish town has the same choice of workshops and stores, a similar men's choir and a similar municipal theater, all clogging up the earth's surface with their foundations and asphalt slabs? Would it be any loss to the biosphere—or to humanity itself—if the area of Äänekoski no longer existed, and instead in its place was an unregulated and diverse mosaic of natural landscape, containing thousands of species and tilting slopes of gnarled, primeval trees mirrored in the shimmering surface of Kuhmojärvi lake? Or would it really be a loss if a small bundle of towns disappeared from the map—Ylivieska, Kuusamo, Lahti, Duisburg, Jefremov, Gloucester—and wilderness replaced them? How about Belgium?

What use do we have with Ylivieska? The question is not ingenious, but it's relevant. And the only answer isn't that, perhaps, there is no use for these places—but rather that the people in Ylivieska town have a reason: they live there. I'm not just talking about the suffocation of life due to the population explosion, or that life and the earth's respiratory rhythm cry out for the productive, metabolic green oases they sorely need everywhere, between the areas razed by man. I also mean that humanity, by squirting and birthing all these teeming, filth-producing multitudes from out of itself, in the process also suffocates and defames its own culture—one in which individuals and communities have to spasmodically search for the "meaning of life" and create an identity for themselves through petty, childish arguing.

I spent a summer once touring Poland by bicycle. It is a lovely country, one where little Catholic children, cute as buttons, almost entirely dressed in silk, turn up around every corner. I read from a travel brochure that in Poland the percentage of people who perished in the Second World War is larger than any other country—about six million, if my memory doesn't fail me. From another part of the brochure I calculated that since the end of the war, population growth has compensated for that loss threefold in forty years. . . On my next trip after that, I went through the most bombed-out city in the world, Dresden. It was terrifying in its ugliness and filth, overstuffed to the point of suffocation—a smoke-filled, polluting nest where the first spontaneous impression was that another vaccination from the sky wouldn't do any harm. Who misses all those who died in the Second World War? Who misses the twenty million executed by Stalin? Who misses Hitler's six million Jews? Israel creaks with overcrowdedness; in Asia Minor, overpopulation creates struggles for mere square meters of dirt. The cities throughout the world were rebuilt and filled to the brim with people long ago, their churches and monuments restored so that acid rain would have something to eat through. Who misses the unused procreation potential of those killed in the Second World War? Is the world lacking another hundred million people at the moment? Is there a shortage of books, songs, movies, porcelain dogs, vases? Are one billion embodiments of motherly love and one billion sweet silvery-haired grandmothers not enough?

All species have an oversized capacity for reproduction, otherwise they would become extinct in times of crisis due to variations of circumstances. In the end it's always hunger that enforces a limit on the size of a population. A great many species have self-regulating birth control mechanisms which prevent them from constantly falling into crisis situations and suffering from hunger. In the case of man, however, such mechanisms—when found at all—are only weak and ineffective: for example, the small scale infanticide practiced in primitive cultures. Throughout its evolutionary development, humankind has defied and outdistanced the hunger line. Man has been a conspicuously extravagant breeder, and decidedly animal-like. Mankind produces especially large litters both in cramped, distressed conditions, as well as among very prosperous segments of the population. Humans reproduce abundantly in times of peace and particularly abundantly in the aftermath of a war, owing to a peculiar decree of nature.

It may be said that man's defensive methods are powerless with regards to hunger controlling his population growth, but his offensive methods for pushing the hunger line out of the way of the swelling population are enormously eminent. Man is extremely expansive—fundamentally so, as a species.

In the history of mankind we witness Nature's desperate struggle against an error of her own evolution. An old and previously efficacious method of curtailment, hunger, began to increasingly lose its effectiveness as man's engineering abilities progressed. Man had wrenched himself loose from his niche and started to grab more and more resources, displacing other forms of life.

Then Nature took stock of the situation, found out that she had lost the first round, and changed strategy. She brandished a weapon she hadn't been able to employ when the enemy had been scattered and small in numbers, but one which was all the more effective now against the densely proliferating enemy troops. With the aid of microbes—or "infectious diseases" as man calls them, in the parlance of his war propaganda—Nature fought stubbornly for two thousand years against mankind and achieved many brilliant victories. But these triumphs remained localized, and more and more ineluctably took on the flavor of rear-guard actions. Nature wasn't capable of destroying the echelon of humanity in which scientists and researchers toiled away, and in the meantime they managed to disarm Nature of her arsenal.

At this point, Nature—no longer possessed of the weapons for attaining victory, yet utterly embittered and still retaining her sense of self-esteem—decided to concede a Pyrrhic victory to man, but only in the most absolute sense of the term. During the entire war, Nature had maintained her peculiar connection to the enemy: they had both shared the same supply sources, they drank from the same springs and ate from the same fields. Regardless of the course of the war, a permanent position of constraint prevailed at this point; for just as much as the enemy had not succeeded in conquering the supply targets for himself, Nature likewise did not possess the capability to take these same targets out of the clutches of humanity. The only option left was the scorched earth policy, which Nature had already tested on a small scale during the microbe-phase of the war, and which she decided to carry through to the bitter end. Nature did not submit to defeat—she called it a draw, but at the price of self-immolation. Man wasn't, after all, an external, autonomous enemy, but rather her very own tumor. And the fate of a tumor ordains that it must always die along with its host.

In the case of man—who sits atop the food chain, yet nevertheless ominously lacks the ability to sufficiently restrain his own population growth—it might appear that salvation would lie in the propensity for killing his fellow man. The characteristically human institution of war, with its wholesale massacre of fellow humanoids, would seem to contain a basis for desirable population control—that is, if it hadn't been portentously thwarted, since there is no human culture where young females take part in war. Thus, even a large decrease in population as a result of war affects only males, and lasts only a very short time in a given generation. The very next generation is up to strength, and by the natural law of the "baby boom" even becomes oversized, as all the females are fertilized through the resilience of just a very small number of males. In reality, the evolution of war, while erratic, has actually been even more negative: in the early stages of its development there were more wars of a type that swept away a moderate amount of civilians as well. But by a twist of man's tragicomic fate, at the very point when the institution of war appeared capable of taking out truly significant shares of fertile females—as was intimated by the bombings of civilians in the Second World War—military technology advanced in such a way that large-scale wars, those with the ability to make substantial demographic impact, became impossible.

[translated by Harri Heinonen and Michael Moynihan]

⚡ ⚡ ⚡

Harold McNeill, illustrator of Pentti Linkola, has a website at <www.third-camelot.com>. Contact: Third Camelot, P.O. Box 194, Beaver, OR 97108. email: third_camelot@hotmail.com

"Ship of Fools" by Hieronymus Bosch

SHIP OF FOOLS

Ted Kaczynski

Once upon a time, the captain and the mates of a ship grew so vain of their seamanship, so full of hubris and so impressed with themselves, that they went mad. They turned the ship north and sailed until they met with icebergs and dangerous floes, and they kept sailing north into more and more perilous waters, solely in order to give themselves opportunities to perform ever-more-brilliant feats of seamanship.

As the ship reached higher and higher latitudes, the passengers and crew became increasingly uncomfortable. They began quarreling among themselves and complaining of the conditions under which they lived.

"Shiver me timbers," said an able seaman, "if this ain't the worst voyage I've ever been on. The deck is slick with ice; when I'm on lookout the wind cuts through me jacket like a knife; every time I reef the foresail I blamed-near freeze me fingers; and all I get for it is a miserable five shillings a month!"

"You think you have it bad!" said a lady passenger. "I can't sleep at night for the cold. Ladies on this ship don't get as many blankets as the men. It isn't fair!"

A Mexican sailor chimed in: "*¡Chingado!* I'm only getting half the wages of the Anglo seamen. We need plenty of food to keep us warm in this climate, and I'm not getting my share; the Anglos get more. And the worst of it is that the mates always give me orders in English instead of Spanish."

"I have more reason to complain than anybody," said an American Indian sailor. "If the palefaces hadn't robbed me of my ancestral lands, I wouldn't even be on this ship, here among the icebergs and arctic winds. I would just be paddling a canoe on a nice, placid lake. I deserve compensation. At the very least, the captain should let me run a crap game so that I can make some money."

The bosun spoke up: "Yesterday the first mate called me a 'fruit' just because I suck cocks. I have a right to suck cocks without being called names for it!"

"It's not only humans who are mistreated on this ship," interjected an animal-lover among the passengers, her voice quivering with indignation. "Why, last week I saw the second mate kick the ship's dog twice!"

One of the passengers was a college professor. Wringing his hands he exclaimed,

"All this is just awful! It's immoral! It's racism, sexism, speciesism, homophobia and exploitation of the working class! It's discrimination! We must have

453

social justice: Equal wages for the Mexican sailor, higher wages for all sailors, compensation for the Indian, equal blankets for the ladies, a guaranteed right to suck cocks, and no more kicking the dog!"

"Yes, yes!" shouted the passengers. "Aye-aye!" shouted the crew. "It's discrimination! We have to demand our rights!"

The cabin boy cleared his throat.

"*Ahem.* You all have good reasons to complain. But it seems to me that what we really have to do is get this ship turned around and headed back south, because if we keep going north we're sure to be wrecked sooner or later, and then your wages, your blankets, and your right to suck cocks won't do you any good, because we'll all drown."

But no one paid any attention to him, because he was only the cabin boy.

The captain and the mates, from their station on the poop deck, had been watching and listening. Now they smiled and winked at one another, and at a gesture from the captain the third mate came down from the poop deck, sauntered over to where the passengers and crew were gathered, and shouldered his way in amongst them. He put a very serious expression on his face and spoke thusly:

"We officers have to admit that some really inexcusable things have been happening on this ship. We hadn't realized how bad the situation was until we heard your complaints. We are men of good will and want to do right by you. But—well—the captain is rather conservative and set in his ways, and may have to be prodded a bit before he'll make any substantial changes. My personal opinion is that if you protest vigorously—but always peacefully and without violating any of the ship's rules—you would shake the captain out of his inertia and force him to address the problems of which you so justly complain."

Having said this, the third mate headed back toward the poop deck. As he went, the passengers and crew called after him, "Moderate! Reformer! Goody-liberal! Captain's stooge!" But they nevertheless did as he said. They gathered in a body before the poop deck, shouted insults at the officers, and demanded their rights: "I want higher wages and better working conditions," cried the able seaman. "Equal blankets for women," cried the lady passenger. "I want to receive my orders in Spanish," cried the Mexican sailor. "I want the right to run a crap game," cried the Indian sailor. "I don't want to be called a fruit," cried the bosun. "No more kicking the dog," cried the animal lover. "Revolution now," cried the professor.

The captain and the mates huddled together and conferred for several minutes, winking, nodding and smiling at one another all the while. Then the captain stepped to the front of the poop deck and, with a great show of benevolence, announced that the able seaman's wages would be raised to six shillings a month; the Mexican sailor's wages would be raised to two-thirds the wages of an Anglo seaman, and the order to reef the foresail would be given in Spanish; lady passengers would receive one more blanket; the Indian sailor would be allowed to run a crap game on Saturday nights; the bosun wouldn't be called a fruit as long as he kept his cocksucking strictly private; and the dog wouldn't be kicked unless he did something really naughty, such as stealing food from the galley.

The passengers and crew celebrated these concessions as a great victory, but the next morning, they were again feeling dissatisfied.

"Six shillings a month is a pittance, and I still freeze me fingers when I reef the foresail," grumbled the able seaman. "I'm still not getting the same wages as the Anglos, or enough food for this climate," said the Mexican sailor. "We women still don't have enough blankets to keep us warm," said the lady passenger. The other crewmen and passengers voiced similar complaints, and the professor egged them on.

When they were done, the cabin boy spoke up—louder this time so that the others could not easily ignore him:

"It's really terrible that the dog gets kicked for stealing a bit of bread from the galley, and that women don't have equal blankets, and that the able seaman gets his fingers frozen; and I don't see why the bosun shouldn't suck cocks if he wants to. But look how thick the icebergs are now, and how the wind blows harder and harder! We've got to turn this ship back toward the south, because if we keep going north we'll be wrecked and drowned."

"Oh yes," said the bosun, "It's just so awful that we keep heading north. But why should I have to keep cocksucking in the closet? Why should I be called a fruit? Ain't I as good as everyone else?"

"Sailing north is terrible," said the lady passenger. "But don't you see? That's exactly why women need more blankets to keep them warm. I demand equal blankets for women now!"

"It's quite true," said the professor, "that sailing to the north imposes great hardships on all of us. But changing course toward the south would be unrealistic. You can't turn back the clock. We must find a mature way of dealing with the situation."

"Look," said the cabin boy, "If we let those four madmen up on the poop deck have their way, we'll all be drowned. If we ever get the ship out of danger, then we can worry about working conditions, blankets for women, and the right to suck cocks. But first we've got to get this vessel turned around. If a few of us get together, make a plan, and show some courage, we can save ourselves. It wouldn't take many of us—six or eight would do. We could charge the poop, chuck those lunatics overboard, and turn the ship to the south."

The professor elevated his nose and said sternly, "I don't believe in violence. It's immoral."

"It's unethical ever to use violence," said the bosun.

"I'm terrified of violence," said the lady passenger.

The captain and the mates had been watching and listening all the while. At a signal from the captain, the third mate stepped down to the main deck. He went about among the passengers and crew, telling them that there were still many problems on the ship.

"We have made much progress," he said, "But much remains to be done. Working conditions for the able seaman are still hard, the Mexican still isn't getting the same wages as the Anglos, the women still don't have quite as many blankets as the men, the Indian's Saturday-night crap game is a paltry compensation for his lost lands, it's unfair to the bosun that he has to keep his cocksucking in the closet, and the dog still gets kicked at times.

"I think the captain needs to be prodded again. It would help if you all would put on another protest—as long as it remains nonviolent."

As the third mate walked back toward the stern, the passengers and the crew shouted insults after him, but they nevertheless did what he said and gathered in front of the poop deck for another protest. They ranted and raved and brandished their fists, and they even threw a rotten egg at the captain (which he skillfully dodged).

After hearing their complaints, the captain and the mates huddled for a conference, during which they winked and grinned broadly at one another. Then the captain stepped to the front of the poop deck and announced that the able seaman would be given gloves to keep his fingers warm, the Mexican sailor would receive wages equal to three-fourths the wages of an Anglo seaman, the women would receive yet another blanket, the Indian sailor could run a crap game on Saturday and Sunday nights, the bosun would be allowed to suck cocks publicly after dark, and no one could kick the dog without special permission from the captain.

The passengers and crew were ecstatic over this great revolutionary victory, but by the next morning they were again feeling dissatisfied and began grumbling about the same old hardships.

The cabin boy this time was getting angry.

"You damn fools!" he shouted. "Don't you see what the captain and the mates are doing? They're keeping you occupied with your trivial grievances about blankets and wages and the dog being kicked so that you won't think about what is really wrong with this ship—that it's getting farther and farther to the north and we're all going to be drowned. If just a few of you would come to your senses, get together, and charge the poop deck, we could turn this ship around and save ourselves. But all you do is whine about petty little issues like working conditions and crap games and the right to suck cocks."

The passengers and the crew were incensed.

"Petty!!" cried the Mexican, "Do you think it's reasonable that I get only three-fourths the wages of an Anglo sailor? Is that petty?"

"How can you call my grievance trivial?" shouted the bosun. "Don't you know how humiliating it is to be called a fruit?"

"Kicking the dog is not a 'petty little issue'!" screamed the animal-lover. "It's heartless, cruel and brutal!"

"Alright then," answered the cabin boy. "These issues are not petty and trivial. Kicking the dog is cruel and brutal and it is humiliating to be called a fruit. But in comparison to our real problem—in comparison to the fact that the ship is still heading north—your grievances are petty and trivial, because if we don't get this ship turned around soon, we're all going to drown."

"Fascist!" said the professor.

"Counterrevolutionary!" said the lady passenger. And all of the passengers and crew chimed in one after another, calling the cabin boy a fascist and a counterrevolutionary. They pushed him away and went back to grumbling about wages, and about blankets for women, and about the right to suck cocks, and about how the dog was treated. The ship kept sailing north, and after a while it was crushed between two icebergs and everyone drowned.

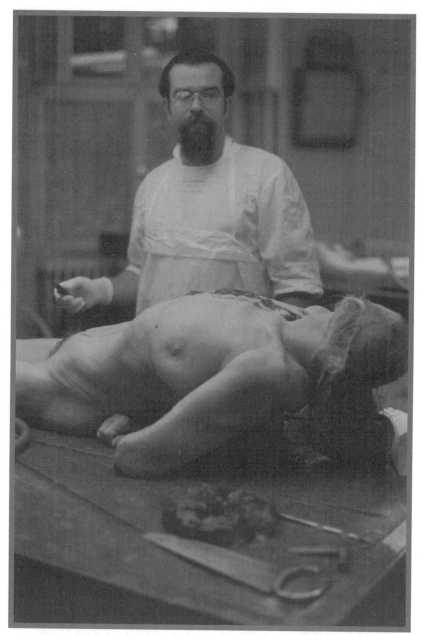

Joe Coleman's painting appears on the cover of the first *Apocalypse Culture*, and his "Ecce Homo," seen on this sequel edition, appreciates the ever-intensifying degeneracy of our planet. A close friend for over 15 years now, Joe's work has become more sophisticated, detailed and remarkable, painting by painting. Joe seeks bodies for anatomical dissection and peculiar bounties to become part of his remarkable "odditorium." Contact Joe Coleman by writing P.O. Box 22788, Brooklyn, NY, 11202.